# THE CLINICAL APPLICATION OF PROJECTIVE DRAWINGS

# The
# Clinical Application
# Of
# Projective Drawings

*Sixth Printing*

By

**EMANUEL F. HAMMER, Ph.D.**

*Head, Psychology Unit, Psychiatric Clinic*
*Court of Special Sessions, New York City*
*Psychologist, Child Guidance League, New York City*
*Formerly, Senior Research Scientist*
*New York State Psychiatric Institute*
*Director, Interne Training*
*Lynchburg State Colony, Virginia*

**CHARLES C THOMAS · PUBLISHER**
*Springfield · Illinois · U.S.A.*

*Published and Distributed Throughout the World by*

CHARLES C THOMAS • PUBLISHER

Bannerstone House

301-327 East Lawrence Avenue, Springfield, Illinois, U.S.A.

© *1958, by* CHARLES C THOMAS • PUBLISHER

ISBN 0-398-00768-3

Library of Congress Catalog Card Number: 57-10997

First Printing, 1958
Second Printing, 1967
Third Printing, 1971
Fourth Printing, 1975
Fifth Printing, 1978
Sixth Printing, 1980

*Printed in the United States of America*

*R-1*

To

**DIANE**

who was born the same year as this book

# CONTRIBUTORS

BENDER, LAURETTA, M.D., *Professor of Clinical Psychiatry,*
*New York University College of Medicine*
*Associate Attending Psychiatrist, New York University,*
*Bellevue Medical Center;*
*Senior Psychiatrist, Children's Service, Bellevue Hospital,*
*New York City*

BROWN, FRED, PH.D., *Chief Psychologist, Mount Sinai Hospital,*
*New York City*
*Adjunct Professor of Psychology, New York University,*
*Washington Square College, New York City*

BUCK, JOHN N., *Formerly, Chief Psychologist, Lynchburg State Colony,*
*Lynchburg, Virginia*

HALPERN, FLORENCE, PH.D., *Assistant Professor, New York University,*
*College of Medicine*

HAMMER, EMANUEL F., PH.D., *Head, Psychology Unit, Psychiatric*
*Clinic, Court of Special Sessions;*
*Chief Psychological Consultant, Home Advisory Council,*
*New York City; Lecturer, Child Guidance League,*
*New York City*

HARROWER, MOLLY R., PH.D., *Director, Psychological Testing*
*Program, University of Texas, Medical Branch,*
*Galveston, Texas*
*Research and Consulting Psychologist, New York City*

HEIDGERD, EVERETT, M.A., *School Psychologist,*
*Vocational, Education and Extension Board, Rockland County,*
*New City, New York*

[ vii ]

JOLLES, ISAAC, M.A., *Psychologist, Quincy Public Schools, Quincy, Illinois*

KINGET, G. MARIAN, PH.D., *Assistant Professor, Michigan State University*

LANDISBERG, SELMA, M.A., *Psychologist, Lenox Hill Hospital, New York City*

LEVY, SIDNEY, PH.D., *Director, Research Institute for Personality, Psychotherapy and Education
Lecturer in Psychology, New York University
Private Practice of Psychoanalysis,
New York City*

MACHOVER, KAREN, M.A., *Senior Psychologist, Kings County Psychiatric Division, New York City
Lecturer, The New School of Social Research, New York City
Instructor in Clinical Psychiatry, Long Island College of Medicine*

NAUMBURG, MARGARET, *Formerly, Department of Clinical Psychiatry, New York State Psychiatric Institute
Child Study Group, Institute of Pennsylvania Hospital*

SCHILDER, PAUL, M.D., *Formerly, New York University— Bellevue Medical Center*

SCHNEIDMAN, EDWIN S., PH.D., *Chief for Research, Psychology Service, VA Neuropsychiatric Hospital, Los Angeles, California
Clinical Associate, University of Southern California*

# PREFACE

Pᴿᴼᴶᴱᴄᴛɪᴠᴇ ᴅʀᴀᴡɪɴɢ ᴘsʏᴄʜᴏʟᴏɢʏ has spoken with many voices in the years since its birth, about twenty years ago—years of, at first, uncertain development and, later, more directed and vigorous growth. There is impressive evidence on all sides, as work continues to go forward rather energetically and enthusiastically in the development and modification of projective drawing techniques, that these methods have begun to outgrow their early, provisional form, and that the time for stock-taking of their present, fuller dimensions has now arrived.

Projective drawings, as a clinical tool, have moved relatively rapidly into a secure niche in the projective battery. By virtue of their time economy, ease of administration, and rich clinical yield, projective drawings appear to be the most frequent supplement, along with the TAT, to the Rorschach in the clinician's work-a-day projective armamentarium.

Although there exists a vast body of literature on the subject of the projective significance of drawings, the assembled study of projective drawing with its infinitely subtle language has never before been integrated in one book. In addition, publication concerning the drawing techniques, Machover (5) observes, "has not kept up with the increasing verification and support which (these techniques) have received in their application to clinical problems for more than twenty years" (p. 89).

The present book has been prepared because of the pressing need that exists today to bring within the confines of one volume, for easy reference, the variety of projective drawing procedures that are part of the growing group of tools of the clinical psychologist. This book essays to explore and survey the continental limits and several offshore islands of the present-day state of projective drawings.

The early explorers of this continent were Paul Schilder (6), and later Lauretta Bender (2), John Buck (3), and Karen Machover (4). From them, psychologists have learned the beginnings of the concept of *body image*—the individual's inner conception of his own body and its functions in the social and physical world, and its relation to motility phenomena. This concept escorted psychologists to the observation-point overlooking the field of projective drawings. There a happy marriage of theory and empiricism was made; and it proved to be a productive union, as well.

In addition to the older siblings of this projective drawing family, Buck's House-Tree-Person and Machover's Figure Drawing techniques, there is the Draw-A-Person-in-the-Rain modification of Abrams which attempts to elicit clues to the self-concept under conditions symbolizing environmental stress, Schwartz's Draw-An-Animal approach (useful for disclosing the biological side of the bio-social coin), Caligor's Eight-Card-Redrawing Test which digs down into the deepest layers of the subject's psychosexual identification, the Draw-A-Family procedure, Harrower's Unpleasant Concept Test, Kinget's Drawing Completion Test, and free doodles.

Nurtured on a rich diet of clinical experience and experimental studies, projective drawings are gradually being accepted for what they surely are—*developing* techniques of persistent and fundamental importance in the clinical battery of the projective tester.

This book attempts to deal with projective drawings primarily from a clinical viewpoint, both as an economic diagnostic method in actual practice, and also as an adjunct to psychotherapy. For the most part, it is a *clinical* book, meant primarily to be of practical use to the clinician and the clinician-in-training. "Often, procedure has been long established as useful empirically before experimental science can prove the validity of the method and supply a consistent hypothesis. Thus, the clinical approach is often ahead of the academic one" (1). Therefore, the empirically-based observations that form the backbone of this book are offered as hypotheses which, for the most part, still await experimental investigation and verification.

In addition to the goal of presenting a clinical book, the author and his collaborators hope to set the stage, via the hypotheses presented in this book, for further validating research. (One section summarizes the research, in the field of projective drawings, to date.) The members of the projective drawing family are well out of their swaddling clothes now, but a rich diet of experimental as well as clinical research is needed to insure their continued robust development.

At the present stage of the development of projective drawings, the usefulness of the hypotheses presented in this book will, for clinical purposes, have to be accepted on predominantly empirical grounds (barring the particular hypotheses already supported experimentally). These hypotheses have been established in clinical practice and, like those of the Rorschach technique, may be used pending the conclusion of the extensive investigations that, in part, are still necessary to establish their full validity.

In spite of more than twenty years of development in the field of projective drawings, the present book is to be regarded as a report bearing many of the earmarks of an exploratory nature—and certainly not yet as the full-dress debut of a wholly mature scientific instrument.

Because the field of projective drawings is a rapidly growing sub-discipline in which many clinicians have a voice, the writer has arranged to have certain of the chapters on several of the projective drawing modifications prepared by leading workers whose competence with those techniques has been outstandingly established. In the roster of collaborators, we are fortunate in having the fathers of several of the different techniques present a contribution to the section devoted to their innovations. The result, the writer believes, is a richer one than might have occurred had he himself presumed to present the field of projective drawings from the background of his experience alone.

The author wishes to acknowledge his special indebtedness to the collaborators who, in their contributions, cut beneath the surfaces of outer personality and sought, painstakingly, carefully, and sensitively to see human beings as they are, and to render them truly and sympathetically.

Appreciation is extended to the students, in my annual summer workshops in projective drawings, whose penetrating questions stimulated much of the thinking expressed in the theoretical sections of this book.

The writer is especially thankful to John N. Buck, teacher and friend, not only for his careful perusal of the manuscript and his many fruitful comments, but also for his constant encouragement and ready collaboration, over the years, on problems in projective drawing interpretation. Thanks are also most warmly expressed to Lila K. Hammer for her patience, ever-present assistance, and germane ideas.

E. F. H.

## REFERENCES

1. Bellak, L.: A study of limitations and "failures": toward an ego psychology of projective techniques. *J. Proj. Tech.*, 18:279-293, 1954.
2. Bender, Lauretta: Schizophrenic childhood. *Nerv. Child.*, 138-140, 1952.
3. Buck, J. N.: The H-T-P technique, a qualitative and quantitative scoring method. *J. Clin. Psych.*, Monograph No. 5:1-120, 1948.
4. Machover, Karen: *Personality Projection in the Drawing of a Human Figure.* Springfield, Thomas, 1949.
5. Machover, Karen: Drawings of the human figure, in Frank, L. K., Harrison, R., Hellersberg, Elisabeth, Machover, Karen, and Steiner, Meta: *Personality Development in Adolescent Girls.* Yellow Springs, Antioch Press, 1953.
6. Schilder, P.: *Image and Appearance of the Human Body.* New York, Internat. Univ. Press, 1950.

# CONTENTS

Part III

*Unit 1*

# THE CLINICAL APPLICATION OF
# PROJECTIVE DRAWINGS

# PART I

# SETTING THE STAGE

## CHAPTER 1

## PROJECTION IN THE ART STUDIO

EMANUEL F. HAMMER, PH.D.

TELL ME WHAT YOU READ and I'll tell you what you are—we are relatively sure somebody once said that. This truism can safely be expanded into: Read me what you write or show me what you draw and I'll tell you what you are.

James Barrie, Poe and Kafka can be found quite clearly in their works by even the psychologically uninitiated. The man in the street senses this and then merely speculates upon the *degree* to which Mike Hammer represents the shadow-side of Mickey Spillane's personality, and again how much of the *Old Man of the Sea* is to be found in Hemingway?

Most psychologists do not quarrel with the hypothesis that a writer projects himself in his writings, and that it should be possible, therefore, to build up a personality analysis of a writer from his writings. McCurdy, for one, demonstrates this convincingly in his book *The Personality of Shakespeare* (7).

The same projective hypothesis holds for painters, composers, architects, designers, and anyone who produces something out of his imagination.

In fact, it may safely be said that every act, expression, or response of an individual—his gestures, perceptions, feelings, selections, verbalizations, or motor acts—in some way bears the stamp of his personality.

One's way of walking, whether proudly, boldly, timidly, arrogantly, self-consciously, or stridently; one's way of hammering a nail, whether confidently, impatiently, irritatedly, rhythmically or joyfully; even one's way of lacing a shoe, whether one alloplastically places one's foot on a hydrant or fence post thus bringing the shoe up to one's self, or whether one autoplastically brings

[ 5 ]

one's self all the way down to the ground to encounter the shoe lace—all reflect some facet of one's personality.

*In projective drawings, the subject's psychomotor activities are caught on paper.* The line employed may be firm or timid, uncertain, hesitant or bold, or it may consist of a savage digging at the paper. In addition, as we shall later see, the subject's conscious and unconscious perception of himself and significant people in his environment determine the content of his drawing. In such expression, the unconscious levels of the subject tend to utilize symbols — symbols whose meanings can be unraveled through study and understanding of dreams, myths, folklore, psychotic productions, and so on. The chapters that follow will support and elaborate the thesis that drawing productions are employed as one of the many forms of symbolic speech.

The drawing page serves as a canvas upon which the subject may sketch a glimpse of his inner world, his traits and attitudes, his behavioral characteristics, his personality strengths and weaknesses including the degree to which he can mobilize his inner resources to handle his psychodynamic conflicts, both interpersonal and intrapsychic.

Psychiatric patients, I have found, can frequently express themselves more easily through graphic means of communication than through verbal ones. Freud (4) himself discovered this phenomena. In speaking of the difficulties patients often have communicating their dreams, he writes, " 'I could draw it,' the dreamer says frequently, 'but I don't know how to say it.' "

The case of the well-known dramatist, August Strindberg, also illustrates the greater affinity between feelings and pictures than exists between feelings and words. This individual, so extraordinarily able in verbal areas, made use of drawings during periods in which he felt himself, because of depression and other psychic disturbances, unable to express himself adequately by words. He tried to "say" his otherwise inexpressible mental experiences in pictorial ways (5).

When one observes the drawings of children, one sees conveyed, things that they would never have been able to express in words, even if they had been fully conscious of some of the feelings that toss and distress them. The graphic examples, in the chapters that follow, will illustrate how the subject's feelings frequently float into his drawings unwittingly and/or unwillingly.

Historically, man used drawings to record his feelings and actions long before he employed symbols that recorded specific speech. From the cave man on through the ages, man—both primitive and cultured—has expressed his emotions, feelings, religious ideas, and needs by art work.

It was not until a little more than 2,000 years ago that man reached the stage of employing language composed of written words. Primitive man attempted to give permanence to his expression entirely by means of pictures. Considered in this light, drawing communication is an elemental or basic language.

The individual himself begins to use graphic communication quite early in life. Children draw before they can write. Hence, in projective drawings, as in dreams, subconscious conflicts employ the language of symbolism quite readily. Drawings, like symbolic speech, tap primitive layers of the subject. Freud and his followers have made not only the clinician, but the artist and the general public as well, aware of the fact that the unconscious expresses itself in symbolic images. Psychoanalysis has demonstrated most convincingly that "intellectualization and the exaggerated verbalism of our culture have been imposed on the deeper and more primitive levels of our unconscious mode of imaged expression" (8).

Certainly when one attempts creative activity, one tends to draw upon primitive or deeper levels within oneself. The observer usually feels in a work of art an integral relation between the work and the artist, as though the work embodies what is most personal, sacred or meaningful to the artist.

Man's earliest childhood with all its strivings, yearnings and uncertainties, with all its difficulties in grasping the world and getting in closer touch with others, is still alive in every human being, and "it is possible that man has to go back to it whenever he wants to create"(1). Projective drawings capitalize on this creative stream.

The pressing forward of facets of self-portraiture in art has been recognized for hundreds of years. Leonardo DaVinci, the genius of so many spheres of activity, is credited with the first ob-

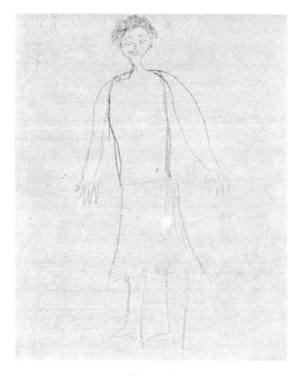

Figure 1

servation of this process of projection. The person who draws or paints, he recognized, "is inclined to lend to the figures he renders his own bodily experience, if he is not protected against this by long study" (6).

That all art contains some element of the artist's intimate personality has long been recognized. Elbert Hubbard, an artist, observed, "When an artist paints a portrait, he paints two, himself and the sitter." Alfred Tunnelle, another perspicacious artist commented, "The artist does not see things as they are, but as he is." For graphic illustrations of this principle of projection, Figures 1 and 2 are presented. Figure 1 was drawn by a male subject who walked with the aid of crutches. His drawing was produced in response to the request, "Please draw a person." Although he did not draw someone leaning upon crutches, he did draw an extra and unnecessary line extending from the base of the feet onto the ground, as if he could not conceive of a standing posture without the aid of some support. The important point is that the subject was not consciously drawing himself, yet he had to project his inner feeling that one cannot stand without the help of something additional upon which to lean. His need for physical bolstering presses forward onto the drawing page and is clearly imprinted onto his picture of a male.

Figure 2 also was drawn by an adult male with a crippling physical condition, in this case missing his left arm. The subject was born without this appendage, and while he did not draw a one-armed person, he did give a distinct treatment to the left arm of the drawn Person which rendered it withered and less effective than the right arm. His chromatic drawing of a Person (Figure 3) again reflects his feelings of insufficiency in the area of the missing limb. When we observe the drawn Tree offered by the same subject, we note a conspicuous truncated limb pro-

Figure 2

Figure 3

truding from the trunk. And if additional support for the projective thesis be needed, the amputated limb of the tree is on the same side as is the missing limb of our subject.

Thus, the truism formulated by Tunnelle to the effect that the artist does not see things as they are but as he is, is confirmed by the projective drawings of patients in the clinic as well as by drawings of artists in the studio.

To return to Leonardo, who formulated his observations on the basis of his own drawings as well as those of the group of students that clustered around him, it has been noted, "The smile on the *Mona Lisa,* in great probability, did not belong to Mona Lisa at all but represented Leonardo Da Vinci's own outlook on life and depicted the amused superiority which he had gained as compensation for his resentment against an unkind deal of fate and a frequent misunderstanding of his place in life" (2).

Into this picture of the *Mona Lisa,* Leonardo projected himself, his psychological penetration, and his puzzling serenity.

Similarly, in Leonardo's *The Last Supper,* the central figure, Christ, has "the grandeur, the imperturable grace and tranquility characteristic of Leonardo himself in his noblest moods" (2).

For purposes of contrast, one has only to observe the widely different moods depicted in the art work of El Greco and Van Gogh. El Greco, with his depressive, dysphoric, and gloomy tones, of which perhaps the most noteworthy treatment appears in his *View of Toledo,* reflects his own dismal and dampened emotional condition. Van Gogh, on the other hand, employs clashing, hot, brilliant, volatile hues which burst forth onto the canvas from the pressure of his turbulent, upheaved, jarring emotions—resulting from a life he attempted to live out by mixing loneliness, madness and a consuming dedication to his art. The contrasting canvasses of Van Gogh and El Greco serve to illustrate the words

Figure 4

of an anonymous artist: "The eye sees what the mind wants it to see."

In the work of Toulouse-Lautrec, we find much the same expressive principle thrown into sharp relief. The legend is well-known: Toulouse-Lautrec, the aristocrat of genius, the misshapen, dwarfed Don Juan thrown head-long by his physical affliction, his self-loathing and search for an impossible love into an association with the "dregs of society," dies of debauchery in the flower of his age after immortalizing the Paris underworld in his art.

Toulouse-Lautrec, himself, was a deeply unhappy individual who covered his tortured existence with a bright veneer of gaiety and wit, just as he attempted to do on his famous canvasses. He was known as a bitter sensualist who groped for beauty in the sordidness of the cafés and brothels of the Montmartre, just as he sought to find something positive in his own essentially negative self-concept. Toulouse-Lautrec's personality handicaps, his defensive coldness of heart and constricting fear of emotional experiences and of deeper interpersonal give-and-take are clearly reflected in his use of flat, almost apathetic tones and his contempt for color, which handicapped his paintings and prevented him from attaining the greater status of an artist that might otherwise have been his. He had been burnt by the fires of fate, and dared not venture deeply into life again, either in actuality or on his canvasses. Instead, he attempted the superficial gaiety of forms in his paintings, just as he attempted the facade of gaiety in his social relations, but he was as incapable of expressing the deeper emotions implied by the free use of warmer colors as he was incapable of making deeper relationships with those in his environment.

In the work of Botticelli, we find expressed another principle of projective or expressive drawings: namely, that one may express a wish-fulfillment motif rather than actual feelings about one's self.

Botticelli had been an invalid from his early youth, and was physically underdeveloped and delicate. Goldscheider remarks that in Botticelli's self-portrait, Botticelli rejected "hateful reality, and represented himself in the handsome and dignified form that he might assume in what the psychologist calls a 'wishing-dream'; just as Durer visualized himself as Christ, so Botticelli saw himself as a strapping young Florentine, who might not be ashamed to appear in the company of the handsomest of the Medici." This principle of expressing an idealized image of one's self will be encountered again, in clinical context in the following chapter, and in developmental or normative context in the chapter on the H-T-P's of adolescents.

To return to examples of artists who project themselves as they feel themselves to be, rather than as they wish to be, we need search no further than the famous contemporary French painter Bernard Buffet. In Buffet's art we find the grimmest of views. This well-fed and prosperous young man of twenty-six translates the scenes around him into such macabre, emaciated images that they become mere specters of his surroundings. The fat loaves of bread and lush fruit that weigh his table shrink away, in his still lifes, to skimpy dried-up shapes. The sturdy gnarled trees on his farm become, in his landscapes, stark gibbets for war victims. And in his self-portraits, even his own face takes on a ghastly appearance. Buffet, recently voted by French critics as the leading painter of his generation, obviously descends to the inner depths within him for his images, rather than accept inspiration only from without. His self-portraits present a starved and staring contrast to the outer appearance of this relaxed and healthy-looking artist.

Nourishment of the meagerest kind is depicted by Buffet in his still life in spite of the fact that in real life he enjoys ample, even luxurious fare on his table. Undernourishment is featured in Buffet's drawing (Figure 5) of a skeletal hare on a platter in contrast to his own pets, plump and pampered.

Buffet's drawings, it becomes apparent, are motivated by what goes on within him, and are incidental to happenings around him.

These examples illustrate the thesis that creative productions reveal inner needs more directly than do other types of activity.

The particular aliveness which distinguishes anything creative from other products of human skill and endeavor, and the relation which exists between the creator and his creation, are the

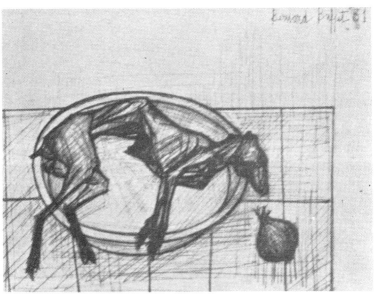

Figure 5

subject of three fables, which Schactel (9) summarizes: one a Greek myth, one an ancient Chinese story, and one a modern fable. Pygmalion, in the Greek myth, having carved the image of a woman out of stone, falls in love with his creation and persuades Aphrodite to give life to the statute. Wu-Tao-Tse, in the Chinese myth, having reached old age, paints a landscape for the last time, mounts his donkey, rides into the mountains of his painting and is never seen again. The modern fable is presented in Jean Cocteau's movie, *Le Sang Du Poete.* In one scene, the protagonist draws a human face, and the mouth in the face begins to speak. The hero wishes to silence the voice of his creation and places his hand over the drawn mouth. However, the mouth now appears on the palm of the artist's hand and tells him to go through a mirror which hangs on the wall. He does this and finds himself in a long dark hallway where, as he peeps through the keyholes of the rooms leading off from this hallway, he observes a series of scenes which represent painful or eventful incidents in his childhood and adolescence.

What the three fables have in common is that *the artist has given life, real existence to his work:* "Pygmalion has achieved this through his prayer; the Chinese painter can ride into his own painting where he will continue to be till the end of time; and the young draftsman finds himself impelled by the voice of his work to delve into the dark corridor of his own past" (9, p. 92). The last of the three stories, expressed with modern sophistication, reflects not only the life-instilling quality of the creative process, but also throws into relief the role played by the dark corridor of one's personal past. It is this personal past, the unconscious layer of the personality, into which, as E. M. Forster says, "Man, in the creative state, lets down a bucket and draws up something which is normally beyond his reach" (3).

Cocteau's fable expresses with penetrating insight the fact that, in creative effort, man gives expression to a whisper within him that leads to, and comes from, his own past and is part of his deeper self.

Somerset Maugham has observed of one who writes: "In giving to the character of one's invention flesh and blood, one is giving life to that part of one's self which finds no other means of expression." This applies equally well to one who draws or paints.

An interesting validity study of the thesis that psychologists can deduce personality traits from the creative effort of a subject was recently reported by Spiegelman (10). He tested the hypothesis that the personality of a communicator can be ascertained from his creative production by trained clinicians. Spiegelman adminstered a Rorschach to the creator of the color film, *Uirapuru*, Mr. Sam Zebba. The film is an enactment, by natives of the Amazon jungle, of a story of a legendary bird of love, and has won international prizes in Europe. With the exception of an introductory narration, there is no dialogue in the film. The Rorschach was interpreted "blind"—that is, with no information other than the fact that the subject was an adult male—by Dr. Bruno Klopfer. From his interpretation, twenty-five "true" statements about the personality of the subject were derived, and mixed-in with twenty-five "false" statements. The entire set was then given to a group of both clinical psychologists and laymen. The clinical group did significantly better than chance and significantly better than the control group in selecting the statements which described the subject on the basis of their viewing of the motion picture created by him.

## SUMMARY

By examining the creative art work of a number of individuals, we have observed that subjects tend to express in their drawings quite unwittingly (and at times, unwillingly) their view of themselves as they are, or would like to be. Drawings represent a form of symbolic speech which taps a relatively primitive layer within the subject. In the words of Tunnelle, "The artist does not see things as they are, but as he is." Hubbard expressed it in much the same way, "When an artist paints a portrait, he paints two, himself and the sitter." Thus, psychologists have, ready-made, the raw material from which to forge a clinical tool. Their efforts to do so constitute the remainder of this book.

## REFERENCES

1. Bender, Lauretta: *Child Psychiatric Techniques.* Springfield, Thomas, 1952.

2. Craven, T.: Leonardo Da Vinci, in Campbell, O., Van Gundy, J., and Shrades, C. (eds).: *Patterns for Living.* New York, Macmillan, 1940.

3. Forster, E. M.: The Raison d'Etre of Criticism in the Arts, in French, R. (ed.): *Music and Criticism.* Cambridge, Harvard, 1948.

4. Freud, S.: *New Introductory Lectures on Psychoanalysis.* New York, Norton, 1933.

5. Hildebrand, A.: *Problems of Form, Painting and Sculpture.* New York, Julian Press, 1932.

6. Kris, E.: *Psychoanalytic Explorations in Art.* New York, Internat. Univ. Press, 1952.

7. McCurdy, H. G.: *The Personality of Shakespeare.* New Haven, Yale, 1953.

8. Naumburg, Margaret: Art as symbolic speech. *J. Aesthetics and Art Criticism, 13:*435-450, 1955.

9. Schactel, E. G.: Projection and its relation to character attitudes and creativity in the kinesthetic responses. *Psychiatry, 13:*69-100, 1950.

10. Spiegelman, M.: Evaluation of personality by viewing a motion picture. *J. Proj. Tech., 20:*212-215, 1956.

## CHAPTER 2

## PROJECTION IN THE CLINICAL SETTING

EMANUEL F. HAMMER, PH.D.

Kʀɪꜱ, ɪɴ ʜɪꜱ ᴏʙꜱᴇʀᴠᴀᴛɪᴏɴ on drawings and paintings by patients, commented that the psychological process at work is similar to that of the "normal" artist. This process he described as "the placing of an inner experience, an 'inner' image, into the outside world, i.e., the mechanism of projection" (17).

As Piotrowski (23) has observed, art products were probably the first device to be treated as projections of both conscious and unconscious personality trends. Burckhardt in 1855 was able to draw some astoundingly accurate deductions concerning the dominant personalities and the sociopsychological atmosphere of a whole epoch, the Italian Renaissance, mainly from an analysis of the works of art of that period.

In the psychopathological field, Nolan D. C. Lewis, in 1928, made a systematic study of graphic projections, which he called, "An Avenue of Projection," not only to identify personality dynamics, but also to further psychotherapy by discussing the patient's graphic productions with him. "The drawing of a patient can be considered subject to analysis similar to that employed in dealing with dreams or other behavior material" (19). Lewis indicated the advantage of drawing and painting over dream material, stating that "frequently the basic unconscious difficulties of certain patients are through this manner of objectification brought to consciousness with greater facility than through dream analysis" (19).

Dorken (6) observes, "The psychological evaluation of graphic art was probably the first established 'projective' technique." One of the first clinicians to note the symbolization in the drawings of his "insane" patients was a 19th century French psychiatrist,

Max Simon, who was also shocked by such "obscene drawings" and ordered the patients to cease making them (25).

In the years following this unwilling investigator of symbolism, the insights of psychoanalysis have led the general public as well as the artist and clinician to become increasingly aware of the phenomenon that the unconscious "speaks" in symbolic images. In the words of Naumburg (22), "The discoveries of psychoanalysis concerning the dynamics of the unconscious, as well as the uncovering of the symbolic art of prehistoric cultures and ancient civilizations, have given a new perspective to the meaning and value of unconscious elements in the symbolic aspects of drawing (p. 441)."

## THE EARLY PHASE OF PROJECTIVE DRAWINGS

Florence Goodenough, having devised an intelligence scale based mainly on the number of details put into the drawing of a man, became aware, along with other clinicians, that her test was tapping personality factors in addition to intellectual capabilities of her child subjects. The "verbalist" type of product with a large number of details; the "individual response" generally incomprehensible to anyone but the subject, the suggestion of a "flight of ideas" as exemplified by the drawing with only one ear, with hair on only one side of the head, and eight fingers on each hand—these were some of the early unique responses of different types of children which were attributed to nonintellectual components in the personality. Bender (1) reports a study in which a group of 450 school children were asked to draw a man. Nine were found who produced drawings with one or more of the above characteristics, namely, a verbalistic, individual, or "flight of ideas" type of reaction. These children were rated by their teachers as showing more psychopathology than the other children in terms of oversensitivity, proneness to worry, muscle-twitches, poor concentration, absentmindedness, timidity, instability, and flightiness. Hanvik (13) also concluded from an experimental study he conducted, "Emotionally disturbed children do not draw the human figure in a fashion commensurate with their intellgence as measured by a standardized I.Q. Scale."

The present writer, in using the Goodenough "Draw-a-Man

Test," also became aware of the fact that emotional factors, more so than intellectual ones, were constantly pressing into view. In checking a drawing for credit for the inclusion of a hand, it soon became apparent that whereas the same quantitative I.Q. credit was given for a balled-up, clenched fist, or a delicate and open hand in a feminine gesture patting the cheek, produced by a male subject in his drawing of a male, more important qualitative clues to the functioning of the total personality were being ignored. The subject was granted identical quantitative credit whether he drew his person with the arms crossed defiantly over the chest, hanging flexibly at the sides, or placed timidly behind the back, but the fact that these several arm positions had vastly different qualitative implications was not taken into account and much valuable diagnostic, and even prognostic, material was overlooked. Similarly, the large range of facial expressions, size, placement on the page, and so on, seemed to offer more information about non-intellectual components than about the intellectual capabilities.

Many clinicians have had similar experience with drawings, experience expressed in the rule so often quoted: "Children draw what they know, not what they see."

Both the House-Tree-Person Drawing device and the Figure-Drawing procedure as a personality tool were born as an outcropping of intelligence scales. Machover's Figure-Drawing technique (20) grew from her experience with the Goodenough tool for appraising children's intelligence. Similarly, Buck's House-Tree-Person procedure (3) was born as an outcropping of an intelligence scale upon which he was working at the time Wechsler came out with his Intelligence Scale. Buck, having had the same experience observing the flooding of the drawings by non-intellectual personality factors, salvaged the House-Tree-Person drawing test from his other intellect-tapping subtests, and developed it into the productive projective technique it has, by now, become. Thus, both Buck and Machover, working independently in Virginia and New York, respectively, took the ancient maxims quoted in the previous chapter, "When an artist paints a portrait he paints two, himself and the sitter," and "The artist does not see things as they are but as he is," and gave them

20th century voice. Buck and Machover were thus the chief achitects and most eloquent spokesmen of the projective drawing field.

## CONVERGING LINES OF EVIDENCE SUPPORTING THE VALIDITY OF PROJECTIVE DRAWING INTERPRETATION

The dynamic personality indications sketched into projective drawings were discovered by using various sources of evidence: namely, information about the subject, free associations, translation of symbols by functional analysis, and comparison of one drawing with another drawing in a series, or of drawings and the Rorschach or TAT data. All of this information was blended together by employing the method of internal consistency, the favorite method of clinically-oriented investigators.

As an example of such internal consistency, I am reminded of a patient, a nine-year-old Negro boy, referred to me after he was discovered stealing toys. There was a history of spying on his mother and step-father in bed at night, masturbation, and homosexual and heterosexual episodes. He shared a bed with two brothers, one seven years old, and one thirteen. There was an older sister of eighteen. The patient was a rejected child, and had only once in his life received a present from his mother. He did not know when his birthday was because of his mother's habitual ignoring of the event. As punishment, he was often deprived of food. When he was enuretic, he was put in cold water to be taught a lesson. He felt rejected by his teacher as well as by his mother, and was beaten-up by his older brother while his mother was at work. For his Person, he drew something which he then described as "a football dummy." This response to the request to draw a person, communicates his feeling that he experiences himself as being forced into the role of a "football dummy" whose only function, we do not have to hazard a guess, is to absorb punishment—to receive the aggression of others without being able in any way to avoid it, much less to retaliate.

Here, we find, consistency is quite evident between the projection of a football dummy as a central element in his self-concept and the beatings and mistreatment afforded by brother, mother, and the outer world in general. Additional consistency was then found between his figure drawing and the responses he offered to the Blacky Test. To many of the Blacky pictures involving the little dog interacting with parental and sibling figures he offered repeated themes of "Father, and brother, and mother, will all punish Blacky," and, "When Blacky comes home he gets nothing but punishment." And, elsewhere, "Blacky thinks it is better to run away than stay home and get punishment."

In an abbreviated way, one might say that the field of projective drawing interpretation rests upon the following foundation stones: (a) The use of common psychoanalytic and folklore meanings of symbols, derived from clinicians' study of dreams, art, myth, fantasy and other such activities influenced by unconscious determination. (b) Clinical experience with the mechanisms of displacement and substitution as well as a wide range of pathological phenomena, especially the conversion symptoms, obsessions and compulsions, phobias, and the psychotic states, all of which become understandable only within the framework of the concept of symbolism. (c) Unraveling of the symbolization employed by inviting the patient's associations. (d) Empirical evidence, which will be best illustrated in the chapters constituting case studies. (e) The flooding of frank symbolization onto the drawing pages from the unconscious of psychotics.[1] (Following these leads, we can then find more subtle murmurings in the same tongue of symbolism in the drawings of non-psychotics). (f) The correlation between projective drawings made at intervals during the course of therapy and the clinical picture at the times the drawings were produced. (Direct correlations are

---

[1] From the standpoint of analytic psychology, psychosis is considered an eruption of the material of the unconscious into consciousness, which floods and overwhelms the ego. Delusions are made up of this material, and their content is treated, by clinicians, in much the same way as is that of dreams. The drawings and paintings of psychotic patients also usually contain representations of the same sort of imagery that constitutes their delusions. In fact, the drawings of prepsychotics often forewarn of the eruption of the unconscious long before overt delusions, hallucinations or autistic thinking become manifest. Such prepsychotic drawings reflect the painful despair, the rasp of jarring emotions, and the uncontainable panic of these conditions. Persons with sightless eyes, gaping mouths, a leering grin, a clutching fist, and other such manifestations appear in the untutored art of those in mental torment.

found between the dropping out of such pain-indicating symbolism and the behavioral changes in therapy, as the psychotherapeutic collaboration begins to correct these patients' distorted picture of themselves and the world.) (g) Internal consistency, as previously illustrated with the nine-year-old boy's response to both the Blacky and the Figure-Drawing test and also the consistency between these data and the case history. (A study by Gallese and Spoerl (9) is pertinent here: Figure Drawings and Thematic Apperception Test stories of twenty-five male students were matched. The comparison was made in terms of the percentage of instances in which the results of each test were corroborated by the results of the other. Agreement was found in 72 per cent of the cases. In that area where agreement was lacking, the authors indicate that the figure drawings tended to uncover "basic needs and conflicts" and the TAT "the manner in which they are integrated and expressed in the total personality situation." Thus, where agreement is not present, the different techniques were found to supplement, rather than contradict, each other.) (h) And, most basically, the interpretative framework of projective drawings rests upon experimental studies. A separate chapter is later devoted to experimental studies of validity and reliability, but perhaps the most central ones should be highlighted here.

Kotkov and Goodman (16) investigated the basic premise that one's body image is projected in one's drawings. They compared the drawing of a person offered by obese women with those of a control group of non-overweight women. The drawings of the obese women, in almost all cases, were larger or wider than those of the control group.

Berman and Leffel (2) compared the somatotypes of 39 males with their figure drawings of a man, and a statistically significant correlation emerged in support of the hypothesis of a projection of the body image.

Ruth Dunnett (7) adds an anecdotal observation: "Unconsciously, children portray themselves in their pictures. Once when I stated my preference for one of two figures in a boy's picture the boy, who was a stocky little fellow with a short neck, said, 'Oh, but I like this one much better,' indicating the one with the head joined almost directly onto the shoulders, in a similar way to his own."

Cleveland and Fisher (4) took as their assumption the observation that arthritic patients unconsciously think of their bodies as covered by a hard outer shell, and conceive of this shell as a barrier against psychological threats, utilizing as a primary defense a stiffening of the musculature of the outer body layer. In contrast, it was assumed that patients developing physical symptoms involving the body interior, such as peptic ulcer, regard the body surface as permeable, as an inadequate defensive area, easily penetrated. Patients of both groups were given projective drawing tests, and the two groups were found to differ significantly in their drawings. The arthritics gave significantly more responses emphasizing body impermeability than did members of the other group. The hypothesis in regard to projection of the body image in one's drawings was deemed supported.

In a study of surgical cases, Meyer, Brown and Levine (21) administered House-Tree-Person drawings before and after surgery. Ear operations, breast-removals, leg amputations, loss of an eye, were all reflected, in the drawings, in conflict indicators in the surgical area. Excessive shading, erasures, tremulous line treatment, or studied avoidance of the area marked the site of operation. Loss of a limb or of a sense organ on one side of the body was projected onto the same side of the drawn figure. For example, if the patient's left arm had undergone surgery, he might express his painful awareness of that fact by drawing his tree with the limbs on the left side broken or sawed off and with the left arm of his drawn person withered or useless, hanging by a thread from the shoulder, or hidden defensively behind the back.

This finding of anatomical laterality and its surprisingly consistent accuracy emphasizes the element of self-portraiture characteristic of projective drawings.

Attempts to substantiate the thesis of projection in drawing by study of the sensory handicapped or physically disabled is quite popular. Machover (20) has noted that deaf people, or those who have abnormal or disturbed auditory experiences, will most often give special attention to their drawing of the ear, emphasizing it in some way. She also reports an individual case of a male adult whose barely perceptible and functionally insignificant polio residual was picked up in the drawing by a conspicuous reinforcement of the line around the right ankle. In this connection, the reader may be reminded of Figures 1 through 4 of the previous chapter, which showed the drawings of a man who walked with the aid of crutches, and those of the subject who was born missing an arm.

Bender's (1) experience with children is in the same direction. She finds that children with a severe defect of the body often depict this defect in their drawing of a person. A child who had had one leg shorter than the other from earliest infancy always drew her person with one leg shorter than its mate. Several children with congenital anomalies of the skull depicted that anomaly in their drawings. A child who had a disabling neurological condition of the feet drew one-legged people or people riding in carts.

It is not only the physical aspects of the body image which are projected, but also the psychological. In an interesting study of sexual role and self-concept, Fisher and Fisher (8) asked 76 female psychiatric patients to draw a female figure. Those who drew figures of a low degree of femininity, according to ratings by judges, tended to have fewer heterosexual experiences, more dysfunctions, and more constricted sexual lives. Those who drew highly feminine figures, on the other hand, had led more promiscuous but unsatisfying lives. The group of women who produced figures of average femininity were found to have derived more genuine satisfaction from their feminine roles.

In a comparison of drawings of overt homosexual and non-homosexual subjects, DeMartino (5) found that high heels and emphasized eyelashes appeared significantly more frequently in the homosexual's drawing of a male than in those offered by the non-homosexuals. This is quite consistent with Machover's observation, "The homosexually inclined male . . . may give large eyes with lashes to the figure of a male, in combination with a well specified high heel" (20). Levy (18) has also observed "If the eyes are very large and if those of the male figure have lashes, the subject is almost surely a homosexual."

In a study of the projection of aggressivity in figure drawings, Katz (15) compared 52 adult males, who had been convicted of assault and/or murder, with a control group. Drawing items which significantly differentiated the aggressive from the non-aggressive group include eyes "piercing" and reinforced, large fingers, arms reinforced, fingers reinforced, legs thrust wide, combination of firm, light, and heavy lines, large arms, and hair reinforced. The reinforcement of the parts of the body capable of aggressive action like arms and fingers, as well as emphasis on eyes which can "give dirty looks" is in accord with the projective drawing hypothesis, as is the reinforcement of the hair, frequently a symbol for virility, assertion or aggression.

In an attempt to see whether clinical psychologists could accurately differentiate well-adjusted from poorly adjusted children on the basis of their figure drawing, Toler and Toler (27) used three fifth-grade classes. The criterion was sociometric data whereby the children rated each other as to popularity. To a statistically significant degree, the clinicians were successful in making the kind of discriminations called for to differentiate between children who were more popular in their groups and children who were less popular. Apparently the self-concept is crucial to one's successful relationship with one's peers, and this aspect of the self-concept reflects itself in the drawings made by popular and non-popular children.

Drawings are also found to quite sensitively reflect situational stress. In the previously mentioned study by Meyer, Brown and Levine (21), it was found that the preoperative drawings of cases awaiting surgery showed many regressive features which improved after surgery. For instance, the preoperative drawn person was often depicted as a child; the postoperative person had "grown up." The preoperative tree was often a sapling which also "grew up" after the operation. A similar impression was conveyed in the house drawing of some subjects: a preoperative house might have resembled a log cabin or four-walled box with few windows and situated in isolation up a mountain, only to be expanded into a suburban residence in the postoperative drawing. Another feature of several of these cases was the suggestion of a striking change of mood from depression to cheerfulness. Drab monochromatic pictures in the preoperative state were replaced by brightly colored ones in the postoperative retest; a window-box with flowers was added to liven-up the house; a huge picture window disclosing a food-laden dining-room table replaced the nearly windowless wall of the preoperative house. Warmth and coziness are implied in the smoke issuing from a sturdy chimney, of which the preoperative counterpart was a smokeless chordee.

Hammer (12) investigated sexual symbolism in the House-Tree-Person projective drawing test. On the assumption that subjects who were about to undergo eugenic sterilization or who had just been sterilized would be prone to reveal strong feelings of castration, the drawings of subjects in this group were compared to a control group for indices of genital symbolization and castration feelings. Significant statistical differences were found between the two groups on twenty-six of the fifty-four items investigated. Elongated objects, such as chimneys, branches, tree trunks, arms, nose, legs, feet, and so on, are susceptible to being utilized as phallic symbols. Circles, triangles, and objects with a vertical split down the center (such as a vertical window sash-line emphasized and the horizontal sash-line omitted) may be employed as reflections of felt castration in the drawings of males. It is in the drawing of these genital symbols that an individual may reveal his feelings of genital inadequacy and castration anxiety. Such feelings may be depicted by his presentation of the symbols as damaged, cut through, broken or otherwise impaired. Hammer concluded, "The rules of symbolic disguise appear to fit into certain generalities or to make up a language of symbolism."

Spoerl (26) matched drawings with personality sketches and was able to demonstrate significant success in judging personality from drawings.

Waehner (28) analyzed drawings of college students and drew up descriptive personality sketches for each student. Teachers were highly successful in recognizing the students from the sketches. There was also a close relationship between Rorschach interpretations and the projective drawing personality sketches.

In another study reported in the same monograph, Waehner studied the drawings of nursery school children. Teachers and psychologists who knew the children matched statements about them (based on blind analysis of the drawing products) with the children. Four out of the five matchers recognized all of the children, and the fifth was 50 per cent correct in her matching. The matchers agreed with 85 per cent of the single specific statements, disagreed with 4 per cent and were neutral in regard to 11 per cent.

A significant correlation between the diagnosis of pathology made on the basis of projective drawings and the psychiatric opinion on those who produced them was yielded in a study by Gunzburg (11). There was a positive correlation between the diagnosis of pathology or non-pathology, based on the eighty sets of drawings, and the diagnosis based upon the clinical picture. It was found that 74 per cent of the cases were placed by the drawing criteria in the same category as the psychiatric opinion and only 12.5 per cent in a category which disagreed with the psychiatric diagnosis. The remaining 13.5 per cent were considered "doubtful" on the basis of the drawing criteria. This result is statistically significant at the one per cent level of confidence.

In the area of reliability, equally good results are found on the basis of experimental studies (6, 15, 26-28). In fact, Machover (20) has stated that consistency is so great that "occasionally drawings of patients obtained over a period of years are so remarkably alike as to constitute personal signatures" (p. 6).

Thus, the statement that the subject draws what he feels, rather than solely what he sees, summarizes the observation of the clinicians and experimenters cited above. The subject, by the size, placement, line pressure, content of the drawing, and the like, conveys what he *feels* in addition to what he sees. His subjective aspects color and define his objective intent.

Naumburg (22) points out that Luquet, the French psychologist, long ago indicated that both children and primitives consistently draw elements which they consider essential, and drop out others which may not concern them, and then include aspects which are known to be there but are not visible. The goal, then of both child and primitive is not "objective realism" but what Luquet calls "mental realism." Our experiments have shown that adult subjects have this same goal, too.

## SOME BRIEF CLINICAL EXAMPLES

To convey the *feel* of projective drawings, and the drama that is frequently unfolded in them, the following brief examples are presented.

Figure 1 was drawn by a twenty-eight-year-old male. The most conspicuous aspect of the subject's drawing performance is the large size he gives the drawn male, causing it to crowd the drawing page at both top and bottom. Along with this, the firm line pressure, the overextended, broadened shoulders, and the stance (with the feet spread apart and the arms hanging away from the body, ready for action) all reinforce the impression one gets of someone who is trying "to prove himself." The subject cannot prove himself big enough in stature (that is, there is not room enough on the page to draw the person as large as he would wish it to be), nor generally impressive enough. The zoot-suit treatment, the stern, hard facial expression, and the almost ape-like, long arms that extend too far down the body length all emphasize the subject's attempt to prove himself on paper—

Figure 1

Figure 2

to prove himself manly, active, deserving of status, and one not to be taken lightly. The broadened shoulders and the height-filling stature remind us most forcefully of Shakespeare's psychological principle that the person, "Doth protest too much."

When we learn that the subject was examined because of a rape offense for which he had been convicted, we then see the close parallel of his trying to prove himself more manly than he actually feels, on paper as well as in real life. The compulsive need to prove his masculine prowess was also evidenced by the fact that he maintained four mistresses simultaneously in different parts of the city. Frequently he would visit all four in one night. On one such night after returning from a visit to the fourth, the inner voice of doubt concerning his virility raised its whisper for a fifth time, and he had to commit rape on the way home to quiet this doubt.

He derived very little pleasure from his sexual activities. He reported that he would much rather go to a movie or read a book than engage in coitus, but something within him just felt "uncomfortable" until he had had intercourse. He did not regard intercourse as "fun" or "pleasurable," but rather as serving to release intolerable anxiety—anxiety that grew out of his fear that he was not man enough. This fear apparently had been reinforced by the physical condition which caused him to walk with a limp. Physically he was small in stature, thin and verging toward the puny, very much the antithesis of his drawn person, whose traits he attempted to emulate in ego-ideal fashion.

For contrast, Figure 2 is presented. Whereas Figure 1 deviated markedly from the statistical norm in regard to size, Figure 2 deviates just as strikingly in the other direction, on this continuum. Figure 2 is drawn inadequate not only in size, but in stance and facial expression. The arms are held away from the sides as if incapable of action. They reflect helplessness and dependency. This is reinforced by the ineffective fingers, only three in number, on each hand. The facial expression is passive, orally-receptive, and round—lacking in feelings of manliness. The entire figure is heavily shaded, reflecting the intense anxiety and tension of the subject.

The placement of the figure on the drawing page supports the implications of the other elements of the drawing. Rather than assume a stance toward the center of the page, the drawn person retreats toward the bottom and the left, as if to seek the security of a corner of the entire field represented by the drawing page. In addition, a sun is added to warm the pathetic little figure which is so greatly in need of emotional warmth and comfort.

Figure 2 was drawn by a thirty-three-year-old male, also a sex offender; but a sex offender of an entirely different nature—one who approached small children rather than mature females for his sexual gratification. Apparently, our second subject suffers inadequacy feelings in psychosexual areas of much more massive proportions than the first subject. The second subject can not even employ compensation to hide his inner feelings of lack of manliness or virility. He gives in to this feeling by approaching little girls instead of adult females, just as he gives in to this same feeling on the drawing page. Thus we can see that one's performance on the drawing page often tends to parallel one's performance in the overt behavioral field. The patient's feelings of inadequacy and helplessness, so clearly sketched into his drawn male, explain his having to turn toward immature sex objects when his psychosexual needs clamor for satisfaction.

As support for the hypothesis of projection in drawing, and to meet the argument that clinicians tend to read into drawings that which they know about the subject, the writer performed a little informal experiment. He gave Figures 1 and 2 to a group of twenty clinical psychologists, explaining that one had been drawn by a rapist and the other by someone who approached little girls for his sexual gratification. The psychologists were then asked to indicate which one had been offered by which subject. Not one of the entire group of psychologists made an incorrect choice.

Since the drawings were so overt in their reflection of the underlying traits of the two subjects, and since they spoke so eloquently of the psychological condition of those who drew them, the two drawings were then also given to thirty freshmen college students of an English class. It was gratifying to note, the students also were 100 per cent correct in their designation of which drawing was made by which subject. Apparently, then, when drawings are particularly clear in their implications, and when they reflect extreme conditions, even the uninitiated layman can understand the language of projective drawing communication.

To continue the exemplification of the continuum in size which the clinician employing projective drawings may encounter, Figure 3 is presented. Figure 3 consists of a male subject's drawing of a male person. The figure is so small, that the reader may have trouble locating it; it will be found at the very bottom, center, of the drawing page.

Whereas Figure 2 is a graphic portrayal of feelings of inadequacy, Figure 3 reflects total feelings of insignificance. Not only by the miniscule size, but also by the light line pressure which causes the drawn person to all but fade from view, our third subject conveys to us his feelings of being wholly without worth, status, or recognition as a person. He feels painfully constricted and capable of being wholly overlooked by others.

This drawing, strange as it may seem at first, was drawn by a twelve-year-old boy with an I.Q. of 150. In spite of his superior I.Q., he felt he was without a grain of worth. His father held a Ph.D. in one of the social sciences, and his mother a Master's degree in an allied area. They so over-pushed the child to attainments above even his clearly superior capabilities that he soon crystalized the self-concept of someone who was, by comparison with these high standards, clearly inadequate. Obvious preference was shown to the subject's younger sibling which served to reinforce the subject's feelings of insignificance as a person. Also, his parents held to the philosophy that watching TV, reading comic books or drinking a soda would spoil the child. Here, too, their behavior led him to believe that his needs were to be forever overlooked, just as the drawn person he renders is so easily overlooked. Close inspection of the drawing reveals inadequate, puny arms that cannot accomplish anything for himself, a head that is bowed down in dejection, and a sad facial expression.

Figure 3

Figures 1, 2 and 3 are chosen to illustrate the wide range of individual differences, at least along a single variable (size), which reflects the individual differences among the subject's themselves.

In passing, it may be noted that the drawing of the human figure (as in Figure 1) can assume the character of an over-emphasized, exaggerated portrait of strength or importance, adequate for self-inflation. Within the normal range, children and adolescents tend to draw themselves as more forceful, glamorous, or bigger and older than they actually are, which appears to be indicative of their own wishes about themselves. They put into the picture drawn a promise of that reality which they desire. Children and adolescents who are capable of compensating, express this compensating capacity in their drawings.

In the opposite direction, on the continuum of size, we find the child with somewhat greater feelings of inadequacy, the child who has suffered more awareness of the fact that he has been born a pygmy in a world of giants. This child is more prone to draw a person as weak, insignificant, and as protected and reinforced by guns, canes, and so on. Whereas the aggressive child draws big, dangerous arms with long fingers, the inadequate or withdrawn child "forgets" to draw hands at all—as though the subject had not experienced helping hands when he needed them or as if hands were guilty things, which may be used to do something which is labeled in our culture as *taboo*.

Hinrichs (14) obtained drawings of a person from delinquent and non-delinquent boys. To a statistically significant degree, the delinquent boys more frequently drew soldiers or cowboys as a reflection of their virility strivings (which frequently pressed them into delinquent acts in an effort to prove themselves more possessed of the stereotyped traits symbolized by soldiers and cowboys, who attain status through the use of force and aggression).

An adolescent boy, for example, referred to the author because of excessive truancy, the flaunting of rules in school, and generally rebellious behavior, reflected his characteristic role in life in his drawing of a person as presented in Figure 4. The drawn male is dressed in a soldier's outfit as a reflection of the subject's need for greater status, prestige and recognition as a male than he feels he possesses. The drawn person turns his back on the world, much as the subject himself has done, and introduces a regulation into the picture merely to break it. He adds the sign, "No Spitting," so that the drawn person may disobey it. This clearly paralleled the subject's seeking out rules and regulations merely to break them, to prove to himself and others that they did not apply to him, that he was outside of the sphere that authority could encompass, that he was bigger and better than the rules and the people who made them.

In sharp contrast to the traits projected in Figure 4, we have those projected by another subject in Figures 5 and 6.

These two drawings were made by a twenty-eight-year-old male. The drawn male is described as a seventeen-year-old boy "asking his mother for money." Here the patient projects himself as immature (that is, much younger than his own age), and

Figure 4

Figure 5

Figure 6

as quite dependent upon a mother-figure. Not only does the drawn person ask his mother for money, but the subject adds a drawn sun to the picture as a reflection of his need never to be without a stronger, warmth-giving figure. For his drawing of a female, he renders a maternal figure, where other subjects his age customarily depict a sex object. Not only is the figure itself maternal in outline, but also engaged in extending succor to the patient. His need for nutrience and a close emotional relationship to a mother-figure was clearly supported by the behaviorial picture. Even though he was twenty-eight, if the patient took a girl to a dance, his mother would pick him up with the family car when the dance was over, drive the girl home, and then bring her son home. The mother's successful efforts to keep the subject immature, dependent, and inadequate were reflected in the subject's psychological make-up and were expressed by (a) his revealing self-portrait and (b) his depiction of female figures.

In contrast to the previous drawings produced by neurotic subjects and those with character disorders, Figure 7 was drawn by a schizophrenic patient. The feelings of depersonalization which form the core of this patient's pathology clearly define and limit his projective drawing. Along with the intense feelings of depersonalization which overwhelm this individual, the subject conveys in his drawing a feeling that he is controlled by outside influences. His drawing assumes the appearance of a mechanical automaton subject to the complete control of someone other than himself. The patient's verbal descriptions are consistent with this graphic portrayal of his feelings: "The face looks very enigmatic, but it doesn't mean anything . . . nothing behind the façade . . . just one box on another."

In contrast to the patient's present schizophrenic reaction, we have the same person's projective figure drawing obtained three years earlier, while the patient was still employing a neurotic character armoring during his first month of admission to the hospital (see Figure 8).

The patient commented about this drawn person that it represented a male clown, whose best part was his "costume or disguise." "The worst part is that he is not much of a person . . . ineffectual . . . he is too old to be helped . . . he is nobody, just a clown in the circus, he is nobody except when he is performing, when he is amusing people." Here the feelings of lack of worth as a person, the extremely negative self-concept and

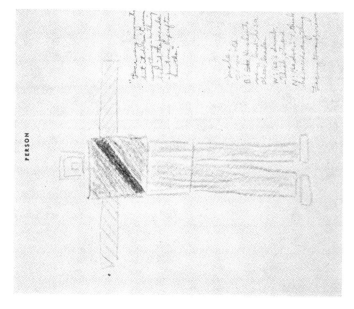

Figure 7

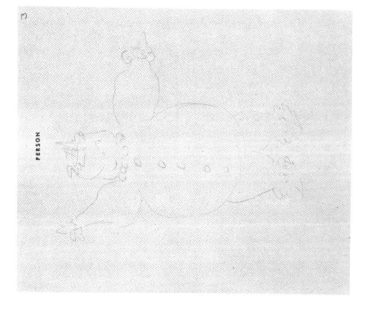

Figure 8

derogatory evaluation of himself foreshadow the later movement across the schizophrenic borderlands. His feelings of inadequacy, insufficiency, futility (particularly about recoverability) also prophesy the later schizophrenic solution, as does his retreat into a "disguise." Already the drawn figure begins to lose human-like proportions and inflates itself into a synthetic-like balloon, somewhat removed from flesh-and-bone qualities, as an early hint of beginning feelings of depersonalization.

Sometimes in a drawing, a sturdy, well-rooted tree shows a strong similarity to the person drawn, who also stands solidly and determined; or, on the other hand, a tree and a person both appear shaky and on the verge of toppling, so that we see that the self-image can be projected onto inanimate as well as animate concepts (see Figures 9 and 10).

The tree was described as, "Dead, it died of some sort of blight, it is an old tree, it has now been dead a long time . . . and

Figure 9

Figure 10

the elements have pushed it over, or are presently pushing it over." The drawn person also topples. In both drawings we have a reflection of the patient's anxious concern about his personality balance and its precarious position.

In responses such as this, in which primarily a fear is expressed, there may be present an element of wishing for the feared event, of wanting to give up active effort and surrender to the disintegrating forces. The psychiatric diagnosis was that of pre-psychosis.

The depiction of wind blowing fiercely, something very infrequently introduced into projective drawings, is a direct expression of the tremendous environmental pressure to which the patient feels subjected. We may deduce from the position of the bent-over tree, that the patient fears this pressure will crack his personality, and precipitate the psychotic condition. (This prophecy was unfortunately verified ten weeks after the projective drawings were obtained.) The puny size of the drawn tree reinforced the tortuously bent-over position in indicating the extremely weak ego-strength of the patient.

Two more examples of projection in the drawing of the tree may be found in Figures 11 and 12.

Figure 11 depicts a severely mutilated, ravaged, scarred tree with broken-off limbs which the patient has labelled by writing in, "Dead limbs." The whole tree itself is further defined by the patient's having written, "Dead tree" beside his drawing. This thirty-eight-year-old male patient was found to have had the most astonishing and shocking childhood. The twelfth child born to his parents, he was neglected as an infant to the point where he was allowed to lie in his soiled diapers for two to three days at a time until sores developed on his body. He had an alcoholic father and a severely disturbed mother who fought and bickered continually. As he grew older, he was subjected to both verbal and physical abuse from his father, including blows on the head with a cane during his father's periods of intoxication. At the age of six, the patient ran away from home and existed by sleeping in doorways and in automobiles while subsisting on the milk he stole from doorsteps. After several weeks of this incredible life, he was picked up and was placed in a welfare home for the remainder of his developmental years. The scarring that his early life experiences had left on his self-concept, the wounds and the traumas, all left their deep mark. And his drawn tree clearly mirrors the ravages on his personality. He presently experiences himself as a beaten, emotionally crippled, aching individual, who lives in a pessimistically-toned, depressive atmosphere of acute discontent.

The other tree (Figure 12) was offered by a twelve-year-old boy who had been referred because of the following behavior: he had been observed picking up baby pigs with the prongs of a pitchfork, throwing down baby chicks and crushing them under the heel of his shoe, and at one time setting fire to a bale of hay underneath a cow. On top of this, he had recently released a tractor to roll down a hill onto some children. (Fortunately, the children dodged the vehicle in time.)

His drawn tree speaks as eloquently as does his behavior. It is a graphic communication saying in distinct and unequivocal language: "Keep away from me!" Spear-like branches with

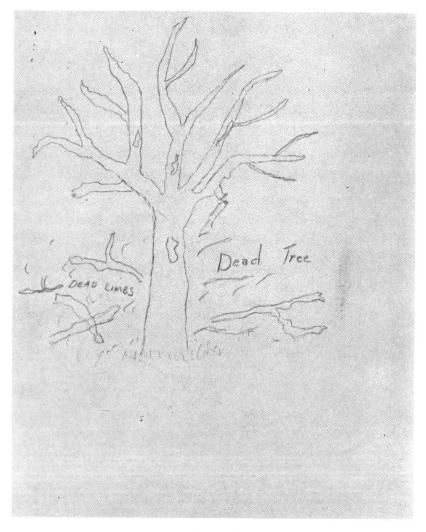

Figure 11

thorn-like "leaves" decorate a sharply pointed tree trunk. The branches reach out aggressively in a promise of inflicting significant harm to all those who come within reach. The drawing is steeped in sadism, aggression, and angry resentments. The depicted tree could well have been used as an emblem for Hitler's Storm Troopers.

The drawing of a person or of a tree is by no means singular for the receiving of the subject's projections. Drawings of animals, houses, and other objects may also be used to communicate deeper feelings. Figure 13 for example, was drawn by a twenty-eight-year-old male subject, in response to the request, "Please draw a house." The lines which so directly convey to the viewer the distinct impression of bars in the windows, the subject rationalized as creases in the window drapes. Not only the barred-like windows but also the entire stockade effect conveys the atmosphere of a prison rather than that of a cozy home.

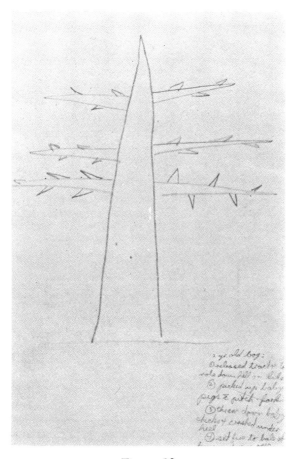

Figure 12

Figure 13

This unconsciously motivated depiction of the subject's home situation directly parallels the existing state of affairs. The subject, at the age of twenty-eight, was engaged to be married but was handicapped in consummating these plans by the fact that he was the sole support of his invalid father and an aging mother. In spite of his many protestations that he enjoyed being able to care for his parents when they needed him, he—at least on lower levels of awareness—perceived his situation as imprisoning.

This drawing of a house, the two drawings of the tree and the eight drawings of persons that preceded it, all offer convincing confirmation of the principle that people draw what they feel within themselves rather than, or at least in addition to, what they see.

Before going further, it should be pointed out that although some clinicians interpret each drawing of a person as a projection of body image or self-concept, not all such drawings involve such self-portraiture. While projection of the felt self or the idealized-self is frequently the case, it is not always necessarily so. A figure drawing may, at times, be a reflection of perceptions of significant people in one's environment. Children are, of course, more prone than adult subjects to depict parental figures in their figure drawings.

The case of Leonard, a twelve-year-old-boy, who stayed away from school because he felt the teachers were picking on him, may serve as illustration. Excessive truancy was his remedy for the feeling that teachers had it in for him, and would make a special scapegoat of him. The tensions within the boy were reflected behaviorally in his doubting eyes, taut face, unceasing and jerky chatter, and complete self-centeredness. Knowing no other way to establish himself, he tried to do it by bravado, belligerence, and a refusal to abide by the rules. It was for this latter reason that he was referred to the writer. Lenny soon earned from his peers the nickname of "Rocky." Behind Rocky's tendency to misinterpret the actions of people in authority was a series of childhood traumatizing experiences with a cold, harsh, and often

Figure 14

Figure 15

brutal set of parents; his mother was bitingly sarcastic and his father physically abusive.

This perception of his parental figures is expressed on paper in the subject's two figure drawings (Figures 14 and 15). The mother is clearly presented as orally aggressive and capable of inflicting severe damage with her mouth. The hands are absent, reflecting Rocky's perception of his mother as not reaching out to him—ungiving and rejecting. She is perceived of in unappealing and frightening tones. Rocky's father figure, on the other hand, while not orally aggressive, is apperceived as capable of inflicting severe physical damage to one's vital parts. The scissor-like fingers seem capable of cutting off anything that protrudes from Rocky's body. The implications of castration anxiety are supported by the drawing of a house (Figure 16) in which Rocky projects onto that which protrudes from the body of the house, the chimney, his feelings that that which protrudes from his own body is likewise flimsily attached and vulnerable to separation from the body. The chimney hangs onto the body of the house

Figure 16

by a mere thread; it is as unattached as one can draw a chimney and still keep it part of the house. Rocky's feelings of vulnerability are also expressed in the house drawing by its quality of thinness, lack of substance, and lack of capability to withstand the pressures and forces of the environment. On one side the house already buckles.

In addition, the subject dresses the male drawing in the authoritarian role (military uniform of the Russians) in which he apperceives his father to parade. He then adds the dictatorial aspects of his father-image by labeling the drawn male "Stalin."

Apparently Rocky's experiences with his parents have torn a deep gash in his feelings of adequacy and left him with no one to turn to for help in tending the aching wound. The drawings suggest the intensity of the dowry of antagonism with which Rocky had to start off in life. And once a boy has suffered rejection, he will find rejection even where it does not exist. The boy's fear of, and expectation of, mistreatment at the hands of authority figures rippled outward to include the teachers with whom he had so much trouble. So Rocky built a wall of isolation and toughness around himself, strong enough—he hoped—to defend himself against the world.

In response to the request to draw an animal, he began by drawing what he described as "a timid rabbit running away" on one side of the page; he then appeared displeased with the drawing, turned the page over and on the other side drew what he described as "a little wildcat." Here we see the two sides of the coin of Rocky's inner view of himself. His basic feeling of fearfulness and lack of adequacy (as conveyed by the concept, "a timid rabbit running away"), he attempts to hide behind the tough-guy façade of "a little wildcat."

Underneath it all, however, he appears as a lonely boy who wears his bitterness and antagonism as a mask to conceal and deny his hunger for human warmth.

One of the early dreams the patient reported was a nightmare in which he tried to kill someone and then fell out of bed. He reported, "I'm always trying to kill someone in my dreams. I was beating up a guy in this dream. I had him on the floor and was kicking him, almost killing him." He then followed this with a degree of insight: "I was afraid of the guy, but I just hit him. When I hit him, I wasn't afraid of him anymore." Thus, in his dreams, Rocky offers us support for the interpretive deductions made on the basis of his animal drawings, where he attempts to hide his feelings of being the "timid rabbit" behind the cloak of "a little wildcat." [2]

A word of caution: although the previous examples were presented as graphic illustrations of projection in drawing, they were meant to be exercises only. In actual clinical practice, the dangers of basing interpretative deductions on isolated bits of data are obvious. In practice, confirmation of interpretative speculation on the basis of one drawing must be checked against not only the other drawings, but the entire projective battery, the case history, the clinical impression gleaned during the interview with the subject and all other available information. If, for example, a subject for his Most Unpleasant Concept draws someone having run over someone else in an automobile, for his house drawing sketches a picture of a cathedral, and for his animal drawing offers a lamb, the sequence suggests a common denominator that one might *speculatively* read as follows: I attempt to conquer the anger and hostility within me by denial and reaction-formation (that is, I say that the most unpleasant thing for me would be to aggressively harm someone else), by restricting myself to what is pure, innocent, good and holy (the drawing of a cathedral) and gentle (the choice of a lamb for an animal drawing) in interpersonal exchange. Rage will not erupt (the most unpleasant thing I can think of, as reflected in the Most Unpleasant Concept Test) if I cling to a saintly ideal (the cathedral drawing and, to a lesser degree, the lamb drawing) to see me through crises which may, at times, arise.

This tentative formulation must then be checked against the Rorschach and the clinical impression. On the behavioral level, the subject may assume a self-effacing, Pollyanna role in which he attempts to present himself as good, sweet and noble. The projective drawing induction may be offered further support by

---

[2] In the therapy relationship, Rocky has begun to learn that not all his future relationships with authority figures are doomed to be the sterile, harsh and traumatizing ones he has experienced in the past with the principle authority figures in his life. Hence, he is now more able to evaluate teachers in an objective light—as he was surprised to find out: "You know, some of them really aren't such bad Joes, I guess." He is beginning to discover a world which can be a good place in which to live.

the Rorschach content of aggression, hostility, "explosions," blood and gore. Thus, if the drawings fit in persuasively with the overt behavior and the Rorschach content to make a continuous pattern of the reaction-formation variable within the subject's personality, we may, with greater confidence, accept their implications.

Interpretations should ordinarily represent the convergence of several, or many paths, of data. This *principle of convergence* is essentially no different from that which guides dream analysis, psychoanalytically-oriented therapy, Rorschach interpretation, and thema analysis of Thematic Apperception Test data. In fact, it is a basic principle of all scientific methodology.

## THE EFFECT OF ART TRAINING ON PROJECTIVE DRAWING

A frequent question that students ask me concerns the interfering effect of art training, in the elementary and secondary schools, upon drawings as an unhampered or free personality reflection. For the answer to this question, one has only to look at the speed with which individuals throw off the repressive effects of the Palmer handwriting style once they pass the sixth grade, the last school level at which this artificial mold is applied to cast unnaturally one's true personality expression as it bursts through on the psychomotor level. By the eighth grade, students' handwriting is again as varied as is the range in their personalities. Their handwriting has squirmed out of the hampering mold to move into freer congruency with their own personality, whether constricted in size, timid in pressure, bold in size or aggressively savage in its attack of the paper, flexible and smoothly functioning or grandiose in its flourishings.

Art training, by its very nature, favors free expression more than does handwriting training, and as such it probably contaminates projective drawing interpretation even less than handwriting training does handwriting analysis.

In fact, it has frequently been observed that one's skill as an artist serves to enhance the capacity for expressing one's self graphically in the projective media rather than to interfere with it. Figures 17 and 18 may serve as illustrations. Figure 17 was drawn by an overt bisexual with strong feminine identification.

He conveys the fact subtly by the feminine features he gives his male drawing as well as by implying that the clothes are too large for the figure. Thus, he reflects his feeling that the role of a male is an uncomfortable one for him, one which he does not feel "big enough" to fill.

Parenthetically, it might be observed that the conflict this produces within him creates the need for stability reflected in his seeking the very base of the page as the line on which to stand his figure.

Figure 18, because of the artistic capabilities of the subject, clearly conveyed the opposing poles in the subject's self-concept. The crew-cut, the dangling cigarette, and the flattened, pugilist-like nose, clash in direct fashion with the sissified, prissy, Little Lord Fauntleroy outfit.

This jibes with the information in the case history. The subject, when he was a child, was forced to take violin lessons. He

Figure 17

Figure 18

lived in a delinquent, slum area and when carrying his violin case through the neighborhood, he was subject to the taunts and jeers of his contemporaries. The "tough guy" component assimilated through association with his peers before he was forced into studying music, is reflected in the drawing, as is the effect on his self-concept—still prevalent, years later at the age of 43—of the sissified element also ingrained into his inner view of himself.

The artistic capabilities of the two subjects who drew Figures 17 and 18, we may observe, aided rather than hindered self-portraiture.

Waehner (28) investigated the effect of advanced art training on projective drawings. He found that there was no difference between students with and without art training (or art interest) in the degree of accuracy with which they were psychologically diagnosed, on the basis of their projective drawings.

## THEORETICAL POSTULATES

The theoretical orientation followed in the present book has been expressed elsewhere (24) in the following formulations:

(A) There is a tendency in man to view the world in an anthropomorphic way, in his own image—and this facilitates the projective aspects involved in drawing a house, a tree, a person, an animal, or any other concept, for that matter.

(B) The core of the anthropomorphic view of the environment is the mechanism of projection. Projection is defined as that psychological dynamism by which one attributes qualities, feelings, attitudes and strivings of one's own to objects of the environment (people, other organisms, things). The content of the projection may or may not be known to the person as part of himself. In this respect the concept of projection endorsed here is broader than Freud's early one which assumed that the content of the projection always is repressed and that the function of projection is to enable the person to deal with an outer danger when it becomes too difficult to deal with an inner danger which, therefore, has to be first repressed and then projected (such as is involved in denying a trait in one's self and attributing it to other people or objects).

(C) Distortions enter into the process of projection to the extent to which: (a) the projection has a defensive function (projection in Freud's sense); (b) tangential, partial, or superficial data from the object are invested with meanings from the subject's own life which do not correspond to the real or total picture of the object, and (c) qualities are ascribed to the object, the presence of which the subject denies in himself (again projection in Freud's sense).

Distortions in the mechanism of projection are very much like the situation of a man who, according to the analogy of Gondor (10), "has only a limited number of slides for a projection machine, and, and no matter what the situation or the type of screen, can project only his available pictures" (p. 11).

The emotionally disturbed person's perception of the world is not always accurate. It may give him distorted views—and one's characteristic distortions of the world are sampled by projective drawings and recorded on paper.

## SUMMARY

Projective drawings tap the stream of personality needs as they flood the area of graphic creativity. Certain concessions must, however, be made to psychology's demand for standardization: hence, the same concepts (house, tree, person, animal) are asked for from the subject, on the same size paper with standard material.[3]

Armed with the knowledge that man's deeper needs (a) color his creative efforts and (b) show an affinity for speaking in pictorial images, the clinician and/or experimenter has at his disposal a rapidly and easily administered technique for eliciting submerged levels of human feelings. Basically, the subject's relative emphasis of different elements within his drawings, in addition to his global drawing performance, tells us a good deal of what matters to him, what it does to him, and what he does about it.

In the field of projective drawing, interpretation empirically rests upon the following foundation stones: (a) The use of common psychoanalytic and folklore meanings of symbols, derived from study of dreams, myth, art, fantasy and other such activities steeped in unconscious determination. (b) Clinical experience with the mechanisms of displacement and substitution as well as a wide range of pathological phenomena, especially the conversion symptoms, obsessions, and compulsions, phobias, and the

---

[3] A "number two" pencil is employed for the achromatic phase of projective drawings and eight crayons of standard colors for the chromatic phase. This will be more fully described in a subsequent chapter.

psychotic states—all of which become understandable only within the framework of the concept of symbolism. (c) Unraveling of the symbolization employed in drawings by inviting the patient's associations. (d) Empirical evidence with previous patients' drawings. (e) Following the lead provided by the frank flooding of symbolization onto the drawing page, from the unconscious of psychotics, we can then detect more subtle murmurings in the same tongue of symbolism in the drawings of non-psychotics. (f) The correlation between projective drawings made at intervals during the course of therapy and the clinical picture at the times the drawings were produced. (g) Internal consistency between one drawing and another, between the drawings and the other techniques in the projective battery, between drawings and dreams, between drawings and the behavioral picture, and between drawings and the case history. (h) And, lastly but most importantly, experimental studies.

The field of projective drawing interpretation also rests upon several theoretical postulates: (a) There is a tendency in man to view the world in an anthropomorphic manner, in his own image. (b) The core of the anthropomorphic view of the environment is the mechanism of projection. (c) Distortions enter into the process of projection to the extent to which the projection has a defensive function, that is, the projection is in the service of ascribing to the outer world that which the subject denies in himself.

## REFERENCES

1. Bender, Lauretta: *Child Psychiatric Techniques.* Springfield, Thomas, 1952.
2. Berman, S., and Leffel, J.: Body type and figure drawing. *J. Clin. Psych.,* 9:368-370, 1953.
3. Buck, J. N.: The H-T-P technique, a qualitative and quantitative scoring method. *J. Clin. Psych.,* Monograph No. 5:1-120, 1948.
4. Cleveland, S., and Fisher, S.: Body-image boundaries in various psychosomatic illnesses. APA Convention, California, 1955.
5. DeMartino, M. F.: Human figure drawings by mentally retarded males. *J. Clin. Psych.,* 10:241-244, 1954.
6. Dorken, H.: The reliability and validity of spontaneous fingerpaintings. *J. Proj. Tech.,* 18:169-182, 1952.
7. Dunnett, Ruth: *Art and Child Personality.* London, Methuen, 1948.
8. Fisher, S., and Fisher, Rhoda: Style of sexual adjustment in disturbed women and its expression in figure drawing. *J. Psychol.,* 34:169-179, 1952.
9. Gallese, A., and Spoerl, Dorothy: A comparison of Machover and Thematic Apperception Test interpretation. *J. Social Psychol.,* 40:73-77, 1954.

10. Gondor, E.: *Art and Play Therapy.* New York, Doubleday, 1954.
11. Gunzburg, H. C.: Scope and limitations of the Goodenough drawing test method in clinical work with mental defectives. *J. Clin. Psych., 11*:8-15, 1955.
12. Hammer, E. F.: An investigation of sexual symbolism. *J. Proj. Tech., 17:* 401-413, 1953.
13. Hanvik, L. J.: The Goodenough Test as a measure of intelligence of child psychiatric patients. *J. Clin. Psychol., 9*:71-72, 1953.
14. Hinrich, W. E.: The Goodenough drawing test in relationship to delinquency and problem behavior. *Arch. Psychol., 175*:1935.
15. Katz, J.: The projection of assaultive aggression in the human figure drawing of adult male Negro offenders. Ph.D. Thesis, New York University, unpublished, 1951.
16. Kotkov, B., and Goodman, M.: The draw-a-person tests of obese women. *J. Clin. Psych., 9*:362-364, 1953.
17. Kris, E.: *Psychoanalytic Explorations in Art.* New York, Internat. Univ. Press, 1952.
18. Levy, S.: Figure drawings as a projective test, in Abt, L. E., and Bellak, L.: *Projective Psychology.* New York, Knopf, 1950.
19. Lewis, N. D. C.: Personality factors in alcoholic addiction. *Quart. J. Stud. Alcohol, 1*:21-44, 1940.
20. Machover, Karen: *Personality Projection in the Drawing of a Human Figure.* Springfield, Thomas, 1949.
21. Meyer, B., Brown, F., and Levine, A.: Observations on the House-Tree-Person Drawing Test before and after surgery. *Psychosom. Med., 17:* 428-454, 1955.
22. Naumburg, Margaret: Art as symbolic speech. *Journal of Aesthetics and Art Criticism, 13*:435-450, 1955.
23. Piotrowski, Z. A., and Abrahamsen, D.: Sexual crime, alcohol and the Rorschach Test. *Psychiat. Quart.* (suppl.), *26*:248-260, 1952.
24. Schactel, E. G.: Projection and its relation to character attitudes and creativity in the kinesthetic responses. *Psychiatry, 13*:69-100, 1950.
25. Simon, M. P.: Les écrits et les dessins des aliénés. *Arch. anthrop. crim.* (Paris), *3*:318-355, 1888.
26. Spoerl, D. T.: Personality and drawing in retarded children. *Character and Personality, 8*:227-239, 1940.
27. Toler, A., and Toler, Belle: Judgment of children's personality from their human figure drawings. *J. Proj. Tech., 19*:170-176, 1955.
28. Waehner, T. S.: Interpretations of spontaneous drawings and paintings. *Genetic Psychology Monograph, 33*:3-70, 1946.

# PART II

# EXPRESSIVE COMPONENTS

## CHAPTER 3

## EXPRESSIVE ASPECTS OF PROJECTIVE DRAWINGS

EMANUEL F. HAMMER, PH.D.

THE MUSCLES of an individual are honest. When we try to hide what is in our minds, the muscles of our face and shoulders and our bodily posture, give us away. It is hard to smile when our hearts tell us to cry.

In fact, very often our psychomotor expression is more eloquent than words. Fidgety fingers or taut facial muscles frequently belie the words we might try to hide behind. In giving a speech, for example, only the shaking of the paper in our hands may give our tension away.

Goldsmith once commented, with his characteristic penetration, "The true use of speech is not so much to express our wants as to conceal them." Our muscles can not similarly be controlled.

In the realm of projective drawings, even the attitude with which the subject approaches the task offers a wide range in which the personality can manifest itself: the subject might draw cheerfully or sourly; silently or garrulously; in a tense manner or with the calm poise of a man who cooks pancakes in a restaurant window; with confidence or hesitancy, with one eye on the examiner, or with apparent complete disregard of the other person's potential opinion. The clinician also is interested in whether cooperation is basic or only superficial as in the case of a subject who offers a stick-figure as an index of his compliance with the examiner's request but actually as a disguised evasiveness and/or negativism.

In addition, the clinician is interested in the structure and content of the drawings produced. The size of the drawing, the pressure of line, the quality of line, the placement on the drawing page, exactness, degree and area of completion and detailing, symmetry, perspective, proportions, shading, reinforcement, and erasures comprise the structural, or expressive, phase of the drawing. Content analysis, on the other hand, considers the postural tone of the figures, the facial expression, the emphasis upon various individual aspects such as the chimney, the window or door of the house, the branches or the roots of the tree, the individual parts of the body with its clothing and accessories, and the like. The present chapter will be devoted to the expressive components of drawings, and the remaining chapters which follow will be devoted predominantly to content.

To further differentiate the expressive from the content elements of communication, we may take an example from language expression. The meaning of any sentence depends to a great extent on what word, or words, are emphasized, in addition to what words are employed. The meaning changes as different words are emphasized. For example, the sentence, "I didn't say he stole the cow," can be given a variety of meanings by employing different expressive emphasis: 1. *I* didn't say he stole the cow. (But somebody else said so.) 2. I *didn't* say he stole the cow. (But I'm perfectly willing to say so.) 3. I didn't *say* he stole the cow. (But that is what I thought.) 4. I didn't say *he* stole the cow. (But somebody did.) 5. I didn't say he stole the *cow*. (But he stole everything else.)

In similar fashion, the expressive emphasis in drawings conveys different nuances of meaning. In fact, children will at times reflect their feelings on paper in purely expressive manner without employing any form whatsoever. Some children will draw what they label a "happy line" or a "lazy line," or even a "nervous line." And certainly they will employ colors, throwing them onto the page without any content, to express fun, excitement, quiet time, fear, love, or hate. In speaking of color, a child once commented that red was "a party feeling" and pale blue was "sleepy."

More formal investigation by Allport and Vernon (1) has indicated that the rich ore of expressive movements is worthy of being dug out, refined, and forged into a handy tool, for, as they conclude, expressive movements really constitute "brain writing" (p. 187).

Children's expressive movements have diagnostic potential whether they are gross (as in the play-therapy room) or confined (as on the drawing page). A child might withdraw into a corner of the room, or sit on the edge of the chair, as though he were ready to run away, and if he were given a big sheet of paper, he might follow suit by drawing cautiously in one corner of the page only. At the other extreme, a child might sit at a table as though he wished to occupy the whole space showing no consideration for the other children there. No paper is big enough for him either, and his drawings expand beyond the drawing sheet.[1]

Adults tend to express their constrictive, expansive or aggressive patterns more in their handling of the space on the paper than in overt, obvious withdrawal or expansion in the clinician's office. Therefore, projective techniques are frequently found to be more useful with adults than children since the former have more sophisticated defensive layers covering their basic needs. Children, on the other hand, employ less defensive facades and are more apt to reveal themselves in frank or direct fashion.

Each individual, whether child or adult, however, expresses himself in movement patterns which are characteristic and which reveal the unity (or disunity) of his personality, and which also express the cultural movement patterns which he has molded in his idiosyncratic way.

The difficulties of capturing, recording, and measuring the transient qualities of overt movement are obvious; it becomes necessary to seek some means of doing so. Projective drawings appear to answer this need, for they "capture" movements on paper.

Wolff (21) has made an interesting contribution in his discovery of the "rhythmic quotient" by careful measurements of drawings made by pre-school children, blind persons, epileptic children, and African children. He has discovered that there are

---

[1] We may assume, even before we communicate directly with these children, that the behavior of the former expresses mistrust, loneliness, and fear; that the behavior of the latter expresses pseudo self-confidence to aggressive proportions or else the compensation of the show-off in an effort to cover weakness.

definite proportional ratios in the size of form elements which are characteristic of each individual, which do not vary with his age, and which appear relatively early in life. His findings tend to demonstrate the reliability of expressive movements.

This correlation between personality and psychomotor patterns has long fascinated the student of psychological dynamics.

## SEQUENCE

By analyzing our drawing test data in terms of the sequential emergence of drive derivatives, defense and adaptation, we witness dynamic and economic shifts which at the same time lay bare structural features of the subject. By examining samples of ongoing drawing processes we have an opportunity to study in slow motion, as it were, the structural features of conflict and defense.

In the microcosm of the interaction between a subject and the drawing page we may, for example, see a subject give tiny shoulders to his drawn person, then erase them, and finally endow the drawn person with compensatory, overly-broad shoulders. From this we may postulate that the subject's first reaction to a new situation is one of inferiority feelings which he then quickly attempts to cover-up with a façade of capability and adequacy, which, however, he overdoes to the point of "protesting too much."

It is quite as important to compare one whole drawing with another in sequence, as it is to note the sequence in which the details of a single drawing are produced.

For example, a male, thirty-eight years of age, first drew a large, threatening female with feet placed in a broad stance and with face wearing a stern expression. She was clothed in a riding habit and carried a large whip in her hand. Following this depiction of a threatening, stern, and punitive female figure, the subject gazed at his drawing for a long time and then hesitantly reached for the next sheet of paper and drew a small, puny male who stood with shoulders drooped dejectedly, head bent, arms behind the back: all-in-all a most submissive, subjugated posture. The subject thus views females as menacing, and attempts to placate them by assuming a passive, appeasing role.

At times it is the line quality to which the subject's sequential treatment gives diagnostic significance. An initially timid, tentative and hesitant line may be reacted to by some subjects with erasure and a subsequent still more sketchy, insecure line or, on the other hand, may be reinforced by going over it again and again to the point where it assumes a superficial veneer of confidence and boldness.

Sequential analysis thus provides us with a series of behavior samples recorded on paper.

Perhaps the most deviant sequence observed (5) occurred in the drawing of a person in which first the feet were drawn, then the head, then the knees, and then the legs, and finally all these disjointed segments were connected. The finished product, however, gave no indication of such deviant concept formation. It was only in the sequence that the subject revealed the disordered thinking produced by the deep psychopathology that surged within him and threatened to overwhelm him.

Sequential analysis of the set of drawings may provide clues to the amount of drive or energy of the subject. And it may provide data which allow an appraisal of the subject's control over this drive. Does the subject, for instance, break down under the emotionally-tinged associations that are presumably aroused by the different drawing concepts, or is he able to handle himself well in these spheres. Progressive psychomotor decrease, as he proceeds from one drawing to the next in the set of projective drawings, suggests high fatiguability. Progressive psychomotor increase suggests excessive stimulability. Frequently subjects are somewhat disturbed initially, but soon become calm and work efficiently as they proceed from the first to the last drawing. This is presumably simply "situational anxiety" and is not indicative of anything more serious.

If the subject, however, initially accepts the drawing task without much protest, produces a fairly good drawing for his first offering (the House in the House-Tree-Person test), shows obvious fatigue on the next drawing (in this case, the Tree), and after having laboriously produced, say the head of his Person abandons the task, the clinician would have to consider, among other things, a definite depressed state. (The drawings of significantly depressed subjects are characterized by either a marked paucity of details or an inability to complete all of the drawings, however scantily, or both.)

Sometimes borderline psychotics will reveal their disorder by their emotional reaction, in the sequence from one drawing to the next. As they get into the more obviously interpersonal areas, in their progression from the drawing of a House to that of a Tree to that of a Person, annoyance may give way to fear, and fear to panic.

## SIZE

The size of the drawn concept contains clues about the subject's realistic self-esteem, his characteristic self-expansiveness, or his fantasy self-inflation. Figures 1, 2 and 3 of the preceding chapter serve to illustrate the correlation between the size of the drawn figure and the degree of adequacy of the subject.

Tiny drawings are presented by subjects with feelings of inadequacy and perhaps with withdrawal tendencies. On the other hand, the too large drawing, the drawing that tends to press out against the page's borders, denotes feelings of environmental constriction with — and, this is noteworthy — concomittant overcompensatory action or fantasy (see Figure 1, drawn by the rapist, in the preceding chapter). This finding of Buck's (5) in regard to overly large drawings is supported by Hammer's study, The Frustration-Aggression Hypothesis Extended to Socio-Racial Areas (9). Four hundred House-Tree-Person (H-T-P) drawings were obtained from Negro and white children in the South, ranging in grade level from first to eighth. The assumption upon which the study was based was that for a Negro child, the white world is often found to be full of disappointments, frustrations and threat, both covert and overt. The environment was assumed to be more constricting, and conducive to frustration and aggression, for the Negro than for the white child. The drawings of the Negro children were found to be conspicuously too large for the drawn page, without adequate space framing them. They tended to touch the page's side margins, whereas those of the white children did not, thus supporting the hypothesis that the feeling of frustration produced by a restraining environment is reflected in the size of the drawing. The hypothesis that the subject who draws an overly large figure has a strong aggressive stream was offered support by the fact that the Persons drawn by the Negro children more often than not carried weapons, had sharply squared shoulders, aggressive fingers, or well-defined teeth.

Precker (18), too, found that exaggerated size may be considered as evidence of aggressiveness or motor release. Zimmerman and Garfinkle (22) also found that lack of restraint in the size of drawings correlated with aggressiveness and a tendency toward the release of this aggressiveness into the environment.

In regard to small size, Traub (3) and Lembke (3) who independently studied the drawings of bold and timid children, observed that extremely small drawings were associated with feelings of inferiority.

Waehner (19) reports that girls whose free drawings were very small, were, on the basis of other criteria, found to be anxious, shy, constricted, or highly self-controlled. Alschuler and Hattwick (2) found that children who drew small figures, or who worked with restricted masses in their drawings, tended as a group to show more withdrawing, emotionally dependent behavior than did the total group. Elkisch (7) found that compression in drawings conveys a feeling of discomfort, of being shut in, of pressure.

## PRESSURE

Pressure of pencil on paper has been found, like size, to be an indication of the subject's energy level (12, 18, 10). In regard to reliability, it was found by Hetherington (10) that subjects are rather remarkably constant in their pressure.

Alschuler and Hattwick (2) reported that children who drew with heavy strokes were usually more assertive than other children. Light strokes were the result of either (a) low energy level or (b) restraint and repression.

In an investigation of the drawings of abnormal subjects, Pfiester (3) found that fearful neurotics, chronic schizophrenics, and advanced catatonics showed little pressure, resulting in small, faint lines. Psychopaths, organic cases, epileptics, and encephalitics characteristically employed heavy pressure. Variation in pressure was found among the more flexible, adaptable individuals, in contrast to the greater uniformity of pressure displayed by catatonics and the feeble-minded.

Buck (5) also found that heavy lines drawn with great force were usually produced by organics. Extremely tense subjects at times, may, however, also draw the sort of line for which organic subjects show a prediliction.

At the other end of the continuum, light, very faint lines are preferred by inadequate and/or depressed individuals.

## STROKE

Alschuler and Hattwick (2) found that children who drew with long strokes stood out for their controlled behavior, whereas children who worked with short strokes showed more impulsive behavior.

Mira (17) also writes, "In general, the length of movement of a stroke tends to increase in inhibited subjects and decrease in excitable ones."

Children who used straight-line strokes tended to be assertive; those who used circular strokes tended to be more dependent and more emotional (2). Krout (14) found that rounded lines were associated with femininity and straight lines with aggressive moods. Jagged lines—which incidentally appeared as the symbol of the most aggressive unit in Hitler's army—were associated with hostility.

Buck (5) indicated that broken, indecisive lines, or lines that were continuous only because they had been frequently reinforced, were usually indicative of insecurity or anxiety. The present writer has found tight lines (thin and stretched long), which radiate a feeling of tension, to be offered in the drawings of those subjects whose emotional state was taut as an improperly tuned, discordant violin. Sketchy lines, if overemphasized, reflect anxiety, timidity, lack of self-confidence, hesitancy in behavior and in the meeting of new situations.

Some subjects draw pictures in which every set of lines is disconnected: the eyes may not be inside the face, and fingers and hands are attached to the wrong places or not at all. There is stress or purposeless direction in every line. The rhythmic, fluent lines of healthier subjects are absent. This type of distance from reality, confusion, and bizarreness in drawing strongly suggest psychotic trends.

Erasures, if excessive, are found to be a graphic correlate of (a) uncertainty and indecisiveness, or (b) self-dissatisfaction.

Within the area of normality, we find that good adjustment is implied by drawings made predominantly with decisive, well-controlled, free-flowing lines.

### DETAILING

Inadequate detailing has been found to be the preferred drawing reaction of subjects with distinct withdrawal tendencies (5). The absence of adequate detailing conveys a feeling of emptiness and reduced energy, so characteristic of subjects employing defenses of withdrawal, and at times depression.

Excessive detailing, on the other hand, as might be expected on the basis of general empirical contact with an emotionally disturbed population, occurs in the obsessive-compulsive. Brick (4) found that compulsive children tended to detail every cobblestone, every rail in a fence, and every minute aspect of the concept drawn. Waehner (19) reports that students who made minutious details were described by their peers as overly neat, pedantic and constricted.

Neurotic children or adults who have the feeling that the world around them is uncertain, unpredictable and/or dangerous, tend to seek to defend themselves against inner or outer chaos by creating a rigidly ordered, highly structured world. The drawings of these subjects will be very exact. These people will create rigid, repetitious, elements in their drawings. There is nothing flowing or relaxed in the lines, the drawings, or in their total presentation. Everything is put together by force—as though they feel that without this pressure everything would fall apart.

Too perfect a drawing performance, executed with unusual, exacting control and care, is offered by patients who range from obsessive-compulsive to incipient schizophrenics or early organics. The "too-perfect" performance reflects the effort of these types of patients to hold themselves together against the threat of imminent disorganization. It is a direct manifestation of their hyper-vigilance, and implies the presence of a relatively weak ego, so afraid of a break-through of forbidden impulses that it dares not relax its constant vigilance.

The most frequent emotional accompaniment of the excessive detailing of one's drawing, is a feeling of rigidity. Stiffly drawn trees or animals parallel the same quality in the drawn person. In this regard, the latter may be presented as standing rigidly at attention, with body and head very erect, legs pressed closely together, and arms straight and held close to the body. The kinaesthetic emphasis, in these projections, is on the erect posture and on the rigid tension with which the posture is held, keeping the self closed off against the world around. These drawing performances often express a most unfree, rigidly controlled, and basically defensive attitude. This is the characteristic drawing performance of people to whom spontaneous relations to others and the world around them are an acute threat.

The most recent drawing of this nature seen by the writer was offered by an eight-year-old boy who suffered the effects produced by over-pushing, demanding, high aspiring parents. The tightness underscored in the boy's drawings reflected his feeling of constriction and helplessness, his feeling of being packed like a bird's egg in the cotton of his parents' ambition for him.

Such drawings, with their suggestion of rigidity of defense and limited adaptiveness, have been found in the projective data of subjects usually unable to relax, or to perform casually or impulsively. Instead, they do so dutifully, cautiously or perfectionistically. Such defensive rigidity precludes the spontaneity and self-assertiveness that allow a legitimate amount of irresponsibility, "laziness" and self-indulgence.

### SYMMETRY

Symmetry has long been regarded as one of the most elemental gestalt principles. It is not surprising, therefore, that drawings which display an obvious lack of symmetry have been found to indicate equivalent inadequate feelings of security in the subject's emotional life. Werner Wolff's (21) study of the abstract drawings of children offers objective support for this observation.

At the other extreme, when bilateral symmetry is stressed to the point of producing an effect of rigidity, it signifies an obsessive-compulsive system of emotional control (much as does the rigidity factor discussed in the section above) which may express itself in repression and overintellectualization. Waehner (19) found another clinical group to show rigid symmetry: depressed patients. Sixty per cent of the pictures of depressed neurotics showed rigid symmetry, compared to 25 per cent of a control group.

## PLACEMENT

Children who centered their work on the drawing page, according to Alschuler and Hattwick (2), tended to show more self-directed, self-centered and more emotional behavior than did the total group. Children who did off-center work tended to show more uncontrolled, dependent qualities.

If not carried to meticulous extremes, the centering of graphic elements was found by Wolff (21) to indicate "high security."

In regard to placement on the horizontal axis of the page, Buck (5) hypothesizes that the farther the mid-point of the drawing is to the right of the mid-point of the page, the more likely is the subject to exhibit stable, controlled behavior, to be willing to delay satisfaction of needs and drives, to prefer intellectual satisfactions to more emotional ones. Conversely, the further the mid-point of the drawing is to the left of the mid-point of the page, the greater is the likelihood that the subject tends to behave impulsively, to seek immediate, frank, and emotional satisfaction of his needs and drives. Koch (13) independently, on the basis of his projective drawing work on the "Tree Test" in Switzerland, identifies the right side of the page with "inhibition," which is consistent with Buck's concept of emphasis on the right side of the page suggesting intellectual control. Wolff's (21) finding that subjects who were attracted to the right side of the page in their drawings showed introversion, and those to the left side of the page extroversion, is consistent with Buck's findings, in that introversion is associated with the capacity to delay satisfaction, and extroversion the seeking of more immediate gratifications.

Concerning placement along the vertical dimension of the drawing page, Buck offers the following hypothesis: the higher the mid-point of the drawn concept is above the mid-point of the page, the greater the implication (a) that the subject feels he is striving hard, that his goal is relatively unattainable; (b) that the subject tends to seek satisfaction in fantasy rather than in reality; or (c) that he tends to keep himself aloof and relatively inaccessible.

The further below the average mid-point of the page that the mid-point of the drawing is located, the greater the likelihood (a) that the subject feels insecure and inadequate, and that this feeling is producing a depression of mood, or (b) that the subject finds himself reality-bound or oriented toward the concrete.

Levy's (15) findings are consistent with Buck's. Children whose drawings are placed in the upper half of the sheet usually have high standards of achievement, for the attainment of which they constantly strive. Adults whose figures are placed in the upper half of the page frequently are those who feel unsure of themselves ("up in the air"). Subjects whose drawings are placed at the bottom of the page seem to be more firmly rooted, though occasionally depressed and harboring a defeatist attitude.

Anthropological investigations concur in indicating the universal equating of "up" with ideation or fantasy or the world of ideas, and "down" with the terrestrial, the firm, the solid, and the concrete.

If a corner is chosen for placement, it most often is the upper left. Normative studies show a negative correlation between age and preferred use of this quadrant. Weider and Noller (20) and Jolles (11) found that the youngest children in an elementary school preferred the upper left quadrant, that as they progressed from first to eighth grade, they gradually moved their drawings until the normative placement was just about page center for the eighth-grade children. These normative studies are consistent with Buck's findings (5) that regressed individuals manifest a tendency to hide their drawings away in the upper left corner.

Figures which cling to the edge of the paper (like windows drawn clinging to the edge of the walls) reflect a need for support, fear of independent action, and lack of self-assurance on the part of the subject. In a recently completed, as yet unpublished, study of the writer's this type of placement was found to differentiate dependent from independent children. The tendency to edge the drawing over to an end of the page correlated .74 with teachers' ratings of the childrens' dependency needs on a 5-point continuum.

## MOTION

Motion is occasionally indicated in projective drawings, and most frequently done so by children. Waehner (19) observed that gifted children produced the most pictures including motion (people walking or running, dogs leaping, birds flying, trees swaying and the like). Depressives had few, and psychotics had either few or many motion elements. Feeble-minded children had the least motion elements.

In a study comparing movement on both the Rorschach and in free drawings, de Assis Pacheco (6) studied 751 free drawings and 666 Rorschach interpretations obtained from children ranging from seven to twelve and one-half years of age. Animal Movement on the Rorschach correlated positively with motion in the drawings, although Human Movement on the Rorschach did not. This is consistent with the fact that the childish needs feel more at home in the animal content.

## DEFECTIVE SYNTHESIS AND OTHER
## PSYCHOTIC SUGGESTIONS

Defective synthesis is characteristic of the drawings of those with major emotional upheavals. Examples are known of highly gifted artists who, during periods of mental derangement, regressed to the level of a child's artistic powers, and produced pictures consisting of a muddled and disordered mass of details, without any leading idea. Some of the works of Josephson, the Swedish painter, furnish all too apt illustration of this fact.

The twisted landscape of the minds of psychotic patients is reflected in the equally disorganized production on the drawing page. In addition, profuse smudgy shading is not unusual as a direct reflection of the atmosphere of psychosis, gray with secret discontentment.

In a study of the spontaneous drawings of psychotics, Mohr (3) found perseveration and repetition of subject matter to be characteristic of schizophrenics.

Not only are the productions of the psychotic apt to be fantastic, peculiar, and bizarre, and even of apparent bewildering purposelessness (8), but they are often characterized by a mixture of mediums, such as a combination of writing and drawing (3). One is tempted to speculate that this mixing of mediums reflects efforts at compensation for a feeling of breakdown of capacity for basic communication.

Malraux (16), years ago, formulated the view that the "insane" artist holds an "inner monologue" with himself in which he speaks solely for himself, whereas "the genuine artist holds a dialogue with the world." Such an interpretation of psychotic art is related to the pre-dynamic psychology of the epoch before Freud. The recent findings of psychoanalytic, projective technique, and other approaches have rejected the view that psychotic art is meaningless. It is now recognized that the symbolic projections of mental patients are all meaningful whether or not clinicians, at the present time, have yet attained the capacity for understanding such communication.

In conclusion, it may be said that the pencil stroke, at the moment of contact, carries inevitably, in the words of the American artist, Robert Henri, "the exact state of being of the subject at that moment into the work, and there it is, to be seen and read by those who can read such signs."

## REFERENCES

1. Allport, G. W., and Vernon, P. E.: Studies in Movement. New York, Macmillan, 1933.
2. Alschuler, A., and Hattwick, W.: Painting and Personality. Chicago, Univ. Chicago Press, 1947.
3. Anastasi, A., and Foley, J.: A survey of the literature on artistic behavior in the abnormal. Psychol. Monographs, 52:71, 1940.
4. Brick, Maria: Mental hygiene value of children's art work. Am. J. Orthophychiat., 14:136-146, 1944.
5. Buck, J. N.: Richmond Proceedings (mimeographed copy) Calif., Western Psychological Services, 1950.

6. de Assis Pacheco, O.: The symbolism of movement in children. *Crainco Portug.*, 11:129-139, 1952.
7. Elkich, Paula: Children's drawings in a projective technique. *Psychol. Monographs*, 1:58, 1945.
8. Guttmann, E., and Maclay, W.: Clinical observations on schizophernic drawings. *Brit. J. M. Psychol.*, 16:184-205, 1937.
9. Hammer, E. F.: Frustration-aggression hypothesis extended to socio-racial areas: a comparison of Negro and white children's H-T-P's. *Psychiat. Quart.*, 1:11, 1953.
10. Hetherington, R.: The effects of E.C.T. on the drawings of depressed patients. *J. Ment. Sc.*, 98:450-453, 1952.
11. Jolles, I.: A study of the validity of some hypothesis for the qualitative interpretation of the H-T-P for children of elementary school age. Presented at the H-T-P Round Table, APA Convention, Washington, D.C., 1952.
12. Kadis, A.: Finger painting as a projective technique, in Abt, L. E., and Bellak, L.: *Projective Psychology*. New York, Knopf, 1950.
13. Koch, C.: *The Tree Test*. Berne, Hans Huber, 1952.
14. Krout, J.: Symbol elaboration test. *Psychol. Mono. AMA*, 4:404-405, 1950.
15. Levy, S.: Figure drawing as a projective test, in Abt, L. E., and Bellak, L.: *Projective Psychology*. New York, Knopf, 1950.
16. Naumburg, Margaret: Art as symbolic speech. *Journal of Aesthetics and Art Criticism*, 13:435-450, 1955.
17. Mira, E.: *Psychiatry in War*. New York, Norton, 1943.
18. Precker, J.: Painting and drawing in personality assessment: Summary. *J. Proj. Tech.*, 14:262-286, 1950.
19. Waehner, T. S.: Interpretations of spontaneous drawings and paintings. *Genetic Psychology Monograph*, 33:70, 1946.
20. Weider, A., and Noller, P.: Objective studies of children's drawings of human figures. *J. Clin. Psych.*, 6:319-325, 1950.
21. Wolff, W.: *The Personality of the Pre-School Child*. New York, Grune & Stratton, 1946.
22. Zimmerman, J., and Garfinkle, L.: Preliminary study of the art productions of the adult psychotic. *Psychiat. Quart.*, 16:313-318, 1942.

## SUGGESTED READING

Abel, T. M.: Free design of limited scope as a personality index. *Character & Personality*, 7:50-62, 1938.

Allen, Grant: *The Color Sense—Its Origin and Development*. London, Kegan Paul, Trench, Trubner & Co., 1892, p. 282.

Allport, G. W., and Odbert, H. S.: Trait names. A psycho-lexical study. *Psychol. Monog.*, 47:171, 1936.

Allport, G. W., and Vernon, P. E.: *Studies in Expressive Movement*. New York, 1933.

Anastasi, A., and Foley, J. P.: A survey of the literature on artistic behavior in the abnormal: III. Spontaneous productions. *Psychol. Monogr.*, 52: No. 237, 1941.

Anastasi, A., and Foley, J.: An analysis of spontaneous drawings by children in different cultures. *J. Appl. Psychol.*, 20:689-726, 1936.

Anastasi, A., and Foley, J.: A study of animal drawings by Indian children of the North Pacific Coast. *J. Social Psychol.*, 9:363-374, 1938.

Appel, K. E.: Drawings by children as aids to personality studies. *Am. J. Orthopsychiat.*, 1:129-144, 1931.

Asch, S. E.: Forming impressions of personality. *J. Abnorm. & Social Psychol.*, 41:258-290, 1946.

Ayer, F. C.: *The Psychology of Drawing.* Baltimore, 1916.

Ballard, F. B.: What children like to draw. *J. Exper. Pediat.*, 2:127-129, 1913.

Barnes, E.: A study of children's drawings. *Pediat. Sem.*, 2:451-463, 1843.

Bataille, G.: L'art primitif. *Documents*, 7:389-397, 1930.

Baynes, H. G.: *Mythology of the Soul; A Research Into the Unconscious from Schizophrenic Dreams and Drawings.* London, Ballière, Tindall & Cox, 1939.

Belo, J.: *Balinese Children's Drawing.* Djawa, 5 and 6, 1937.

Bender, L.: Gestalt principles in the sidewalk drawings and games of children. *J. Genet. Psychol.*, 41:192-210, 1932.

Bender, L., and Schilder, P.: Form as a principle in the play of children. *J. Genet. Psychol.*, 49:254-261, 1936.

Bender, L., and Rapaport, J.: Animal drawings of children. *Am. J. Orthopsychiat.*, 14:521-527, 1944.

Berger, E.: Der sandersche phantasietest im rahmen der psychologischen eignungsuntersuchung jugendlicher. *Arch. psychol.*, 103:499-543, 1939.

Berrien, F. K.: A study of the drawings of abnormal children. *J. Educ. Psychol.*, 26:143-150, 1935.

Best, Mangard Adolf: *Method for Creative Design.* New York, Alfred A. Knopf, 1927.

Biber, Barbara: *From Lines to Drawings.* New York, 1930.

Biber, Barbara: Children's drawings: from lines to pictures. New York, Bureau Educ. Experiments, 1934.

Billings, M. L.: A report of a case of inverted writing and drawing. *Child Development*, 6:161-163, 1936.

Brill, M.: Study of instability using the Goodenough drawing scale. *J. Abnorm. & Social Psychol.*, 32:288-302, 1937.

Broom, M. E., Thompson, B., and Bouton, M. T.: Sex differences in handwriting. *J. Appl. Psychol.*, 13:159-166, 1929.

Brown, D. D.: *Notes on Children's Drawings.* Univ. of California Publ., 1897.

Bullough, E.: Recent work in experimental aesthetics. *Brit. J. Educ. Psychol.*, 12:76-99, 1934.

Burk, F.: The genetic versus the logical order in drawing. *Pedag. Sem.*, 9:296-323, 1902.

Cailli, Ruth Kennedy: *Resistant Behavior of Preschool Children.* Child Development Monographs, No. 11. New York, Teachers College, Columbia University, 1933.

Calkins, M. W.: The self in scientific psychology. *Am. J. Psychol.*, 26:496-524, 1915.

Calkins, M. W.: The self in recent psychology. *Psychol. Bull.*, 13:20-27, 1916.

Cameron, N.: Individual and social factors in the development of graphic symbolizations. *J. Psychol.*, V:165-184, 1938.

Cane, F.: The gifted child in art. *J. Educ. Sociol.*, 10:67-73, 1936.

Cantril, H., and Rand, H. A.: An additional study of the determination of personal interests by psychological and graphological methods. *Char. & Pers., 3:* 72-78, 1934.

Cattell, R. B.: *Description and Measurement of Personality.* Yonkers, World Bk. Co., 1946.

Child, H. G.: Measurement of the drawing ability of 2177 children in Indiana city school systems by a supplemented Thorndike Scale. *J. Educ. Psychol., 6:*391-408, 1915.

Cockrell, D. L.: Design in the paintings of young children. *Sch. Arts Mag., 30:* 33-39, 112-119, 1930.

Cohen, J.: The use of objective criteria in the measurement of drawing ability. *Pediat. Sem., 27:*137-151, 1920.

Cole, N. R.: *The Arts in the Classroom.* New York, Day, 1940.

Danz, Louis: *It is Still the Morning.* New York, William Morrow & Co., 1943, p. 273.

Dillon, M. S.: Attitudes of children toward their own bodies and those of other children. *Child Development, 5:*165-176, 1934.

Dixon, C. Madeleine: *High, Wide, and Deep.* New York, Day, 1943, p. 273.

Dorcus, R. M.: The experimental study of forms of expression. *Char. & Pers., 2:* 168-176, 1933.

Downey, J. E.: *Graphology and the Psychology of Handwriting.* Baltimore, 1919.

Drever, J.: The Analytical study of the mechanism of writing. *Proc. Roy. Soc., 34:* 230-240, 1913-1914.

Dummer, Ethel S.: *Why I Think So: The Autobiography of an Hypothesis.* Chicago, Clarke-McElroy Pub. Co., 1937, p. 274.

Eng, Hilda: *The Psychology of Children's Drawings: From the First Stroke to the Color Drawing.* London, Kegan Paul, Trench, Trubner & Co., 1931, pp. viii and 393.

Estes, S. G.: Judging personality from expressive behavior. *J. Abnorm. & Social Psychol., 33:*217-236, 1938.

Eagleson, O. W.: The success of sixth subjects in attempting to recognize their handwriting. *J. Appl. Psychol., 21:*546-549, 1937.

Findley, W. G.: Factor analysis of a short item drawing test. *Psychol. Bull., 33:* 605, 1936.

Florina, A.: Research into the drawings of preschool children. *New Era, 9:*37-38, 1928.

Frank, L. K.: Projective methods for the study of personality. *J. Psychol., 8:* 389-413, 1939.

Freeman, F. N.: An experimental analysis of the writing movement. *Psychol. Monog., 17:*4, 1914.

Gallagher, M.: Children's spontaneous drawings. *Northwestern Monthly, 8:* 130-134, 1897.

Garma, A.: The origin of clothes, *Yearbook of Psychoanalysis.* N.Y. Internat. Univ. Press, 1950.

Gerald, H. J. P.: Inverted positions in children's drawings. Report of two cases. *J. Nerv. & Ment. Dis., 68:*449-455, 1928.

Gesell, A. L.: Accuracy in handwriting as related to school intelligence and sex. *Am. J. Psychol., 17:*394-405, 1906.

Gesell, Arnold, et al.: *The First Five Years of Life: A Guide to the Study of the Preschool Child.* Harper & Bros., p. xiii and 393.

Gesell, Arnold, Ilg, Frances L., and Others: *Infant and Child in the Culture of Today: Guidance and Development in Home and Nursery School.* New York, Harper, 1943.

Goodenough, Florence: *Developmental Psychology.* New York, Appleton, 1934.

Goodenough, Florence: *Measurement of Intelligence by Drawing.* New York, World Bk. Co., 1926, p. xi and 177.

Goodenough, F. L.: Studies in the psychology of children's drawings. *Psychol. Bull.,* 25:272-279, 1928.

Goodenough, F. L.: Children's Drawings, in *Handbook of Child Psychology.* Worcester, C. Murchison, Ed., 1931.

Gridley, P. F.: Graphic representation of a man by four-year-old children in nine prescribed drawing situations. *Genet. Psychol. Monogr.,* 20:183-350, 1938.

Griffiths, Ruth: *A Study of Imagination in Early Childhood.* London, Kegan Paul, Trench, Trubner & Co., 1935, p. xiv and 367.

Grippen, V. B.: A study of creative artistic imagination in children by the constant contact procedure. *Psychol. Monogr.,* 45:63-81.

Hallowell, A. I.: The child, the savage, and human experience. Child. Res. Clinic. *Proc. 6th Inst. Except. Child.,* 8:34, 1939.

Harms, Ernst: Child art as an aid in the diagnosis of juvenile neuroses. *Am. J. Orthopsychiatry,* XI:191-209, 1941.

Hattwick, La Berta A.: Sex differences in behavior of preschool children. *Child Development,* December, 1937.

Hattwick, La Berta A., and Alschuler, R. H.: *Painting and Personality,* Vols. I and II. Chicago, Univ. Chicago Press, 1947.

Herrick, M. A.: Children's drawings. *Pediat. Sem.,* 3:338-339, 1893.

Hicks, M. D.: Art in early education. *Kindergarten Mag.,* 6:590-605, 1894.

Hildreth, G.: The simplification tendency in reproducing design. *J. Genet. Psychol.,* 64:1944.

Hinrichs, W. E.: The Goodenough drawing test in relation to delinquency and problem behavior. *Arch. Psychol.,* 175:1-82, 1935.

Homberger, Erik: Configuration in play. *Psychoanalyt. Quart.,* 6:139-214, 1937.

Hull, C. L., and Montgomery, R. P.: Experimental investigation of certain alleged relations between character and handwriting. *Psychol. Rev.,* 26:63-74, 1919.

Hunt, J. M.: *Personality and the Behavior Disorders,* Vol. I, by Robert W. White. New York, Ronald, 1944.

Hurlock, E. B.: The spontaneous drawings of adolescents. *J. Genet. Psychol.,* p. 63, 1943.

Hurlock, E. B., and Thomson, J. L.: Children's drawings: An experimental study of perception. *Child Development,* pp. 127-138, June, 1934.

Jacobs, Michel: *The Art of Color.* New York, Doubleday, 1931, p. 90.

Jacoby, H. J.: *The Handwriting of Depressed Children.* London, New Era, January, 1944.

Kato, M.: A genetic study of children's drawings of a man. *J. Exper. Psychol.,* 3:175-185, 1936.

Katz, S. E.: The color preference of children. *J. Appl. Psychol.,* 6:225-266, 1922.

Katz, S. E.: Color preference in the insane. *J. Abnorm. Psychol.,* 26:203-211, 1931-1932.

Kerr, M.: Children's drawings of houses. *Brit. J. Psychol., 16:*206-218, 1936-1937.
Klopfer, Bruno: Personality differences between boys and girls in early child-hood: Report before the American Psychological Association. *Psychol. Bull., 36:*538, July, 1939.
Klopfer, Bruno: Rorschach reactions in early childhood. *Rorschach Research Exchange, V:*1-23, 1940.
Knauber, A. J.: Art ability in children. *Child Development, 2:*66-71, 1931.
Krotsch, W.: *Rhythmus und Form in der freien Kinderziehung.* Reported by Victor Lowenfeld, Leipzig, 1917. *The Nature of Creative Activity.* New York, Harcourt, 1939.
Land, A. H.: Graphology, a psychological analysis. *Univ. Buffalo Stud., 3:*81-114, 1924.
Lecky, P.: *Self-consistency, A Theory of Personality.* New York, Island Press, 1945.
Lewis, N. D. C.: Graphic art productions in schizophrenia. *Proc. A. Res. Nerv. Ment. Dis., 5:*344-368, 1928.
Liss, E.: The graphic arts. *Am. J. Orthopsychiat., 8:*95-99, 1938.
Long, W. F., and Tifflin, J.: A note on the use of graphology by industry. *J. Appl. Psychol., 4:*469-471, 1941.
Lorand, Sandor: *Psychoanalysis Today.* New York, Interna. Univ. Press, 1944.
Lowenfeld, Margaret: *Play in Childhood.* London, Gollancz, 1935.
Lukens, H.: A study of children's drawings in the early years. *Ped. Sem., 4:*79-110, 1896.
Lundholm, H.: The affective tone of lines. Experimental researches. *Psychol. Rev., 28:*43-60, 1921.
McAllister, C. N.: Researches on movements used in handwriting. *Yale Psychol. Lab. Studies, 8:*21-63, 1900.
Machover, Karen: A case of frontal lobe injury following attempted suicide. (drawings, Rorschach). *J. Proj. Tech., 11:*1, 1947.
Maitland, L.: What children draw to please themselves. *Inland Educator, 1:*87, 1895.
Maitland, L.: C. Ricci's the art of little children. *Pediat. Sem., 2:*302-307, 1895.
Manuel, H.: Talent in Drawing: An experimental study of the use of tests to discover special ability. *School & Home Educ. Monogr., 3:* 1919.
Manuel, H., and Hughes, L. S.: The intelligence and drawing ability of young Mexican children. *J. Appl. Psychol., 16:*382-387, 1932.
Mathias, Margaret C.: Encouraging the art expression of young children. *Childhood Education, 15:*293, 1939.
McCarthy, D.: *Children's Drawings.* Baltimore, 1924-1925.
McDermott, L.: Favorite drawings of Indian children. *Northwestern Monthly, 8:* 134-137, 1897.
McElwee, E. W.: The reliability of the Goodenough intelligence test used with subnormal children fourteen years of age. *J. Appl. Psychol., 18:*599-603, 1934.
McIntosh, J.: An inquiry into the use of children's drawings as a means of psycho-analysis. *Brit. J. Educ. Psychol., 9:*102-103, 1939.
Melcher, W.: Dual-personality in handwriting. *J. Crim. Law & Criminol., 11:* 209-216, 1920.
Miller, J.: Intelligence testing by drawings. *J. Educ. Psychol., 29:*390-394, 1938.
Mira, E.: Myokinetic psychodiagnosis: A new technique for exploring the conative trends of personality. *Proc. Roy. Soc. Med., 33:*9-30, 1940.

Morgenstern, S.: Le symbolisme et la valeur psychoanalytique des dessins infantiles. *Rev. franc. Psychoanal.*, 11:39-48.

Newhall, S. M.: Sex differences in handwriting. *J. Appl. Psychol.*, 10:151-161, 1926.

Oakley, C. A.: The interpretation of children's drawings. *Brit. J. Psychiat.*, 21: 256-270, 1930-1931.

Oakley, C. A.: Drawings of a man by adolescents. *Brit. J. Psychiat.*, 31:37-60, 1940.

Oberlin, D. S.: Children who draw. *Delaware State M. J.*, 10: 1938.

Oldham, H. W.: *Child Expression in Form and Color.* London, John Lane, 1940.

Omwake, K. T.: The value of photographs and handwriting in estimating intelligence. *Pub. Personnel Stud.*, 3:2-15, 1925.

O'Shea, M. V.: Children's expression through drawing. *Proc. Nat. Educ. A., 1015:* 1894.

O'Shea, M. V.: Some aspects of drawing. *Educ. Rev.*, 14:263-284, 1897.

Paset, G.: Some drawings of men and women made by children of certain non-European races. *J. Roy. Anthrop. Inst.*, 62:127-144, 1932.

Pfister, H. O.: Farbe und Bewegung in der Zeichnung Geisterkranker. Schweiz. *Arch. Neurol. & Psychiat.*, 34:325-365, 1934.

Pinter, R.: Aesthetic appreciation of pictures by children. *Pediat. Sem.*, 25: 216-218, 1918.

Pintner, R., and Toops, H. A.: A drawing completion test. *J. Appl. Psychol.*, 2: 164-173, 1918.

Poffenberger, A. T., and Barrows, B. E.: The feeling value of lines. *J. Appl. Psychol.*, 8:187-205, 1924.

Powers, E.: *Graphic Factors in Relation to Personality: An Experimental Study.* Dartmouth Coll. Library (unpublished), 1930.

Prince, M.: *Clinical and Experimental Studies in Personality.* Cambridge, Mass., Sci-Art. 1929.

Prinzhorn, H.: *Bildnerei der Geisterkranken.* Berlin, Springer, 1923.

Read, Herbert: *Education Through Art.* London, Faber, 1944. pp. xxxiii and 320.

Review of Educational Research (Washington, D.C.: National Education Association of the United States, 1201 Sixteenth St., N.W.), Vol. XIV, No. 1 (February, 1944), Chapter vi.

Reitman, F.: Facial expression in schizophrenic drawings. *J. Ment. Sc.*, 85:264-272, 1939.

Sachs, Hans: *The Creative Unconscious.* Cambridge, Mass., Sci.-Art Publishers, 1942.

Saudek, R.: *Experiments with Handwriting.* New York, 1928.

Sears, R. R.: Experimental studies of projection. 1. Attribution of traits. *J. Soc. Psychol.*, 7:151-163, 1936.

Schube, K., and Cowell, J.: Art of psychotic persons. *Arch. Neurol.*

Schubert, A.: Drawings of orphan children and young people. *J. Genet. Psychol.*, 37:232-244, 1940.

Spoerl, D. T.: Personality and drawing in retarded children. *Char. & Pers.*, 8: 227-239, 1940.

*The Visual Arts in General Education: Report of Committee on Function of Art in General Education, Progressive Education Association Commission on the Secondary School Curriculum.* New York, Appleton, 1940, pp. x and 166.

Thorndike, E. L.: *The Measurement of Achievement in Drawing.* Teach. Coll. Record, 1913.

Traube, T.: La Valeur diagnostique des dessins des enfants difficiles. *Arch. Psychol.*, Geneve, 26:285-309, 1937.

Wachner, T. S.: Interpretation of spontaneous drawings and paintings. *Genet. Psychol., Monogr.*, pp. 3-70, 1946.

Wolff, W.: Projective methods for personality analysis of expressive behavior in preschool children. *Char. & Pers.*, 4:309-330, 1942.

Wolff, W.: *The Expression of Personality.* New York, Harper, 1943.

Wolff, W.: *The Personality of the Preschool Child.* New York, Grune & Stratton, 1946.

Yepsen, L. N.: The reliability of the Goodenough drawing test with feeble-minded subjects. *J. Educ. Psychol.*, 20:448-451, 1929.

# PART III
## CONTENT COMPONENTS

### Unit 1
#### Human Figure Drawing

# CHAPTER 4

# PROJECTIVE FIGURE DRAWING

SIDNEY LEVY, PH.D.

## INTRODUCTION

"THE PROFESSION of psychology is much like living, which has been defined by Samuel Butler as 'the art of drawing sufficient conclusions from insufficient premises.' Sufficient premises are not to be found, and he who, lacking them, will not draw tentative conclusions, cannot advance" (1, p. 22).

The psychologist who attempts to capture the infinite complexity of a human being, and having captured it, strives to communicate what he perceives, is doomed to failure. He is in the desperate position not only of arriving at sufficient conclusions from insufficient premises, but in the process he is forced to use a primitive language which lacks sufficient precision or adequate extension; and all are in the service of abstractions which are too crude and lack an undetermined number of dimensions. Thus he is doomed to final failure. "There *is* no conclusion," said William James (2).

However, not all inconclusiveness is equally so. It may be said that there is a hierarchy of ignorance and of failure and although the latter inevitably overshadows any attempt to come to climactic understanding of a human person, excitement, insight, knowledge and even glory may sometimes attend such failure.

The interpretation of projective figure drawings is without sufficient experimental validation, rarely yields unequivocal information and frequently misleads the unwary, the naive, the reckless and the impulsive. All this is equally true of the Rorschach Test, or any other psychological technique or, for that matter, any technique in natural or social science.

Notwithstanding these limitations the use of Projective Figure Drawings may be so fruitful, economical and profound a source of information and insights about a personality, that with each passing year my fondness for it grows, and the returns from the use of this technique become ever more satisfying. For pure drama and excitement the figure drawings, and the story they tell, in The Case of Mr. P. (Chapter 7) is not often equalled.

Freud has said "nothing is too trifling as a manifestation of hidden psychic processes" (3, p. 91).

Under the impact of Freud's ideas, "art has become, next to dreams, the acknowledged via regia into the depths" (4, p. 10).

He dignified the trivial acts of ordinary life by elevating them to something meaningful, and through his investigations he laid the groundwork on which this most trivial form of art, figure drawing, assumes incredible significance. But a word of warning! In his early researches Freud sometimes committed errors of simplistic interpretation, e.g., "the hat has been adequately established as a symbol of the genital organ. . ." (4, p. 143).

Freud, a searching genius, quickly corrected this error having discovered the complexity of symbol and symptom formation, and very early in his investigations revealed that any given symbol, symptom, act or product, may be produced by 57 different combinations of circumstance. In short, the single dimension, dictionary or "pat" approach to meanings quickly yielded to a multi-dimensional, field approach in his work. Thus, a "hat," whether it be in a dream, a fantasy, or in a *drawing* may have *n* number of different meanings depending on the "field" or organizational matrix, which produces it. In one case a hat may signify a male genital, in another case it may suggest a female genital, in a third it may signify *social prestige*, in a fourth it may express *depression*, in a fifth perhaps concealment of impotency, in a sixth repression ("clamping the lid on") and on, and on, and on (see section on the Head, p. 105).

At this point many timorous individuals who would like to impose upon phenomena a "simplicity which does not in fact exist" may throw their hand high in protest. "If a datum can mean male in one case, and female in another and something else another time, then it can have no real meaning. It's a 'heads you win, tails I lose' situation." This is a cry of anguish in the face of a complicated universe, only the anguish is disguised as skepticism and is wed to ignorance.

The truth, as I see it, is that:

1. Every drawing, symptom, fantasy or act has a history out of which it was produced.

2. This history is a dynamic, organized field of vectors.

3. The drawing or symbol in a given case is produced by a unique field.

4. The same drawing or symbol in another case may be the resultant of a different field.[1]

5. The field which produces a particular drawing or symbol is "layered," i.e., multidimensional.[2]

6. That a drawing or symbol is economic and over-determined.[3]

7. A particular psychodynamic in one matrix of factors may produce drawing symbol A; in another matrix it may produce non-A; in still another it may produce contra-A; in another reciprocal-A.

The amount of information which may be secured from this projective technique varies with the psychologist's apperceptive mass, i.e., his understanding, experience, and skill. The best kind of preparatory training for the drawing analyst may be courses in the pluralism of William James, the multidimensional linguistic symbols of James Joyce (5), the dream interpretations of Freud (6), the explorations in symbolism by Stekel and Jung, and a personal psychoanalysis!

## ASSUMPTIONS

1. The basic assumption is that figure drawings are determined. As Rieff (7) has stated, Freud and his contemporaries

---

[1] E.g., A headache may be "caused" by various fields of vectors. In one case it may be produced by hypoglycemia, in another by hypotension, in a third by repressed hostility, etc.

[2] On one level an armless individual may represent a "wish to be castrated"; on a "layer" under this level, it may represent a strong genital drive associated with guilt, etc.

[3] A particular part of a drawing may be the economic resultant of training factors, biological engineering factors, cultural factors, and psychodynamic factors.

and descendants have convinced us that every act is determined, e.g., rage, compulsion, dream, trivial error, or slip of the tongue. However, none of these can be dignified or institutionalized as a psychodiagnostic technique. To merit inclusion as such, a technique must be concerned with segments of behavior which are nuclear.

2. The second assumption is that a figure drawing *is* determined by *nuclear* psychodynamic factors. To understand this concept one may refer to chemistry where the color of a chemical substance is determined but is peripheral for most purposes and not of central significance. However, the atomic configuration of a chemical *is* nuclear.

3. The third assumption is that this nuclearity comes about as a result of the "body image" concept (8). According to this concept, each of us carries about in his psychic apparatus an image, physical in structure and largely unconscious, of the kind of a person he is. Furthermore, this image is based in part on convention, in part on body sensation and structure, and in part on symbolic translation from attitude into bodily characteristic. That this translation takes place is readly ascertainable by a study of cartoons where a "square jaw" for example stands for the characteristic of determination and strength, etc.

4. Although a figure drawing is determined by a combination of cultural, personal training, biomechanical, transitory, and characterological factors, the latter may be isolated, identified and to some extent quantified.

For example, the following drawings were obviously executed by subjects who had art training (Figures 1 and 2).

However, the art training does not disguise the characterological aspects but blends with them. Rouault, Renoir, Picasso all had art training—but how different their art! A study of the life of each of these artists reveals the intimate relationship between his life experiences and personality on the one hand, and his art on the other (9).

5. There are intermediating operations between the details of a drawing and the forces which determine them; these operations have a grammar and a syntax similar to that which governs dream symbols, fantasy formations and somatic displacements.

Some other factors are worthy of consideration. Attempts to evaluate the reliability and validity of a psychological procedure are desirable and necessary. However, techniques for so doing must be adequate to the subject matter; otherwise, the validity index may refer not to the subject matter being investigated, but rather to the naïveté or shallowness of the validating technique. For example, at one time the reliability of the Rorschach was investigated by using the odd-even technique applied to the Rorschach cards! Anyone who knows a smattering about the Rorschach can see that this would yield a low coefficient of reliability which would be related not to the Rorschach but to the investigator's lack of information. One kind of validation study which may be meaningful is suggested in the Case of Mr. P. (Chapter 7) where sequential figure drawings parallel the subject's own changing life situation, dreams, fantasies, associations and external behavior.

Figure 1

Figure 2

In the section on human figure drawings first the basic Draw-A-Person technique will be described and then elaborated and discussed.

## DRAW-A-PERSON TECHNIQUE

This may be regarded as a type of situational test in which

the subject is presented not only with the problem of drawing a person, but with the problem of orienting, adapting and behaving in a situation. In his efforts to solve these problems he engages in verbal, expressive and motor behavior. This *behavior*, as well as the drawing itself, provides the data for psychological analysis.

## The Basic Procedure

The following paragraphs present the equipment, directions, observations and interpretations of the Draw-A-Person Technique.

*Equipment.* The basic procedure consists in presenting the subject with a moderately soft pencil and blank paper approximately 8½ by 11 inches in size. The paper should be placed in a pile within arm's reach so that the subject may select the sheet and place it in any position he prefers. There should be an adequate flat desk surface and sufficient illumination. The individual must be comfortably seated, with sufficient room for arms and legs. At this point it seems appropriate to caution against the frequently observed practice of permitting the subject to be seated along the side of a desk so that it becomes necessary for him to twist his body and shoulders. It is also undesirable to use a surface area so limited that the subject cannot rest his arms upon it. It is desirable to permit the subject to assume his usual state of relaxation so that any physical tensions may be assumed to be endogenous rather than imposed upon him by the external physical situation.

*Directions.* It will be assumed that rapport has been established between examiner and subject. The examiner says: "Will you please draw a person." This may result in a number of questions, such as "The whole person?" "What kind of person?" and in many protestations about the artistic ineptitude of the subject. In response to the class of questions relating to the kind of drawing, the examiner should limit himself to a very general statement, such as "Draw whatever you like in any way you like." This may be repeated in an effort to encourage and stimulate the subject, but no more specific directions should be given. In response to expressions of doubt about the artistic competence of the subject, the examiner may say: "That's all right; we're not interested in how well you draw as long as you draw a person." This may be repeated and rephrased, but may not be made more specific.

At this point the subject may respond in any one of a number of ways. For example, he may draw a complete person, an incomplete person, a cartoon, a "stick" figure, a stereotype, or an abstract representation of a person. Or he may express continuing reluctance. Each of these kinds of behavior yields information about the individual and is not to be regarded as wasteful of time. The clinician is just as much interested in the subject's behavior preliminary to and during the drawing as he is in the resulting artistic production. If the subject continues to be reluctant, the examiner may use whatever skills, techniques or persuasion are available to him without giving any additional specific information. The fact that artistic talent is not important and that "whatever you do is all right" should be stressed. I have used this procedure with more than 5,000 individuals and have faced very few persistent refusals to draw a person.

If the subject draws an incomplete figure, he is asked to take another sheet and draw a complete one. (The examiner must remember to number each sheet consecutively.) A word of explanation is necessary about what is meant by a complete figure." A figure that includes the major part of all of the four major areas of the body is acceptably complete. The four areas of the body are the head, the torso, the arms, and the legs. If any *one* of these areas is *completely* omitted, the figure is incomplete. If only a part of an area is omitted, however—for example, the hands or the feet or one of the facial parts—the drawing is acceptably complete.

If the subject draws a cartoon, "stick" figure, stereotype, or abstract representation, he is asked to select an additional sheet and to draw a person; but stereotypes, cartoons, etc. (as the case may be), are not acceptable, and the instructions are repeated until a satisfactory figure drawing results.

The examiner now has in his possession one or more consecutively numbered drawings, at least one of which is an acceptably complete figure. If this figure is a male, the examiner now says: "This is a male figure; now please draw a female." If the first

② Draw a person of the opposite sex

figure is a female, the examiner now says: "You drew a female figure; now please draw a male." The reactions of the subject may vary in ways similar to those previously described, and the examiner's responses are appropriate.

*Observations and Interpretations.* This aspect of the technique consists in recording descriptive and interpretive statements about the subject's behavior and drawing.

### Behavior

The behavior of the subject may be described with respect to its orientative, verbal, and motor aspects. He is presented with a somewhat unstructured situation. How does he orient himself? Does he express an acute need for more direction, and, if so, is this need expressed directly and verbally or indirectly through expressive movements and motor activity? Does he venture comfortably and confidently into the task? Does he express doubts about his ability, and, if so, does he express these doubts directly or indirectly, verbally or through motor activity? Is he insecure, anxious, suspicious, arrogant, hostile, negative, tense, relaxed, humorous, selfconscious, cautious, impulsive? The astute clinician will be able to form a fairly illuminating impression of the subject as a result of his preliminary behavior.

### Analysis of the Drawing

In the following paragraphs the steps in analysis are described, along with other relevant information and drawings. The drawings are not presented as proof of the interpretive principles described but are included solely for *illustrative* purposes.

### Figure Sequence

Does the subject draw the male or female figure first? Of 5,500 adult subjects examined, 89 per cent drew their own sex first. These 5,500 include drawings secured from college students, from high school students, from clinic patients, neuropsychiatric hospital patients, and patients in psychoanalytic and psychotherapy practice. If the 280 drawings secured from patients in clinics and hospitals are treated separately, the percentage of those who draw their own sex first is reduced to 72 per cent

Figure 3A

Figure 3C

Figure 3B

Figure 3.  Figure Drawings by Overt Homosexuals

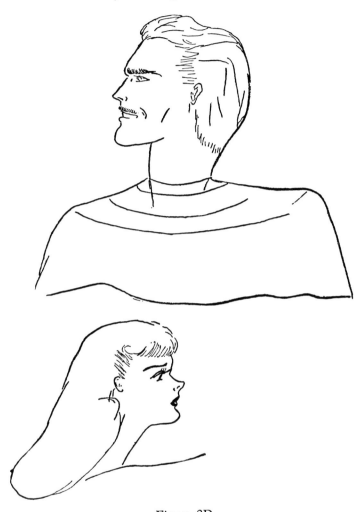

Figure 3D

Figure 3 (*Cont.*) Figure Drawings by Overt Homosexuals

of the latter group. Most of the research reported in the literature verifies that: (1) the great majority of people draw their
own sex first; (2) the incidence of deviation from this rule is
greater among individuals who request or require psychotherapy. There has been some variation in the actual percentages
reported.

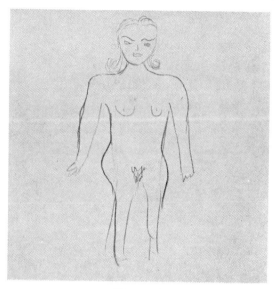

Figure 4

In my own collection I have noted that this variation generally is a function of: (1) the kind of population tested (random, clinic, etc.), and (2) the size of the population under consideration. Up to the point where I had 1,500 drawings, the range of the percentage was as much as 18 per cent with each succeeding 100 drawings. Since the collection of drawings reached 4,000 the variation has been limited to plus or minus 5 per cent. The percentage of those in the clinic-hospital group has not yet stabilized.

Of sixteen overt homosexuals, thirteen drew the opposite sex first. These two facts suggest that it is usual for people to draw their own sex first, and that it may be usual for a small selected group of homosexuals to draw the opposite sex first. This obviously does not mean that every individual who draws the opposite sex first is a homosexual or neurotic. The experienced clinician knows how dangerous it is to apply normative generalizations to an individual. If a subject draws the opposite sex first, however, the clinician should be interested in exploring the reason for this atypical procedure. I have found the following explanations for some of the cases cited above in which the first figure drawn was of the opposite sex: sexual inversion; confusion of sex identification; strong attachment to or dependence on parent of opposite sex; strong attachment to or dependence on some other individual of opposite sex; regression to an infantile narcissistic stage where one is "one with mother" (see Case of Mr. P). There are probably other explanations as well.

Subjects will occasionally verbalize their indecision by asking such questions as: "Which sex shall I draw first?" The clinician should consider the possibility that the subject who raises these questions may be indicating confusion as to his own sexual role. Figures 3A, 3B and 3C were drawn by overt homosexuals; Figure 3D by an individual who has had both homosexual and heterosexual experience. Figure 4 is that of a person who had developed, as a defense, an unconscious fantasy of being castrated and of possessing female organs (12).

Figure 5

*Figure Description*

I have found that by simply describing each figure, illuminating insights are enticed into consciousness. The following are examples of descriptive statements:

Figure 3A. "This is a muscular female ballet dancer in a toe-dancing position with her left foot pointing and extending horizontally from the body." This subject was an "active, aggressive," homosexual.

Figure 3B. "This looks like a male acrobatic figure in a half-crouching position similar to that assumed by dancers before they receive their partner. He is apparently unclothed except for tights, and the facial features are omitted." This subject was a passive homosexual.

Figure 5. "This is a very unusual drawing of a large-eyed, long-haired, fancifully clothed, and bearded individual. He is not a contemporary, and his appearance is not masculine despite the beard and clothing." The figure looks like "empty" clothing. The person who drew this was an ambulatory schizophrenic whose relationship to people and the world was empty, manneristic and full of cliches. He was often described as "unreal" and very effeminate.

It is the experience of most clinicians that even untutored and unskilled individuals, including young children, draw figures that convey expressive ideas. It is interesting to note that the person who drew Figures 6A and 6B protested: "I have never been able to draw anything, I just don't know how to draw." Later, while discussing her father, John, she described him as follows:

A very stern man who loved to go out dressed up. He was always meticulous about himself and insisted upon doing the right thing at the right time and criticized other peole who do things for the fun of it or because they just want to. Margueritte (Figure 6A) is a young girl who really does not look the way she is pictured to be. But that's the way John makes her feel. John made her feel as though her evening gown were a house dress. She hesitated to accompany him to functions for fear of being criticized.

It is interesting to observe that, in spite of her protestations about lack of drawing skill, the two figures she drew convey with astonishing clarity and economy her feelings about herself and her father.

The precise way in which this is used by the clinician cannot be specifically formulated. The technique of studying the drawing for a few moments in order to describe the attitudes and feeling tones conveyed by it has proved productive. Perhaps the clinician's mind-set is so structured that the threshold for responding to subliminal cues is lowered. But this is speculation. The fact is that drawings do vary in their expressive aspects, and that recognition and conscious formulation of these differences seem to facilitate further interpretation.

### Comparison of Figures

Virtually everybody is able to draw two figures that differ

Figure 6A

Figure 6B

Figure 7A

Figure 7B

from each other in some ways. The particular ways selected (consciously and unconsciously) by a subject are usually informative with respect to psychosexual attitudes. For example, in Figure 7A the male figure is much smaller and less mobile and has shorter arms than the female shown in Figure 7B. That is a descriptive statement of the differences between the two drawings. One possible interpretative statement based upon these objective differences is that the male is a smaller, more passive individual than the female. This interpretation is based upon the following elements: the woman's stance, posture, and arms suggest activity, whereas the male figure's posture, arms, and hands convey the impression that he is not in motion, that he is standing, with his hands in his pockets, watching. From this we may proceed a step further away from the objective drawing to the interpretation that the subject sees the man as inactive (passive), introverted, whereas the female appears to him as active, extroverted, aggressive. That this is the general feeling conveyed by these drawings can easily be verified in ways similar to the technique used by me. This pair of drawings was presented to five clinicians with a request that they describe each of the figures as succinctly as possible. From the five statements made about the male (all five agreed in the essential characterization), the descriptive words that appeared with most frequency were tabulated. Words implying spectatorship rather than active participation (observer, onlooker, thoughtful, watching) occurred in each of the five descriptions. Words implying passivity or dependence (less competent, dependent, feels small) occurred in four of the descriptions.

Descriptive words implying activity (aggressive, protective, active) appeared in all of the statements about the woman; and the implication of extroversion (takes care of others, not self-centered, motherly, competent) appeared in all the statements. When the five statements were boiled down into one descriptive passage about each figure, the following descriptions resulted.

"Figure 7A is that of a somewhat retiring, sensitive, dependent, thoughtful, idealistic, introverted, gentle individual."

"Figure 7B is that of a competent, energetic, active, protective, generous, firm person who is accustomed to taking charge."

These two statements, with sexual identification omitted, were presented to five other clinicians with the request that they match each statement with the drawing to which it seemed to apply. In every case the former statement was matched with the male figure and the latter with the female.

There are other factors in each drawing to support these characterizations. Hands and arms are the parts of the human body that "do things," establish contact (shake hands), punish, or defend. In the male drawing, the arms are relatively short (limited contact possibilities), pressed close to the body, and the hands are placed in the pockets. In this position there is no suggestion of readiness for activity, attack, manipulation, aggression, or other forms of contact.

The woman's arms are rather long, bent away from the body, with hands outlined. They are in a position from which it is quite easy to establish contact with people or objects. The kinesthesia expressed in the position of the arms suggests activity, whereas arms resting along the sides of body with hands in pockets imply a lack of muscular tension, ego passivity. The hair in the female drawing is sketched in firm strokes and gives the over-all impression of energy. What kind of woman wears her hair in this way? Observe that the man's hair is not drawn from the center of the head away from the body (as is the woman's), but is drawn from the head toward the body for the most part. In my experience with figure drawings stroking toward the body is suggestive of introversive tendencies, whereas stroking away from the body is often associated with extroversive tendencies.

Observe the difference in size. What is the usual association with respect to relative size? Is not the adult bigger and more competent than the child? The interpretation may be made that the subject is identifying with the male figure, that his attention is directed toward himself (introverted), and that the female figure incorporates his apperception of women, which may be assumed to be derived from his relationship with his mother or mother surrogate.

The fact that the woman as well as the man is somewhat carefully detailed, with belt and neckline outlined, suggests that the subject who drew these figures is a somewhat compulsive individual with some regard for detail and order. The way in which the outline of the male figure is traced and retraced—the jacket is drawn and then redrawn to correct proportion—reinforces the intepretation of compulsiveness and orderliness. Thus by comparing the man-woman drawings the following interpretative statements may be made about the male subject who drew them:

"S is an introverted, anxious, thoughtful, compulsive, sensitive, passive individual; a spectator rather than a man of action;

has a need for nurturance and support and expects to receive these from maternal figure."

He feels himself to be small in relation to women who are aggressive and threatening. He is preoccupied by anal derivatives (this represents a long leap into psychoanalytic theory, without which one cannot travel far, above the ground) and has conflicted psychosexual identification.

SIZE

The relationship between the size of the drawing and the available space may parallel the dynamic relationship between the subject and his environment or between the subject and parent figures. Size is suggestive of the way the subject is responding to the environmental press. If the self-concept figure is small, the hypothesis may be formulated that the subject feels small (inadequate) and that he is responding to the demands of the environment with feelings of inferiority. If the figure is large, then the subject is responding to environmental press with feelings of expansion and aggression.

A word is in order about the meanings of "large" and "small." The average drawing of a full figure is approximately seven inches long, or two thirds of the available space. More important than absolute size is the impression conveyed by the relationship between the figure and the surrounding space. If the *impression* of smallness is conveyed in a drawing, then the interpretation may be made that the subject feels small (inferior) or lost (rejected).

Figures 8A and 8B were both drawn by six-foot tall adolescent boys. The individual who drew Figure 8A expresses his feelings of inferiority and wraps this feeling in self-deprecatory humor. He is, in effect, poking fun at himself. One may assume from this drawing that he feels foolish and attempts to beat the other person to the punch by making fun of himself. His feelings of impotence are suggested by the use of substitute masculinity symbols which express compensatory wishes. Instead of drawing a strong, "phallic" person, he draws a weak one with a mustache (virility wish) and a long nose (virility wish). The yo-yo suggests: (1) that the subject has not relinquished childish ways; (2) that he has masturbatory wishes. A yo-yo is manipulated

Figure 8A

Figure 8B

with the hand and goes up and down (note placement of hand).[4]

Figure 8B was drawn by a boy who feels large in his environment, who does not poke fun at himself, but is having the usual conflict (Oedipal?) about his sexual feelings. He has resolved it by reinforcing his superego, i.e., by repressing the forbidden im-

[4] This is an example of the law of misplaced concreteness, i.e., an object or act which has one or more characteristics of another may represent the other.

pulse. However, the psychoanalytic cliché "the return of the repressed through the repressed" is illustrated. The left hand ends in a "circle" which states in effect "there is nothing here," but note the phallic form of each hand. This individual in his therapy is in the process of a successful resolution of the oedipal-conflict.

Figure 9

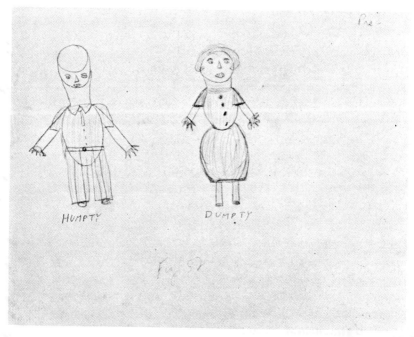

Figure 10

## Movement

Almost all figure drawings suggest some kind of kinesthetic tension, ranging from rigidity to extreme mobility (see Figure 9). A drawing that is suggestive of much activity is frequently produced by those individuals who have a strong impulse toward motor activity. The restless individual, the man of action, the hypermanic, the hysteric, produce drawings that contain considerable movement. Figures that convey the impression of extreme rigidity are frequently produced by individuals with serious and deep-seated conflicts over which a rigid and usually brittle control is maintained (see Figure 10). Occasionally the drawing will be that of a seated or reclining individual, in which case it is frequently indicative of low energy level, lack of drive, or emotional exhaustion. If a drawing is a mechanical kind of figure completely lacking in kinesthetic implications, the analyst should be alert for other signs of depersonalization and psychosis. Figures 11A and 11B are mechanical and lifeless and were produced by a schizophrenic.

## Distortions and Omissions

A distortion or omission of any part of the figure suggests that conflicts may be related to the part so treated. For example, voyeurists frequently omit the eyes or close them (see Figure 12). Individuals with sexual conflicts will omit or distort the areas associated with sexual parts. Infantile individuals with oral needs usually draw enlarged breasts. In a study of World War II leg amputees I found that the lower parts of the body were frequently omitted (see Figure 13). Remarks, erasures, shading, and reinforcement are all in the same direction as distortions and omissions and should be explored for possible relationships to conflict areas (see Case of P).

*Head Region.* This is usually drawn first. Most individuals' concept of self is focused in the head and face. If the head is markedly enlarged, the subject may either be very grandiose, have intellectual aspiration (or have head pains or other somatic symptoms) be introspective or phantasy ridden. If the head and face are dimmed out, the subject may be extremely self-conscious and shy. If the head is drawn last, the possibility of severe thought disturbance should be explored. If the head is very clearly drawn

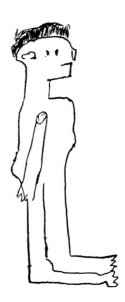

Figure 11A                    Figure 11B

Figure 12

in contrast with a vaguely sketched or rejected body, the individual may habitually resort to fantasy as a compensatory device or may have feelings of inferiority or shame about his body parts and function.

The hair is given a great deal of attention and care by narcissistic or homosexual individuals. Hair on the face (beard or mustache) is usually associated with a compensatory striving for virility by those who have feelings of sexual inadequacy or doubts about masculinity (see Figures 3D and 5). The mouth may be portrayed by a straight line, a curved line, an oval, and sometimes with teeth. If teeth are included, the subject may be orally aggressive and sadistic; other characteristics associated with this stage of development should be looked for. If the mouth is indicated by a single line, the individual may be verbally aggressive. If the mouth is excessively oval or full and open, the subject may be an oral erotic, dependent individual.

If the eyes are very large and if those of the male figure have lashes, the subject is almost surely a homosexual. If the eyes are large in outline but the pupils are omitted or absent, the subject may be expressing guilt in relation to voyeuristic tendencies. If the eyes are large and have the quality of staring, the clinician should investigate the possibility of paranoid trends.

The nose may portray a social stereotype or may be interpreted as a phallic symbol. If the nose is hooked or broad and flared, the subject is expressing rejection and contempt. If the nose is especially large, it is usually associated with feelings of sexual impotency. Male involutional melancholics usually draw extremely large noses. Adolescents who are attempting to establish their male role but feel inadequate for it, almost invariably draw large noses.

The chin is a social stereotype for strength and determination. If a self-concept drawing has an enlarged chin, it may be an expression of strong drive, aggressive tendencies, or if very exaggerated, compensatory feelings for weakness and indecisiveness.

The ear is rarely detailed. If it is enlarged or emphasized, the clinician should explore the possibility of organic damage in the auditory area, or auditory hallucinations in a paranoid individual, a hearing disability, or a passive homosexual conflict (see Case of Mr. P).

The neck separates the head from the body and may be regarded as the link between intellectual control and id impulses. A long neck may suggest that the subject is having difficulty in controlling and directing instinctual drives (see discussion of this in Case of Mr. P, p. 146). A long neck may also indicate somatic

Figure 13

symptoms in this area. Individuals who have difficulty in swallowing, globus hystericus, or psychogenic digestive disturbances may draw figures with extremely long necks. Schizoid individuals also frequently draw figures with an exaggerated neck (see Figures 11A and 11B).

*Arms and Hands.* The arms and hands are the contact and manipulatory organs of the body. If the hands are hidden, the subject is expressing contact difficulties or feelings of guilt for manipulatory activities (masturbation). If the hands are shown but are exaggerated in size, this may be interpreted as compensatory behavior for feelings of manipulatory insufficiency, contact difficulties, or inadequacy. If the hands have considerable shading, then the subject may be expressing anxiety with respect to manipulation or contact activities. If the arms are pressed close to the body, the subject may be expressing passive or defensive feelings. If the arms are overly long and extended away from the body, the subject may be expressing externally directed aggressive needs. If fingers, fingernails, and joints are carefully sketched, the subject is either compulsive or is expressing difficulties with relation to body concept (as in early schizophrenia). Closed fists suggest repressed aggression.

*Other Parts of the Body.* If the legs and feet are drawn first and given considerably more attention than the rest of the body, the subject may be expressing discouragement or depression. If the hip and buttocks of the male figure are rounded and larger than they should be or given an unusual amount of attention, the subject may have strong homosexual trends. If the trunk is rounded or wasp-waisted, a similar interpretation may be made. If the elbow joints and other articulatory regions are delineated, the subject is either a compulsive individual, in which case this trait will be manifested in many other ways, or he is a dependent, uncertain individual who needs familiar perceptual cues for reassurance. If internal anatomy is drawn, the subject is almost surely schizophrenic or manic. If the body is vaguely or bizarrely drawn (Figures 11A and 11B) the subject may be schizophrenic.

The treatment of the feminine figure, by male subjects, should be carefully observed. Is the drawing a representation of a child, a dream girl (Petty model), a maternal figure? What parts of the female body are emphasized? If the breasts are extremely enlarged and carefully drawn, the subject may be expressing strong oral dependent needs. If the arms and hands are long and prominent, the individual may be expressing the need for a protective mother figure. If femininity in the female figure is indicated through the use of superficial or symbolic details, the subject may be expressing severely repressed forbidden sex feel-

1.

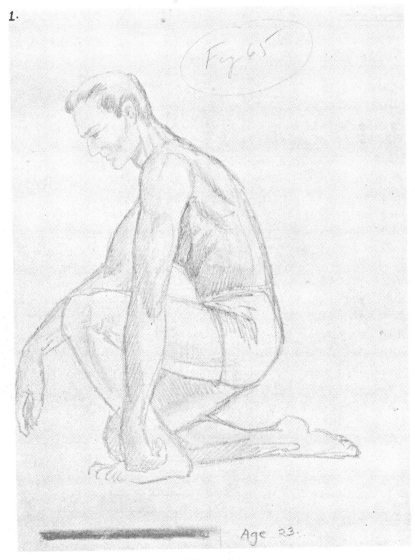

Figure 14

ings. If the shoulders and other masculine indicators in the male figure are exaggerated, the subject may be expressing his own insecurity with respect to masculinity (12).

*Clothing.* Most drawings are clothed. If the figures are nude and the sexual parts prominently displayed, the subject may be expressing rebellion against society (parent figures) or may be consciously aware of sexual conflicts. Individuals in whom there is a large voyeuristic element may draw glorified nude figures. If the self-concept figure is nude and given a great deal of attention, the subject may be expressing body-narcissism. (See Figure 14.) On the other hand, if the self-concept drawing is carefully clothed, the individual may be expressing clothing—or social— narcissism. Both forms of narcissism are found in infantile, egocentric individuals.

Button emphasis is usually an indicator of a dependent, infantile, inadequate personality. If the buttons are emphasized along the mid-line, the subject may have somatic preoccupations. If buttons are drawn on cuffs and other equally inconspicuous areas, the subject is probably an obsessive-compulsive individual. The latter will also draw shoelaces, wrinkles, etc. The particular detail selected to express the compulsiveness may be significant, for example—creases in the trousers suggest a tendency to masculine display.

Pockets, when placed on the breast, are indicators of oral and affectional deprivation and are usually found in the drawings of infantile, dependent individuals. They may also express a psychosexual identification with the mother, with the pocket being a symbolic receptor organ, i.e., vagina. An exaggerated tie is frequently interpreted as a phallic symbol. If a great deal of care and attention are lavished upon the tie and if the figure is somewhat effeminate, the subject may be a homosexual. A small tie may suggest repressed feelings of organ inferiority. Earrings are frequently drawn by subjects who have sex preoccupations of an exhibitionistic nature. Cigarettes, pipes, and canes are usually interpreted as symbols of striving for virility.

## Graphology

The stroking may be described with respect to pressure, direction, continuity, angularity, rhythm. The pressure of the stroke is usually related to the level of energy. Thus an individual with a great deal of drive and ambition will usually draw firm lines. The individual whose energy level is low because of physical or psychic reasons will draw rather light lines. The cyclothymic, unstable, or impulsive individual will show fluctuating pressures.

The direction of the stroke may be vertical or horizontal, determined or undetermined. A marked preference for horizontal movements is frequently associated with weakness, femininity, fantasy living. A marked preference for vertical stroking is often associated with determination, hyperactivity, and assertive masculinity. If the direction of the stroke is determined and unhesitating, the individual may be a secure person with perseverance and persistence in working toward goals. Strokes that are indeterminate or vacillating in direction are frequently associated with a lack of the foregoing qualities. Thus, vague, insecure individuals who lack opinions and points of view will draw figures in which the stroking has no determined direction. Uninterrupted straight lines are frequently the product of quick, decisive individuals. Interrupted curvilinear lines are often associated with slowness and indecisiveness. Very short sketchy strokes are often associated with anxiety and uncertainty. If the stroking is performed in a free and rhythmic way, the subject may be an unconstricted, responsive individual. If the stroking is constricted, the individual may be a tense, withdrawn, coarcted person. If the outline of the figure is sharp and clear with an unbroken reinforced line, the individual may be expressing his isolation and a need to protect himself from external pressures. Shading is usually an anxiety indicator. If the shading is found in sexual areas, the anxiety may be in relation to sexual function.

Undue emphasis on strokes drawn from the page toward the subject may suggest self-involvement, introversion, or anxiety. Exaggerated strokes drawn from the subject toward the upper part of the sheet may suggest aggression or extroversion. Emphasized strokes drawn from right to left are frequently associated with introversion or isolation. When the direction is from left to right, the figure-drawing analyst may look for tendencies toward extroversion, social stimulation, need for support.

At the risk of repetition, the clinician is again cautioned against using any one area of interpretation as reliably diagnostic unless supported by the total patterning of the drawing analysis. *Miscellaneous.* If the subject draws "stick" figures or abstract representations, they may be interpreted as indicative of evasion. This is frequently characteristic of insecure, self-doubting individuals. If the figures are clowns, cartoons, or silly-looking, the subject is expressing his contempt and hostility for himself. This is frequently found in adolescents who feel rejected or inadequate. Witches or similar characters are drawn by individuals who are hostile toward females and express their feelings extrapunitively.

Frequently ancillary material such as lines to represent the ground or a fence to lean on are included. These may be interpreted to express the need for support or succorance. Compulsive individuals are very easily recognized by their drawings. They are unable to leave them alone, and they go over and over an area, adding more and more detail. The hysteric, impulsive, unstable individual presents drawings that reveal these qualities in their lack of preciseness and the lack of uniformity of performance.

## REFERENCES

1. Murray, H. A., *et al.*: *Explorations in Personality.* New York, Oxford, 1938.
2. James, William: *Principles of Psychology.*
3. Freud, S.: *Leonardo Da Vinci.* New York, Random House, 1947.
4. Freud, S.: *Delusion and Dreams.*
5. Tindall, W. Y.: *James Joyce, His Way of Interpreting the Modern World.* New York, Scribner, 1950.
6. Freud, S.: *The Interpretation of Dreams.* (Translated by Strachey.) New York, Basic Books, 1955.
7. Rieff, Philip: In Freud, S. (4).
8. Schilder, P.: *The Image and Appearance of the Human Body.* London, Kegan Paul, Trench, Trubner & Co., 1935.
9. Untermeyer, L.: In Rouault, G.: *Makers of the Modern World*, p. 420.
10. Levy, S.: Figure drawing as a projective test, in Abt and Bellak: *Projective Psychology.* New York, Knopf, 1950.
11. Bettelheim, B.: *Symbolic Wounds.*
12. Levy, R. A.: Confusion of sexual role in schizophrenic children, a study involving figure drawings. Study completed at State University of New York College of Medicine, 1956.

## CHAPTER 5

## CHILD CASE STUDY:
## A TROUBLED EIGHT-YEAR-OLD

Florence Halpern, Ph.D.

### GENERAL REMARKS ON CHILDREN'S DRAWINGS

Like the adult, the child's concept of the human body derives from the experiences he has had with his body, the sensations he has known in connection with it, the pains and pleasures it has afforded him, the uses to which he has put it, and the perceptions which have resulted from these experiences and from his observations of and contacts with others. From the developmental point of view it is probably the human face that the child first abstracts out of the mass of impressions impinging on him when he is approached by another person. Thus the face is probably the most significant area of the human body for the young infant and child, the one through which social contact is made and satisfactions attained. By observing facial expressions, the child soon learns what he can anticipate, what the nature of any particular set of circumstances is likely to be, long before he has any understanding of speech. In view of the importance of the face in the young child's life and in his adjustive efforts it is not surprising that the drawings of very young children concentrate on the head and face, and little else.

Next in importance to the face are the limbs since they too play a primary part in making social contact and also constitute a means of extending, contacting, exploring and mastering the environment. Thus the early drawings of children, that is, three- and four-year-olds, consist largely of a head and limbs, often inappropriately placed, and little else. If a body is indicated it rarely consists of more than a single line.

With increased experience of himself and others, the child

learns to incorporate the body into his concept of the human figure. The body is generally represented by a large circle or oval, oft times not any larger, if as large, as the head. Certainly it bears little true resemblance to the human form. It is the rare child who before the age of eight gives indication of shoulders or neck. At five it is not unsual for the arms to be treated as extensions of the head rather than the body. This tendency disappears at about six, and drawings with arms coming from the head in children seven years, and older, generally reflect developmental lags or pathological conditions.

One of the most consistent findings in the drawings of four- and five-year-olds is the appearance of a large dot in the center of the body, which on questioning turns out to be the navel. A number of explanations for this phenomenon are suggested. In his early explorations of his body and body openings the child generally discovers his navel, and then asks questions about it. Depending on the explanation offered him, the navel comes to have varying significance. Where the question is brushed off or answered unsatisfactorily the navel acquires a certain secret, mysterious quality and is associated in the child's mind with other strange and secret matters. It is therefore not surprising that some children consider the navel a kind of keyhole to the abdomen and regard it as the door to the mother's body, the way the child emerges from the mother's body. When the explanation given the child accords with the biological realities and is presented in simple, understandable and confident fashion the navel comes to represent to the child his physical separation from the mother. From the idea of physical separation there emerges the concept of psychological separation, the growing awareness of the possibility of an independent "self," physically and emotionally. Thus the navel represents the child's concern with basic issues which seem to reach their peak at about four to five years of age. By the time the child is six this concept of the independent self is no longer new, and therefore much less likely to be startling and disturbing. So the navel disappears but the dependency needs are certainly not yet fully satisfied and the child is not yet ready to give up completely his tie to the mother figure. Instead, the navel is replaced by a row of buttons. These buttons are common in the drawings of children up to about eight years of age and are then likely to disappear, provided the child has successfully resolved his problems in relation to dependence and independence.

Whereas three- and four-year-olds rarely give their figures hands and fingers, growing ability in manipulating the environment and the awareness of the need for such manipulation, both from the physical and psychological points of view, results in the appearance of hands and fingers sometimes as early as five and one-half to six years of age. The hand is first drawn as a circle and the fingers indicated by one dimensional, straight lines stuck in all around this circle. Feet tend to appear somewhat later than fingers, also often in one dimension.

The separation between the head and the body, between the intellect and the so-called grosser functions of the human being, finds reflection in the figure drawings at about the age of eight. It is then that the child's awareness of his need for intellectual control results in attempts at drawing a neck. The length and width of the neck and the general emphasis given it constitute a measure of the subject's need for and emphasis on control. It can be assumed that the more the neck is stressed, the more threatening the bodily impulses are and the greater the need to defend against them by intellectual control.

Other factors typical of the eight to ten year old group are the appearance of two dimensional arms and legs, often occurring around eight; and the generally better integrated and proportioned body. At eight, and continuing through to puberty, we find efforts at enhancing security and prestige through the addition of symbols of strength and importance. Thus in the drawings of boys, there is likely to be considerable emphasis on guns, fishing rods, cowboy hats, etc.; while baskets, pocketbooks, hair ribbons and similar adornments begin to appear in the drawings of girls. The hair which actually appears early in the drawings of young children now tends to be treated as an adornment rather than as just another body feature.

The improvement in the figure drawing as far as their integrative aspects are concerned stems from the fact that sometime during the eight-to-ten-year period, depending upon the intellectual and emotional maturity of the child, as well as his artistic ability, the segmented nature of the figure which characterizes the productions of very young children gives way to an awareness of the body as a unit rather than a series of parts added to one another. This latter concept of the human figure which is typical for most children under eight is well reflected in the verbalizations which frequently accompany their drawing efforts. Thus one child said while drawing, "First the head, then the stomach, then the legs. And now what does he need? What should I give him now? What does he need? Oh, yes, the hands." The concept of the body functioning as a single unit, with one direction and purpose, is not within the scope of the young child's understanding. He is not so far removed from the time when, in response to his oral and exploratory impulses, he bit his own toes, unaware until he experienced pain, that they were actually a part of his body. While he soon learns what belongs to him and what is apart from himself, different aspects of his body still make very separate and distinct impressions on him. At any given moment, different parts of his body may well be concerned with different needs and problems, often pulling him in opposing directions. This lack of a true sense of unity finds expression in his drawings in the portrayal of each area of the body as a unit by itself, and it is the agglomeration of these individual units that makes up the young child's concept of his body.

By the time the child reaches puberty not only has the fragmented concept of the human body disappeared, but the drawings acquire considerable sophistication. This is the period when the body acquires new and very special importance, and in consequence, depending upon the sex of the subject, the drawings emphasize such attributes as size, strength, grace, physical attractiveness, etc.

While the changes that occur in the figure drawings all through childhood can certainly be attributed in considerable measure to the psychological development of the child, his increasing facility in manipulating the pencil and in graphic representation must be taken into account. It is possible that the young child actually has a somewhat more mature concept of the human body than he is able to express in his drawing.

As in the case of the adult, sex differences play an important part in determining the type of figure that the child will produce. Only in the very youngest group, that is, the three- and four-year-olds, is this factor of little or no importance. For most children five years of age or older, there is an awareness of some differences between the sexes and this awareness is reflected in their drawings. At first, the difference may be expressed by the presence or absence of a skirt, or the length of the hair. However, not until pre-puberty or even puberty is there likely to be any recognition of the difference in body form. Rather, the drawings of children until puberty rarely show any awareness of bodily contours. Instead, the figures are generally presented without curves, revealing the child's body, not the adult's.

Since the needs and problems of the child vary not only from month to month and year to year, but actually from week to week and day to day, it can be assumed that once the child's needs and perceptions advance beyond a very infantile stage, his concepts of himself will become more complicated and variable. However, he is handicapped in his ability to communicate these changing self concepts by his limited skill in portraying himself through drawings. Instead, his figures are likely to have a certain stereotyped quality, but careful inspection will reveal variations in small details from one drawing to another, and these variations are often of prime significance. They reflect the child's shifting perceptions of himself and his environment, even when the basic figure remains unaltered.

With a knowledge of what is fairly typical for a given age group and what constitutes the particular psychological problems of that group, the child's drawing can be evaluated in terms of its similarity to and deviations from what is usual at a given age. However, certain factors are of special importance in interpreting the child's representation of the human body. One such factor is the source of never ending wonder that the body holds for the child. As he experiences it, there are new sensations constantly stemming from it. All kinds of mysterious things take place within the body and happen to the body. For example, it becomes larger if one eats correctly and is likely to shrink if one does not. It can provide pleasant sensations and a sense of well being, but it can also cause much pain and discomfort. By using, or failing to use, certain areas of his body or by emphasizing or neglecting certain bodily functions, the child learns early in life how he can win attention and approval or disapproval from the environment. Thus, the body also becomes an important instrument of power with which to manipulate those about him. For the child then, there is a certain magic about the body, and it is therefore not strange that for the very young child with his limited acceptance of reality, the body is sometimes endowed with supernatural qualities. So it is not unusual for a four-year-old to draw a person with an enormous, balloon-like body or with a grossly exaggerated head. However, by six or seven such striking distortions are not likely to appear. Instead, there is an increasing recognition and acceptance of the basic realities in so far as the nature of the human body is concerned, although it is still used in power operations.

Another factor that plays an important part in the evaluation of the child's drawing is his own physical place in the environment. The child is a small figure in a world that for him frequently appears to be peopled with gigantic objects. Similarly, psychologically he is at the mercy of the environment which is stronger and more effective than he is. On the other hand, the child is not without opportunity for experiencing himself as equal to, possibly even bigger and stronger than, certain figures in his world, namely his peers. The child who consistently draws a tiny figure is therefore not reacting in terms of all of his experiences and opportunities, but rather is focusing on his relationships with adult figures. These relationships have apparently been so overwhelming that they have made it impossible for this particular child to view himself as other than small and helpless, regardless of the nature of the circumstances in which he may find himself. Similarly, the child who draws an overly large figure is capitalizing on whatever moments of strength and importance he has enjoyed. Apparently his need for such moments and such a reassuring concept of himself causes him to keep out of awareness any other perceptions of himself that he may have had. As in the case whenever extremes are employed, neither the child with the overly small drawing nor the one with the exaggeratedly large drawing is responding in well-rounded healthy fashion to his experiences, and he will therefore have a biased perception of himself, and others, with resulting difficulty in adjusting to the realities of many experiences.

Still another factor comes into consideration in interpreting the drawings of children. This concerns itself with the test situation itself, what the assignment "draw a person" means to the child, how this differs in the child as compared with the adult. The fact that, in clinical practice, testing of a child is frequently introduced with the request to draw (something that is practically never done with an adult), bears witness to this difference in the child's attitude toward drawing as compared with that of the grown-up. For the child, the request to draw is very likely to reduce tension, whereas in the adult it frequently mobilizes tension and anxiety. Since one of the cardinal assumptions underlying all projective testing is that the unstructured nature of the situation tends to arouse anxiety and mobilize defenses, the question naturally arises, is the request to draw actually an unstructured, unfamiliar and anxiety-arousing circumstance for the child or does the frequency and pleasure with which most children draw rule out such a possibility. The chances are that for most children the assignment "draw a person" is not a particularly disturbing one, and therefore does not produce a strengthening of defenses. Yet the child's drawings do definitely reveal his problems because for him, as for the artist, drawing is one of the channels through which he can express his fears, hopes and fantasies. In fact, except for those children who are fearful of any form of manipulative activity and any situation which calls for free, spontaneous self-expression, the drawing is likely to be the way in which the child communicates much that is important to him and much that troubles him. It also constitutes a way in which he can release pent-up feelings and impulses. Like with the dream, that which is created deals with matters that are in a state of tension, that are unresolved; it deals with feelings, experiences and relationships for which the individual longs or which fill him with anxiety and dread, not with matters which have been resolved. Viewed as a creative act, the child's drawings become highly meaningful and communicative.

## CASE STUDY

The drawings to be interpreted here were produced by a boy eight years eight months old, with an I.Q. of 117 on the Revised Stanford-Binet, Form L. He is the older of two children; his sister is three and one-half. The family falls in the middle income bracket, his father being a relatively successful salesman. The child was referred for psychological examination because he is a chronic bedwetter and a stutterer. In school he does well and apparently is liked by his teachers, although one teacher indicated that although he tends to show certain feminine mannerisms, he does occasionally become quite self-assertive and try to take over the situation. On the whole, however, the school has no complaints. The subject has friends both at school and at home, but makes no great effort to be with the other boys. If they come to him he will play with them, but he is unlikely to take the initiative in this connection. Toward his sister he shows ambivalent feelings, at times appearing to be quite interested in her and fond of her, at other times resenting her, pushing her out of his way and on occasion treating her roughly.

During the testing session the child was quite pleasant, responsive and cooperative, although physical restlessness was marked. He was given the drawing assignment first and this was followed by the intelligence test, the Rorschach and Thematic Apperception Test. The man was drawn first, but without the hat, pointer or black board. At this point he called the figure a robot. He then drew the female figure and said "She's eight years old, standing up and talking to the teacher." He then insisted on returning to the male figure, adding the mortar board, the pointer and the blackboard, and labeling the man a "professor."

While these figures have certain features in common with what is ordinarily found in the drawings of eight-year-olds, they also show departures from the more typical drawings of this age group. The absence of bodily curves and the stance of the figures with the legs well apart are the aspects of the drawings that mark them as the work of a child of this age. On the other hand, the well-drawn, carefully shaped features of the girl's face and the profile presentation of the man's face point to greater maturity than is indicated by the structure of the body. Similarly, the detailing of the sexual area of the female figure reveals a sexual precocity not ordinarily encountered at this age. On the other hand, the absence of hands is, in a sense, a lag in development. Hands are likely to be emphasized at this age because they play such an important part in the child's general activity and in his efforts to manipulate his environment as well as relate to it. Uneven development is further suggested by the fact that while the girl has a large, strong, well-articulated neck, the neck is com-

pletely absent in the man. Instead of manifesting the maturity that is suggested by the presence of the neck the man is portrayed as a dependent figure with a row of buttons on his blouse. In general then this boy's drawings emphasize the variable nature of his development and suggest that unresolved problems make it impossible for him to function in a reasonably consistent fashion.

The variable development and functioning that finds expression in this boy's drawings is also reflected in his performance on other tests. For example, on the Stanford-Binet he has several successes at Year XIV, but he also has failures at Year VIII. Furthermore, his successes and failures do not follow any consistent pattern, nor do they correlate very highly with the difficulty of the task. Thus he has only one success at the eleven-year level and three successes at the fourteen-year level. On the Rorschach his instability is manifested in his sudden, sporadic breaks in control and judgment, as reflected in occasional poor form responses, and in unexpected reactions revealing emotional turmoil ("like bombs and they're exploding").

The unevenness in development and adjustment that are evident in this boy's drawings are a reflection of the severe conflict that he is experiencing in regard to himself and his relations with others. His problems, as portrayed in his figure drawings, can be subsumed under three headings: 1) his confusion about his own role and sexual identification, and along with this his general uncertainty about what is involved in being a man or being a woman, that is, which attributes and traits are male and which female; 2) his marked sexual preoccupation and the anxiety and guilt that this preoccupation evokes in him; 3) his desire to set up relationships with his environment while simultaneously fearing the establishment of such relationships.

The differences that exist between this child's drawings of the male and female figure bear witness to his marked role confusion. The strong neck that he has given the female figure along with the carefully encapsulated hair portrays the girl as markedly controlled. The male figure on the other hand is seen as highly variable in his capacity to control his impulses and feelings. While he too has encapsulated hair he is completely without a neck. It can be assumed therefore that for this boy the female is by far the more controlled and therefore probably also the more controlling figure. This concept of controlled and controlling also finds expression in his comments about the figures. The man is first described as a *robot*, in other words something that has no will of its own but simply acts under the direction of others. The female figure on the other hand is functioning independently, "standing up and talking to the teacher."

Apparently this boy was unable to tolerate the concept of an independently functioning, controlling female and a dependent, helpless male. He therefore felt compelled to go back to his drawing of the man and enhance his position, giving him symbols of achievement and authority, namely the mortar board and the pointer. By so doing he finally places the male figure in a far more important role than the one he has ascribed to the female. She is only a child talking to a teacher, while the man is an adult exercising wisdom and power.

Judging by the figures he drew and the way he went about this, it can be inferred that this boy is not at all sure of the position of the male and frequently perceives the male as helpless and dominated by the female. However, he certainly has not given up his masculine strivings (note the broad, square shoulders) and has a strong need to establish the importance and power of the male. However, his choice of the role of professor for his male figure suggests that his rebellion against female authority is likely to follow intellectual channels rather than more directly aggressive ones.

The subject's treatment of the lower half of both figures reveals his very marked sexual preoccupation. In drawing the girl, he first covered the genital area with faint, barely discernible, random lines, not unlike the lines used to indicate the presence of hair. It certainly seemed as though he were furtively attempting to give the figure pubic hair. He suddenly stopped drawing the faint, vague lines and covered the area which they occupied with strong, heavy lines that went in both the horizontal and vertical direction. The resulting crisscross gave the effect of prison bars. Apparently this boy has a strong need to picture for himself what the female body looks like, and is concerned with the appearance of female genitalia. However, these preoccupations, this interest and curiosity, also mobilize intense guilt and anxiety. In order to alleviate this anxiety he tries to keep his sexual curiosity and sexual impulses under strong control. His controlling efforts, as reflected in the heavy cross-barred effect that constitutes the girl's skirt, are of a compulsive order. The very way in which he drew these lines, the pressure that he exerted, and his need to reinforce the vertical lines with horizontal ones, all reveal his compulsive need to defend himself against these impulses.

The male figure also reveals this boy's sexual disturbances and preoccupation. Thus the legs of the man are also covered with hair-like lines, possibly in an effort to indicate masculinity. Certainly they reflect the patient's concern with the lower half of the body. However, the man's chest area is adorned with a yoke that has a v-shape, almost like a displaced vagina. Once again there is evidence of the subject's confusion about masculinity and femininity.

With so much concern about sexual impulses and sexual curiosity, the absence of the hands in both figures takes on special significance, pointing strongly to the possibility of masturbatory guilt. This impression gains some support from one of the stories that the subject tells on the Thematic Apperception Test, in response to the picture of the boy and the violin. Here he says, "Well, this boy looks like he has—well, it looks like a big canteen of some kind and it looks like the boy is mad at it. He's in a *dark room.*" Urged to make a story he finally says, "Once upon a time there was a boy with something that looked like a canteen and he was mad and he never combed his hair." Asked why the boy was mad the subject answers, "Because he did something wrong in the dark room and he's disgusted. That's what I see." Nothing more could be elicited even with considerable urging. Certainly the drawings suggest that this boy ascribes to his hands and arms the burden of the guilt he experiences in connection with his sexual activity and fantasies. Actually the arms of the male figure look like phalluses, while those of the female figure look like breasts.

Tied in with this boy's role confusion and his guilt because of sexual preoccupation and activity there is the whole question of his adequacy. Having cut off his hands in order to avoid the distress caused by his indulgence in masturbatory activity he is left without the means of manipulating his environment or coping with many of his needs and problems. Helpless, he can only see himself as a dependent figure (witness the buttons), yet he has not ceased to strive for power and importance. He gives himself a substitute hand, the pointer, which while not as effective as a real hand, enables him to carry out some functions, primarily intellectual and exhibitionistic ones.

The basic helplessness that characterizes this boy's feelings about himself is also reflected in the presence of the open, orally receptive mouth. This is in definite contrast to the firmly closed mouth that he has given the female figure. In general then, this boy's perception of himself is that of someone who has not received adequate oral satisfaction, who has therefore never felt fully loved and accepted and in consequence has questioned his adequacy. He frequently feels pushed about and overwhelmed by others, particularly the mother. His sense of inadequacy finds expression in his Rorschach interpretations as well as in his drawings. Thus, one of his human responses on the Rorschach is that of "A man with arms and everything, but no head." Once again, in this response, there is stress on arms, indicating how important this area of the body is for this boy. The presence or absence of arms and hand is given an importance afforded no other part of the body except perhaps the head. This emphasis finds graphic reflection in the heavily blacked-in nature of the man's arms. Compulsive control and depressive trends are suggested by these arms, and the arms are obviously associated with the specific activities that are responsible for this boy's deep sense of guilt, depression, and anxiety.

Finally, there is the subject's ambivalence about relating to the environment. The short, handless arms with which he endows both figures certainly argue against the existence of any impulse toward reaching out to the outside world. In the case of the girl, the arms are actually pressed close against the sides, suggesting that from the subject's point of view the female figure does not extend a hand to others, does not make contact with others, but rather is encased in herself. Along with the firmly closed mouth, the picture that emerges is that of a tight, withholding mother from whom this child has experienced little in the way of warmth and emotional support.

In the case of the male figure, it is significant that those parts of the body which come in contact with the environment, especially the arms and the feet, are emphasized. While the emphasis on the arms is certainly tied in with the child's feelings of depression and guilt, it also reflects his need to reinforce his own body limits, to assure himself of his own boundaries and correspondingly of his independence from the environment. In fact, all the lines that define the two figures are quite firm and strong. Such emphasis on body limits reflects this boy's anxiety about own "self" and his fears that that self might become absorbed by external forces. Thus, he hesitates to reach out and become involved with the environment, yet at the same time has a need for contact with others, wants to relate to them and find comfort in his association with them. Certainly the arms of the male figure are not as close to the body as are those of the female figure, and one arm is actually reaching out, although the reaching is associated with intellectual rather than with social or emotional activity.

Furthermore, the direction of the arm is away from the environment, away from the audience or class in front of him. Withdrawal tendencies are certainly suggested.

The retreat from the outer environment pointed up by a number of factors in this boy's drawings receives further support from his handling of the eye. His male figure actually cannot view the environment or absorb what it has to offer since the eye is without a pupil, an "unseeing" eye. In contrast to the man's inability to make contact with the enviornment by means of what he sees and absorbs, the female figure is given a "seeing," penetrating eye which appears to be taking in all that goes on around her, although other aspects of the drawing indicate that she gives nothing in return.

The emphasis on control, intellectualization, detachment and withdrawal which find expression in this boy's drawings are paralleled by the nature of his reactions to the Rorschach test. His efforts at control are reflected in his high F%, while his retreat into his fantasy life is indicated by the fact that his Experience Balance is weighted on the introversive side, an atypical finding in an eight-year-old. Similarly, his confusion about masculinity and femininity is expressed through such interpretations as "Two men shaking hands"; when questioned as to why he thought they were men rather than women, the subject said, "They don't have any long hair. But they have high heel shoes on. Maybe its just a masquerade." Again his disturbance in relation to dependence and independence, his need for response from the environment at the same time that he has a desire to break away from that enviornment and establish himself as an individual in his own right, are symbolized in the response, "The orange part is opening up and a giant egg is coming out. There's a giant egg inside and the orange is the skin that protects it." Not only does this interpretation express the child's need for "birth" and separation from the mother, as well as protection from her, but also points up once again his interest in and curiosity about female organs and female functions.

While the findings on all the tests, Rorschach, Thematic Apperception and figure drawings are in agreement in regard to the basic personality structure and the nature of the subject's specific problems, each test reflects these problems in a different way and in a different idiom, thus enriching the over-all picture. In this particular case, the drawings highlight this boy's compulsive need to see himself as powerful and achieving, thus compensating for his basic feelings of inadequacy, dependency and "badness." Also, the specific way in which the arms are portrayed express the child's feelings of separation from the environment and the lack of emotional security that is an inevitable part of that separation. Finally, the emphasis on the sexual areas of the body and on the truncated arms pinpoints one specific factor in this boy's disturbance and explains much of his guilt, anxiety and depression.

In summary, this child's figure drawings give the picture of a boy who is confused in regard to his identification, riddled with guilt and anxiety because of masturbatory activity and sexual preoccupation, and conflicted about his relationships with his environment. He apparently perceives the feminine figure, namely the mother or mother surrogate, as withholding and controlling. At the same time that he feels rejected by the mother figure he manifests great curiosity about her as a sexual object. This curiosity generates all kinds of sexual fantasies and also probably increases masturbatory activity. In contrast to his perception of women as strong and ungiving, masculine figures are seen as likely to be inadequate, less capable of control and more dependent than are feminine ones. Unable to tolerate such an unsatisfactory concept of himself, this boy seeks to build up his self-image and enhance his self-esteem by withdrawing from intense emotional involvement which will probably only result in frustration and increased feelings of weakness and rejection. Instead, he finds his compensations in his fantasy life where he identifies with figures that represent prestige and power. The nature of his conflicts, and the way he goes about dealing with them, point to the beginnings of an obsessive-compulsive character structure.

As far as his specific symptoms are concerned, the bedwetting would certainly seem to be tied in with his masturbatory activity and sexual fantasies. His stuttering most probably constitutes a defense against oral release of sexual impulses and aggressive power strivings. His relative indifference toward the establishment of peer relationships is in line with his tendency to withdraw into his inner life and find his satisfactions there rather than in his contacts with his environment. Yet he obviously needs an audience to appreciate what he is exhibiting and teaching. Without such an audience his achievements would afford him little satisfaction. Thus he does not cut himself off from others but rather lets them seek him out, in this way establishing for himself his own importance.

Finally there is his ambivalent attitude toward his sibling. Over and above the customary resentments found in any sibling relationship, this boy's variable behavior suggests that he displaces onto the sister his highly fluctuating attitudes and feelings toward the mother. This impression gains strength from the very nature of his female figure. Although he describes it as a girl of eight it actually looks like a much older woman.

From the prognostic point of view, the outlook for therapy seems to be a relatively good one. There is sufficient guilt and anxiety, sufficient discomfort and unhappiness, to provide motivation for the acceptance of therapy and participation in treatment. Moreover, despite the fact that the subject is somewhat fearful of interpersonal relationships, he actually has not shut himself off from his environment but rather indicates a need for that environment. It therefore seems likely that a constructive type of relationship can be developed in the therapeutic sessions without too much difficulty or delay.

## CHAPTER 6

# ADOLESCENT CASE STUDY:
# A DISTURBED ADOLESCENT GIRL[1]

KAREN MACHOVER, M.A.

GROWING FROM childhood to maturity involves a constant change of the structure and function of the body of the young girl, which bears heavily upon her consciousness. New roles are borrowed from those about her and others are woven by a fantasy excited by the compelling urgency and stress created by her changing body world. In its wake have come the extremes of restlessness, indecision, sudden enthusiasms, and just as sudden discouragements, that have earned for adolescents the label of "normal psychosis."

In drawings of adolescent girls, we find attitudes toward sexual maturation reflected in the treatment of the breast area, the pelvis, conflict beneath the waistline, at the crotch of the male figure, and subtle disturbance about the hemline of the skirt due to uncertainty about how long to make it or how much to grow. Diffidence toward maturation may be projected by an underestimation of the sexual characteristics. The young pre-puberal, rather than indicate breasts, will not infrequently reinforce the outer contours of that area to indicate conflict.

Efforts at control and integration of body impulses with rational considerations may be recorded by conflict in the neck area, since the neck connects the head with the body. Forced restraint of body impulses may be indicated by a tight waistline, a common feature in drawings of adolescents. Other graphic devices of control may be seen in the tight stance, the encased or "mittened" fingers, or in the tidy restraint of a bow, barrette,

[1] Part of a study of *Personality Development in Adolescent Girls.* Yellow Springs, Antioch Press, 1953.

or just a line to encase active hair excitement. The stance of the figure, the treatment of the legs and feet may reveal the subject's attitude toward movement and activity, toward security of his footing, or toward sexual matters. Hands and fingers, organs basically involved in grasp, manipulation, and contact with objects, other people, and one's self, reveal the level of the subject's aspiration, his confidence, his aggressiveness, his efficiency, and often his guilt or conflict concerning interpersonal relationships. The length of arms, their robustness, the direction and vigor with which they extend from the body out toward the "environment" give additional evidence of the nature of the subject's contact.

Most of the adolescents assign an age to the depicted character older than themselves, which is testimony to their forward growth interests.

### RUTH

The subject is a Negro, adolescent female whose parents were born in South Carolina. For this family, the transition from the South to New York resulted in great confusion with regard to understanding the world around them.

Ruth is presented as an example of a maladjusted adolescent, but in considering her as such we must bear in mind that she is Negro and that some of the individual traits projected in the draw-

ings refer to general cultural characteristics of a minority and essentially discriminated group. Such features, that will later be brought out, as identification with the stronger masculine role assigned to a forceful and matriarchal mother, the sense of traumatization and feelings of rejection by the environment, the reaction of retreat into fantasy, drive, ambitions, and self-inflation, and the not unlikely paranoid tinge to Ruth's social reactions, are all to be viewed in the light of the realistic disadvantages that beset her racial group.

Ruth does not embrace the traditional female role with any warmth. She draws the male first, which is an expression of some sexual protest. She openly acknowledges that she would like to be like him, while in regard to the female, she limply answers the question if she would like to be like her, "I am." Both characters, male and female, are described as determined to acquire a professional education. Intelligence is highly rated and precisely estimated in terms of achievement for both characters. The male will become an engineer, and the female will become a doctor. They will both marry mates on their educational level. The male is permitted to marry at 28, while marriage of the female is postponed to from 30 to 33 years of age, and then only "maybe." This is indicative of personal discouragement in regard to her future as a desirable female and also of a compulsive drive for career achievement and distinction. It is not clear which is primary, and in what dynamic way the two factors are related. Dissatisfaction with her body and her personal charms is apparent in the drawings. Also, an enormous drive for self-expression on a large social canvas, as retaliation for the social rejection that she has suffered, is projected (in the large size) independently of her sense of body inferiority.

The drawings are especially outstanding for their force of ego expansion locked in fantasy chambers. The figures are space-filling in all dimensions, and the female does not even have enough room on the page. The environment given to her is not copious enough for her expansive and expressive needs. The initial line she at first employed is timorous and uncertain, but Ruth later encloses the figures and all details with a decisive and protective heavy line. She is very defensive and reactive to her feelings of weakness and inferiority. The abundant and rather precise detailing points to obsessive-compulsive characteristics.

Ruth gives considerable emphasis to the hips, breasts, and

midline of the skirt, which, in combination with the coquettish facial expression, suggests that she is inclined to use her sexual characteristics aggressively. The disturbed treatment of the breasts and the greater virility and robustness of the female figure convey the impression of intense mother attachment and identification. The male is a weak reflection of the female figure. Shoulders are narrower; the face, grooming, and clothing detail are more effete and dandyish in the male than in the female. Insecurity, in terms of a placating facial expression, the use of a ground line, and shaded shoes, is projected upon the male figure, as are graphic indications of dependency (buttons, buckle), affectional deprivation (pocket), and body preoccupation (midline).

Shading, which is indicative of anxiety, is largely concentrated on the trousers of the male, an area of sexual connotations, and hair of both figures, which has sensual implications. Thus, considerable anxiety is expressed in regard to sexual impulses and sensual needs. The female figure is given an especially short and revealing skirt, while the neckline is brought tightly up to the neck in excessive restraint. Ruth has a tendency to impulsive self-indulgence, and then sudden and severe restraints. Exhibitionistic needs are strong. Clothes elaboration and general interest in grooming indicate the importance of social prestige and possessions in Ruth's system of values.

Arms of both figures are long and powerful. This accords with the repeated expression of ambition noted in her associations. Fingers are aggressively speared and well articulated, but compressed in tension. Achievement and mastery of the physical world is very important to Ruth but she is anxious, oversensitive to social opinion to the point of mild paranoid colorings (the eyes of the female are large, over-alert, and somewhat frightened), and is vigorously compensating for a traumatized and deprived childhood. The somewhat weaker male who is given more display value is not uncommon in the tradition of a race whose men have been socially discouraged from achievement. The impulses toward movement, which are so marked in the posture of the two figures, suffer from inhibition and doubt, resulting in static and blocked movement effects.

In summary, we see in Ruth a very intensive drive for self-expression, sensual satisfaction, and achievement, which have for cultural reasons and reasons of specific environmental background been continuously frustrated. This has served to intensify the self-protectiveness, the tight defenses, the suspicion, and the drive to master the environment with whatever means that prove to be effective. A certain ruthlessness has risen out of her deprivations and fear, with aggressive impulses that are only weakly contained. The anxiety, aggression, turmoil, and tense conflict between self-expression and restraint that we see in Ruth's drawings are so great as to raise the question of the advisability of psychotherapeutic help in weathering the storm of adolescence. The impulse drives are as forceful as the restraints, resulting in emotional wear and tear that are leading to considerable frustration and depression. For Ruth, adolescence has come upon more hardened realism and frustration than occurs for better adjusted, sentimental girls of the higher socio-economic brackets.

## CHAPTER 7

## CASE STUDY OF AN ADULT: THE CASE OF MR. P.

SIDNEY LEVY, PH.D.

THE FOLLOWING case study is one of the most fascinating and instructive experiences since I first began to experiment with figure drawings in January, 1945. The nine drawings reproduced were collected from Mr. P. during the course of five years of psychoanalytic therapy administered by the present writer beginning in December, 1951. The drawings are *individually* instructive since each reveals in a clear and dramatic way how internal conflicts, symptoms, fantasies and character structures reveal themselves in a figure drawing; the *sequence* of drawings reveals how *changes* in personality and integration are reflected in figure drawings; finally, the *sequence* of drawings tends to support theoretical postulates about personality development involving aspects of the primary process and the channeling of this process into so-called ego-structures.

The patient was a most interesting and complicated person who had received a Phi Beta Kappa at college, majoring in English Literature as an undergraduate and changing to Accountancy as a graduate student. As a hobby he had pursued, independently, a study of Eugene O'Neil and H. L. Mencken with both of whom he had considerable empathy. His exegesis of *The Iceman Cometh* which he presented in dreams and in conscious thoughts was astonishing for his deep insights of an analytic character before he had any experience with or knowledge of depth psychology. Some of the complications of his character are further suggested by the following facts: he was a post office employee doing very unskilled and undemanding work in spite of his Phi Beta Kappa key, accounting degree, and I.Q. of

165. He was married to a girl of impoverished intellectual background and with no interest in anything except the most commonplace and trivial, and with no understanding or sympathy for the patient. Her family with whom he spent much time was of laboring, peasant background. His wife thought his interest in books to be a sign of queerness. But let's begin at the beginning:

In December, 1950 the receptionist of Dr. H., a physician specializing in disorders of the ear and hearing, whose office adjoined my own, placed a "case file" on my desk and asked if I could see the patient who was at that moment in his waiting room. The history note indicated that the patient had come to Dr. H. that same morning with the complaint that he had "pains in his ears" and that he "could not hear very well." The patient stated that this all began some years previously while he was under anti-aircraft attack from enemy ground-fire during an Air Force combat mission. He returned to his base safely except for minor abrasions and contusions suffered during the rough and bumpy flight. Dr. H.'s thorough otoscopic examination revealed no organic pathology. Complete and detailed audiometric examination including Psychogalvanic Skin Reflex techniques revealed normal hearing but "peculiar behavioral reactions." At the conclusion of the examination Dr. H. informed the patient that as far as he could determine, there was nothing wrong with the patient's ear. (When so informed patient became "angry and shouted about the pain in his ear" in response to which Dr. H. said "I can't *see* your *pain.*" The patient's response to this was "so peculiar" that Dr. H. at once sent his receptionist off to my office and told patient he was arranging for further examination. Dr. H. could not specify details about the patient's "peculiar behavior" except to say "he looked at me in such a strange way that I felt the hair rise along my backbone." [1]) The physician's "backbone" showed excellent clinical judgment because the patient was suffering from a paranoid schizophrenic condition and later exploration revealed that the physician was rather close to a personal exploration of questions of immortality and the like when he said "I can't see your pain."

According to the case history, patient was thirty-six years old, married for twelve years, had two female children aged three and six, had served for four years in an Air Force combat crew

---

[1] The information in parentheses was given to this writer in personal conversation immediately after first session with patient.

in European Theatre of Operations. There were no other note-worthy findings.

When I first saw him he remained just inside the office and at once communicated that feeling of "uncanniness" which E. Jones and H. S. Sullivan have both described at various times. He was like a coiled spring, full of controlled tension. His eyes darted all over the room and it appeared that thoughts and conversations were going on between the patient and his private world of objects. He was about 5'8" tall, very stocky, and very motionless except for his eyes, but the lack of motion was a kind of paradox because the most prominent thing about Mr. P. was the sense of highly charged energy about to explode. The next two hours, largely devoted to reducing some of this tension, were the beginning of five years of analytic therapy with a most interesting person.

During this session, the patient had remained standing and only gradually had the feeling of tension dissipated itself. When I felt it to be safe and useful I made the gesture to the desk and then to the pencils while inviting him to draw. On my desk were several piles of paper, pencils, a box of crayons and various other stationery supplies. A chair was placed at one end of the desk for the patient. After a moment's hesitation he sat down, shot a glance at the desk and another at me and then reached past the pencils over to the box of crayons and with a slight mirthless smile, took out a red crayon and a yellow crayon and then closed the box and put it back exactly where it had been. He then began to draw, in red crayon first, and in yellow crayon after, the figure represented in Figure 1.

How does the drawing analyst think about this? First of all we recall that Figure-Drawing is an experiment in which all aspects of the subject's behavior *as well* as the drawing itself are observed, described and interpreted. When the patient reached past the pencils toward which I gestured and instead took the crayons, we have an increment of behavior which needs, first to be observed and then to be explained. He was complying with my request to draw a person but in doing so he *changed* the situation somewhat. He resisted my gesture to the pencils and selected the crayons. Every instant of behavior is meaningful [2] and has *more than* one determinant, all participating in the outcome,

---

[2] Reference 1, page 91: ". . . to him (the psychoanalyst) nothing is too trifling as a manifestation of hidden psychic processes."

Figure 1

just as, in physics, vectors of force all participate as components in determining the direction and intensity of the resultant force. What then are the determinants here? Before answering this, it is well to interpose a prior question, i.e., What are *all* the alternative explanations one can think of?

1) He thought I gestured to the crayons.
2) He thought the figure-drawing was what I wanted and it didn't matter whether he used the pencil or crayons.
3) It was just "chance" that he selected crayons.
4) He *likes* to draw with crayons.
5) He thought he could do a better drawing with crayons.
6) He was being negativistic, i.e., disobedient.
7) Some combination of these, as for example 4 and 6.

After evaluating all of these alternatives it was decided tentatively that this last explanation was most credible. This lowered the threshold of perception for me with respect to similar aspects of behavior. Item 4 states "he likes to draw with crayons." My basic assumption in this field is that all things are determined, therefore "liking it" must be determined by a more basic level of need. From previous experience and other investigation, it is known that the color red is related to strong, primitive, relatively unmodified emotionality which has closer kinship to id than to superego (I use these shorthand symbols with considerable diffidence). We also know that yellow is often preferred by young children, by very immature young adults and by regressed older adults. An additional determinant appears to be negativism, i.e., in the very act of complying he resists and modifies the request.

One other "evidential fact" before we launch into further interpretation. He replaced the crayon box *exactly* in its original position. What alternatives may we postulate to explain this? Repudiating the explanation that it was just "chance" so often offered by students, I came to the conclusion that this was determined by a *compulsive* need for order, conformity and to "undo," i.e., to restore the situation which existed prior to his thought or act. At this point, the less experienced student or psychologist may be tempted to close his mind and reject this explanation. But life is not simple and neither are people, and Mr. P. like most of us, is very complicated, full of seeming contradiction and conflict. To weave what we have thus far into a tentative pattern: Mr. P. is rebellious but unable to express it directly and completely, but instead projects his rebelliousness into the minor details of his life situations, a sort of glancing blow, or resistance by indirection. In addition, he has so much primitive feeling (red) which has no satisfactory or adequate way of expressing itself (ego defenses) that it has broken through the repressions and is causing disintegration (the figure itself) and regression (yellow). The regression is not complete and a remnant of the former compulsive defenses remains (placing the crayon box back in its pile). To put it into shorthand technical jargon, the id is pushing hard, the superego has almost surrendered and a vestige of the ego (compulsion) remains to try to contain the forces of the id.

Thus far, these are somewhat vague generalizations of an abstract nature and can be applied to many people. We want to know more about Mr. P. himself. Let us look at drawing No. 1.

As so often happens, what Comenious used to call "apperceptive mass," will determine your response to drawing No. 1. Naïve students have often said "He must have been kidding." Experienced psychologists who have worked in State Hospitals for a long time immediately say "This man is psychotic." It is, on occasion, wise to heed the innocent. Although the experienced psychologist may be right ninety times out of a hundred in designating a drawing which has this degree and quality of distortion as being the production of a psychotic person, he may be wrong several times in a hundred. I have received this amount of distortion from:

1) People who were "kidding," i.e., expressing hostility.

2) People who had excellent ego contact but were skilled in abstract or symbolic communciation under conscious control.

3) People who were extremely impulsive, psychopathic, or psychotic and who tended to seriously misinterpret their world but who still retained the ability to "second guess" themselves, that is, who were aware at some level, of the inconsistency between their perception of the world and the nature of the world itself.

4) People who were so troubled and disorganized that this kind of drawing represented their best perception of self and of reality with no specific awareness of its inadequacy.

When I get this kind of drawing I always ask the subject to "criticize the drawing; if you were an artist and this were somebody else's drawing, how would you change it; what fault would you find with it?" Since I started using this question I have occasionally been surprised to observe the subject criticizing the distortions very accurately, indicating an unexpected level of reality-testing. When this has happened the subject has fallen into categories 1, 2 or 3 above. (For each of these subjects, for example the case of the person expressing hostility, exegesis along specific lines to differentiate him from others in his class is still required.)

Mr. P. was completely unable to criticize his drawing in any meaningful way and when he was asked to draw a woman he drew Figure 2. We therefore conclude that this drawing represents Mr. P.'s genuine though subjective perception of himself and that, akin to psychotic language, there is a code which will explain the features of his drawings.

Remembering the rule that requires identification of fact and evidence before supplying meaning, let us look at Figure 1 and Figure 2 and describe them as accurately and perceptively as possible. (If you have cheated a little and looked at Figure 3, your task will have been made easier.) The red outline of Figure 1 is a somewhat continuous outline and is essentially independent, that is, separate from the yellow outline. The red outline was drawn first, the yellow second. The outline may roughly be subdivided into areas that resemble arms, legs and a head region. The head region has a cleft in the center. In the first drawing, which is that of a female, the red outline not only was drawn on the outside (defining the external limits), but was drawn first and is more prominent than the red used in Figure 2 which he identified as the male. We assume that to the subject, red is associated with the female and yellow with the male. I will now add together the facts that:

1) The female is drawn first.
2) Red is associated with female and yellow with male.
3) Red outline surrounds yellow in Figure 1.
4) Shape of red outline has a cleft which in a symbolic way suggests femaleness.
5) Yellow outline has an arrow or bullet shaped anterior end, which is a symbolic way of representing maleness.

Thus, we arrive at the following statement:

The patient is sexually confused. He feels himself to be essentially a female within which there is imprisoned a regressed (helpless, infantile) male.

Subsequent psychoanalytic sessions involving free association and dreams revealed very clearly that the drawing interpretation of Figures 1 and 2 were correct. The qualities, characteristics and dynamics of the "primary process" had overwhelmed his ego. He actually felt himself to be in his own words "a large penis,

Figure 2

helpless and imprisoned inside of my mother, she's all around me
—I *am* my mother . . ." etc.

The psychodynamic laws of symbol formation dictated the
specific features of the drawing. The patient first somatized his

feelings of maleness and femaleness (translated the *ideas* into body feelings), then by the primitive process of misplaced concreteness where a part of an idea or experience becomes the whole, maleness became somatically *identical* with a phallic outline and femaleness with the cleft outline. The feelings of being imprisoned and overwhelmed by mother are clearly portrayed as is the relative strength of the female feelings as compared with the male feelings. In clinical practice one often comes across this process whereby the whole body becomes a part of the body or represents a single function. This happens not only in psychosis but in neurosis and in normal sublimations. For example, an integrated person with some of the same problems as Mr. P. may become a ballet dancer in which case he may display his whole body which primitively represents a phallus (see Fenichel on the "castration complex").

At this point one may, justifiably, be tempted to take a flyer into the dynamics of the "chief complaint" of the patient, i.e., his "ear pains" and his "difficulty in hearing." We know from Freud's work that one "receiving" organ is often substituted for another (and that receptacles of all kinds and shapes may be substituted for a receiving organ). Freud, Jung and Stekel have also demonstrated very clearly that penetration of any kind often symbolizes the basic penetrating organ. Thus a voice often symbolizes a phallus (at least at the primitive level, or in neurotic symptomology, and in artistic creation). Thus it was possible to speculate rather early in the analysis that the ear pains and the difficulty in hearing were symptom formations resulting from conflict between masculinity and femininity, between wish and fear associated with a passive homosexual conflict.

At this point we know from the first two figure drawings that the patient is psychotic, that his reality testing is extremely disturbed, that the primitive process has largely displaced his ego, that he has very bizarre body sensations, that he feels like both male and female, phallus and vagina, that his masculinity is subordinated, that aggressive actions or symbols of any kind stimulate the already intolerable conflict between passive homosexual wishes and the fears opposing these wishes, that a vestige of compulsive defense remains, that there is extreme regression, that emotionality is largely uncontrolled. In spite of this, the writer decided not to recommend hospitalization but to recommend

Figure 3

continued functioning on the job, in his home and in the community.[3]

---

[3] In many discussions of the ethics and wisdom involved in treating very ill people extramurally, it has become clear to the author that if the focus remains "what is good for the patient" rather than "what is comfortable or safe" for the therapist, considerably less hospitalization and better therapeutic results obtain.

The early months of psychoanalytic therapy were devoted to:
1) restoring ego; 2) permitting opportunities for expressing disturbing feelings and conflicts in peripheral areas (so that accompanying guilt would not be released before patient could handle
it); 3) reducing anxiety, the latter largely by the fact that his
inadequate ego was now reinforced and aided by the ego of the

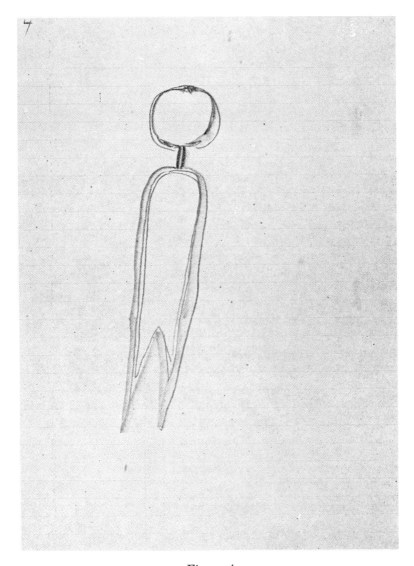

Figure 4

therapist. Figure 3, drawn after one month of therapy, indicates a sharpening of the basic conflict, less confusion about the conflicting impulses, more anxiety and less regression, and the *beginning of a third outline!* Let us look at this third outline which was lightly sketched in after the basic two outlines were completed. Notice the head and the ear on the outside of the two previous outlines; also the arms and legs outside the two previous outlines. These are sketched in lightly, uncertainly, incompletely. The feeling is that this third outline is less integrated, less a central part of the person, is more recent and more like a garment than a part of the central core of the person. But it represents the beginnings of integration. Patient is beginning to take a chance on hearing, rather tentatively at this point.

Figure 4 is interesting in many ways. First, notice how entirely different the whole gestalt is. The neck is long and thin and like the rest of body, heavily reinforced with thick black lines. This represents the growth of ego control. The neck is the connecting channel between the body and the head. In language akin to that of the primary process, the neck mediates between the body (impulse and feeling) and the head (thought and control). In the attempt to repress the feelings which heretofore have overwhelmed the patient, he has instituted very forcibly, repressive measures. In somatic symbols (thin, narrow neck), he has expressed the psychic process of allowing a small part of his feeling life to find expression, but only as much as he can control. He has indicated how he has reinforced this channel of communication (heavy lines of neck) lest it be destroyed (as it was in Figures 1 and 2) by too wide a torrent of feeling. This drawing further indicates that almost all other activities have been sacrificed to this basic protective maneuver, a sort of Maginot Line. There are no arms, indicating that whatever control has been achieved has been purchased in part, as least, by withdrawal from the world of objects. The arms and hands are organs for establishing contact with people and things, but they have stimulated so much conflict in the past that the floodgates were opened. Now he is blocking these out until he can build up his controls. Note that the experiment suggested by Figure 3 has been abandoned as too dangerous. The ear and arms are now completely eliminated. The patient has tried another approach. Instead of reaching out to the world, he has excluded it and concentrated entirely on forces of repression and control of internal drives. External stimuli were found to stir up more affect than could be handled so energy is now concentrated on building up defense.

Mr. P.'s external life reflected the changes mirrored by his drawing. He stopped seeing people; on the job instead of having furious quarrels with everybody, he kept to himself, not noticing or reacting to others. Instead of the overt aggression he had expressed against so many people before, he was now depressed. Also more pronounced anxiety and more obsessive-compulsive behavior began to be apparent.

In this drawing, we notice the shading between the heavier outlines. This represents the anxiety he is experiencing and points the way to one of the major defenses he may be expected (and encouraged) to develop, i.e., rationalization. The basic two outlines are still clear and separated but the distance between them is being obliterated by "shading," in other words, he is rationalizing, explaining away the separation. The way in which this defense of rationalization is reflected in succeeding drawings is most fascinating and instructive (see the treatment of the cleft which becomes a part in his hair).

The several layers of heavy black lines, not *one* line but *two* heavy lines and in some places three lines; the way in which he reinforced the neck outline over and over again, indicate another line of ego building, i.e., of defensive formation—the obsessive-compulsive mechanism.

Remember in the original interview, the way in which he placed the crayon box back in place suggested that a tatter of the obsessive-compulsive defensive structure was left at the end of a long and serious regression. Now we seem to be moving in the opposite direction with repression, obsessive-compulsive behavior and rationalization building up in the drawing. This drawing not only mirrored very accurately what was happening to the patient *at that moment* in his intra-psychic life and in his relationship to the world, but when viewed in the perspective provided by the prior three drawings, charted the path along which future progress was to be expected.

Figure 5 was completed one year later at the same time that he reported a dream in which there was a man known as Mr. P. who lived in Granite City. The gist of the dream involved repeated attempts on the part of Mr. P. to escape from buildings, from law enforcement authorities, from criminals, from dangers of all kinds and how in each attempt he was forced to return for

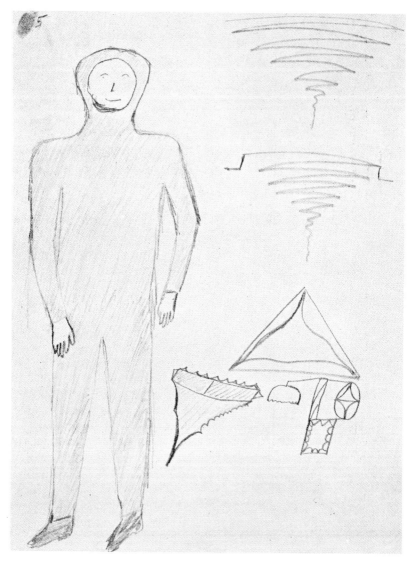

Figure 5

shelter to a stone building on the outskirts of the city in which there were a number of strange objects. In his associations the strange objects became the couch, drapes, etc., of the therapist's office and Mr. P. became Mr. Prisoner. At the same time he developed a series of somatic symptoms including a stiff neck, "arthritis" of the left side, a feeling of carrying a great weight and of being encased in cement. The ways in which the dream and the drawing reflect his feelings and thoughts are worth study. The drawing reflects the "Mr. P. in Granite City" symbol. Granite City in the dream is a symbolic externalization of his intrapsychic life, i.e., being encased in granite of his own making (repression). The "criminals" are his destructive feelings and impulses; the law enforcement officers are symbols for superego, the cement room is the safe room to which he can escape. His feelings are thoroughly repressed, even his body participates in the repression (stiff neck and arthritis). There is a little less fear of the aggressive primitive forces getting out of control and a greater desire to deal with his feelings (the criminals) and the outside world of objects and superego representation, so that Mr. P. may now draw hands. Shortly after this drawing he began to make attempts to get a new job. There is still repression, anxiety, and depression but the obsessive-compulsive defense is becoming more noticeable and better rationalized. The shading is obsessive in character; the patient's pencil went over and over the body.

There is obviously some pathology being expressed in terms of the left side—note the left foot— the extra stroking on the left upper arm. The left side (distaff side) often symbolizes the feminine part of our identification with parents. Perhaps the all-encompassing mother figure has now been sufficiently integrated so that she can be limited to the left side, but is still giving trouble there. Remember the rule that the strength of a drive can be estimated by the intensity of the repression necessary to contain it. Mr. P.'s left side has "arthritis," i.e., it is disabled. (How often in clinical practice, a symptom such as "arthritis" has been taken away medically or psychotherapeutically only to leave instead a psychosis! From this drawing some light is shed on this reversible reaction.)

The doodles adjoining the figure are worthy of note. Those in the upper right hand corner are in the nature of obsessive-compulsive rituals. The triangle underneath these designs stimulated associations about the "trinity" at first related to religious symbols and eventually to the mother, father and son. The saw-like triangle, to the side, is a symbol suggesting first, compulsiveness and secondly, aggression. His associations to it were "like a buzz-saw," "like teeth," "the lower jaw and sharp teeth." The object next to it stimulated the following associations: "intricate design," "balanced," "scales." We interpreted this, on the struc-

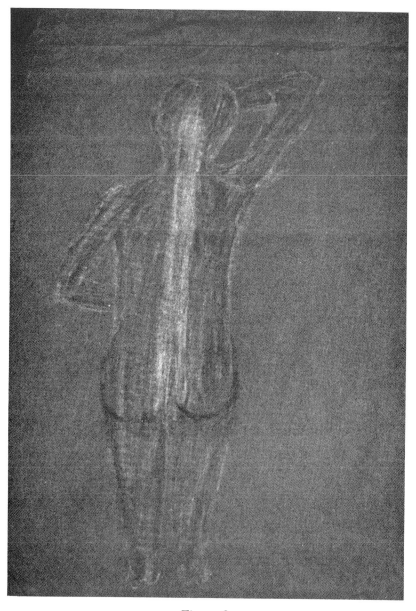

Figure 6

tural level, to represent an obsessive-compulsive binding up of anxiety and on the symbolic level to represent the "scales of justice," i.e., the superego in juxtaposition to the destructive impulses represented by the "oral-sadistic" drives in the ajoining triangle.

The period following drawing No. 5 was characterized by increased release of affect, replacement of repression by expression of feelings in the form of fantasy and dreams, depression, in obsessive-compulsive behavior and in occasional direct insight. Things were under sufficient control to begin to allow a little tentative freedom. The prisoner will soon attempt to escape from his Granite City.

Drawings 6, 7, 8 and 9 reflect a very marked change in Mr. P.'s level of integration. To help us understand the process that is developing it may be useful to consider a crude analogy for a moment. Let us think of the Spring season when the snow begins to melt in the mountains, and the heavy Spring rains begin to fall, all contributing to a flood tide which causes rivers to burst out of their accustomed channels, destroying nearby structures, roads and normal operations. Now let us impose a TVA system of floodgates, turbines and sluice-ways which cooperate to direct the floodwaters in ways which provide for a fairly regular flow of the water and to use up the energy contained in the rushing waters not to destroy but to turn turbines, etc.

The Spring flow of water may be likened to the basic, primitive affects in man. These affects can be stimulated or intensified in a number of ways, internally and externally. Excessive internal repression or excessive external deprivation or exacerbation may both contribute to the building up of the "flood-waters" of feeling. If there are inadequate "sluice gates," i.e., channels through which to discharge the affective energy, there will be a flooding over of uncontrolled feeling. Beginning with drawing No. 6 the primitive affects are substantially directed through the "turbines" of the ego. The energy is "used up" in socially acceptable, i.e., controlled ways. Now, let us become more specific and less fanciful.

In drawing No. 6 the same basic conflict between being male and female exists, but it is now expressed through an integrated and rationalized form. There is only one clear outline of a person, and the other outline is now a "stiff backbone like an iron bar going through my back; stiff as a ramrod!" Consider how artistically the psyche works. The internal figure has always been the "male" outline. Now this outline is a phallic-like object which is "stiff as a ramrod!" Compare this with idiomatic expressions such as "Don't you have a backbone?" meaning, "Are you weak?" i.e., feminine. How can the psyche rationalize the external (feminine) outline? The drawing under consideration supplies an answer to this question. The figure has "his" back to the observer. Clinical experience has corroborated the interpretation suggested in this sequence, that is to say, a male figure with his back to the observer has been found by this writer to mean, without exception up to the present moment, that the subject suffers from a problem in the area of psychosexual identification in the form of a conflicted wish to be a woman. Underlying this wish is often found a more basic impulse. For opposing explanations of this basic impulse see Bettelheim (2) and Nunberg (3). The dynamics of symbol formation in this instance follows the rule that two objects which share some essential form quality may be interchanged one for the other. Thus, a man's unclothed back clearly bears a "form" similarity to a woman.

Note the flaring hips. When a subject has more effective control over the psychosexual conflict now being discussed, he is able to rationalize it and disguise it even more skillfully in which case the male figure may be presented in a ventral view but the *hips may flare*, or if the problem is very thoroughly and effectively rationalized, there may simply be some disproportionate anxiety expressed by the stroking in this area (see Figure 9).

Let us spend a few more moments on Figure 6. Note the position of the left hand on the hip and the right hand on the head. This communicates a strong sense of empathy with a posture that is essentially feminine. If you visualize a continuum of postures ranging from, at one end, the posture presented in Figure 6, and, at the other end, the most minimal kinesthesia in *either* arm, you will make available to yourself a key to Figure-Drawing Analysis which ordinarily accrues only after extensive study and experience.

To put this figure on black paper, the patient had to ignore a convenient pile of white paper. Whenever in any projective situation, a subject "changes" the structure in form or substance, in major part or minor detail, it suggests a tendency toward negativism. Negativism ranges the "value continuum" all the way from independent, critical skepticism through stubbornness, to a self-destructive, world-destructive, catatonia.

In addition, negativism is a descriptive term and is itself multiple-determined. Therefore, the use of the term is not satisfactory unless it is filled-in with a matrix of determinants and needs. In the present case, the patient had been so controlled and dominated by his mother (and later his wife and her family; the post office and the Military Service) that it became necessary for his own sense of identity, his salvation as a person, to begin to "feel his own feelings" and seek his own satisfactions. At this moment he is not able to do this in any substantive way so he displaces this need to a minor aspect of his world. Even toward this minor detail his drive toward self-assertion is so dominated by superego (fear, guilt, mother's strength, and habit) that it requires reinforcement from other needs. In this case his feelings of guilt sought external representation in the sheet of black paper. Another reinforcing determinant is the shame (guilt) associated with the problems reflected in the drawing under consideration. It is too early, and the defenses described above not sufficiently integrated to display themselves in the "full light of day."

The psychic organization revealed in the drawing was also revealed in his dreams and in his life. The consciously perceived and everpresent feeling of being a weak little man inside of a woman, both somatically and psychologically, began to yield to the feeling of being *one* person with a "stiff ramrod of a backbone like an iron bar." His posture became stiff (he constantly rubbed and stretched his back). He became more and more assertive in minor situations. For example, his wife wished to visit her married sister on a Friday night when patient had begun to go to a "Great Books" reading group on Friday nights. He suggested she go without him. A power struggle ensued in which patient was quickly vanquished. But he insisted that he first had to return a book to the library, delaying their leaving for 30 minutes (assertion in minor details). At the post office he began to change from a confused, docile person to one who rebelled in little situations. For example, the employee was required to get permission from his supervisor to go to the men's room. He formed the habit of asking one of the *other* supervisors. In many ways he tried to "lose himself in the shadows" and had a number of paranoid ideas of being "found out in broad daylight."

In executing the present drawing, the patient stroked the body over and over again, holding the pencil in such a way that not the tip but the side of the exposed lead left a broad stroke and the tip of his finger as well as the edge of the lead caressed the body.

This is an excellent illustration of the aphorism, "the return of the repressed through the repressed." The repetitious stroking is, descriptively, an obsessive-compulsive defense. It serves to bind up, or channel, the anxiety associated with a tabooed impulse, in this case a libidinal drive toward the "body" of the drawing. Note how the repressed drive is dynamically expressed in the stroking. The body represents "the female as part of himself." At this stage of treatment the hearing symptoms subsided and compulsive masturbation replaced them. The drive toward his own body (narcissism) in this instance is a drive toward the "female part of himself."

As treatment continued, the patient gradually became more and more interested in a woman who was a neighbor. She was a "big, buxom woman who has a big behind." This woman began to occupy his night dreams and his fantasies. At the same time his voice became more and more strident and louder and louder until he was shouting most of the time, not letting anybody else speak. He described his feelings as follows: When I speak in a loud and resonant voice it gives me a very exciting sensation in my ears. I like to experience it. I don't like to hear other people. I drown them out. Certain voices like my mother's and my sister's-in-law used to "go through my ears and transfix me to the spot."

Earlier in this discussion mention was made of the phallic significance of the voice, phallic woman, etc. The patient was now becoming more and more aggressive in more and more areas. The conflict between passivity and aggressivity is now beginning to be resolved in favor of the latter; not only in voice and behavior, but in figure drawing as well. In Figure 7 there is an assertion of self as an "undivided" and more phallic person. This is the first one in the series which *looks* like a person, face view. Let us examine this minutely. First look at the neck. For the first time, the neck is neither "wide open" nor "narrowly constricted," nor "strongly reinforced" as in Figure 4. This indicates a feeling of increasing comfort and confidence in the relationship between his emotions and his control of them.[4]

---

[4] Everything is overdetermined, and there are other layers of meaning associated with the neck which for the moment are set aside. See my previous chapter for discussion of "neck."

If attention is turned to the limbs it is noted that there are legs, shoes, arms but no hands. Why should there be no hands? In evaluating a part which is omitted, distorted or displaced, it is advisable to consider the function, the structure, symbols and idioms associated with the part; and, by derivation through the law of misplaced concreteness or Von Domarus' principle (4),

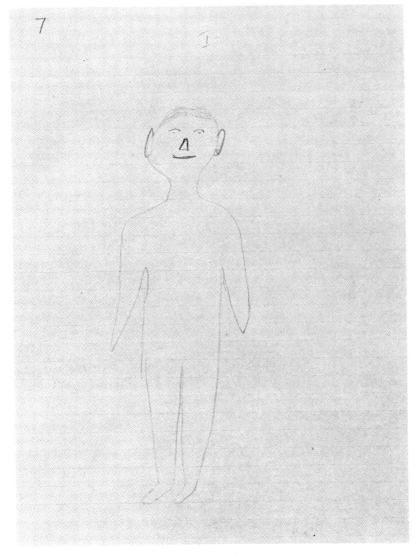

Figure 7

other meanings. (This opens wide the sluice gates!) Functionally, hands are used for hand shaking (establishing contact with others), hitting (expressing aggression), love making (stroking, masturbating, etc.), and *personal associations*, such as painting, farming, etc. Since the patient is still experiencing difficulty in direct aggression, direct social relationship and sexual aggression, he expresses the attempt to repress these drives by cutting off the hands. But the repressed affects are expressed in the form of the arm. The arm looks even more an aggressive phallus than do fingers.[5]

If we examine closely the hip region we note there is a slight break on one side. It is a truism that to understand anything, one must understand its history. This break in the hip line is the present indicative of the flaring hip in Figure 6, the two blended outlines in Figure 4, and the two separate outlines in Figure 2. Thus the sexual conflict is now expressed in the slight break in the line in this area.

Now let us examine the head itself. The hair is parted in the middle. This is a socially acceptable and rational way of reflecting the same dynamic in the primary process which is expressed in an undisguised, uncontrolled way in the split-head of the earlier drawings. How would the reader feel if, without the benefit of this clear sequence, he were presented with the statement that "a hair combed with a part in the middle indicates a strong feminine identification and a partial resolution of such a conflict through obsessive-compulsive mechanisms and narcissism"!

Full, front face is now portrayed for the first time. This means that he is ready to face up to the world. The "sense of self" is often focused in the face. A little reflection will indicate how that develops. Compare this face with the faceless previous drawings. One side of the face (which matches the broken hip-line) is fuller (fatter) than the other side.

The nose, mouth and ears are emphasized by size or pencil pressure or both. This indicates that the patient's orientation to the world is largely through these three organs, and not through the hands or eyes. Hands and eyes are *primarily* externally directed (i.e., aggression) in their orientation. Ears and mouth

---

[5] The return of the repressed through the repressed.

are usually receivers. But a word of caution here. Ears are *usually* receivers (passive). The voice enters the ear, there is an *opening* in the ear. But if *location* is the psychodynamic principle then the ears may become male genital symbols (testes, one on either side). Symbols are chameleon in nature depending upon which laws are observed in their formation, i.e., function, structure, location, direction, idiosyncratic experience, etc. In spite of all our obsessive systems, the *world* and nature remain fairly flexible, fluid and changeable.[6]

At any rate, Mr. P.'s major contact with the world is through his ears (hearing), mouth (talking, eating, swallowing, biting), and his nose (smelling, poking, blowing, etc.). In his behavior, thought and feeling Mr. P. verified these conclusions. Patient continually talked, shouted and ate. In therapy, at home, on the job, he kept "shouting everybody down." He sought out people with deep, resonant voices and provoked them into talking. He became acutely aware of smells and continually complained about "nasal congestion."

Viewed from a slightly different conceptual level, the original all-encompassing problem of male vs. female is now diverted to and contained in the problem of receiving or giving in terms of facial organs.

There is now a relative freedom from anxiety (slight shading), very little depression (neck is not narrow), and instead of rigid repression (reinforced lines, etc.), there are now adequate ways of expressing and fulfilling emotional drives through the hearing, talking, eating and smelling (without guilt).

Figure 8 was executed at the same time as Figure 7. Since the very first pair of drawings, patient had refused the request to "now draw a person of the opposite sex." That direction had never had any real meaning to him. He has now externalized

---

[6] I have been trying to learn what determines the psychodynamic principle which is selected for symbol formation, i.e., location, form or function. The current hypothesis I am exploring, without having arrived at a resolution, is that these three principles stand in hierarchical relationship to each other, similar to id, superego and ego; with function being most primitive and form more advanced. I am not yet satisfied. I have been unable to find this problem explored elsewhere, not even Freud where one may find almost all else. Communication relevant to this problem is invited.

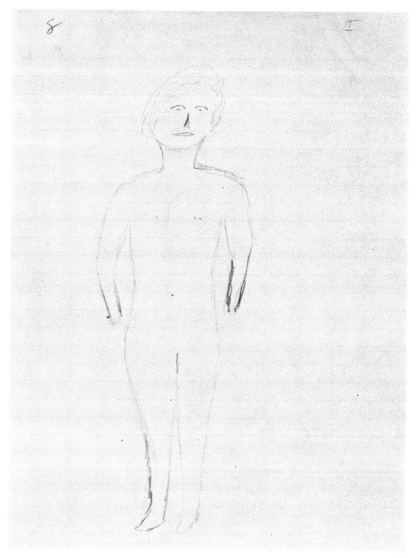

Figure 8

the female component sufficiently to present a separate woman figure-drawing. Note how much more anxiety is suggested by the broken lines and the shading in the "woman drawing." Although he is finally substantially "free" and has established separate identity, there is still much anxiety associated with the female figure. Figure 8 shows the left arm and right leg to have special meaning to the patient. The forearm is reinforced, as is the right leg. Patient's own left arm and right leg were giving him trouble at this time. They were stiff, numb (almost paralyzed) and sometimes painful. Dreams and associations revealed that when patient was very young he slept with his father, his own

Figure 9

left arm in contact with his father who slept on the left side of the bed and his right arm often thrown over his father. Fantasies of being a woman are associated with those memories. At this stage in therapy, strong transference feelings developed in which he confused therapist with an uncle who had replaced his own father on the latter's death.

The final drawing, Figure 9 was completed by the patient in May, 1955. At this stage of therapy patient was very much aware of himself as a person, presented the picture to the world of a somewhat obsessive, aggressive person who now had a number of friends, had left the post office one and a half years earlier, and in his new, responsible job had received a promotion after one year. He now has considerable hostility to his wife and other women and constantly seeks "intellectual gratification" from male companions with whom he "can speak and be understood." He reads voraciously, attends plays, takes a "Great Books" course and wants to find "work that is more fulfilling." His hatred toward wife, mother and sister is in central awareness, freely ventilated in therapy and under control in personal contact. Figure 9 not only reveals his present stage of integration and the nature of his character structure, but clearly reveals the "scars" or traces of early trauma.

If Figure 9 were presented for drawing analysis without benefit of the prior sequence or any special knowledge of patient's history, the following would be said of him. He is an obsessive-complusive individual. The evidence for this is in the clothing detail (pockets, tie, tie pin, lapels, shoe laces, part-in-hair, handkerchief in breast pocket). There is evidence of strong oral-dependent needs and a repressed passive homosexual conflict. These are expressed symbolically in the number of pockets (receiving organs), buttons (dependency symbols—nipples, umbilicus), and the absence of ears (denial) replaced by shading.

There is evidence of a conflict between male and female identification (left foot shorter, left arm "damaged," hip area reinforced, part-in-hair). There is evidence of some strain involving the intensity of anger and its control (somewhat elongated neck, reinforced with collar and narrow opening at chin). There is some difficulty in reaching out to and establishing relations with other people; there is fear connected with his hostile impulses (arms pressed to side). Patient's feeling of being inadequate (unfinished tie, shading) and up in the air (placement of figure) is rationalized and controlled by obsessive devices (line placed under feet and another under that; stick-pin in tie to anchor it). In short, Mr. P. has exchanged a chaotic body image for a granite prison and exchanged the latter for a set of details (button and pockets and hair-part). In retrospect we see the relationship between the part in his hair and the cleft in Figure 1; between the pointed handkerchief in the pocket and the male figure inside the female figure; between the tie and the stiff backbone in Figure 6; between the shading around the ears as compared with the wide-open ears in Figure 7; the shading in the hip area as compared with the flaring hips in Figure 6. Thus, "where id was, there is now ego."

## REFERENCES

1. Arieti, S.: *Interpretation of Schizophrenia.*
2. Bettelheim, B.: *Symbolic Wounds.*
3. Freud, S.: *Leonardo Da Vinci.* New York, Random House, 1947.
4. Nunberg, H.: *Problems of Bisexuality as Reflected in Circumcision.* London, Imago Pub. Co., Ltd., 1949.

PART III

CONTENT COMPONENTS

Unit 2
House-Tree-Person Drawings

## CHAPTER 8

# THE HOUSE-TREE-PERSON PROJECTIVE DRAWING TECHNIQUE: CONTENT INTERPRETATION[1]

EMANUEL F. HAMMER, PH.D.

I~ HIS DRAWING of a House, a Tree, and then a Person (the H-T-P Test) it is the subject's inner view of himself and his environment, the things he considers important, the things he emphasizes, and the things he neglects to include that interest the clinician.

In the previous chapters we have seen how the psychodynamic imperatives of both the subject's self-concept and his perception of his environment press forward onto the drawing page. Symbolically potent concepts such as House, Tree and Person are saturated with the emotional and ideational experiences associated with the personality's development, and the drawing of these images compel projection on the part of the drawer.

### ADMINISTRATION

The H-T-P taps the stream of personality as it floods the area of artistic creativity. Certain restrictions have been placed upon completely free expression in the interest of standardization. The same concepts, for example, are requested from each subject, on the same size paper, with similar materials. A number two pencil with eraser is employed on a four-page form sheet[2] of white paper, each page 7 by 8½ inches in size (2). Only one surface is exposed at a time to the subject. His drawing of a House is

[1] The present chapter focuses on a consideration of the qualitative interpretation of the H-T-P. Buck's quantitative scoring system of the H-T-P may be found in his more detailed presentation of his technique (1, 2).

[2] These form sheets may be ordered from Western Psychological Services, 10655 Santa Monica Boulevard, West Los Angeles, California.

[ 165 ]

requested with the longer axis of the sheet placed horizontally before the subject, and his drawing of a Tree and Person, in turn, are then obtained on separate sides with the longer axis the vertical way.

The subject is asked to draw as good a House (and later Tree and Person) as he can. He is told that he may draw any kind he likes, he may erase as much as he wishes, and he may take as much time as he chooses.

If the subject protests that he is not an artist, I generally assure him that the H-T-P is not a test of artistic ability at all but that I am interested, rather, in how he does things. If the subject asks permission to use, or attempts to use, any mechanical aid, he is told that his drawing must be free-hand.

The order of presentation of the stimuli: House, then Tree, and then Person, always remains the same. This provides the most gradual introduction into the drawing task, in that in step-by-step manner, it leads up to the entities that are psychologically more difficult to draw. The subject is gradually led along from the more neutral to the "closer-to-home" self-portraits. Thus, the drawing item which arouses the most conscious associations is left to the last.

### THE CHOICE OF HOUSE, TREE AND PERSON AS DRAWING CONCEPTS

In regard to his choice of the specific items, House, Tree and Person, Buck (1) states that: (a) they were items familiar to all, even the very young child; (b) they were found to be more willingly accepted, than other items, as objects for drawing by subjects of all ages; and (c) they stimulated more frank and free verbalization than did other items. In addition, one might add that these concepts are symbolically fertile in terms of unconscious significance (to be discussed under the separate sections of this chapter: House; Tree, and Person).

In regard to Buck's choice of drawing items, Griffiths' (5) study of the free drawings of young children in England indicates houses, trees and people to have the highest personal significance. "The favorite [drawing] object [of young children] is . . . the human figure" (p. 199). "[After] the human figure . . . the drawing of the house is the next favorite object drawn by children" (p. 219). "Then the child begins to draw trees in particular, and also flowers . . . [and] seems to notice for the first time colour in its true application" (p. 222). Eng's (4) findings offer parallel confirmation: "The first and favorite subject that children draw is human beings, but next to that, according to my observations, the house."

Independently of Buck, Emil Jucker (9), in Europe, discovered that the free drawing of a tree also carried a wealth of projective possibilities. He evolved it as a projective device, not by chance, "but after mature consideration and long study of the history of cultures and more especially of myths" (p. 5). His student, Charles Koch (9) further developed it into a projective drawing instrument to obtain "an idea of the total personality in its deeper layers of being" (p. 5).[3]

Studying children's house building with blocks, Pichon Rivière (13) found that houses were capable of symbolizing: (a) the child's body; (b) the womb; (c) the parental home. Empirical data with the H-T-P projective drawing technique tend to support the first and third of these symbolic meanings more frequently than the second, although deteriorated psychotics will at times give a distinct womb-like flavor to their House drawing.

In regard to the first symbolic meaning (the House drawing representing the body image), subjects with problems in phallic areas will frequently project this onto their depiction of the chimney, subjects with oral emphasis in their character structure tend to emphasize the outline of the windows, and so on.

In reference to the last-named symbolic meaning, a depiction of the parental home, one adolescent girl who felt heavily oppressed by the frictions and constant heated arguments at home mirrored this in her drawing of the House by adding a profusion of thick, bellowing smoke pouring forth from the chimney. In this manner, the drawing reflected her view of her home as a hotbed of turbulence, unrest and stirred-up emotionality. Also the previously shown drawing (p. 44) of the prison-like House, in which the subject mirrored his inner view of himself being imprisoned in the home situation by virtue of his obligations to

---

[3] He reported his findings in a book called *The Tree Test* (9).

postpone marriage and support his aging and invalid parents, illustrates the use of the drawn House to depict one's perception of the home situation.

When house-building seemed to symbolize the child's body, Pichon Riviere found that anomalies in the construction of houses were symbolically related to the alterations in the body image resulting from the particular form the child's emotional disturbance assumed. This confirms Buck's (2) findings with the drawn House.

Rosen (14) points out that the house, which is symbolically so closely related to the human figure, plays an important part, not only in children's drawings, but also in primitive art. This can be seen not only in the uncovered cave man drawings but later in the early cultural development of man. The close relationship of the House to the chief object of representative art, the human body, occurs in the early Renaissance of the 13th Century, becomes more rare in the 14th Century, and in the 15th Century, when art had lost its child-like character, it disappears almost entirely (4).

The concept of the Person, of course, is most obviously flooded with the emotional experiences associated with the individual's development. This was independently and simultaneously recognized by Machover (12), Buck (2), Levy (11), and perhaps in its deepest theoretical implications, by Paul Schilder in his contribution of the concept of the Body-image (16).

Thus, there appears to have been some striking independent confirmation of the high personal significance of the three concepts, House, Tree and Person, which Buck chose as the entities to use in forging his tool with which to tap deep personality areas. The intense symbolic potential of the House, as rooted in basic childhood and adult experiences, was simultaneously singled out by Griffiths (5) in England, Pichon Rivière (13) in South America, and Buck (2) in the United States. In addition to Buck, the clinical usefulness of the drawing of the Tree was realized by Jucker (9) in Europe, and Koch (9) in Switzerland, while that of the drawing of a Person was independently arrived at by Machover (12), Levy (11), Schilder (16), and following the theoretical insights of the latter, by Lauretta Bender (1).

## THE PROJECTIVE ASPECTS OF THE
## HOUSE-TREE-PERSON DRAWINGS

Traditionally, a clinical technique qualifies as a projective device if it presents the subject with a stimulus, or series of stimuli, either so unstructured or so ambiguous that their meaning for the subject must come, in part, from within himself.

The structuring involved in asking the subject to draw a House, a Tree and a Person is more ambiguous than one might think at first. Although the subject is asked to draw a House, a Tree and a Person, he is not told *what* House, Tree and Person to draw. Since he is given no cue from the examiner, it is from within the subject that the response flows: as to the size, type, placement or presentation of the House, kind, age, size, placement or presentation of the Tree, or sex, facial expression, body stance, age, race, size, clothing, presentation (side, three-quarter or full view placement) or action of the Person. One need only recall the wide variety of the drawings presented in the preceding chapters, for graphic illustration of the validity of this thesis.

In addition, the inclusion or exclusion of the various details of a House, Tree and Person are left wholly to the subject, as is his relative emphasis therein. To borrow an example from the writer's recent H-T-P study on sex offenders (6), whereas normal subjects tend to draw an unnoteworthy (clinically) chimney on the House, sex offenders have been found either (a) to display their feelings of phallic inadequacy directly [4] by drawing a chimney in the following cluster of ways: with the upper part missing as if sliced away on the diagonal; with the roof showing through the chimney which is presented as transparent (thus reflecting the subject's feelings of flimsiness in regard to his phallus); with the chimney depicted as toppling or falling off the edge of the roof; or with a two-dimensional chimney presented on a House which is treated three-dimensionally (thus conveying the subject's feelings that there is less substance to the phallic than to the other parts of his body-image), or (b) to mask their feelings

---

[4] This projection of direct feelings of phallic inadequacy occurred in the pedophile sub-group of sex offenders in whom a sexual approach to a child occurred as a substitute sexual outlet because of crippling feelings of psychosexual inadequacy in regard to approaching adult females.

of phallic inadequacy under a cloak of compensatory virility strivings [5] by drawing several chimneys (rather than the more conventional number of one) on a roof; an elongated oversized chimney; a chimney phallically shaped with a rounded tip; a chimney overemphasized by line pressure, shading or prominent placement (as a full-length chimney extending to the ground and in some drawings made the central focal point of the entire picture).

This does not, however, mean that the chimney must be a phallic symbol in drawings. In well-adjusted subjects, the chimney usually represents only a necessary detail in the depiction of a House. But if a subject suffers from psychosexual conflicts, the chimney—by virtue of its structural design and its protrusion from the body of the House—is susceptible to receive the projection of the subject's inner feelings about his own phallus.

Thus, it may be seen that in the House-Tree-Person drawing technique the subject is presented with stimuli which are completely familiar, but at the same time so completely nonspecific that in order to respond, he must *project* or at least *select*. Sir John Lubbock once said, "What we see depends mainly on what we look for." And we choose that House, Tree or Person to draw for which we have a certain affinity or, at times, identification.

In his lifetime, the subject no matter how young he may be, has seen such an infinite variety of houses, trees and people, that only those that are the most symbolically meaningful compete to press forward onto the drawing page. Whether the subject chooses a sturdy oak, a drooping, weeping willow, an immature sapling, or a tree bent almost down to the ground by the environmental pressures and cracking under the strain, whether a stern-faced, night-stick wielding policeman, a nurturant maternal figure offering a bowl of hot soup held in her hands, a helpless child-like figure standing with arms amputated, a nude figure in a frank position of legs spread apart in invitation, or a disheveled tramp sprawled against the curb—the subject is making a choice on the basis of what is emotionally meaningful to him.

As with the thematic apperception tests, the subject selects a

---

[5] Rapists who attempt to prove their masculinity through an over-assertive, forceful sexual approach convey this compensatory phallic trend in their distortions of the chimney in their drawn Houses.

theme out of his past experience which reflects his own needs. Clinicians have learned that when a subject offers a theme, from a past movie he has seen, in response to one of the TAT cards, the subject is still providing information of interest to the clinician. That particular theme stuck in the subject's mind originally and was later selected from the shelf of these remembered themes, because, in all probability, it reflected needs or traits of significant proportions.

In responding to the H-T-P, TAT, or Rorschach, the subject's inner eye looks upon and then decides which pictures his needs shall select from the gallery of remembered things.

## SYMBOLISM INHERENT IN THE HOUSE-TREE-PERSON TRIAD

Before turning to a consideration of the dynamic significance of various essentials *within* the drawings of House, Tree and Person, it would be profitable to consider the broader areas of the personality tapped by these three concepts.

The House, as a dwelling place, has been found to arouse within the subject associations concerning home-life and intrafamilial relationships. In children, it has been found to tap their attitude concerning the home situation and relationships to parents and siblings. The previously mentioned drawing with profuse and over-heavily shaded smoke pouring forth from the chimney of the house as a reflection of the hot and turbulent emotional atmosphere in the home situation, illustrates this relationship of the House drawing to the perceived home conditions.

For married adults, the drawings of the House may reflect the subject's domestic situation in relationship to his spouse. With many married, adult subjects, however, the childhood relationship to parental figures is still apparent as residual attitudes revealed in the House drawing. And the more neurotic, regressed or fixated the subject, the more likely the latter, rather than the former, depiction is to occur.

As to the Tree and the Person, both these concepts tap that core of the personality which theorists, notably Paul Schilder (15), have labeled the body image and the self-concept. The drawing of the Tree appears to reflect the subject's relatively deeper and more unconscious feelings about himself, whereas the drawn Person becomes the vehicle for conveying the subject's closer-to-conscious view of himself and his relationship with his environment. In this manner, a picture of the conflicts and defenses as set in the hierarchy of the subject's personality structure is provided.

The Tree, a more basic, natural, vegetative entity has been found to be a more suitable symbol upon which to project the deeper personality feelings, feelings about the self residing at a more primitive personality level than what one has learned about people. The latter, including the subject's methods of dealing with others and his feelings toward them, is more apt to be projected onto the drawn Person.

This view, that the Tree taps more basic and long-standing feelings, is supported by the fact that the Tree is less susceptible to change on retesting (2, 7a). Whereas psychotherapy of a nonintensive kind will frequently bring improvement as indicated by a decrease of the psychopathological signs in the drawn Person, only deep and extensive psychoanalytic collaboration (or highly significant alterations in a life situation, particularly of children whose personalities have enough resiliency to improve along with situational improvements) will produce any but minor changes in the Tree.

Clinical experience also suggests that it is easier for a subject to attribute more conflicting or emotionally disturbing negative traits and attitudes to the drawn Tree than to the drawn Person because the former is less "close to home" as a self-portrait. The deeper or more forbidden feelings can more readily be projected onto the Tree than onto the Person, with less fear of revealing oneself and less need for ego-defensive manuevering.

A subject may, for instance, more readily and unwittingly portray his feeling of emotional trauma by scarring the drawn Tree's trunk and truncating its branches, than by a parallel mutilation of the drawn Person's face and body and similar distortion of the drawn Person's arms.

The clinical finding that forbidden feelings can be projected more readily onto the Tree than onto the Person drawing is similar to the rationale behind Blum's Blacky Picture Test, Bellak's

Children's Apperception Test and the Despart Fables. It has been my experience that the animal figures on these thematic techniques, in parallel fashion to the relationship between the drawn Tree and Person, are more susceptible for the projection of the deeper and more negative feelings (with less threat to the subject) than are the human figures of the TAT.

Thus, a comparison of the subject's responses to the animal as opposed to the human TAT-type stimuli, and a comparison of the subject's drawn Tree with his drawn Person, provide data which enable the clinician to appraise the hierarchy of the subject's conflicts and defenses.

## INTERPRETATION OF ELEMENTS WITHIN HOUSE, TREE AND PERSON

It is the content of the drawings, more so than the expressive movements employed in the drawing, which express the more unconscious qualities that exist at the heart of personality.

### House

*Roof:* Empirical findings with the H-T-P indicate that the roof of the drawn House may be employed by subjects to symbolize the fantasy area of life. Colloquial expressions such as "bats in the belfry," "something wrong upstairs," or "a few shingles loose" tap the same symbolism in which the roof area is equated with mental life. Thus, a condition whereby fantasy distorts one's mental functioning is spoken of in terms of an impairment in the individual's roof.

A House which is drawn with an overly large roof, overhanging and dwarfing the rest of the House (see Figure 1), is given by patients over-immersed in fantasy and relatively withdrawn from overt interpersonal contact. These subjects most frequently yield a Rorschach experience-balance heavily weighed on the intratensive side (with average proportions of seven to twelve *M* to a *Sum of C* of zero to two). The number of their Human Movement responses almost invariably exceeds their Sum of Color by four or five times.

Occasionally schizophrenic or distinctly schizoid patients draw a roof and then place the door and windows within this roof outline, so that what is produced is essentially a House which is all roof (see Figure 2). And the schizophrenic and markedly schizoid individual exists in a world which is largely fantasy. In a relative way, these subjects are more withdrawn into their fantasy life than the subjects who draw an overly large roof overhanging the walls of the House. In the latter group, there is an exaggerated emphasis on fantasy life which throws the personality structure out of balance, whereas patients who draw a House which is all roof live predominantly a fantasy existence.

The absence of a roof on a House, or a roof consisting of only a single line connecting the two end walls so that there is no height to the roof (it is essentially one-dimensional rather than two-dimensional) occurs at the other end of the use-of-fantasy continuum. The group most noted for the single-line roof are imbeciles, individuals who lack the capacity to daydream or in other ways fantasize. Within the normal intellectual range, the one-dimensional roof depiction occurs in those with constricted personalities and concrete orientation. In clinical practice it most commonly appears hand-in-hand with a coarctated Rorschach record.

Thus, extremes in the relative size of the roof drawn tend to reflect the subject's degree of devoting his time to fantasy and of his turning to this area in his satisfaction seeking.

A roof reinforced by heavy line pressure, or by repeated retracing of the roof outline (where this does not occur in the other areas of the drawn House), is offered by subjects who are attempting to defend themselves against the threat of fantasy breaking away from control (see Figure 3). Its most frequent occurrence is in the drawings of pre-psychotics, although it also occurs to a lesser extent with anxiety neurotics. At any rate, it represents heightened concern with the fear that those impulses presently discharged in fantasy will flood into overt behavior or distort the perception of reality.

*Walls:* The strength and adequacy of the depicted walls of the House have been found to be directly related to the degree of ego-strength in the personality. Crumbling walls have occurred in the drawings of patient's with overtly disintegrating egos, and a reinforced boundary of the walls is frequently offered by incipient psychotics who are employing an all-out, hypervigilant, and often-times conscious effort to maintain ego intactness.

The outline of the walls of the House portrayed with a faint and inadequate line quality also connotes a feeling of impending personality breakdown and weak ego control, only without the employment of compensatory defenses. Patients who offer this inadequate wall periphery are more reconciled to their impending pathology (they have accepted defeat as inevitable and have ceased to struggle) than are the patients who overly reinforce the outline of the walls. Instead of attempting to fend them off, the former group adopt an attitude of passive sufferance toward the disintegrative forces which threaten.

Transparent walls in the drawings of adults are direct evidence of a reality-testing impairment. Young children frequently draw walls that are transparent (with objects within the House allowed to show through the wall material), and in so doing they

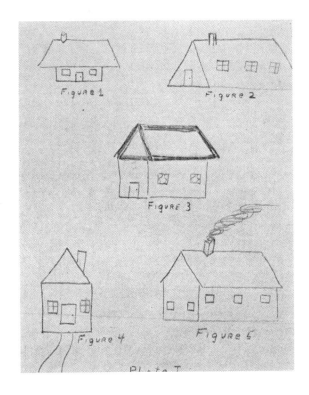

merely indicate their immaturity of conceptual ability, taking a gross liberty with the presentation of reality. With adults, defects in reality testing of this magnitude occur, in my experience, only in the drawings of (a) low grade defectives, and (b) psychotics.

**Door:** The door is that detail of the House through which, in actuality, direct contact is made with the environment. A door that is tiny in relation to the size of the windows in particular and the House in general, reflects a reluctance to make contact with the environment, a withdrawal from interpersonal give-and-take, and an inhibited capacity for social relations. Timidity and fearfulness in one's relationship with others are the behavioral correlates of the tiny-door depiction. Occasionally a subject who draws an excessively small door in his House also offers the "burnt child" reaction on the Rorschach. Emotional exchange with others has been found to result in pain, and the subject is reluctant to expose himself again.

The door placed high above the House's baseline and not made more approachable by steps (see Figure 4) is another way in which subjects may indicate their attempts to keep their personality inaccessible. This depiction is common in those who tend to make contact with others in the environment on their own terms only.

The overly large door (here, as elsewhere in psychology, it is the both extremes which are deviant) is drawn by those who give other clinical evidence of being overly-dependent upon others. The drawing of the door as open, a statistically infrequent occurrence, conveys an intense thirst to receive emotional warmth from without (if the Post-Drawing Inquiry * reveals the House to be occupied). If the House is said to be vacant, the open door connotes a feeling of extreme vulnerability, a lack of adequacy of ego defenses.

Emphasis upon locks and/or hinges demonstrates defensive sensitivity of the type not infrequently found in paranoids.

**Windows:** In the drawing of the House, windows represent a secondary medium of interaction with the environment. Emphasis upon window locks, as with parallel treatment of the door locks, occur in those who are over-defensively fearful of danger from without—again found most frequently in paranoid orientations.

---

* See pages 239-245 for the questions in the Post-Drawing Inquiry.

Similarly, shutters or curtains added to the windows, and presented as closed, also convey withdrawal needs and extreme reluctance to interact with others.

Shutters, shades or curtains put on the windows but presented as open, or partially open, mirror an attitude of controlled interaction with the environment. These subjects suffer a degree of anxiety, manifested as tact, in interpersonal relations. Social workers, examined in connection with a study of personality patterns of various vocational groups, showed a predilection for depicting this attribute of controlled emotional give-and-take with others (4a).

Windows completely bare, without not only curtains or shades but also cross-hatching, occur in the drawings of individuals who interact with those in the environment in an overly blunt and direct fashion. The exercise of tact is minimal in their behavior, and they tend toward being a bit of a "bull in a China shop" type of social participant.

Reinforcement of window outlines, if similar reinforcement does not occur elsewhere in the drawing, has most frequently been presented by subjects with oral fixations or oral character traits. Occasionally, however, the window outline is also emphasized by those with anal orientations; and frequently the oral as opposed to buttock emphasis on the drawn Person will allow a differential interpretation.

In regard to size of the windows, convention decrees that the living room window be presented as the largest and the bath room window as the smallest. Where deviations from this rule occur, we have an index of a strong emotional need pressing forward. A distinct distaste for social intercourse is behind the attempts to minimize the importance of the associations to the living room by drawing the window of this room the smallest in the House.

Undue importance given to the bathroom by making the window to that room the largest of all the windows, tends to reflect experiences involving severe toilet training in the childhood background of the subject. It has also been found in those suffering masturbation guilt and in those with compulsive hand-washing as a symptom.

Placement of windows which does not conform from wall-to-wall (which suggests that the height of a floor as viewed from the front of the House is not the same as if viewed from the side of the House, as in Figure 5) directly reflects an organizational and form difficulty, empirically found to be suggestive of early schizophrenia.

*Chimney:* This was previously discussed in the introductory section of this chapter in illustrating the wide variety of treatments which might be accorded a single detail of the drawings.

*Smoke:* A profusion of dense and excessive smoke pouring forth from the chimney reflects either considerable inner tension *in the subject,* or conflict and emotional turbulence *in the home situation,* or both, since the latter may well produce the former condition, and vice-versa.

Smoke veering sharply to one side, as if indicating a strong wind, reflects a feeling of environmental pressure and has been frequently associated, in my experience, with child reading disability cases where parental pressures, both causatively and reactively, are massive. Adolescents who experience undue parental pressure toward social conformity and/or scholastic achievement, have also made use of this depiction, as have some individuals shortly after their induction into the armed services.

*Perspective:* The House drawn as if the viewer is above and looking down upon it (labeled by Buck the "bird's-eye view") is produced by subjects who basically reject the home situation and the values espoused therein. Such subjects combine compensatory superiority feelings with a revolt against the traditional values taught at home. Iconoclastic attitudes go along with a feeling of being above the demands of convention and conformity. In a study by Buck (3a), comparing different professional groups, this "birds-eye view" was relatively more common among medical students.

The "worm's-eye view," in which the House is presented so that it is as if the viewer is below and looking up at it, is a perspective employed by subjects who feel rejected and inferior in the home situation. Feelings of lack of worth mingle with low self-esteem and feelings of inadequacy; happiness in the home situation is considered largely unobtainable.

The perspective of the House presented as far away, that is, as distant[6] from the viewer, is employed by two groups of subjects: (a) those who project a self-portrait in the drawing of the House and thus disclose their feelings of withdrawal and inaccessibility; (b) those who convey a perception of the home situation—a home situation with which the subjects feels unable to cope. In this latter use of the "far-away" perspective, the subject is displaying his view that feelings of comfort are unattainable in relationship to those at home.

The "absolute profile" presentation of the House is another personally-meaningful deviation from the usual perspective. The term "absolute profile" refers to the House drawn with only the side presented to the viewer. The front of the House, including the door or other entrance, is turned away making it unseen and less accessible. Withdrawn, oppositional or interpersonally-inaccessible subjects project these traits in the House drawing by offering this perspective. Evasive paranoid subjects also have a preference for seeking refuge, during their H-T-P performance, in the "absolute profile."

The House drawn from the rear, and particularly if no back door is indicated, mirrors the same withdrawal and oppositional tendencies as does the "absolute profile" presentation, only to proportions of greater pathology. The only "rear view" depictions the writer has seen, have been in the drawings of paranoid schizophrenics, most frequently while they were still in a prepsychotic state when the need to protectively withdraw is most acutely felt.

*Groundline:* The relationship of the drawn House, Tree or Person to the groundline reflects the subject's degree of contact with reality. The same symbolic stream equating the ground with practical reality is also evident running through colloquial speech: "He has his feet firmly planted on the ground." Whether the contact with the ground is either firm or tenuous is of major diagnostic interest. Latent or borderline schizophrenics invariably

---

[6] A tiny House may be drawn lost in a vast expanse of white space; a fair-sized House may be drawn high on a hill; or a House may be separated from the viewer by a multitude of interposed irrelevant details: trees, shrubs, fence, animals, road, river, etc.

have difficulty presenting their drawn whole in firm contact with reality (as represented by the groundline). They either offer a drawing resting tenuously on a choppy or sporadically drawn groundline (see Chapter 9, Figure 9), on an amorphous, cloud-like groundline (see Chapter 9, Figure 7), or as being up-rooted (in the case of the Tree) from the ground and toppling (see Chapter 9, Figure 14). A greater degree of schizophrenic pathology and phantasy-absorbing distance from reality is displayed by a drawn whole that hovers over but nowhere touches a ground-line drawn beneath it.

*Accessories:* Some subjects directly reveal their lack of feelings of security by having to surround and buttress their House with bushes, trees and other details unrelated to the instruction.

A walkway, easily drawn and well proportioned, leading up to the door, is commonly added by individuals who exercise a degree of control and tact in their contact with others. A long and winding walkway, on the other hand, occurs in the drawings of those who are initially aloof in their interpersonal relations but eventually warm-up and do establish emotional rapport with others. They are slow and somewhat cautious in making friend-ships, but when relationships with others develop, they tend to be of a deep quality.

A walkway excessively wide at the end toward the viewer and leading in a direct line to the door, but with the width of the walkway narrowing too sharply so that it is considerably less than the width of the door where they meet, reveals an attempt to cloak a basic desire to remain aloof by employing superficial friendliness.

Fences are placed around the drawn House in a maneuver of defensiveness. A shy, eight-year-old boy recently offered the writer a picture in which the most conspicuous elaboration of the drawing of the House was a fence "to keep everybody away." It was as if he were trying to insure that nobody should interfere with what little security he did feel.

*Summary:* Thus, in an abbreviated way, one might say that the drawn House most frequently represents two major entities: (a) a self-portrait with fantasy, ego, reality contact, accessibility, oral, anal or phallic emphasis as elements thereof, and (b) the perception of the home situation—past, present, desired future, or some combination of all three.

## Tree

As Schactel (15) has pointed out: The fully matured and highly differentiated adult mind is capable, up to a certain extent, of voluntarily assuming different attitudes in his perception and experience of the environment. He can be at one moment the detached observer; the next moment he can open himself receptively to all the impressions from the environment and the feelings and pleasures aroused by them; and in the next he can project himself in emphatic experience with some object of the environment.

In looking at a tree, for example, he can in one moment be the detached botanist who observes, compares, classifies what he sees; in the next moment he may surrender to the color of the foliage and bark, the sound of leaves rustling in the breeze, their fresh scent after a shower of rain; and in the next moment he may try to feel, inside of himself, kinesthetically, how slight or solid the trunk stands and rises up, how calmly the branches spread, or how gracefully they move and yield to the wind.

In the drawing of a Tree, we have found that the subject chooses from his memory of the countless number he has seen, the one with which he has the greatest empathic identification and in drawing, the subject modifies and recreates the Tree further along in the direction of his kinesthetic reaction fed by his own inner feelings.

It is no surprise to anthropolgists that one's "view" of a Tree is personally meaningful. In myth and folklore and even everyday parlance, the tree has always symbolized life and growth.

In Scandinavian folklore, the old myths tell of Ygdrasil, the "tree of life." In German stories, the tree is said to have its roots in the bowels of the earth, in the nether regions of our primitive past; its trunk on the earth among the mortals; and its branches reaching into the heavens where the Gods dwell and rule mankind (9).

The symbol-seeped meaning of the tree carries through to the 20th Century and is apparent in our speaking of the "family tree" and in sayings like "As the twig is bent, so grows the tree."

In the drawings of a Tree, as we shall later see, a subject will neglect the branches if he does not "branch out," mingling with and enjoying other people. In this manner, the subject projects during the process of drawing the Tree, and makes it a veritable self-portrait.

Sometimes subjects will draw a Tree that is tossed by the wind and broken by storms—a reflection of the effects of environmental pressures *they* have endured.

> The unconscious etching-out of the self-image via the Tree drawing was most evident in a recent case of a woman who drew a basket under the Tree with five shining fruits in it. She had five children, and the drawing quite clearly represented her basic pride in her maternal role.
>
> Her positive evaluation of her maternal achievements is in sharp contrast to that revealed in the Tree drawn by a woman who was seen for a clinical evaluation in connection with the psychotherapy program of both her children, one a twenty-year-old overt homosexual and the other an eleven-year-old boy with a severe remedial reading disability. The mother's unconscious rejection of her children as well as her negative evaluation of herself as a mother came through with graphic impact in her drawing of a fruit Tree with two conspicuous apples resting on the ground beneath it. Her spontaneous comment, "These are two rotten apples which have fallen to the ground" brought this picture from her unconscious to sharp focus.

"A tree drawing may be grasped as a whole, intuitively; even without investigation of the details one can receive an impression of harmony, or unrest, of emptiness, of baldness or of fullness, or one may receive an impression of hostility and be warned. This, too, is the first stage in the learning of the method. One should passively submit oneself to the effect of a very large number of tree drawings, 'contemplate' them, simply look at them without any critical attitude. Thus, slowly, looking becomes seeing, distinctions are recognized, the picture begins to differentiate itself, one becomes more intimately acquainted with the subjects. . . .

Some drawings enable an adequate character study to be worked out. Others provide mere contributions to a personality diagnosis" (9, p. 31).

In speaking of the line of development of the Tree from bottom to top, Koch (9) points out that the drawing as it grows in development from the roots upward parallels the subject's felt development in time, that is, the psychological life history of the subject. He observes that traces of early experiences tend to be shown at the bottom of the trunk and those of more recent occurrence at the top. This is congruent with Buck's (3) experience that the lower the scarring on the Tree trunk, the earlier the traumatizing experience took place.

This hypothesis was investigated by Levine and Galanter (10) who employed hospitalized paraplegics and compared the height of the trunk at which scarring occurred in their drawing of a Tree with the subject's age at the time of the onset of the paraplegic condition. An analysis of this relationship led the investigators to conclude that ". . . the hypothesis may have some degree of validity in terms of a broad approximation of the time of injury."

The most extreme instance of scarring the writer has encountered was offered by a twelve-year-old boy. He placed a ravaging wound approximately half-way up the height of the Tree trunk. Subsequent psychotherapeutic collaboration with the youngster revealed that his mother's death, occurring when he was five years of age, was unconsciously felt as an abandonment, and left him with a deep hurt. The child was secretly angry with the parent for having "deserted" him. At the same time he felt that he must have been really bad, or his mother would not have left him. This feeling of his aching wound was etched into the self-portrait his drawn Tree represented.

The Tree, a living or one-time living thing in an elemental environment (rain, wind, sleet, storm, warmth or sunshine), is the most likely of the three drawings to convey the person's felt image of himself in the context of his relationship to his environment.

Buck (2) adds to this the postulations that: (a) the trunk represents the subject's feeling of basic power and inner strength (in analytic terminology, his "ego-strength"); (b) the branch structure depicts his feeling of ability to derive satisfaction from his environment (tapping a more unconscious level of the same area tapped by the adequacy of the arms and hands on the drawn Person), and (c) the organization of the drawn whole reflects the subject's feeling of intra-personal balance.

There is a striking parallel to the first two of these postulates of Buck in the experience of Koch in Switzerland: "The trunk frequently represents the basic area of the self-concept, the ego-strength. . . . It is to be assumed that when a tree is drawn, knowledge of the essential nature of the wood will cause every-thing relating to inherent endowment to be projected into these parts of the tree more clearly than into the foliage. 'He is carved from good wood.' 'The wood is good.' and similar expressions are indeed habitually used by German-speaking people in reference to a person's inherent nature" (9, p. 15).

To these examples from the German language, we might add the American colloquialism, "A chip off the old block."

In independent agreement with Buck's second postulate, Koch observes: "The outer parts of the crown, the extremities, form the zone of contact with the environment, the zone of relation-ship and exchange between what is within and what is without" (9, p. 15).

Now as to the dynamic significance of the subject's differential treatment of the details within the drawing of the Tree:

*Trunk:* In support of the concept of the trunk serving as an index of the basic strength of the personality, reinforced periph-eral lines in this area of the Tree have been found to reflect the subject's felt need to maintain personality intactness. Here, he employs compensatory defenses to cloak and combat his fear of personality diffusion and disintegration. He attempts to guard against this eventuality with all available resources.

On the other hand, faint, sketchy or perforated lines employed for the Tree trunk, and not elsewhere in the drawing, depict a more advanced state of feelings of impending personality collapse or loss of identity—a stage at which compensatory defenses are no longer looked to with any real hope of staving off the immi-nent breakdown. Acute anxiety is invariably present.

Holes have been placed in the trunk and animals shown

peeping out of them by those who (a) inwardly feel that a segment of the personality is pathologically free from control (dissociated) and potentially destructive (the most frequent instance of this depiction is offered by those wracked by obsessive guilt feelings), or (b) are identifying primarily with the animal within the Tree trunk, rather than with the Tree, and are thus depicting their regressive yearnings for a withdrawn, warm, protected, uterine existence. In the writer's experience, the former identification with the Tree occurs more frequently with adult subjects, and the latter identification with the animal within is more usually employed by children. The safest guide, however, for making the differential interpretation is the Post-Drawing Inquiry, the other projective data, and the clinical history, in that overlap of the two age groups, in the identification figure, occasionally is found in immature adults (with withdrawal needs) and obsessive or phobic children (with a potential for dissociation).

*Roots:* If the subject is unduly concerned about his hold upon reality, he may express this by an overemphasis upon the roots of the Tree as it makes contact with and takes hold of the ground. A talon-like grasp (the roots depicted as if straining to hold onto the ground) was recently drawn by a subject who subsequently suffered an overt psychotic break and had to be institutionalized. At the time the H-T-P was administered, two weeks prior to his overt break, the adhesive clutch of his Tree roots reflected his hypervigilant clinging to reality and panic-like fear of losing contact with reality.

Roots drawn as showing through transparent ground serves as direct evidence of an impairment of the subject's reality testing ability. If the subject is of average intelligence, or better, and in the adolescent or adult age range, this reality testing impairment has been found to be an item which should serve to alert the clinician to the possibility—but only the possibility—of other suggestions of a schizophrenic process.

*Paper-Based Tree:* Employment of the bottom edge of the paper as the groundline, with the drawn whole resting on that edge, is a favorite presentation of insecure subjects who suffer feelings of inadequacy. They cling to the bottom of the page for compensatory security. Depressed subjects who drop the placement of their drawing down to the lower section of the page may also allow it to come to rest on the bottom edge. The use of faint lines, reflecting the depressive's sapping of energy and drive, as well as his favorite Tree content—a Weeping Willow —may provide clues to aid in the differential interpretation.

*Branches:* The branches represent the subject's felt resources for seeking satisfaction from the environment, for reaching out to others, and for "branching out" achievement-wise. The Tree *limbs* represent a more unconscious parallel, in the subject's self-concept, to the drawn Person's arms. Joyce Kilmer, in his epic piece, had a poet's finger on the pulse of symbolism in his analogy: A tree who "lifts her leafy arms to pray."

Occasionally a subject will try to mask with superficial and compensatory optimism his deeper feelings of inability to obtain satisfaction. For example, he may draw his Person with overly long arms extending away from the body as if striving manfully, but his Tree will show clearly by its truncated and broken branches that basically he feels he has no real hope of success.

Branch structures presented as tall and narrow, reaching unduly upward and minimally outward to the sides, have been seen in Tree drawings of subjects who are afraid to seek satisfaction from, and in, the environment and, hence, over-reach into fantasy (upward toward the top of the page) for substitute gratification. These depictions are employed most commonly by those in the introverted-to-schizoid range. A better balance in the distribution of one's satisfaction-seeking pursuits occurs in those whose Tree branches extend laterally outward into the contemporary environment as well as upward into the fantasy area.

At times, a subject will emphasize the upward reaching of the branch structure to the point where the top of the Tree extends off beyond the page's top. This is an extreme example of a subject over-extended into fantasy. Whereas introverted and schizoid subjects both tend to overemphasize the upward extension of their Tree's branches, only those subjects near the frankly schizoid end of the continuum extend branches beyond the page's top. And certainly this is so when the trunk itself goes above the page top.

Occasionally a subject will abruptly flatten the top of the

foliage area or crown of the Tree, as if he were attempting to deny or reject the fantasy area entirely. This recently occurred in one patient who was panicked by the emergence of homosexual fantasies, and in another patient who was attempting to deny the site of his painful guilt produced by obsessive thoughts of killing his younger brother. Both wished to repress their fantasy life, and to deny the threatening-content forcing its way into that area.

One-dimensional branches which do not form a system, and are inadequately joined to a one-dimensional trunk (segmentalization), make the presence of organicity suspect (see Figure 6). Whether or not organicity is suggested by the flavoring of the rest of the drawings, the other projective techniques, the case history, and the neurological findings, this type of Tree reflects feelings of impotence, futility, and lack of ego-strength with poor integration of the satisfaction-seeking resources—all contributing to a graphic picture of feelings of inadequacy.

Flexibility of the branch structure, with the organization of the branches proceeding from thick to thin in a proximal-distal direction, is a favorable finding and bespeaks a feeling of a high ability on the part of the subject to attain satisfaction from his environment. This tends to be so, providing, of course, the branch structure is of adequate size in relation to the trunk.

Branches which appear club-like, or look spear-like with excessively sharpened points at the ends, or appear to have barb-like thorns along their surface, underscore the presence of intense and ready impulses of hostility and aggression. If the behavioral picture indicates that the subject is not acting out these impulses, but on the contrary he appears to be a relatively mild and meek individual, we may rest assured that this surface adjustment is made at the expense of massive efforts at repression with concomitant inner tension of considerable proportions. In such instances, the clinician might do well to inspect the drawings for indications of lack of control to appraise the likelihood of incipient and catastrophic acting-out of these impulses.

If the signs of control are very much overemphasized, they may of themselves be regarded as indicating an approaching impulse-eruption into overt behavior, since the individual may well be on the verge of exhausting his defensive potentials.

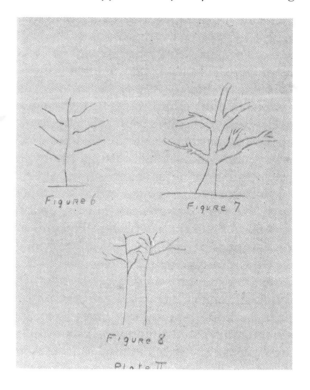

Within the Tree drawing, two-dimensional branches drawn and unclosed at the distal end mirror a feeling of little control over the expression of one's impulses (see Figure 7). One deteriorated, back-ward, schizophrenic, with the intuitive sensitivity of one whose formerly unconscious processes have flooded into consciousness, commented in reference to his drawn Tree with its open-ended branches: "This is a picture of me, with no control over what comes out of me, the things that I do."

Branches that are drawn so that they actually look more phallic-like than branch-like, are offered by those with sexual preoccupations and/or virility strivings.

Broken branches and cut-off branches depict the subject's feelings of being traumatized and not a complete unit within himself. Feelings of "castration" exist, whether on a psychosocial level resulting in feelings of inadequacy, helplessness, and enforced passivity, or on a psychosexual level where feelings range from lack of virility to impotency.

If the Tree trunk itself is truncated, and tiny branches grow from the stump, it is the core of the self which is felt to be damaged. I have seen this depiction only twice, in both cases from children with whom I had begun therapeutic collaboration. This type of Tree drawing reflected stunted emotional growth, but with beginning—although tentative and rather feeble—efforts at regrowth, stimulated, perhaps, by the initial phase of the therapeutic relationship.[7]

Buck (3a) reports a similar experience: A middle-aged neurotic patient having a very rough climateric, received testosterone; following this, his previous large and branch-bare trunk was adorned with tiny, lacy, one-dimensional limbs.

Branches that turn inward toward the Tree instead of reach outward toward the environment reflect egocentricity, and strong introverted, ruminating tendencies. Thus far, this portrayal has been seen only in obsessive-compulsives.

An overly large branch structure placed on top of a relatively tiny Tree trunk suggests an overemphasis on satisfaction seeking. This was most recently seen in the drawing of a subject the writer tested one week-day evening.

The patient gave a rather rich and lengthy projective protocol, and it was midnight before we were finished with the entire battery. The patient asked if he might phone his wife, and I offered him my apologies to add to what I thought would be his own for going home so late. It was with some surprise that I learned that he was phoning his wife to discuss whether to meet at the Stork Club or the Twenty-One Club, at one A.M., to begin the evening. When I inquired as to the time of his business appointments the following day, he replied quite casually, "Nine o'clock." His frantic pleasure seeking, in his efforts to quiet, or at least mask, the inner voice of doubt concerning his essential feelings of worth and significance (the tiny Tree trunk), supported the interpreta-

---

[7] One of these cases interrupted therapy when she moved to another city, but the other drew a Tree, at the completion of therapy, whose full bloom expressed her returned feeling of capability, fulfillment, and optimism regarding future growth.

tion (over-emphasis on satisfaction seeking) his overbalanced branch structure suggested.

If the opposite extreme occurs, i.e., a tiny branch structure topping an overly large trunk, it tends to imply that the subject experiences frustration due to an inability to satisfy strong basic needs.

This type of Tree was recently produced by a twenty-two-year-old woman who had been married but a short time before her husband was drafted. Feelings of sexual, as well as emotional, frustration also pervaded her Rorschach and TAT protocols.

In children's drawings particularly, branches are sometimes drawn reaching appealingly to the sun. This has occurred in the drawings of those youngsters who have shown other evidence of marked and frustrated needs for affection. The Tree stretches out its arms hungrily for the warmth from some significant authority figure (in this case, represented by the sun) for which the subject is starved.

Occasionally a child will draw a Tree as bending away from a large and low-placed sun, drawn as bearing down upon the Tree. This depiction is offered by subjects who shy way from domination by a parental, or other authority, figure who makes the subject feel painfully controlled, subjugated, and inadequate.

Before leaving the section devoted to the discussion of the branches, a relatively rare, but symbolically clear, treatment deserves mention: secondary branches drawn spike-like and imbedded like thorns into the flesh of the primary branches. The points of the secondary branches, rather than being at the outer end, are at the point of contact with the Tree trunk or with the branches from which they grow. These small branches appear to dig into, rather than grow from, the larger branches. The reader has correctly anticipated the interpretation of masochistic tendencies.

The writer recalls one such instance in a drawing made by a woman who at one time was complaining of the inconvenience resulting from the plumbing in her kitchen being out-of-order and of the many times within a few days she had had to call in the plumber. "If I have to call him just once more . . ." (and the writer expected to hear the sentence finished with some extrapunitively directed expression of her anger not too far short of hitting the plumber over the head with the kitchen sink) . . . "I'll pull *my* hair out." The intrapunitive direction of the release of her aggression was consistent with the masochistic orientation apparent in her branch treatment.

Midway between an intrapunitive and extrapunitive role in life, a predominantly impunitive subject may portray his orientation by wrapping the ends of his branches in cloudlike balls. The hard expression of the branch is covered up, as though wrapped in a cushioning pad of cotton. Although aggression with this person is not discharged inward, inhibitions prevent its discharge outward. Pleasant manners and a soft-spoken way frequently accompany this "impunitive branch treatment."

In a general way, the overall impression conveyed by the branches correlates with the broad personality setting of the subject, whether the branch or foliage treatment is composed of lively, animated and soft effects, or angular, harsh and stern outlines, or jerky, irritable, anxious and insecure treatment — the drawing page serves as a canvas upon which the subject sketches his more enduring personality mood.

*"Keyhole" Tree:* The depiction of the trunk and foliage area as if by one continuous line, without a line separating the crown from the trunk, is so called because of its resemblance to a keyhole. Actually the presentation is one of enclosed, unrelieved white space, and like the *Space* response on the Rorschach, has been found to be offered by oppositional and negativistic subjects. In drawing this type of Tree, subjects are complying with the examiner's request, but only in a minimal manner. Such subjects do the least they can short of refusing outright to render the drawing.

*"Split" Tree:* The name for this drawing response comes from the fact that the sidelines of the trunk do not have any lines connecting them to each other; they extend upward, each one forming its own independent branch structure (see Figure 8). The impression is that of a Tree split vertically down the

middle, giving the appearance of two one-dimensional Trees side-by-side. It suggests a shattering of personality, dissociation of major personality components, a breakdown in defenses and the danger of inner impulses spilling over into the outer environment. If there is any single sign in the H-T-P which can be regarded as pathognomonic of schizophrenia, it is this one. Koch (9, p. 80), in addition to Buck (3), has observed this "splitting" of the Tree as an index of schizophrenia.

*Theme:* The implications of a sense of doom in the drawing of a Tree with a buzzard hovering over it; the utter lack of worth, abysmally low self-esteem and sense of degradation apparent in the drawing of a Tree with a dog urinating on it; and the terror of a feeling of imminent bodily mutilation conveyed by the drawing of a Tree with a man identified as a father-figure threatening total destruction by chopping upon it are self-explanatory.

Pregnant women, we have found, to a noteworthy degree offer fruit trees, and depressed patients show a propensity for weeping willows.

Young children will frequently draw apple trees; the frequency is 35 per cent at the kindergarten age, 9 per cent by the tenth year of age, and close to nothing by the fourteenth year of life (9). With young children, the identification is apparently with the fruit of the Tree, the Tree itself representing the mother-figure, for we find that children who suffer from feelings of rejection will draw one apple as falling (having been cast off), or having fallen, from the Tree.

*Age Ascribed to the Tree:* The implications of feelings of immaturity apparent in an adult's drawing of a tiny sapling rather than a full-grown Tree are clear. To get a more refined index, however, of the developmental level meant to be conveyed by the drawn Tree, when the subject is finished he is asked how old a Tree his drawing represents. Our experience suggests that the age projected is related to the felt level of psycho-social-sexual maturity of the subject. This was supported by an experimental study (6) conducted by the writer.

Sixty-four sex offenders at Sing Sing Prison served as subjects, half of them had been convicted of the offense of rape of an adult female, and the other half of a sexual approach toward a female child (pedophilia). The rapists served as a contrast group to the pedophiles in regard to such factors as the experience of having been detected, tried and incarcerated for a sexual offense as well as living in a more or less common prison environment at the time of the study.

Clinical investigation (8) has shown that pedophiles are people who feel psychosexually immature. They are fixated on, or regressed to, a childhood level—a level at which sexual urges, normative studies tell us, are expressed in the form of mutual seeing, touching and manual manipulation. These practices are the extent of the sexual activities of the overwhelming majority of the pedophiles. Because of his immaturity, when the pedophile's sexual needs clamor for release, he seeks out immature sex objects of approximately the age at which he himself feels psychosexually adapted. In his sex play, he attempts to choose *another* child—as it were—as his companion.

If we grant this assumption, then, that the pedophile approaches children, whereas the rapist approaches adults, because the pedophile feels psychosexually more immature than the rapist, a comparison of the ages ascribed to the drawn Trees by both groups would allow us to investigate the validity of Buck's (3) hypothesis concerning *the age ascribed to the Tree as a reflection of the subject's felt psychosexual maturity level.*

The results were highly significant and in the predicted direction. The mean age assigned to their Trees by the rapists was 24.4 years, whereas that of the pedophiles was 10.6 years. The age ascribed to the drawn Tree differentiates the pedophiles from the rapists at the one per cent level of confidence, and serves to support Buck's hypothesis.

***Tree Depicted as Dead:*** A question in the Post-Drawing Interrogation is aimed at eliciting the subject's feelings concerning the live or dead quality of his Tree. Subjects who respond to the question, "Is that Tree alive?" by indicating that the Tree is dead have been found to be significantly maladjusted. This response is most prevalent in the withdrawn, the schizophrenic, the depressed, and the severely neurotic who have given up hope of ever achieving a comfortable adjustment. Hence, its occurrence is of negative prognostic significance, as are all other signs suggesting feelings of futility.

In another study on sex offenders (7), the writer found that there was an increasing progression from rapists to heterosexual pedophiles to homosexual pedophiles in regard to the number who saw their drawn Trees as "dead" which parallels the increasing distance from an appropriate sex object. On the one hand, these parallel data tend to support the view that the sickest people psychologically see their drawn Tree as "dead," and, on the other hand, tend to describe the hemosexual pedophiles, who deviate from the norm in *both* age and sex of the partner chosen, as the sickest sub-group of sex offenders studied. An increasing distance from an appropriate sex object goes hand-in-hand with an increase in the likelihood of serious psychopathology. And the occurrence of "dead" Trees on the H-T-P is supported as an index of the likelihood of serious pathology.

In the Post-Drawing Inquiry, if the Tree is said to be dead we are interested in finding out whether the death is perceived as caused by something external or something internal. If the death of the Tree is said to have been caused by such things as parasites, wind, elements, lightning, etc., the subject holds something in the outer environment responsible for his difficulties, and usually suffers acutely from feelings of traumatization. If the death is said to have been caused by something internal such as rotting of the roots, trunk or limbs, the subject regards his self as unwholesome and unacceptable. Generally the writer found much more intense pathology and guilt to be present in those who perceive the Tree as rotting away from the inside than in those who see the Tree as killed by outside agents.

All else being equal, the prognosis is generally better when the damage is ascribed to external agents. If the Tree is perceived as "dead," the subject is asked how long ago it may have died. It has been found that the time said to have elapsed since the death of the Tree can serve as a clue to the relative duration of the subject's feelings of maladjustment, disability, or massive feeling of futility and loss of hope, whichever the case may be.

In ending this section on the discussion of the Tree it is perhaps appropriate to do so with a word of caution: "It is admittedly not always possible to make sure, from the drawing alone, which of the possible meanings is correct in the individual case. Some meanings, naturally, are always correct in a general formulation; others, on the contrary, are provisionally to be regarded as indications, the more exact meaning being discovered in a full examination, from the results of inquiry, of observation, of test findings, etc." (9, p. 33).

### Person

The Person is that concept in the House-Tree-Person Test which is most often submitted incompletely or rejected entirely; it is the least commonly debased because it is most "close to home" as a self-portrait. Since it is at times the most difficult to draw, it may arouse in the subject a fear of failure, particularly the subject who feels he will not do adequately on this "test." Hence, it is during the drawing of the Person that the subject most frequently needs emotional support from the examiner.

In regard to theme, the drawing of a Person tends to elicit principally three types: a self-portrait, an ideal-self, and a depiction of one's perception of significant others (parents, siblings, etc):

(a) A self-portrait depicting what the subject feels himself to be. Body contours, whether obese or thin, physiological areas of sensitivity such as a hooked nose, a cauliflower ear, a pockedmarked skin, or a club foot are often reproduced faithfully and exactly in the drawn Person. Subjects of average or below average I.Q. will usually reproduce these features upon their drawn Persons in mirror image, i.e., if the subject has a withered right hand, he will reproduce this condition on the drawn Person's left hand. Abstract ability allows the non-mirror image depiction (i.e., the subject's right side to be portrayed by the drawn Person's right side) and is seldom found in subjects of less than high average intelligence.

It has been noticed that physiological flaws or physical disabilities are reproduced in the drawing of the Person *only* if they have impinged upon the subject's self-concept and have created an area of psychological sensitivity.

Along with his projection of feelings of physical defects, the subject *also projects his assets:* broad shoulders, muscular development, attractive physiognomy; this is done to the point where even in artistically incapable individuals, an amazing likeness frequently results.

In addition to the physical self, the subject projects a picture of the psychological self into his drawing of the Person. Subjects of adequate or superior height may draw a tiny figure, with arms dangling rather helplessly away from the sides and a beseeching facial expression. Here, the subject is projecting his psychological view of himself as tiny, insignificant, helpless, dependent and in need of support, his physical self not withstanding.

A helplessly compliant adult male, living at home and controlled by a domineering mother drew for his Person a puppet with strings attached.

A nine-year-old boy, drew a football dummy for his Person. The social worker reported that as punishment, the boy was often deprived of food and severely whipped with a cat-of-nine-tails. When he was enuretic he was put into cold water to be taught a lesson. While his mother was at work, he was frequently beaten by his older brother. Hence, in his self-concept, he portrays his unconscious view of himself as a "football dummy" whose only function, we may deduce, is to absorb punishment. (See Chapter 2.)

The self-disdain of one subject was reflected by his drawing "a man asking for a handout" as his Person. His feelings of futility about matching up to the expectations of the male role were made apparent in the drawing of a man with clothes much too large for him, clothes hanging essentially unfilled from his shoulders.

Other examples are: the aggressive simian-like Person drawn by a rapist; the toppling Person losing equilibrium offered by a pre-schizophrenic; the manikin-like clothes dummy suggesting feelings of depersonalization; the adolescent's drawn Person carrying a baseball bat in one hand, a tennis racket in the other and wearing a mustache on his lip, revealing by his yearning for so many badges of virility, his underlying feelings of inadequacy in this area; the exhibitionistic female subject who managed to expose a good deal of her drawn female Person by the expedient of having a strong gust of wind blowing the drawn Person's skirt over her head; the drawing of a clown as a fusion of the subject's attempts to depict the harmlessness of his instinctual impulses and his secondary use of this concept in an attention-getting maneuver; the reduced energy and drive suggested by a draw Person slumped into an arm chair rather than standing on his feet (as is statistically the norm) and the need for emotional warmth and security implied by the placing of the seated figure in front of a conspicuously-detailed roaring fireplace; the narcissism reflected by the drawing of a woman with her hands thrust ecstatically in her hair, while dancing alone to music (supported by the Rorschach response: "Animal looking at his reflection in the water"); and a paranoid's drawing of a male with rigidly erect body, with the side of the body presented to the viewer depicting both the subject's refusal to face reality squarely and his rigid unadaptiveness—all these themes support the thesis that the drawn Person may represent a psychological self-portrait.

(b) An ego-ideal rather than a picture of what the subject presently feels himself to be.

A slender, rather frail, intensely paranoid male drew a boxer whose shoulders, before he was through, extended to the dimensions of a Hercules.

An unmarried, pregnant, young girl, suffering feelings of terrible shame in regard to the stomach contour which was so revealing of her condition drew a lithe, graceful, slender dancer twirling unencumbered by any burden.

Adolescent boys frequently draw muscular athletes attired in bathing suits, and adolescent girls draw female movie star figures wearing evening gowns—the ideal states for which the adolescents of both sexes long.

With patients who come into therapy with obesity as their presenting symptom, I have found that those who still cling to their ego-ideal (i.e., draw a slim rather than an obese Person) have a considerably better prognosis.

(c) A depiction of a significant person in the subject's contemporary or past environment, usually because of either strong positive or negative valence for the subject.

The pressing forward onto the drawing page of the subject's perception of significant figures in the environment, in contrast to the perception of one's self,[8] occurs more often in the drawings of children than of adolescents or adults. And the Person children represent in their drawing is almost invariably a parental figure. The occurrence of the depiction of one's view of a parental figure more frequently in the drawings of children than of adults probably represents the greater importance of the parent to the child's life, the child's need for a model to identify with, incorporate into his self-concept, and after whom to pattern himself.[9] Thus, the kind of perception of mother- or father-figure the child reveals in his drawing is frequently a prophesying element predicting the traits which retest drawings, years later, indicate the child incorporates.

One eight-year-old boy, referred because of excessive bullying of his classmates, drew a man, menacing in every aspect: bared teeth sharpened to a point, a club in one hand, and the other hand coming to an end not in conventional fingers but in a clear depiction of what looked like the ends of scissors—a weapon which might shear off and do damage to vital parts of the subject. The social worker's investigation of the father revealed that he was a despot in every way, cruel, punitive and domineering. The bullying attitudes the subject had picked up suggested that he had already begun to defend himself against .the threat of the destruction-invested father through the universal mechanism of incorporation. In an understandable self-protective maneuver he donned his enemy's cloak so that he could put himself out of harm's way. He became the bully, rather than the bullied. The process of incorporation became the bridge across which the subject sought to travel to comparative safety.

In this manner, projective drawings tend to reveal the felt

---

[8] At times both may occur simultaneously in the same drawing yielding a fused image of self and others.

[9] Adults who produce parental figures for their drawn Persons are usually found to be "past-ridden," never having fully achieved independence from parental control.

Plate III

Plate III (*Continued*)

self, the ideal self, and—one is tempted to say—the future self (barring the intervention of psychotherapy or significant changes in the environmental situation).

At this point, the reader is referred to Chapter 4 on Figure Drawing by Sidney Levy for a discussion of the significance of various elements within the drawn Person.[10]

Before concluding the present chapter, we may profitably glance at the sets of drawings in Plate III which are borrowed from one of Buck's manuals (3) as a sampling of drawings from "normal" subjects.

The drawings are of adult subjects of different intelligence levels ranging from "Imbecile" to "Superior." Secondary neurotic elements in some of the drawings might be pointed out in passing: the occurrence of multiple chimneys, the anxiety-steeped shading of the Tree on the "adult average" level, and the seated figure suggesting a certain lethargy and dampening of vitality with pipe added in possible compensatory fashion. All in all, the drawings represent relatively efficient personality functioning at the different intelligence levels. They may serve as a rough frame of reference from which to judge deviant drawing treatments.

The projective drawing of House, Tree and Persons, the verbal responses to the Post-drawing Inquiry period, the repeated drawing of the House, Tree and Persons, this time with crayon (see chapter on the Chromatic H-T-P), and the responses to the Post-drawing Inquiry following the chromatic drawings, with pertinent indications provided by other tests, and with orienting biographical data, provide a pool of information from which it is possible to estimate—at least grossly, at times more specifically—the areas of the subject's conflicts and the type and adequacy of his adaptive operations. Within the frame of reference of the individual psychological analysis of the subject's entire mode of functioning, projective drawings provide an opportunity for the psychologist to raise the shade on the window to the patient's inner personality.

## REFERENCES

1. Bender, Lauretta: *Child Psychiatric Techniques.* Springfield, Thomas, 1952.
2. Buck, J. N.: The H-T-P technique: A quantitative and qualitative scoring manual. *Clin. Psychol. Mono.,* 5:1-120, 1948.
3. Buck, J. N.: *The House-Tree-Person Test.* Colony, Virginia, 1947.
3a. Buck, J. N.: Personal communication.

---

[10] When the writer received Levy's chapter, he noticed such close consistency and congruent agreement concerning the various drawing items that, in the interest of space economy, the corresponding section of the writer's treatment of the H-T-P technique was deleted. The independent confirmation of that area of overlap of the two projective drawing approaches, originating in different geographic areas, is reassuring.

4. Eng, Helga: *The Psychology of Children's Drawings.* London, Kegan Paul, Ltd., 1954.

4a. Frankel, A.: Personal communication.

5. Griffiths, Ruth: *A Study of Imagination in Early Childhood.* London, Kegan Paul, Trench, Trubner & Co., 1935.

6. Hammer, E. F.: A comparison of H-T-P's of rapists and pedophiles. *J. Proj. Tech., 18:*346-354, 1954.

7. Hammer, E. F.: A comparison of H-T-P's of rapists and pedophiles: the "dead" tree as an index of Psychopathology. *J. Clin. Psychol., 11:*67-69, 1955.

7a. Hammer, E. F.: The role of the H-T-P in the prognostic battery. *J. Clin. Psychol., 9:*371-374, 1953.

8. Hammer, E. F., and Glueck, B. C.: Psychodynamic patterns in the sex offender, in Hoch, P. H., and Zubin, J.: *Psychiatry and The Law.* New York, Grune & Stratton, 1955.

9. Koch, C.: *The Tree Test.* New York, Grune & Stratton, 1952.

10. Levine, M., and Galanter, E.: A note on the "tree and trauma" in interpretation in the H-T-P. *J. Consult. Psychol., 17:*74-75, 1953.

11. Levy, S.: Figure drawing as a projective test, in Abt, L., and Bellak, L. (eds).: *Projective Psychology.* New York, Knopf, 1950, pp. 257-297.

12. Machover, Karen: *Personality Projection in the Drawing of the Human Figure.* Springfield, Thomas, 1949.

13. Pichon Rivière, A. A.: El juega de construir casas: su interpretacion ye su valor diagnostico. *Rev. psicoanál., 7:*347-388, 1950.

14. Rosen, F.: Darstallende kunst im kindesalter der volker. *ZAngPs, 1:*93-118, 1907.

15. Schactel. E. G.: Projection and its relation to character attitudes and creativity in the kinesthetic responses. *Psychiatry, 13:*69-100, 1950.

16. Schilder, P.: *Image and Appearance of the Human Body.* London, Kegan Paul, 1935.

## H-T-P BIBLIOGRAPHY [11]

Beck, H. S.: A study of the differences between normals and mentally handicapped organics in the drawing of the house. Unpublished manuscript.

Beck, H. S.: A study of the applicability of the H-T-P to children with respect to the drawn house. *J. Clin. Psychol., 11:*60-63, 1955.

Bieliauskas, V. J.: Current and proposed research designed to validate the H-T-P. Paper read at *Am. Psychol. A.,* Cleveland, September, 1953.

Bieliauskas, V. J.:   Theory and method in H-T-P research (abstract.) *Virginia J. Sc., 4:*321-322, 1954.

Bieliauskas, V. J., and Pennington, L. W. Jr.: Developmental trends in children's H-T-P drawings of a person (abstract). *Virginia J. Sc., 4:*323, 1954.

Bieliauskas, V. J. (chairman), Brown, F., Hammer, E. F., Landisberg, Selma, Machover, Karen, and Piotrowski, Z. A.: An evaluation of the H-T-P in relation to other projective techniques. Symposium at the East. Psychol. A., Philadelphia, April, 1955.

---

[11] Compiled by V. J. Bieliauskas.

Bieliauskas, V. J.: Scorer's reliability in the quantitative scoring of the H-T-P technique. *J. Clin. Psychol.*, in press.

Boring, R. O., and Topper, R. C.: *A Psychodiagnostic Screening Technique.* V. A. Hospital, Tuscaloosa, Alabama, 1949, pp. 24-30 (mimeographed).

Brown, F.: A statistical analysis of some inter-relationships between discrete wholes of the H-T-P Test. Paper read at *Am. Psychol. A.*, Washington, D.C., September, 1952.

Brown, F.: House-Tree-Person and Human Figure Drawings, in Brower, D., and Apt, L. E. (eds.): *Progress in Clinical Psychology*, Vol. 1. New York, Grune & Stratton, 1952, pp. 173-184.

Buck, J. N.: JNB drawing test. *Virginia Ment. Hyg. Surv., 2:* No. 12, 1940.

Buck, J. N.: The use of psychological tests in institutional personnel work. *Am. J. Ment. Deficiency, 4:*559-564, 1941.

Buck, J. N.: The H-T-P: a measure of adult intelligence and a projective device. *Virginia Ment. Hyg. Surv., 9:*3-5, 1946.

Buck, J. N.: The H-T-P, a measure of adult intelligence and a projective device. *Am. Psychologist, 1:*285-286, 1946, (abstract).

Buck, J. N.: *The H-T-P.* A projective device and a measure of adult intelligence. Lynchburg State Colony, Virginia, 1947 (mimeographed manual).

Buck, J. N.: The H-T-P, a projective device. *Am. J. Ment. Deficiency, 51:*606-610, 1947.

Buck, J. N.: The H-T-P Test. *J. Clin. Psychol., 4:*151-159, 1948.

Buck, J. N.: The H-T-P technique; a qualitative and quantitative scoring manual. *J. Clin. Psychol., 4:*317-396, 1948.

Buck, J. N.: The H-T-P technique: a qualitative and quantitative scoring manual. *Monogr. Suppl., J. Clin. Psychol.*, No. 5, 1948.

Buck, J. N.: The use of the H-T-P in personality analysis. *Am. Psychologist, 3:* 284, 1948 (abstract).

Buck, J. N.: The H-T-P technique. *J. Clin. Psychol., 5:*37-74, 1949.

Buck, J. N.: The present and future status of the psychologist in the field of mental deficiency. *Am. J. Ment. Deficiency, 2:*225-229, 1949.

Buck, J. N.: *Administration and Interpretation of the H-T-P Test: Proceedings of the H-T-P Workshop held at Veterans Administration Hospital, Richmond 19, Virginia, March 31, April 1, 2, 1950.* (Better known as: *The Richmond Proceedings*). California, Western Psychological Services, 1950 (mimeographed).

Buck, J. N.: The use of the H-T-P in differential diagnosis in mental deficiency. Paper read at Am. Psychol. A., Pennsylvania State Coll., September, 1950.

Buck, J. N.: The use of the House-Tree-Person Test in a case of marital discord. *J. Proj. Tech., 14:*405-434, 1950.

Buck, J. N.: Directions for administration of the achromatic-chromatic H-T-P. *J. Clin. Psychol., 7:*274-276, 1951.

Buck, J. N.: The quality of the quantity of the H-T-P. *J. Clin. Psychol., 7:*352-356, 1951.

Buck, J. N.: Una descripcion breve de la tecnica C-A-P. *Rev. psicol. gen. apl.*, Madrid, 7:11-28, 1952.

Buck, J. N.: Tests of personality: picture and drawing techniques. D. House-Tree-Person drawing technique, in A. Weider (ed.): *Contributions Toward Medical Psychology; Theory and Psychodiagnostic Methods.* New York, Ronald, 1953, pp. 688-701.

Butler, J. M., and Fiske, D. W.: Theory and techniques of assessment, in C. P. Stone and Q. McNemar (eds.): *Annual Review of Psychology*, Vol. 6. California, Annual Reviews, 1955, pp. 327-356.

Cowden, R. C., Deabler, H. L., and Feamster, J. H.: The prognostic value of the Bender-Gestalt, H-T-P, TAT, and Sentence Completion Test. *J. Clin. Psychol.*, 11:271-275, 1955.

Deabler, H. L.: The H-T-P in clinical practice with adults. Paper read at Am. Psychol. A., Cleveland, September, 1953.

Demming, J. A.: The H-T-P test as an aid in the diagnosis of psychopathic personality. Unpublished master's thesis, Kent State. Univ., 1949.

Diamond, S.: The house and tree in verbal fantasy: I. Age and sex differences in themes and content. *J. Proj. Tech.*, 18:316-325, 1954.

Diamond, S.: The house and tree in verbal fantasy: II. Their different roles. *J. Proj. Tech.*, 18:414-417, 1954.

Digiammo, J. J.: Relationship between performance on visual-form perception measures and drawings on the H-T-P technique. Unpublished master's thesis, Richmond Professional Inst., 1955.

Duffy, F. X.: The development of form concepts in the drawing of a tree by children: kindergarten through the ninth grade. Unpublished master's thesis, Richmond Professional Inst., 1953.

Ellis, A., and Rosen, E.: H-T-P: a projective device and a measure of adult intelligence, in O. K. Buros (ed.): *The Fourth Mental Measurements Yearbook.* New Jersey, Gryphon Press, 1953; pp. 178-181.

Freed, H., and Pastor, Joyce T.: Evaluation of the Draw-A-Person Test (modified) in thalamotomy with particular reference to the body image. *J. Nerv. & Ment. Dis.*, 114:106-120, 1951.

Gibson, Katherine V.: Maturation of perspective in children's drawings of houses. Unpublished study, School of Clinical and Applied Psychology, Richmond Professional Inst.

Guenzburg, H. C.: Maladjustment as expressed in drawings by subnormal children. *Am. J. Ment. Deficiency*, 57:9-23, 1952.

Guertin, W. H., and Sloan, W.: A comparison of H-T-P and Wechsler-Bellevue IQ's in mental defectives. *J. Clin. Psychol.*, 4:424-426, 1948.

Hammer, E. F.: An investigation of sexual symbolism: a study of H-T-P's of eugenically sterilized subjects. *J. Proj. Tech.*, 17:401-413, 1953.

Hammer, E. F.: Frustration-aggression hypothesis extended to socio-racial areas: comparison of Negro and white children's H-T-P's. *Psychiat. Quart.*, 27:597-607, 1953.

Hammer, E. F.: Negro and white children's personality adjustment as revealed by a comparison of their drawings (H-T-P). *J. Clin. Psychol.*, 9:7-10, 1953.

Hammer, E. F.: The possible effects of projective testing upon overt behavior. *J. Psychol.*, 36:357-362, 1953.

Hammer, E. F.: The role of the H-T-P in the prognostic battery. *J. Clin. Psychol.*, 9:371-374, 1953.

Hammer, E. F.: A comparison of H-T-P's of rapists and pedophiles. *J. Proj. Tech.*, 18:346-354, 1954.

Hammer, E. F.: Comparison of the performances of Negro children and adolescents on two tests of intelligence, one an emergency scale. *J. Genet. Psychol.*, 84:85-93, 1954.

Hammer, E. F.: Guide for qualitative research with the H-T-P. *J. Genet. Psychol.,* 51:41-60, 1954.

Hammer, E. F.: Relationship between diagnosis of psychosexual pathology and the sex of the first drawn person. *J. Clin. Psychol.,* 10:168-170, 1954.

Hammer, E. F.: A comparison of H-T-P's of rapists and pedophiles; III. The "dead" tree as an index of psychopathology. *J. Clin. Psychol.,* 11:67-69, 1955.

Hammer, E. F.: *The H-T-P Clinical Research Manual.* California, Western Psychological Services, 1955.

Hammer, E. F., and Piotrowski, Z. A.: Hostility as a factor in the clinician's personality as it affects his interpretation of projective drawings (H-T-P). *J. Proj. Tech.,* 17:210-216, 1953.

Hammer, E. F.: *Projective Drawing Interpretation.* Springfield, Thomas, 1957.

Harris, D. B.: Child psychology in C. P. Stone and D. W. Taylor (eds.): *Annual Review of Psychology,* Vol. 4. California, Annual Reviews, 1954, pp. 1-30.

Hurley, J. F.: The H-T-P as a rigidity-flexibility indicator. Paper read at South. Soc. Phil. & Psychol., Roanoke, Va., March, 1951.

Jolles, I.: *A Catalogue for the Qualitative Interpretation of the H-T-P.* Beverly Hills, California, Western Psychological Services, 1952.

Jolles, I.: A study of the validity of some hypotheses for the qualitative interpretation of the H-T-P for children of elementary school age: I. Sexual identification. *J. Clin. Psychol.,* 8:113-118, 1952.

Jolles, I.: A study of the validity of some hypotheses for the qualitative interpretation of the H-T-P for children of elementary school age: II. The "phallic tree" as an indicator of psycho-sexual conflict. *J. Clin. Psychol.,* 8:245-255, 1952.

Jolles, I., and Beck, H. S.: A study of the validity of some hypotheses for the qualitative interpretation of the H-T-P for children of elementary school age: III. Horizontal placement. *J. Clin. Psychol.,* 9:161-164, 1953.

Jolles, I., and Beck, H. S.: A study of the validity of some hypotheses for the qualitative interpretation of the H-T-P for children of elementary school age: IV: Vertical placement. *J. Clin. Psychol.,* 9:164-167, 1953.

Kelly, E. L.: Theory and techniques of assessment, in C. P. Stone and Q. McNemar (eds.): *Annual Review of Psychology,* Vol. 5, California, Annual Reviews, 1954, pp. 281-310.

Kirkham, Sandra L.: The identification of organicity using the House-Tree-Person Test on an institutionalized population. Unpublished master's thesis, Richmond Professional Inst., 1956.

Krugman, M., and Wilcox, Katherine W.: H-T-P: house, tree, and person: a measure of adult intelligence and a projective device: preliminary edition, in O. K. Buros (ed.): *The Third Mental Measurements Yearbook.* New Jersey, Rutgers Univ. Press, 1949, pp. 84-86.

Landisberg, Selma: A study of the H-T-P Test. *Train. Sch. Bull.,* 44:140-152, 1947.

Landisberg, Selma: A personality study of institutionalized epileptics. *Am. J. Ment. Deficiency,* 52:16-22, 1947.

Landisberg, Selma: Relationship of the Rorschach to the H-T-P. *J. Clin. Psychol.,* 9:179-183, 1953.

Leach, Joy: An analysis of the use of space constriction in drawings of the house on H-T-P Test by children by means of a space constriction index. Unpublished study, School of Clinical and Applied Psychology, Richmond Professional Inst., 1953.

Levine, A., Abramson, H. A., Kaufman, M. R., Markham, S., and Kornetsky, C.: Lysergic acid diethylamide (LSD-25): XIV. Effect on personality as observed in psychological tests. *J. Psychol., 40:*351-366, 1955.

Levine, A., Abramson, H. A., Kaufman, M. R., and Markham, S.: Lysergic acid diethylamide (LSD-25): XVI. The effect on intellectual functioning as measured by the Wechsler-Bellevue intelligence scale. *J. Psychol., 40:*385-395, 1955.

Levine, M., and Galanter, E.: A note on the "tree and trauma" interpretation in the H-T-P. *J. Consult. Psychol., 17:*74-75, 1953.

Lyons, J.: The scar on the H-T-P tree. *J. Clin. Psychol., 11:*267-270, 1955.

Markham, Sylvia: An item analysis of children's drawings of a house. *J. Clin. Psychol., 10:*185-187, 1954.

Meyer, B. C., Brown, F., and Levine, A.: Observations on the House-Tree-Person Drawing Test before and after surgery. *Psychosom. Med., 6:*428-454, 1955.

Michal-Smith, H.: The identification of pathological cerebral function through the H-T-P technique. *J. Clin. Psychol., 9:*293-295, 1953.

Morris, W. W.: Other projective methods, in H. H. Anderson, and Gladys L. Anderson (eds.): *An Introduction to Projective Techniques.* New York, Prentice Hall, 1951, pp. 513-538.

Nazario-Ortiz, I.: Quantitative differences between Puerto-Rican and resident American college students on H-T-P drawings. Unpublished master's thesis, Richmond Professional Inst., 1956.

Payne, J. T.: Comments on the analysis of chromatic drawings. *J. Clin. Psychol., 5:*75-76, 1949.

Payne, J. T.: *Observations on the Use of Color with the H.T.P.* Morganton, North Carolina, North Carolina State Hospital, 1950 (Mimeographed).

Payne, J. T.: The drawing process and the hue-space unit. Unpublished manuscript.

Pennington, L. W., Jr.: Space constriction in drawings of a person on the H-T-P test by children from 4 years 6 months to 14 years 5 months of age. Unpublished study, School of Clinical and Applied Psychology, Richmond Professional Institute, 1953.

Pennington, L. W., Jr.: Developmental patterns in drawings of a Person by children from the age 4½ to 15. Unpublished master's thesis, Richmond Professional Inst., 1954.

Perkinson, Patricia R.: Shading on the H-T-P drawings and its relationship with anxiety and intelligence. Unpublished master's thesis, Richmond Professional Inst., 1956.

Radke-Yarrow, Marian, and Yarrow, L. J.: Child psychology, in C. P. Stone and Q. McNemar (eds.): *Annual Review of Psychology,* Vol. 6. California, Annual Reviews, 1955, pp. 1-28.

Reagan, B. V., Jr.: The H-T-P Test: a reading aid, in *Claremont College Reading Conference, Fourteenth Yearbook, 1949.* Claremont, California, Claremont Conference Curriculum Laboratory, 1949, pp. 154-156.

Repucci, L. C.: A quantitative scoring system for children's drawings of a house in the H-T-P. Unpublished master's thesis, Richmond Professional Inst., 1954.

Robben, Camille S.: A study of the validity of some hypotheses for the qualitative interpretation of the H-T-P Test for children of elementary school age: vertical measurement of space constriction of the tree. Unpublished study,

School of Clinical and Applied Psychology, Richmond Professional Inst., 1953.

Rubin, H.: A quantitative study of the H-T-P and its relationship to the Wechsler-Bellevue Scale. *J. Clin. Psychol., 10*:35-38, 1954.

Sarason, S. B.: *Psychological Problems in Mental Deficiency,* 2nd Ed. New York, Harper, 1953, pp. 260-261.

Schneck, J. M., and Kline, M. V.: Clinical psychiatric status and psychological test alterations following hypnotherapy. *Brit. J. M. Hypnotism, 2*:30-41, 1950.

Schwartz, A. A.: Some interrelationships among four tests comprising a test battery: A comparative study. *J. Proj. Tech., 14*:153-172, 1950.

Siegel, J. H.: A preliminary study of the validity of the House-Tree-Person Test with children. Unpublished master's thesis, Southern Methodist Univer., 1949.

Singer, R. H.: A study of drawings produced by a group of college students and a group of hospitalized schizophrenics. Unpublished master's thesis, Pennsylvania State Coll., 1950.

Sloan, W.: A critical review of H-T-P validation studies. *J. Clin. Psychol., 10:* 143-148, 1954.

Smykal, A., and Thorne, F. C.: Etiological studies of psychopathic personality: II. Asocial type. *J. Clin. Psychol., 7*:299-316, 1951.

Sullivan, Anne, and Bondy, C.: Psychologische test in den Vereinigten Staaten von Amerika. *Sammlung, 3:*408-424, 1948.

Vernier, Claire M., Whiting, J. F., and Meltzer, M. L.: Differential prediction of a specific behavior from three projective techniques. *J. Consult. Psychol., 19:* 175-182, 1955.

Wagner, Nancy J.: The use of perspective in the chimney in the H-T-P drawings of children four through fourteen years. Unpublished study, School of Clinical and Applied Psychology, Richmond Professional Inst., 1953.

Waxenberg, S. E.: Psychosomatic patients and other physically ill persons: a comparative study. *J. Consult. Psychol., 3:*163-169, 1955.

Woods, W. A., and Cook, W. E.: Proficiency in drawing and placement of hands in drawings of the human figure. *J. Consult. Psychol., 18*:119-121, 1954.

Woods, W. A., and Repucci, L. C.: The developmental aspects in drawing of the house. *Virginia J. Sc., 4:*322, 1954, (abstract).

Young, Helen R.: A comparison of differences in performance on psychological tests between diploma and degree student nurses. Unpublished master's thesis, Richmond Professional Inst., 1956.

Zimmer, H.: Validity of sentence completion tests and human figure drawings, in D. Brower and L. E. Apt (eds.): *Progress in Clinical Psychology,* Vol. 2. New York, Grune & Stratton, 1956, pp. 58-75.

## CHAPTER 9

## THE CHROMATIC H-T-P, A DEEPER PERSONALITY-TAPPING TECHNIQUE

Emanuel F. Hammer, Ph.D.

Consideration of the concept of "levels" or "layers," and the reflection of these different *depths* of personality structure in projective techniques, has moved into the center of clinical concern of late (4, 9, 11, 13, 15, 18, 20, 21).

In this chapter, the writer intends to share a series of clinical observations, to the end that further study by investigators in various insitutions can eventually more firmly establish, or refute, the deductions forced upon the writer, first in an atmosphere of skepticism and ultimately in an atmosphere of increasing empirically-based conviction.

The data, a liberal sample of which is presented in this paper, suggest the deduction that the achromatic (pencil) and chromatic (crayon) drawing phases of the H-T-P actually tap somewhat different *levels* of personality. The chromatic H-T-P cuts through the defenses to lay bare a deeper level of personality than does the achromatic set of drawings, and in this manner a crude hierarchy of the subject's conflicts and his defenses is established and a richer personality picture derived.

The chromatic series is designed to supplement the achromatic series, to take advantage of the fact that two samples of behavior are always better than one. But the chromatic series is more than a second H-T-P sample because the subject who produces it must, I believe, be in a somewhat more vulnerable state than he was when he produced his achromatic drawings. Even to the best adjusted subject, the achromatic H-T-P and the subsequent searching Post-Drawing-Interrogation is an emotional experience, for many memories, pleasant and unpleasant, are aroused, at the least.

Thus the chromatic series becomes a behavioral sample that is obtained with the subject at a level of frustration that is different from that which pertained when the achromatic series was sought. If the achromatic (as it frequently is for the well-adjusted subject) was a welcome catharsis, the subject may be far less tense than he was at the beginning. In the average clinical case seen for differential diagnosis, however, this will scarcely be the case—such a subject will almost inevitably be so emotionally aroused that his chromatic series will reveal still more about his basic needs, mechanisms of defense, etc., than the achromatic, and point up the disparity between his functioning and his potential pattern of behavior.

But I shall allow the data to speak for themselves; this they do rather eloquently, I think:

## CASE ILLUSTRATIONS

### A Brief Description of the Chromatic H-T-P Administration

After the achromatic set of H-T-P drawings has been completed, the examiner substitutes a fresh set of drawing blanks for the completed set, and a set of crayons for the pencil. The pencil is taken away so that the subject is not tempted to do the outline of the drawing in pencil, and then color in the drawing as one might in a coloring book. A set of Crayola® [1] crayons are employed; the set consists of eight crayons, colored respectively, red, green, yellow, blue, brown, black, purple and orange.

The initial instructions are, "Now, will you please draw a House in crayon." with parallel requests then following for Tree and Person. The subject is purposely not asked to draw another House, another Tree or another Person, for to most subjects the word "another" would imply that they must not duplicate their achromatic drawings. The intent is to provide the subject with the widest latitude of choice.

---

[1] A popular commercial brand put out by the American Crayon Company, Sandusky, Ohio, and easily obtained at any children's toy counter or stationery store.

Case A: Achromatic

The subject is allowed to use any or all of the eight crayons, with all questions as to how he should proceed handled in a non-directive manner, thus maximizing the subject's self-structuring of the task.

In the achromatic series, the subject is afforded every opportunity to employ corrective measures: he may erase as much as he likes, and the pencil is a relatively refined drawing instrument. In the chromatic drawings, the only corrective measure available is concealment with heavy shading and the drawing instrument, the crayon, is relatively crude.

Thus, at the beginning, with the subject in as full possession of his defensive mechanisms as he will presumably be, he is given tools which permit expressive defensiveness; in the second phase, by which time the subject will be more likely to have lost at least part of his defensive control (if he is going to lose it at all), he is provided with a grosser instrument, and with an opportunity to express symbolically (through his choice and use of color) the emotions which have been aroused by the achromatic series and Post-Drawing-Interrogation.

### Case A: A Pseudo-energetic Man

The subject, a thirty-one-year-old, married male, had had two and one-half years of college and was employed as a draftsman.

Case A: Achromatic

Case A: Chromatic

Roof and chimney, shaded black; walls, brown and black; ground, brown and green.

For his achromatic House he drew a slightly pretentious and showy House, suggesting a degree of status consciousness. His achromatic female Person is depicted as dancing, conveying buoyancy and activity. The achromatic male Person is likewise a picture of energy and action. The suspicion may arise in the clinician's mind as to whether or not the subject, in Shakespeare's words, "doth protest too much" by his so emphatic underscoring of the components of energy and activity in his projections.[2] On the other hand, it is still conceivable that this may actually be a man of outstanding vitality and buoyancy, and the clinician is uncertain as to whether to take the drawings at face value or to view them as a defensive personality blanket.

The introduction of the chromatic phase of the H-T-P resolves the issue as neatly as it does dramatically.

[2] Particularly when we note the spindly shank protruding from the trouser cuff and the fact that the suit—the cloak of social behavior—fits very badly. The latter conveys the strong implication that his role is not an essentially satisfying one.

Hair, brown; blouse, green; skirt, red.

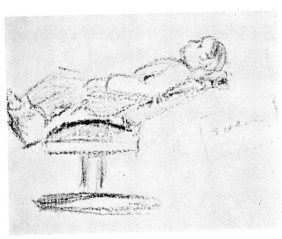

Hair, brown and black; beard, shaded brown; pants, brown and black; chair cushion, green.

Case A: Chromatic

Case B: Achromatic

On the deeper chromatic level, a crude log cabin replaces the elaborate, over-adorned, and impressive achromatic House. The patient's pretentious front collapses into a portrayal of insufficiency and, by comparison, almost abject insignificance. The picture of wealth and "have" is replaced by poverty and "have not," comfort is replaced by bare essentials, ornateness by barrenness, and an expansive, many-roomed home by a tiny, one-room log cabin. The patient's prestige-hungry front, conveyed by the achromatic drawing, which compensates for his essential lack of worth (deserving no better than a crude log cabin as a home), was also supported by his flashy dress, conspicuous jewelery, and his use of pedantic vocabulary.

His chromatic female collapses into a sitting position, and even then has not the strength to keep her head erect, but must lean it against something. A sapping of energy and drive may thus be seen to actually exist beneath the patient's energetic front. By the time the patient comes to the task of drawing the chromatic male, his basic feelings of the futility of overstriving come to the fore and he depicts a Person who reclines still further to a horizontal position, and one who is described as "sixty years old," thus reflecting a mixture of feelings of impotency, decline and decrepitude along with his underlying passivity. On deeper symbolic levels, we note that he will lose his beard and possibly be in the hands of a razor-wielding adult.

The chromatic House and two Persons are devalued concepts which mirror the subject's depression and depreciated self-concept beneath his three achromatic projections.

The underlying picture of the patient's pathology might have been largely lost without the chromatic redrawings. Similarly, the compensatory front of energy and activity, as the other side of the personality coin, is clearly demonstrated in the achromatic, more superficial, level. It is in the integration of the two levels, that the richness of the personality picture is derived.

### Case B: A Pre-psychotic Female

The subject, a thirty-six-year-old unmarried female, was referred for a psychological evaluation because the psychiatrist was in doubt about the differential diagnosis. He wished a projective examination done to help evaluate a neurotic, against a latent psychotic, picture.

Her achromatic House is presented as insecurely anchored to an amorphous cloud-like ground line. The presentation thus suggests that contact with reality, as symbolized by the ground, is at best uncertain.

The achromatic drawing of the House implies the presence of a latent psychotic condition, but it does not do so with any of the dramatic certainty of the chromatic drawing. The subject's lack of firm contact with reality on the achromatic level gives way to an

Case B: Chromatic

Sun, red; house, brown; ground, orange.

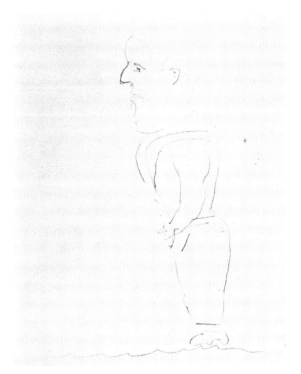

Case C: Achromatic

obvious and catastrophic loss of emotional equilibrium when a deeper personality level was tapped with the chromatic phase of the H-T-P. The House, now presented as frankly toppling over, suggests that the latent psychotic condition is of the incipient or pre-psychotic, rather than of a stabilized, chronic, form. Although the person may now be adjusting on a borderline level with the psychosis not being overt, the indications are that in the immediate future there will be a clear-cut loss of contact with reality.

The patient's subsequent confinement to an institution, four months after the administration of the psychological examination, provided empirical proof of the deeper, and prophesying, level of the chromatic drawings.

### Case C: A Pre-psychotic Male

The subject, a twenty-three-year-old, single, male, was also referred for purposes of establishing a differential diagnosis.

This case also illustrates the thesis that personality clues hinted at in the achromatic drawings, often come through full-blown, in more clear-cut fashion, in the chromatic drawings. The tenuous contact with reality, as suggested by the choppy groundline and the drawn Person's spotty contact with it, in the achromatic drawings, gives way (as with the case of the previous pre-psychotic) to a more frank loss of personality balance under the impact of color. (Also noteworthy as pathology indicators are the absolute profile and the progressively less realistic proportion from massive head to tiny feet.)

A large number of sets of drawings, which Cases B and C illustrate, have served to convince the writer that *incipient or latent psychopathological conditions are most frequently presented by being hinted at in the achromatic drawings and then more vividly and dramatically overtly portrayed in the chromatic expression.*

### Case D: An Overtly Psychotic Patient

A comparison of the achromatic and chromatic sets of drawings produced by the patient, a twenty-eight-year-old male, confined to an institution, again illustrates the relatively stronger

Case C: Chromatic

Entire drawing in brown.

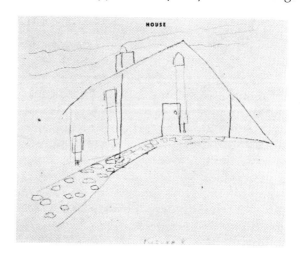

Case D: Achromatic

stimuli represented by the chromatic phase and its greater efficacy in cutting through the patient's defenses.

In spite of the psychotic process, strongly suggested by the gross distortion of reality apparent in the depiction of smoke blowing simultaneously in two directions and the window shades extending outside the window down the front of the building, a degree of personality intactness is suggested by the over-all integration of the remaining achromatic drawings which are of a progressively healthier quality. The only evidence of frank psychosis apparent in the achromatic Tree is the unusual similarity between root network and branch structure; psychotic patients occasionally offer a drawing such as this which just as appropriately represents the concept asked for if it is viewed upside down. The desperate clutching grip of the roots is suggestive of a fear of losing one's hold on reality. The personality picture which evolves from a consideration of the achromatic drawings only is one of severe maladjustment of probably psychotic proportions with certain delusional areas, but a degree of personality integration and some fair defensive resources upon which to fall back. There appears to be a degree of "give" to his personality structure, and the clinician may wonder whether when the patient is driven over the line into the borderlands of psychosis he is not able to recover and return to reality once again.

The later introduction of the chromatic drawings into the clinical consideration, however, shatters the clinician's prognostic optimism by revealing the patient's defenses to be actually paper thin.

Under the emotional impact of color, the patient's defenses do not strengthen, but totally crumble. The House disintegrates entirely, the stones composing the pathway to the door appear to float up off the ground, and the patient himself may be presumed to fall apart on the spot. The patient projects this inner feeling verbally by commenting spontaneously that the branches of the chromatic tree are "falling off." Chaotic emotional impulses are clearly indicated by his inability to contain his coloring within the outline of the drawn Tree as well as by his choice of clashing red, green, orange and yellow heaped helter-skelter onto the page. The Tree itself topples. The wind is bizarrely described as blowing not from the left and not from the right, but straight down upon the Tree from above, reflecting the terrible feelings of pressure which beset the patient. Thus, the projection of himself clinging hard to reality, as conveyed by the overemphasized

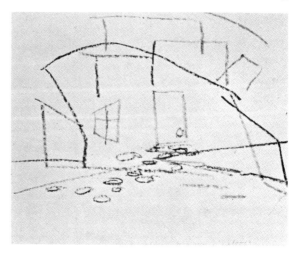

Roofline in bizarre purple; chimney, walls and windows, green; rock path, brown.

Top, orange and yellow; center, yellow and green; base, red.

Case D: Chromatic

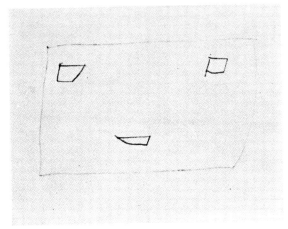

Case E: Achromatic (Figure 15)

roots of the achromatic Tree clutching at the ground, is replaced by the self-portrait of total personality collapse and disintegration on the chromatic level.

## Case E: A Mentally Defective Psychotic

Still another example of the chromatic drawing phase bringing forth into fuller relief that which generally comes through in less intense fashion in the achromatic drawings, is offered by a seventeen-year-old male psychotic functioning on an intellectual level of "imbecile" to "moron."

Case E: Chromatic (Figure 16)

Walls and windows, blue; chimneys, orange.

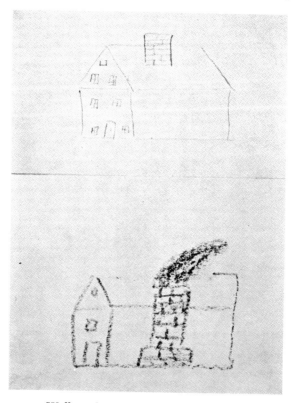

Walls and smoke, black; chimney, red.

Case F: Top, Achromatic; Bottom, Chromatic

His face-like achromatic House reflects the anthropomorphism with which psychotics will frequently endow inanimate objects. The achromatic House (Figure 15) is doused so heavily in anthropomorphism that it seems to leave no latitude for any more human quality to come through on the chromatic level. But the crayons can, and do actually, stimulate a still more anthropomorphic House: two twin, ear-like chimneys, now complete the face (Figure 16).

## Case F: An Exhibitionist

The subject, a forty-two-year-old, married male, had gotten into trouble with the law by exposing his penis to a group of twelve-year-old girls who were playing across the street from his window.

In the achromatic House, his need for drawing attention to

protuberances is hinted at by the somewhat oversized chimney. In his drawing of the chromatic House, however, his exhibitionistic needs are thrown into fuller relief by the tremendous full-length chimney, with smoke pouring forth, presented as the focus of the drawing. His choice of colors follows the same pattern of spot-lighting the phallic symbol. Black crayon is employed to devalue everything but the chimney, which he then colors in a bright, erotic, attention-getting red.

All of the above cases have been presented to carry the thesis that the chromatic level brings forth the deeper personality picture, as a rather direct contrast to the achromatic level. The cases thus far have all been examples of deeper pathology surging beneath the relatively more calmly rippling surface.

Perhaps an even more important clinical yield occurs when the chromatic drawings uncover relatively greater health, rather than sickness, within. The next two cases are presented as illustrations of this type of clinical finding.

### Case G: A Reactive Condition

The patient, a twenty-three-year-old male, was referred by a psychiatrist for personality evaluation because of recurring nightmares following an elevator accident. The accident, which occurred eight months earlier, had resulted in the loss of the patient's

Case G: Achromatic

Case G: Chromatic

Chimney, red; walls and roof, yellow; windows, green.

right leg. The achromatic House, reflecting the more recent and superficial personality picture, reflects the patient's feelings concerning precariously attached appendages by the placement of the chimney overhanging the roof in a position easily susceptible to toppling. On the deeper, chromatic level, he moves his chimney into a position of more secure footing away from the dangerous *edge* of the roof. Thus, it is suggested that the anxiety he is discharging in his nightmares is rooted in a relatively reactive, rather than earlier developmental, situation. This was subsequently supported in the psychiatrist's later therapeutic collaboration with the patient, as well as the case history data indicating loss of the patient's limb during adulthood.

### Case H: A "He-man" Character Disorder

The subject, a twenty-eight-year-old male, presents a set of drawings of a type not infrequently obtained from adolescent males.

Subjects of the adolescent age group, frequently convey, in their drawings, their need to demonstrate virility as compensation for their lack of full maturation and growth, and for their delayed attainment of status. In a subject of the patient's age, however, the persistence of such a need reflects immaturity, as well as the same compensatory character-armoring suggested by

Entire drawing in black crayon.

Case H: Top, Achromatic; Bottom, Chromatic

Case I: Achromatic

his various vocational choices which included truck driving, boxing, and during the war, volunteering for paratrooper duty.

The projective drawings were administered five years after the
patient had been in service; hence his achromatic drawing of a
soldier conveys his clinging to the self-concept of a warrior as a
badge of virile manliness. His defensive masculine strivings then
intensify and become still more frank in his chromatic drawing of
a muscular weight-lifter exhibiting his prowess. Beneath the
compensatory muscles of the drawn Person, however, exists a
somewhat short and organically less adequate frame, a hint of
the inner doubts beneath the patient's virility strivings.

Whereas the achromatic soldier suggests the twin possibilities
of either virility strivings or aggressive impulses, the chromatic
data throws the evidence on the side of the need to demonstrate
manliness.

Whereas this subject's defenses deepen on the chromatic level
(showing a consistency with the diagnosis of character disorder),
the next case presented is one whose defenses, in neurotic fashion,

give way rather than intensify as the subject proceeds from the achromatic to the chromatic levels.

### Case I: A Child in the Cloak of a Warrior

The subject's drawings proceed from the achromatic surface of an Indian brave whose conspicuous headdress testifies to his being a leader among hunters and warriors, to the deeper chromatic level which eloquently conveys the core of his self-concept: a little boy masquerading in the garb of a virile adult (i.e., wearing a sailor suit). On the achromatic level, some hint at lassitude and passivity beneath the virile front comes through in the position of the drawn Indian, who sinks into a sitting posture.[3] But

---

[3] His inner doubts concerning his virility and sexual adequacy are also reflected in his Unpleasant Concept Test where he draws what he later describes as: "A judge telling a man his wife is an adulteress. The judge has just found this out from a lab report indicating that the husband did not really conceive the child."

Case I: Chromatic

Entire drawing in green.

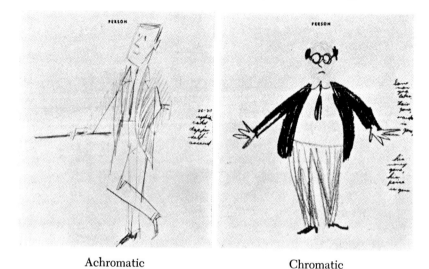

Achromatic                                    Chromatic

Hair, black; face, orange; jacket, black; tie, black; pants, brown; shoes, black.

Case J

it is in the chromatic phase that the basic person—a child playing at being a man—is seen. The "shrinkage" in size of the figure is as striking as the change in content. Once again, a hierarchy of conflict and defense has been contributed to the clinical picture.

### Case J: A Mild Case of Don Juanism

The patient, a 30-year-old, married male with two children, entered psychotherapeutic collaboration because of a heavy sense of guilt which pervaded a recent onset of extramarital activities.

The subject, for his achromatic male Person, drew a well-dressed person in a nonchalant pose, whom he then described as about his own age, or leaning a bit on the younger side (i.e., "twenty-six to thirty"), and as "sophisticated, dapper and self-assured." From merely the achromatic level, one would get little impression of the extent of the basic problem lying beneath the surface (and brought up by the impact of color). Beneath this surface impression of himself, the chromatic male which he later drew indicates that the patient is beginning inwardly to entertain grave doubts concerning his youth, vigor and virility. In the chromatic drawing, the male figure loses his confident and self-assured casualness of pose. The hands are held in a position of helpless ineffectuality, and the facial tone changes to a pathetically empty and depressed one. The achromatic Person's smile is replaced by a morose frown and his bright, alert facial expression gives way to a vacuous one. A premature fear of decline, impotency and decrepancy, associated with "old age," is dramatically conveyed in his description of the chromatic male: "This is the same man years later, his hair is gone, his money is gone, his waist is gone, and his poise is gone. (The drawing is complementary to the Rorschach response the subject gave on Card VI, of a "penis with a beard on it.")

The inner doubts generated by this self-concept appear as the motivational mainspring behind this attempt to recapture his earlier "sophisticated, dapper, self-assured" picture of himself through extramarital activities with his twenty-two-year-old secretary, his nineteen-year-old clerk, and another twenty-one-year-old woman.

In his achromatic and chromatic drawings of Trees, the two levels of his self-concept again are graphically and dramatically portrayed. Thus, his Tree drawings parallel his Person drawings. For his achromatic Tree he drew a sturdy oak which he then describes as "full-grown, stately and very solid." Beneath this surface impression of himself, he apparently inwardly harbors a self-concept actually possessed of just the opposite traits: for his chromatic Tree he draws a weeping willow (conveying his

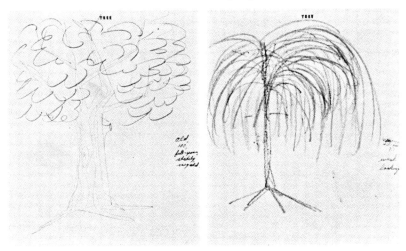

Achromatic                    Chromatic

Foliage, green and brown; trunk, brown.

**Case J**

underlying depression) which he then describes as "weak-looking."

The patient is presently panicked by the cracks he is beginning to experience in his self-esteem. The conspicuous sawed-off limb protruding from his otherwise sturdy and intact achromatic Tree might suggest that he is beginning to experience his feelings of impairment, inadequacy and "castration" on increasingly closer-to-conscious levels.

## DISCUSSION

In its concern with the deciphering of the symbolic meaning of the different individual colors in various projective art techniques, psychodiagnostic psychology has by-passed an awareness of the perhaps richer clinical yield: the tapping of the generally deeper level of the personality by chromatic, as compared to achromatic, projective drawings. The two levels thus contribute to a more definite picture of the stratification of the subject's personality structure.

The chromatic drawing phase strips away the closer-to-conscious personality layers; it more easily raises the deeper layers of the unconscious to eye-level.

Observation of subjects engaging in the achromatic and chromatic drawing tasks suggests a three-factor rationale to go along with the empirical data presented.

Firstly, the crayon drawing task tends to elicit reactions to, and tolerance for, emotional stimuli. In this manner it supplies an impact similar to the Rorschach chromatic cards in getting beneath the subject's defenses.

The second factor probably operative in the chromatic phase of projective drawings, which enables it to dig down deeper into the personality structure, is the associative value of the crayons, which tends to elicit childhood adjustment levels in adult subjects. It seems almost as if crayons appeal in some degree to the residue of childish layers in the adult's personality, and cut-through to tap this level.

The third factor which probably contributes to the efficacy of the chromatic phase, in descending deeper beneath the subject's defenses than the achromatic phase, is a temporal factor.

As routinely administered, the chromatic H-T-P is asked for after the subject has produced an achromatic set of drawings and has been questioned at length concerning them. Thus, by the time he is asked to enter the chromatic phase, he may be psychologically in a more vulnerable position, with his conflicts stirred up, his emotions aroused and, as is the case with some subjects, his defenses ajar. It is through this chink in his armor that the chromatic phase penetrates.

Thus, a three-factor hypothesis is offered in explanation of the clinically-observed phenomenon that chromatic drawings reveal a deeper personality picture than achromatic drawings: (a) the emotional impact of colors; (b) the childhood associations to crayons, and (c) the repetition of the drawing task[4] (after a questioning period).

With colored pencils, crayons that leave a pencil line (achromatic), and a procedure in which the chromatic drawing phase precedes the achromatic one, the writer is presently following through a research design which attempts to separate the three factors and thus evaluate their relative contributions to the, as presently conceived, more potent chromatic clinical instrument.

## COLOR SYMBOLISM ON THE H-T-P

In the foregoing section, the chromatic drawings were discussed as if they were merely deeper-tapping pencil drawings. In the present section, a consideration of the specific use of different colors will be added to round out the total picture of the chromatic contribution.

Some subjects approach the crayons with the hesitant anxiety so characteristic of their customary everyday patterns of behavior. Their crayon lines are faint and uncertain with the color choices restricted to the safer black, brown, or blue. They reveal their personality constriction and interpersonal uncertainties by not daring to open up with the bolder reds, oranges and yellows. This color usage reveals those subjects to be at the end of the personality continuum where over-cautiousness in exchanging pleasure or pain with others prevails.

---

[4] This last factor is the basis upon which the Eight-Card Redrawing Test (see Chapter 17) is effective in providing successively deeper personality pictures.

Psychologically healthier subjects, by contrast, plunge more deeply into the chromatic task, confidently employ the warmer colors, utilize a firm, sure pressure on the crayon, and thus reflect their greater self-assurance in the emotional areas that colors represent.

On the other side of this healthier range in the continuum, are those subjects who employ an almost savage pressure (frequently bearing down so heavily that they snap the crayons) and a clash of inharmonious hot colors. Excessive lability, turbulent emotions and jarring inner needs, in a tension-laden setting, characterize the psychological state of the subjects in this group.

From a normative standpoint, the use of from three to five colors for the House represents the average range, as does two to three for the Tree, and three to five for the Person.

An inhibited use of color, below this average range, is exhibited by subjects unable to make warm, sharing personal relationships freely. The most "emotion-shy" subjects tend to use crayon as if it were a pencil, employing no coloring-in whatsoever.

A more expansive use of color than the normative middle range, particularly if combined with an unconventional employment of the colors, occurs most frequently in those manifesting an inability to exercise adequate control over their emotional impulses. One psychotic recently indicated his inadequate control, as well as his break with conventional reality, by drawing each of the eight windows in his House a different color.

Anastasi and Foley(3) found that an extensive variety of color usage occurred almost exclusively among schizophrenic patients and manic-depressives in the manic phase. Both Lindberg (14) and Eysenck (9), among others, demonstrated a decrease of number of colors employed with increasing age in children, evidence in accord with the increase of emotional control with age. England (8) differentiated problem children from normal children by the former's inappropriate use of color. Since the younger, more uncontrolled child and the adult with lessened control (schizophrenics and manics) manifest a more expansive color usage, they supply support for the projective drawing hypothesis relating this type of color employment with inadequate control over emotionality.

John Payne (17) offers an interesting and fruitful four-fold scheme for the classification of the color output on the H-T-P:

(a) "Empathic intensity" is defined as color emphasis of a particular item, and is reported to occur in the drawings of normal, flexibly-adjusted subjects.

(b) "Tensional intensity," which refers to repeated reinforcement of a color by going back over it again and again, is found in the drawing productions of anxious subjects in the normal and neurotic ranges, particularly in anxiety states.

(c) "Clash intensity," an intensification of conventionally inharmonious color combinations, is evidence of a disturbance of a more profound degree, approaching and within the psychotic range. The schizophrenic patient, previously mentioned, who drew each of his eight windows a different color illustrates this classification. Manics also frequently exhibit "clash intensity."

(d) "Pressure intensity," refers to improperly modulated and excessively heavy pressure on the crayon. Payne finds this in the chromatic H-T-P's of mental defectives and organics. The present writer finds "pressure intensity" occurring also with two other groups of patients: aggressive "psychopaths" and paranoids.

In regard to the specific symbolic connotations of the individual colors, research in the area is in general agreement that the use of reds and yellows is a more spontaneous form of expression (22) than an emphasis on the blues or greens, which are more representative of controlled behavior (1, 2, 12).

Black and brown are more common to states of inhibition (5), repression (16), and possibly regression (19).

Brick (6), in his study of 200 children between the ages of two and fifteen, found an overemphasis upon yellow to be significant as an expression of hostility and aggression. This finding may be related to the study of Griffiths (10), in which yellow was found to be the preferred color at the earliest stage of a child's engaging in drawings. This may be viewed as consistent with Brick's finding, in that young childhood is the stage of the freest experience of rage and open release of hostility.

Buck (7) has found purple to be the preferred color of paranoids and regards any considerable use of it as presumptive evidence of strong power-striving drives, usually paranoid-tinged. Whether the grandiose need of the paranoid taps the same associative stream which links purple with royalty is not presently known. The idea, even if highly speculative, is certainly engaging.

## SUMMARY

Empirical data has been presented which suggests that by the addition of the chromatic phase to the projective drawing task, the clinician is provided with an instrument which taps a deeper personality layer and, hence, when taken with the achromatic drawings, provides a richer and more accurate picture of the hierarchy of the patient's conflicts and defenses. A three-factor rationale, offered along with the empirical data, views the emotional impact of color, the childhood association with crayons, and the repetition of the drawing task as all working in the same direction to enable the chromatic drawings to penetrate deeper beneath the patient's defenses and bring the more basic personality levels to view.

Inhibited or expansive color usage has been related to the corresponding personality correlates. Overemphasis upon any of the eight colors has been discussed and the research correlating color preference with personality traits has been presented. Much more research, it goes without saying, needs to be done.

## REFERENCES

1. Alschuler, and Hattwick, W.: Easel painting as an index of personality in preschool children. Am. J. Orthopsychiat., 13:616-625, 1943.
2. Alschuler, and Hattwick, W.: Painting and personality. Chicago, Univ. Chicago Press, I and II:590, 1947.
3. Anastasi, A., and Foley, J. P.: An analysis of spontaneous artistic productions by the abnormal. J. Gen. Psychol., 28:297-313, 1943.
4. Bellak, L.: The Thematic Apperception Test and the Children's Apperception Test in Clinical Use. New York, Grune & Stratton, 1954.
5. Bieber, I., and Herkimer, J.: Art in psychotherapy. Amer. J. Psychiat., 104:627-631, 1948.

6. Brick, M.: The mental hygiene value of children's art work. *Amer. J. Ortho.*, 14:136-146, 1944.
7. Buck, J. N.: The H-T-P technique: A quantitative and qualitative scoring manual. *Clin. Psychol. Monogr.*, 5:1-120, 1948.
8. England, A. O.: Color preference and employment in children's drawings. *J. Child Psychiat.*, 2:343-349, 1952.
9. Eysenck, H. J.: *Dimensions of Personality.* London, Kegan Paul, 1947.
10. Griffiths, R.: *A Study of Imagination in Early Childhood.* London, Kegan Paul, Trench, Trubner & Co., 1935.
11. Hammer, E. F.: The role of the H-T-P in the prognostic battery. *J. Clin. Psychol.*, 9:371-374, 1953.
12. Kadis, A.: Fingerpainting as a projective technique. In Abt, L., and Bellak, L.: *Projective Psychology.* New York, Knopf, 403-431, 1950.
13. Klopfer, B., Ainsworth, M. D., Klopfer, W. G., and Holt, R. R.: Developments in the Rorschach Technique. In Vol. I, *Technique and Theory.* New York, World Bk. Co., 1954.
14. Lindberg, B. J.: Experimental studies of colour and non-colour attitudes in school children and adults. *Acto. Psychiat. Neurol.*, 16:1938.
15. Murray, H. A.: *Explorations in Personality.* New York, Oxford Univ. Press, 1938.
16. Napoli, P.: Fingerpainting and personality diagnosis. *Genet. Psychol. Monogr.*, 34:129-231, 1946.
17. Payne, J. J.: Comments of the analysis of chromatic drawings. In Buck, J. N.: The H-T-P techniques: A quantitative and qualitative scoring manual. *Clin. Psychol. Monogr.*, 5:1-120, 1948.
18. Piotrowski, Z. A.: Sexual crime, alcohol, and the Rorschach test. *Psychiat. Quart. Suppl.*, 56:248-260, 1952.
19. Precker, J.: Painting and drawing in personality assessment. *J. Proj. Tech.*, 14:262-286, 1950.
20. Rapaport, D.: *Diagnostic Psychological Testing.* Chicago, Year Bk. Co., I and II: 1946.
21. Schafer, R.: *Psychoanalytic Interpretation in Rorschach Testing.* New York, Grune & Stratton, 1954.
22. Zimmerman, J. and Garfinkel, L.: Preliminary study of the art productions of the adult psychotic. *Psychiat. Quart.*, 16:313-318, 1942.

CHAPTER 10

CHILD CASE STUDY:
THE PROJECTION OF A CHILD'S
PERSONALITY IN DRAWINGS

Isaac Jolles, M.A.

Perception and visual-motor activity are affected by the general developmental process. Because of this, these factors are commonly represented by items on individual intelligence tests. Knowing this, one should not be surprised to learn that age is an important factor determining a child's drawing of a house, a tree, and a person. Therefore, the drawings of a very young (although bright) child are usually crude and even resemble rather closely the drawings of older children whose perception and visual-motor activity have been affected by brain damage.

Early in his experience with the H-T-P's of children the writer recognized the influence of developmental factors. This awakening led to the collection of approximately 8,000 sets of drawings from elementary school children ranging in age from five to twelve years. On the basis of this data the writer made four studies for the purpose of investigating the influence of age upon sexual identification, the drawing of the tree, and horizontal and vertical placement of the drawn wholes on the page. The results of these studies indicated a definite age factor which would affect the interpretation of a child's drawings (1).

No attempt will be made here to go into a detailed discussion of these studies. However, mention should be made of some of the significant findings. It was learned that one has to be particularly cautious in interpreting drawn persons of the opposite sex among five-, six-, and seven-year old males and among eleven- and twelve-year-old females because such trends seem to occur too frequently in these age groups to be regarded as significant.

It was found that the "phallic tree" (the basic characteristic of which is the very large trunk in proportion to the branch structure) occurs more frequently among young children than among older children, particularly among the younger in contrast to the older girls.

In spite of the notable influence of age upon the drawings of children, Buck's basic hypothesis concerning interpretation did not seem to be disturbed. It appears that so long as one considers certain minor deviations due to age, the usual interpretations of H-T-P drawings may be applied to those of children. There are rather strong indications that Buck's interpretations of the stimulus value of the House, Tree, and Person and of the significance of horizontal and vertical placement are sound and apply to children as well as to adults. Even the tree labelled by the writer as the "phallic tree" seems to have psycho-sexual significance in many instances.

The fact that concepts pertaining to a drawing technique based upon clinical studies of adults seem to apply to children is an important observation. Drawing is a favorite play activity of many children, and even the Post-Drawing-Interrogation (PDI) resembles a child's play activity. Therefore, the clinician is provided with a most welcome device for probing the feelings and attitudes of the young child. In this respect the H-T-P has much in common with the diagnostic play situation. Thus, in the writer's experience, the H-T-P has excelled other projective techniques in the personality study of pupils in the primary grades (kindergarten, first, second, and third grades).

At this point it would be pertinent to mention the importance of the chromatic phase of the H-T-P. Children are particularly pleased when the clinician spreads before them a group of crayons and asks them to make a house, etc. Even the "color shy" children seem to enjoy this activity, for they have usually had more experience in drawing with a crayon than with a pencil. Such activity is usually a part of the classroom routine.

In a recent publication the writer has pointed out the advantages of using sixteen crayons (No. 16 Crayolas®) instead of the standard eight colors. Not only do the children become very pleased at the sight of so many different colors, but also the various shades of the basic eight add finer nuances to the personality picture.

Before presenting a case study, mention should be made of two other ways in which administration and interpretation of H-T-P's differs from the approaches used with adults. Quantitative analysis is not possible because scoring standards have not been developed for children. Also, the writer has found it expedient to modify the wording of the questions of the PDI and to eliminate some questions which are usually unproductive and thus lengthen the procedure unnecessarily.

## THE CASE OF DAISY MAE

The name, Daisy Mae, is fictitious and was chosen because of similarity to the comic strip character by the same name—low socio-economic status, attractive and reasonably intelligent although naïve and lacking in many basic experiences. The case was selected for presentation here, not because it is typical of cases examined by the writer, but because it illustrates so well the adequacy of interpretations made of rather crude, immature drawings.

At the time of this examination, Daisy Mae was six years ten months of age and in the first grade. She was referred for psychological study because of her inability to understand and follow directions and her academic retardation (kindergarten level in reading and number readiness). She was described by her teacher as a very sensitive child who cried easily and felt that some one was always hurting her. The following psychometric findings were obtained:

1937 Stanford Revision, Form L    CA, 6-10    MA, 5-7    IQ,    82
Arthur Performance Test, Form I    CA, 6-10    MA, 7-1    IQ, 104

These results indicated a normal intellectual potential but a marked deficit in the areas of language development and concept formation. This deficiency appeared to be due to a lack of adequate intellectual stimulation in the home. The following suggestions of organicity were present: deficit in auditory perception; a positive Strauss check list, and poor muscular co-ordination. However, the symptoms of organicity could be accounted for by the lack of home training and her language deficit. History of gestation, birth, motor and speech was negative for organicity. Therefore, this possibility was minimized. Very little was known about the home situation at the time of examination except that the mother was unintelligent, drank a great deal, and took Daisy Mae with her on many of her visits to taverns.

Figures 1, 2, and 3 are the achromatic drawings of the House, Tree, and Person respectively, Figures 4, 5, and 6 the chromatic drawings. The following PDI [1] was obtained.

P1. Is that a man, a woman, a boy or a girl?
    A girl.
P2. How old is she?
    Five.
P3. Who is she?
    Eva.
P4. Who is that?
    A girl in my class.
P5. What is she doing?
    Laughing.
P6. Where is she laughing?
    At the funny person.

T1. What kind of tree is that?
    A bee tree.

[1] P questions deal with the Person; T with the Tree; and II with the House.

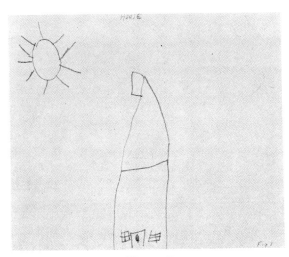

Figure 1

Figure 2

T2. Where is that tree?
    At home.
T3. About how old is that tree?
    Six.
T4. Is that tree alive?
    No.
T5. What do you think caused it to die?
    Cause the bees didn't take care of it.
    Will it ever be alive again?
    No.

---

H1. Does that house have an upstairs to it?
    No.
H2. Is that your own house?
    Yes.
H3. Would you like to own that house yourself?
    Yes.

H4. If you did own that house and you could do whatever you liked with it, which room would you take for your own?

Downstairs. (Which one?) The bedroom.

Whom would you like to have live in that house with you?

Our children and Dad.

Anyone else?

A little girl and a little boy.

H5. As you look at that house, does it seem to be close by or far away?

Close by.

H6. Does it seem to be above you, below you, or about even with you?

Below me.

---

T6. Which does that tree look more like to you, a man or a woman?

A man.

Figure 3

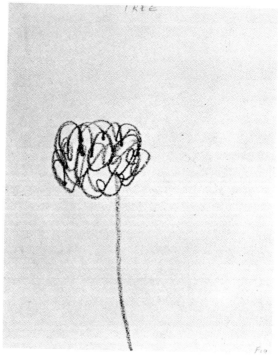

Figures 4 and 5

T7. If that were a person instead of a tree, which way would
the person be facing?
This way. (To subject's left.)

T8. Is that tree by itself, or is it in a group of trees?
By itself.
Would it like to be with other trees?
No.

T9. As you look at that tree, does it seem to be above you, below you, or about even with you?
Even with me.

---

P7. What is he thinking about?
A funny person.

P8. How does he feel?
Terrible. (Why?) She don't want to see no funny
person.

Figure 6

P9. What does that person make you think of?
   Somebody throwed a rock.
P10. Is that person well?
   No.
P11. Is that person happy?
   No.
P12. What is the weather like in this picture?
   Christmas kind.

---

T10. What is the weather like in this picture?
   Cold—winter.
T11. What kind of weather do you like best?
   Warm.
T12. Is there any wind blowing in this picture?
   No.
T13 and 14 pertaining to wind omitted.

---

H7. What does that house make you think of?
   A wasp tree.
H8. Is that a happy, friendly sort of house?
   No.
H9. What is the weather like in this picture?
   Not cold any more.
H10. What person that you know does that house make you think of?
   Happy person.
   But what person?
   (No reply.)
H11. Has anybody or anything ever hurt that house?
   No.
H12. (Subject is asked to draw the sun.) Let us suppose that this sun were some person that you know. Who would it be?
   Next door neighbor.

---

T15. (Subject is asked to draw the sun.) Let us suppose that sun was some person that you know. Who would it be?
   A friend. (What is the friend's name?) Betty.

T16. What does that tree make you think of?
   Of wasps.
T17. Is it a healthy tree?
   No.
T18. Is it a strong tree?
   No.

---

P13. What person that you know does this person remind you of?
   Sun. (No further response could be elicited.)
P14. What kind of clothing does this person have on?
   Blue, grey, pink, brown, yellow (etc.).
P15. What does that person need most?
   New clothes.
P16. Has anybody ever hurt that person?
   No.
P17. (Subject is asked to draw the sun.) Let us suppose that sun were some person that you know. Who would it be?
   Mary.

---

T19. What person that you know does that tree remind you of?
   Wasps might sting.
T20. Has anybody or anything ever hurt that tree?
   No.
T21. What does that tree need most?
   Little birds, baby birds.
T22 and 23 omitted—no irrelevant details, scars, etc.

---

H13. omitted—no irrelevant details.
H14. What does that house need most?
   Happiness.
H15. Where does that chimney lead to in the house?
   (Child could not understand the question.)
H16. Subject questioned regarding rooms represented by the windows of the house.
   (Lower left is subject's room, the right siblings' room.)

---

The horizontal placement of the tree, and to some extent the person, indicates that Daisy Mae has problems controlling her impulses. The personality imbalance suggested by the branch area of the tree and the uncontrolled impulsivity implied in the drawing of the arms on the person tend to substantiate the interpretation of a control problem. The increased size of the chromatic drawings reveal her tendency to overreact to emotional stimuli, and the omission of the trunk of the person, implying a need to repress or deny her body drives, completes the picture of the control difficulty.

The vertical placement of the three wholes reflects the child's insecurity. The narrow, high wall of the house reveals Daisy Mae's withdrawal tendencies, and her inaccessibility is seen in the smallness of the windows and door of the house. Her satisfaction-seeking resources in her environment being limited (branch structure of the tree), she turns to fantasy in an effort to seek satisfaction of her emotional needs. This is indicated by the relatively large roof area of the house and the emphasis on the head of the person.

It is evident that much of the child's emotional difficulty stems from the home situation. In the chromatic drawing Daisy Mae chooses the yellow green crayon for making the wall. This is an unconventional use of the color and reflects the child's hostile attitudes towards her home. In the PDI her reply to H6 suggests a debasing attitude towards her home. Her association of the house with a wasp tree in H7 indicates her feeling that her home is a veritable hornets' nest. Again in H8 and H14 the need for happiness in the home is important evidence of an unsatisfactory home life.

Daisy Mae's need for affection at home is revealed by her use of red to depict the window of her bedroom. Also her erotic fantasies suggested by the use of red for the roof fits into this general pattern. There is evidence of parental rejection in T7, the man facing to the subject's left, and again in T5 where "the bees did not take care of it." The tensions and rejection in the home are so severe that the child actually rejects her mother in H4, omitting her from the family scene.

Daisy Mae's sensitivity to criticism is seen in the large ears on the chromatic drawing of the person. It is interesting to note that in P3 she identifies this person with Eva who was also referred for psychological study because of classroom problems similar to those presented by our subject. From that point on, her problems in interpersonal relationships begin to unfold. In P5, P6, P7, P8 and P9 we get the picture of a child who is made fun of and tormented by other children.

In T4, T17, T18, P10 and P11 Daisy Mae expresses her dissatisfaction with her present state. Her withdrawal tendencies appear again in T8 and T9 in which asocial trends are indicated. In P12 and T10 the lack of warmth in her environment is called to our attention. In H9 the weather changes for the better, but this very likely refers to the home from which the mother is absent.

The expression of her striving for autonomy is reflected in the long legs of the person. This calls our attention to the psychosocial "castration" feelings as indicated by the absence of hands and feet. This is probably the result of undue demands for control placed upon her by her parents. The clue to this is the horizontal placement of the house which does not reflect the control problems as seen in the person and the tree. In other words, she is forced to exercise more control at home than in other life situations.

One cannot overlook completely the symptoms of organicity which appear in Daisy Mae's drawings. The tree with its single line for a trunk and its scribbled lines for branch structure occurs frequently in the drawings of children with brain damage. The scribbled line appears again as hair on the person. The child's control difficulties could be the result of motor-driven behavior which usually has an organic origin. In spite of these symptoms, the writer feels that one must be very cautious in reading organicity into these signs in view of the age of the child and the intellectually impoverished background from which she comes.

In conclusion, Daisy Mae is a withdrawn, inaccessible child who turns to fantasy for gratification of her emotional needs. She is sensitive to the criticism directed towards her by other children which adds to her withdrawal tendencies. These trends are serious in that she not only feels isolated socially but actually prefers an asocial existence. Much of her anxiety and insecurity arise out of the home situation and her control difficulties. Daisy Mae expresses her hostility towards her rejecting mother by rejecting her in turn. In keeping with this pattern, there is her drive to be independent of her family and her fantasies of a home of her own.

Daisy Mae was referred to the Visiting Social Counselor (school psychiatric social worker) for counseling with the suggestion that the home situation be investigated to determine whether work with the family would be feasible. The counselor found the family living in an overcrowded shack which was meagerly furnished and ill-kept. It was learned that Daisy Mae openly rejected her mother and that she had a fair relationship with the father. There was considerable strife between the parents with detrimental effect upon our subject. The father's income was relatively good ($95 per week), but the management of the income was poor. The counselor indicated that the mother was so lacking in satisfactions herself that she could hardly be expected to provide warmth, etc., to the children. In the meantime, play sessions with the child gradually revealed the conflicts (family and social) detected by the H-T-P.

## REFERENCES

1. Jolles, I.: A study of the validity of some hypotheses for the qualitative interpretation of the H-T-P for children of elementary school age. I. Sexual identification. *J. Clin. Psychol.*, 8:113, 1952; II. The "phallic tree" as an indicator of psycho-sexual conflict. *J. Clin. Psychol.*, 8:245, 1952; III. Horizontal placement. *J. Clin. Psychol.*, 9:161, 1953; IV. Vertical placement. *J. Clin. Psychol.*, 9:164, 1953.

## CHAPTER 11

# ADOLESCENT CASE STUDY:
# A LATE ADOLESCENT
# SEX OFFENDER

EMANUEL F. HAMMER, PH.D.

THE INTERPRETATION of projective techniques—or for that matter any diagnostic clinical procedures—on subjects within the adolescent age range involves delicate separation of the normative indices of upheaval from the suggestions of psychopathology above and beyond the developmental disruption.

Adolescence, the emotionally stormiest period of all man's stages, frequently yields clinical data, on Rorschach, TAT and drawings alike, which appear seeped in painful feelings. Raw impulses come through in unvarnished and frank fashion. In addition, the rumblings of the adolescent adjustments being made show themselves in the confusions, tensions, and intense ambivalances picked up by projective examination. Hostility and aggression are more freely expressed than at any other age.

The clear differentiation between heterosexual and homosexual impulses have frequently not yet been made, and show up as tangled together in a confusion which makes the adolescent's psychosexual life so erratic, so fumbling and so bewildering.

Adolescence, the age of physiological maturations and heightened psychic shifts and tensions, provides projective protocols which demand the most parsimonious clinical approach in interpreting pathology from the data. And the closer the subject is, on the adolescent continuum, to the period of puberty, the more imperative is the need for cautious interpretation.

Adolescents' drawings assume the character of over-emphasized, exaggerated portraits of strength and importance, mirroring their self-inflation. The males tend to draw forceful cowboys, athletes or soldiers, the females alluring figures in evening-gowns or shape-accentuating bathing suits.

Because the adolescent is conscious of beginning maturity, he likes to anticipate and experiment with the body form toward which the veering winds of adolescence are shaping him. The adolescent sometimes draws to reinforce the fabric of his day-dreams. He tends to glamorize drawings, and in doing so he also glamorizes his projected appearance and his accomplishments. Thus he reaches toward a hoped-for acclaim.

In addition, the emotional release derived from this type of experimenting with the body image in his drawings helps the adolescent achieve more certainty as to what he is and more definiteness in his self-concept.

The present case study is that of a late adolescent boy who was studied under the auspices of a New York State grant for the investigation of the psychodynamics behind sexual offenses. In an attempt to improve objectivity in the projective interpre-tations, the projective protocol was analyzed "blindly," i.e., with-out the interpreter knowing anything about the subject other than his sex and age. As a demonstration in reliability, the H-T-P protocol was given to both John N. Buck and the present writer for their independent blind analysis. Whereas the writer knew that the subject was a sex offender because of his (the writer's) affiliation with the Sex Offender Research Project (although he did not know what type of sex offense it was, i.e., rape, exhibition-ism, incest, pedophilia, homosexuality, etc.), Buck's analysis was totally blind.

In order to provide the information for an informal check upon both validity and reliability, the psychiatric picture and the social history will be presented, followed by two independent H-T-P interpretative write-ups.

## PSYCHIATRIST'S REPORT [1]

The patient is a nineteen-year-old white male, who has been in and out of reformatories for the past five years. He remembers almost nothing of his childhood. His first memory is of a scene in the courtroom when he was about five or six, when his parents

---

[1] Prepared by Samuel Dunaif, M. D., psychoanalyst, New York City.

were divorced. Thereafter, he had no contact with his parents at all. He spent about a year with foster parents, and then was sent to an orphanage home. He stayed there for a number of years, until he went to live with his older married sister.

The patient's father was a very disturbed man. He would make his daughter urinate into a glass after which he drank the contents.

By the time the patient was nine, he had engaged in fellatio activities. He was forced to leave the orphanage when his fellatio practices were discovered. He was sent to Bellevue to be observed. When he left there, he went to live with his sister.

He began engaging in cunnilingual activities after the mother of one of his girl friends introduced him to this practice. One day the patient went to visit his girl friend, but only her mother was home. The patient gives the following account of this experience:

"One day I went over and my girl wasn't home. Her mother asked me if I was having sexual intercourse with her and I said no. She said why not, I was big enough. She gave me a few drinks and I got dizzy. Then she went into the bedroom and called me in. She was naked. I wanted to go. But then I started to kiss her and I ended up between her legs somehow. I ate pussy. I went back to see my girl and she usually wasn't home. Her mother was usually home and so I kept on doing it. She'd say, 'Come on dear, let's make love.' I just ate pussy—that's all. I never had sexual intercourse." (Patient laughed and giggled in embarrassment while telling this.) "Maybe that's why I'm afraid of older girls."

The patient went with about a dozen girls on whom he performed cunnilingus; usually he would find one girl and she would bring friends to meet him. Patient would kiss girls first, then "feel 'em up" and then "would eat pussy"; the girls were most receptive.

The patient was arrested for "carnal abuse" of a little girl. His sister's children and the child of the neighbor's were in the house. He was good to all of them. Then one day he played with the genitals of the neighbor's girl who then kept coming back for more. This continued for two weeks, until he was caught.

The patient is an extremely disturbed late adolescent. Immature fixations are prominent. Talking to him is like talking to a child. He even has daydreams about cowboys and Indians.

Figure 1: Achromatic

## PSYCHIATRIC SOCIAL WORKER'S REPORT [2]

Supplementary data obtained by the psychiatric social worker, which rounds out the picture presented by the psychiatrist, includes the fact that the patient at one time lived with rather affectionate and warm foster parents. A difference between the religion of the foster parents and that of the patient caused him to be removed from their home, however, and placed back in the orphanage. The removal from the foster home was evidently a traumatic event, for the patient had established a warm relationship with the foster parents.

At the orphanage there was no close relationship with adult figures, and after having experienced parental warmth the patient now was affect-starved.

As to his early development, the patient's sister reports that he used to chase his mother around the house and ask to be breast fed. He wasn't weaned until three and one-half or four years of age; thus his orality was reinforced.

The patient's earliest association in the sexual sphere concerns the age of 8 or 9 when he proposed to a girl in his class that they exhibit their genitals to each other. They did this in the boy's bathroom of the school and he was astonished to observe that she did not have a penis; "I thought it was cut off because she must have done something wrong or that she was born with a deformity."

---

[2] Prepared by Sidney Connell, M.S., New York State Psychiatric Institute.

The patient had "gone steady" with a girl, from ages 12 to 15, whom he had thought of marrying. He seemed particularly attracted to this girl because she "looked exactly like me."

Physically, the patient is a nice looking, somewhat effeminate, but well-built individual. During interviews he tends to be ingratiating, somewhat silly and to giggle inappropriately. He is extremely dependent and eager to talk. There is an inappropriate quality in his responses and he does not appear to be anxious when producing material which usually generates anxiety. He seems extremely infantile, immature, and emotionally impoverished although his fantasy life is pathologically rich and grandiose and he appears to be preoccupied with his fantasies in order to escape from realities. He seems incapable, at the present, of constructive goal directed activities. The immaturity appears to be in the nature of a fixation rather than a regression.

He has offered to bring flowers and plants from the Green House for various staff members. Superficially, he gives the impression of being somewhat exhibitionistic and flirtatious during interviews.

Figure 2: Achromatic

PERSON

Figure 3: Achromatic

Bellevue examination gives the patient an I.Q. of 112 and diagnosis of "schizoid personality, psychopathic personality without psychosis." Kings County examination gives the patient an I.Q. of 116 and diagnosis of "no psychosis, not mentally defective, schizoid personality, with emotional and psychosexual immaturity. Strong anxiety over feelings of inadequacy and preoccupation with immature sexual impulses are present."

## "BLIND" H-T-P [3] INTERPRETATIONS

The following statements are from the "blind analysis" of the H-T-P requested of the writer in 1952.

---

[3] Chromatic drawings were executed with a double line for the House, one line with brown and one with black crayon. The windows were done in blue and the chimney in red. The suns in all three pictures were also executed with a double line, one orange and one yellow. The Tree trunk and branches were done in brown and the foliage line in green. The Person's face and hand were drawn in red, the kerchief in orange, the shirt in blue, and the rest in black. Time limitations, unfortunately, did not permit the administration of the fourth Chromatic drawing.

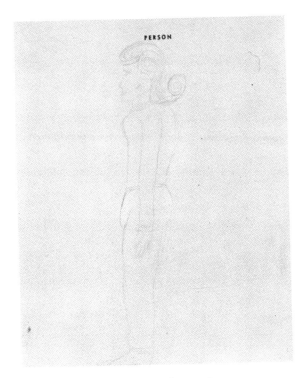

Figure 4: Achromatic

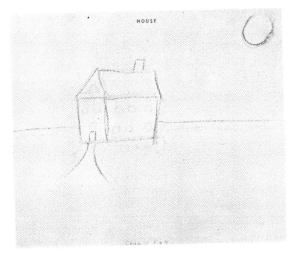

Figure 5: Chromatic

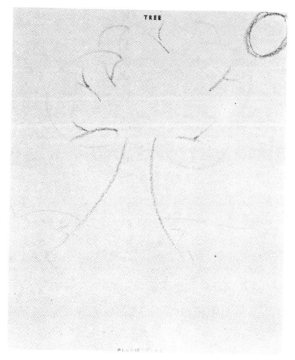

Figure 6: Chromatic

"On the H-T-P, the subject's most conspicuous content occurs in his drawing of a Person: a cowboy. This choice of content suggests a fusion of noteworthy immaturity and a need for the patient to present himself as more masculine than he actually feels. Feelings of insufficiency in regard to virility sink their roots deeply into his personality structure.

"Against this backdrop, feelings of impotency beneath some compensatory efforts are also suggested by the parallel drawing of an erect-like line at the phallic region of the chromatic Person (Figure 7) and the conspicuous gun holster in the achromatic drawing (Figure 3).

"He gives 'nine' as the age of the Tree, thus projecting his own felt immaturity, consistent with the immaturity of the cowboy concept. The combination of immaturity and the feelings of absence of masculine prowess suggest that these two traits may blend to produce psychosexual immaturity with resultant fixations upon, and/or regressions to, pregenital zones. This is supported by the fact that orality is indicated by the open-mouthed depiction of the chromatic Person. The erotic choice of red for the face suggests the possibility of guilt over some sort of oral activities or wishes.[4] The same color usage for the hand plus the fact that the hand is strapped down, as it were, beneath a belt suggests that the patient is attempting to employ defenses against acting out forbidden impulses with his hands, too. Inadequate control over impulses is also implied by the open Tree at the baseline in conjunction with the lack of a line closing off the foliage from the trunk.

"One readily observes the suggestion of the achromatic Person's head drawn with a mask-like covering over it. The Person is drawn in full profile, suggesting a basically evasive attitude on the part of the patient. The mask-like covering over the head further reflects his need to hide his true feelings from others. Thus we may expect that this is an individual who tends to conceal his inner self, to be overly cautious about revealing his inner needs to others, and to rely upon a schizoid character armoring to protect him in his voyage through interpersonal fields. In addition, the mask-like effect is so prominent that we might suspect that the patient feels somewhat a stranger among people and may suffer from depersonalization and estrangement feelings.[5]

"In the drawing of the House (Figure 1), the door of the House does not touch the ground, nor does the path leading up to the door continue up until the House. This tends to imply a need to keep his personlity inaccessible and to keep others from close emotional contact with him, in accord with the full-profile presentation of the Person and the retreat of the head into the mask-like covering. His use of color (the need to use two colors for many of the lines, one warm and one cold) is also consistent with the above in that it suggests that the patient attempts to give the impression that he is much warmer and much more inter-

---

[4] The orality picked up by the H-T-P is consistent with that elicited in a Rorschach administered by the writer approximately a year later, this time not "blindly." On Rorschach Card VI, the patient projected "A baby in a high chair." A self-concept of being a baby who is dependent upon others, regressive wishes, and fear of becoming a man are implied and consistent with the H-T-P picture. The oral connotations of a baby in a high chair, i.e., waiting to be fed, are interesting in that they occur on what is commonly considered to be the "sex card" and thus may be related to the patient's stated preference for cunnilingual behavior. Here, the fear of acting the post-puberty male and his orality unite and result in his flight from penis-vaginal contact into cunnilingus.

[5] "Masks" were also seen in the Rorschach stimuli.

PERSON

Figure 7: Chromatic

ested in interpersonal, emotional contacts with others than he basically feels safe in attempting. This mirrors a superficial accessibility cloaking an underlying, basic mistrust and fear of human relationships which may be expected to limit and define his behavior in psychotherapeutic collaboration.

"In keeping with the other schizoid suggestions, we have the patient's comment that the leaves on the Tree are 'dead.' Feelings of hopelessness in regard to obtaining gratification from the environment reinforce his self-absorption and his retreat from an orientation in which he could readily exchange significant emotional pleasure and pain with others.

"The relative size of his drawings of a male and a female reflects his feeling that women are more dominant and of greater status, as well as capable of 'working at jobs better than men' (as he projects in the Post-Drawing Inquiry). In comparison, the patient feels himself to be more of a boy than a man. Massive feelings of hesitancy in approaching mature females as sex objects probably handicaps his psychosexual adjustment.

"Homoerotic components are clearly reflected in his drawing of a female which appears not only massive but also masculine-looking. If one covers the hair on the drawn female's head, the remainder of the picture is that of a burly, somewhat aggressive male. In addition, the patient has the drawn female wearing pants and there is a distinct impression of a bulge suggesting an erection beneath the pants. In keeping with this, the breast endowment is minimal. Thus, the patient's psychosexual conflicts may generate from severe doubts concerning the precise sexual role he should play. Confused psychosexual identification and strong fear of assuming the active male role produce feelings of psychosexual immaturity and lack of virility.

"Psychotherapy, if pursued with this patient, would have to be both long term and intensive; it would labor under a relatively guarded prognosis."

Buck, as the innovator of the H-T-P technique, was also requested to "blindly" formulate an interpretive picture of this patient. Being a purist, he asked to see the drawings of only House, Tree and first Person drawn—both achromatic and chromatic. Thus, his interpretation was written without having the advantage of seeing the drawn female. His comments follow:

"Qualitative analysis produces the following observations:

"(1) The subject appears to be handicapped by much obsessive thinking—some of it hostile, much of it sexual (it seems not too speculative to comment that a good deal of it involves fantasy about female genitalia: note the unusual crease in the two hats).[6] (2) He finds orificial symbols difficult to deal with. (3) One strongly suspects that the subject was and is overly dependent upon his mother (and he may well revolt strongly against his inability to shrug this off). (4) He would like very much to assume in actuality a virile, robustly masculine role, but his essential femininity forbids this. (5) He feels great guilt over tactile sensory experiences (The red hand is definitely atypical as far as color usuage is concerned. The hand is also pinioned to the side by the belt which adds to its significance. The overall picture of rigidity, with a stance that simply exudes sensual consciousness is often seen in connection with profound guilt feelings. Note, too, the open mouth with the same implications in this area). (6) He is still able superficially to seem capable of functioning in more or less normal fashion, but basically he feels that

[6] We here recall the similar finding in *The Case of Mr. P.*, Chapter 7. [Ed.]

his ability to derive satisfaction from his enviornment is most inadequate (the "dead" leaves), and there is a suggestion that he senses an imminent collapse of ego control (note particularly the proportional imbalance on the chromatic male, the impression one gets that the drawn person faces in one direction, has the chest reversed, the hips and knees in the opposite direction, etc.). (7) His relationship to authority figures is a conflictful one in which he is apparently both hostile and admiring, both rejecting and seeking. (The suns, frequently introduced as a symbol of authority figures in drawings, are relatively small and the chromatic ones are orange and yellow implying a corresponding combination of immature, hostile, rejection and warmth-seeking. His drawings of male figures indicate a simultaneous need to be seen as a virile, rugged male and a desire to rob male figures of their threatening characteristics.) (8) He is presently striving hard for a maintenance of personality integrity, but feels that his effort is likely to fail. (9) Under additional emotional pressure (under the impact of color as compared to the achromatic level) he tends to become more expansive, to behave less conventionally and less affectively, to become a ready prey to panic. (10) He makes use of insulation (the mask effect over the head) and restriction of activity (the rigid posture and full-profile presentation) as defense mechanisms.

"All in all, the subject appears to be rather a sick boy who is in the throes of a very severe neurosis in which schizoid, insulated behavior may be expected to be paramount."

This chapter has consisted of an attempt at a demonstration —though, certainly not a study, or experiment—of *informal* (a) reliability between two sets of independently-derived H-T-P interpretations, and (b) validity, in the comparison between the H-T-P deductions and the criteria provided by the reports of the psychiatrist and psychiatric social worker. Consistency, in the three-way comparison of the two H-T-P write-ups and the criteria, mounts to reassuring proportions.

## CHAPTER 12

# ADULT CASE STUDY:
## CLINICAL VALIDATION OF THE HOUSE-TREE-PERSON DRAWINGS OF AN ADULT CASE (CHRONIC ULCERATIVE COLITIS WITH ILEOSTOMY)

FRED BROWN, PH.D.

### INTRODUCTION

THE MAIN PURPOSE of a psychiatric case study is to present co-ordinated data which will exemplify a basic hypothesis or illustrate the manner in which aetiological factors combine to produce a particular clinical picture. In the field of Clinical Psychology, and especially in psychodiagnostics, the case study serves as an ideographically oriented validative technique from which fruitful hypothesis may emerge. With full cognizance of the pitfalls inherent in this approach, the close matching of a particular projective-expressive technique with a good treatment history and other parts of the battery strikes me as a crucial test of the validity of any instrument which claims to tap significant aspects of the patient's personality.

In undertaking a task of this type, one is tempted to select a case that will be "interesting" and impressive. The hazard involved in such an aim lies in the fact that one might end by exemplifying that which is most atypical in any particular area of psychological practice and least likely to serve the purpose of the presentation. For this reason I have chosen what might be regarded as a routine case on the psychiatric service of a large general hospital. Of course, no case is really "routine" once the test battery is focussed upon the person with an illness, especially after the personality and its unique characteristics have been subjected to detailed test scrutiny. In fact, after a period of almost a decade, I have yet to accumulate a large group of "typical" H-T-P's, Rorschachs, TAT's or whatnot for any particular psychosomatic syndrome. While tests are invaluable in their contribution to the delineation of personality psychodynamics, their value lies precisely in highlighting *individual* pattern nuances.

This is accomplished by adhering to those guiding principles which, in the case of an instrument such as the H-T-P, are derived from clinical observations which have been accumulated over a long period of time. Such observations acquire worth only after they have been tested repeatedly against other criteria. In this way a process of constant refinement takes place which increases the truth value of specific intrepretations, although in every case the perceptive clinician remains the ultimate intergrating instrument.

Our policy at Mount Sinai is to use the test battery (which consists of the Rorschach, H-T-P, Bender-Gestalt test, TAT, Wechsler-Bellevue, and word association test), as a self-contained apparatus for evaluating the patient without resorting to the clinical history until after the study is completed. There is nothing "blind" about this approach if one considers the number of behavior samplings obtained from such comprehensive testing. Inferences and interpretations from one test are cross-checked with other portions of the battery within the framework of projective technique principles and personality theory. If the personality picture so derived differs markedly from the clinical picture or treatment history, then we would have to conclude that the tests fail to justify their existence. This has not yet happened.

In the present study an attempt will be made to co-ordinate the clinical and test material for the purpose of demonstrating how the H-T-P is utilized.

### THE PATIENT

This is a twenty-four-old white girl who was referred to the outpatient division of the department of psychiatry by her group therapist who had been treating her for about a year. Both he and the patient felt that parallel individual psychotherapy was needed. She is described as a very plump and fairly attractive girl with, however, a somewhat plaintive and hostile quality. She has had ulcerative colitis since the age of eight and has been ill for most of her life, so that her education has been very spotty. She had an ileostomy performed about three years ago and since then has been physically improved.

The patient's mother was diagnosed as a paranoid schizophrenic and died in a state hospital after many years of institutionalization. There are two older brothers with whom the patient is living now and one of them is also a paranoid schizophrenic and has been in a state hospital.

She shows evidence of severe psychiatric illness according to the consensus of those who have worked with her. The group therapist characterizes her as a childish person with many infantile traits who reacts with violent emotional upheavals to any sort of deprivation, especially in personal relationships. She has brief episodes of depression, often with thoughts of hopelessness and suicide. Many projective tendencies are noted in conjunction with extremely unrealistic object relationships.

The psychiatrist's impression was formulated as: (1) personality pattern disturbance, unclassified; (2) chronic ulcerative colitis, inactive post-ileostomy. The main features of her personality problem were listed as: (1) severe childhood deprivation and trauma during infancy; (2) secondary effects of severe chronic disabling illness.

## Intelligence Level

In our experience there has been little correlation between the H-T-P and level of intelligence as obtained on the Wechsler-Bellevue Scale. The reason for this is quite obvious when one considers that the H-T-P elicits reactions not always amenable to intellectual control. It might also be hypothesized that the drawing task in the presence of an authority figure might favor regressive manifestations. The following test pattern was obtained on the Wechsler:

| | | | |
|---|---|---|---|
| Information | 13 | Pict. Arrangement | 11 |
| Comprehension | 11 | Pict. Completion | 12 |
| Digit Span | 11 | Block Design | 14 |
| Arithmetic | 9 | Object Assembly | 12 |
| Similarities | 15 | Digit Symbol | 11 |

Verbal scale I.Q.   114
Perform. scale I.Q.   113
FULL SCALE I.Q.   116

The test reveals a girl of bright normal intelligence who places slightly above the 85th percentile for adults. She does exceptionally well on tasks calling for verbal and manipulative conceptualization. It would follow from this that neither visual-motor impairment nor a defect in the ability to conceptualize and abstract would account for flaws in her drawings.

### House-Tree-Person Test

*House.* The House is a patently bizarre conception and is most significant in light of our finding (1) that the very inanimateness of the structure weakens the patient's defenses against damaging admissions even on a projective basis. One is struck at once by the unrealistic fairy tale appearance of the drawing, its divorcement from reality (imbalance and disproportion, shape, number of stories (two), fluid and unstable "ground"), and the manner in which the total concept is surrounded by an encapsulating sac suggestive of a uterine enclosure. There are attempts at solidification indicative of ego-consolidating drives (bricks) which do not cover the building and attest to spasmodic failure of ego functions coupled with sporadic obsessive-compulsive defenses. Although she defensively encircles the structure, line quality is loose enough to indicate moods of elation and the rendering of ground sufficiently dark and unorganized to indicate a basic depressive inclination which carries anal connotations. Periods of disruptive confusion can be inferred from this projection of disorganization, although at the same time she will maintain an extratensive reaction pattern (bold frontward presentation) coupled with considerable impulsivity (M : C, 1 : 3.0, all CF's) and demandingness. She tries to enhance herself narcissistically in order to facilitate oral supplies and can at times stress an optimistic attitude and a need for human relations (window box with flowers), but she is highly apprehensive of the approach of others and is basically distrustful of their motives (broken pathway and vertical approach; [1] brooding appearance of eye-like windows; room hidden away at left side of figure). Intensely hostile and dysphorically tinged impulses press for expression at all times (ground) and the only approach to any kind of stability lies in the distant and inaccessible past (elevated base line on left of figure). While she attempts to control her impulsive behavior in deference to social and conventional imperatives (double line on environment side of house), she feels insecure over her controls and is always vulnerable to regressive outbursts (broken area on left side). The shattered and split tree on the right speaks for her pessimism over meeting strong and dependable figures in the future and suggests that the images of broken parental symbols prevent her from achieving true integration.

The soaring birds inject a note of optimism, ambition, and flight from her limitations, offering a striking contrast to the threatened flooding of her ego by archaic impulses. Her wish for escape is coupled with feelings of inferiority (FK element) and suggests suicidal preoccupations as a final resolution of her difficulties, so that the soaring birds serve a double function in this drawing.

*Post-drawing Interrogation and Supplementary Data.* The figure is a two-story brick "mansion" (unrealistic aspirations and status drive) which reminds her of "luxury, comfort, security"

---

[1] Meyer, Brown, and Levine (1) found that pathways showing this broken "dripping" appearance are frequently associated with some form of anal discharge such as would be found in ulcerative colitis.

(oral-dependency needs). The wish fantasy breaks down when she begins to cry and wonders whether she will ever belong anywhere (depressive intrusion, pessimism).

The fantasied flight and ambitiousness projected in the bird figures is repeated in the Rorschach on Card I, where the central maternal form is described as a figure out of a comic strip, "Wonder Woman," "she could fly and used to help people." In the inquiry she states, "When I was a kid I thought we were going to fly and there was no question about it." She is apparently attempting to substitute an idealized mother with whom she can identify fully in place of the real mother who fled from her responsibilities.

Excerpts from the treatment history support evidence for cyclic mood changes ("I'm restless but not depressed. I would like to do something but don't know what—maybe take a rocket somewhere.") which are linked with the bird thema. On another occasion she begins her session with the remark, "This is my lousy week, I almost committed suicide on Tuesday. My brain was wracking and I was almost confused." Here we have evidence of her mood swings, confusion, and suicidal impulses. Her spasmodic narcissistic enhancement is evident in the following excerpt; "She has a new hairdo and I comment about her looking very nice. She apparently enjoys the comment and talks in a more animated manner."

Regressive manifestations of a uterine type associated with death and rebirth themas are inferred from Rorschach responses, and support House interpretations. Here the wish to rejoin her deceased father is linked with ultimate serenity (IV, Cathedral; inquiry, ". . . quietness, makes me feel it's a peaceful place where you can relax"). Since this card frequently elicits morbidly colored responses from depressively inclined patients it can be inferred that the unconscious reunion thema more than compensates for the latent threatening gloom. On Card IX two responses ("these two things look like babies" and "this looks like a forest, like Paradise") underscore the regressive pull inferred from the claustral House drawing.

Her distrust of people as expressed in the small window, stringy pathway, moat-like area between the observer and the house, and absence of a warmth-symbolizing chimney is brought out directly in the treatment history ("you can't trust any man, even the old ones who act fatherly") and in the Rorschach (Card III, "these look like twins warming themselves over a fire, could be hoboes"). The larger center windows are therefore seen to represent her contact wish, while gloomy forebodings are associated with the parental figures who, like hoboes, gave her no assurance of a fixed domicile. The ambition thema as projected in the "mansion" has its reverberations of unrealism and impracticality in Rorschach and TAT figures and in the clinical material ("Discussion of her job aspirations indicates that she unrealistically involves herself in fantasies of high and unattainable job goals and is invariably disappointed . . ."). Anal obstinacy and blocking are mentioned by her therapist and crop out in the word association test (Breast . . . "buttocks"; Penis . . . "anus"; Mud . . . "puddle").

*Tree.* The tree, as a form of inanimate life, is likely to bring out unconscious strivings which border upon the pre-conscious and can drift over into conscious recognition of ego demands. What is immediately apparent is the large and reality-defying expansion of the trunk which would indicate over-determined and

stressful efforts at ego assertiveness associated with weakness and insecurity (small base), a large oppositional core (center white space), narcissistic self-assertion, impulsivity coupled with lack of delicately modulated interpersonal reach (disjunctive branch rendering), feelings of stagnation (grass at base of trunk), and a massive undercurrent of tension and anxiety stemming from repressed id impulses. She makes a feeble effort to integrate these wild impulses (faint lines at base of foliage), but this fails and she flies off into a fantasy world without aim or direction. It should be noted however that only two of the foliage lines extend beyond the page, so that she remains cognizant of limitations imposed by the environment. The presence of three leaves suggests a rather pessimistic and abortive attempt at more differentiated contact or at least an awareness that this need is present, but the orifice-like opening in the tree's center speaks for feelings of hollowness which would necessitate oral demands of an insatiable nature linked with oral pessimism. The impulsive manner in which the branches are drawn and their spike-like appearance would be associated with intensely hostile and aggressive impulses having their source in the blackened past from which this tormented personality has risen.

Post-drawing Interrogation and Supplementary Data. While drawing the tree she states initially that "it's autumn and the leaves have fallen off . . . this is grass, dry grass because it's fall." Ambivalence concerning her own role is expressed in uncertainty concerning the tree's age ("It's a young tree and it's still growing . . . yet I know big trees like this are generally older trees"), with the suggestion of a reluctance to accept an adult status which would be consistent with her oral-dependency demands. Ambivalence is also noted in relation to her own fund of vigor ("not really dead but sleeping," "some life in the branches, that's where life is, body is dead, life in roots and branches," "I know that Fall is only a temporary time of rest or whatever you call it"), with indications of oscillation between her urge for life and her regressive wish for peaceful extinction. The latter is denied but glimpses of the underlying trend are discernible. Gender differentiation is denied but the hostility theme is revealed in her comment on the branches ("looks like a pin-cushion and these are needles sticking up like a man's hair standing on end"). Not to be inferred from the drawing itself, this comment might suggest fear of the damaging consequences of a man's erection and her own fright reactions which are presented in montage fashion ("hair standing on end"). Emphasis on sleeping carries uterine connotations with hidden implications of being awakened into life by some magical occurrence (Sleeping Beauty fantasy?). And yet, there is a strong affirmation of strength which might underscore a denial component ("strong, very strong and very thick and has firm roots").

The medical social worker reports in 1954 that although she has shown enormous improvement in her social adjustment, "when relationships with the opposite sex become too intimate she withdraws and expresses considerable fear and confusion." The denial elements inferred from the PDI [2] and the underlying feelings of inadequacy (autumnal tree, dry grass, dead body) are also revealed ("Her low self-esteem is marked and she considers herself physically quite repulsive and looks on her future with pessimism") and are consistent with the witches ("black") on Card I and "two ghosts" on Card II of the Rorschach. At a later period the psychiatrist comments, "Ego in this girl is extremely weak and there is a strong self-belittling attitude focussed on her physical appearance." The reaction-formation to ego weakness can therefore be inferred from the massive trunk, while the center orifice and its significance is related to another statement by the psychiatrist ("The patient's manipulative tendencies were reviewed and it was observed that she has somehow managed to be treated specially by every agency"). One can tentatively conjecture that pseudo-ego strength stems from her feeling that she can make demands on others and have them gratified. But the weakness of the branch structure attests to precarious integration which is brittle ($F+100\%/100\%$) and is constantly threatening to fall apart (in December of 1955 the therapist notes "patient was depressed and agitated and stated that she had had a very difficult week. She feared that she would have a nervous breakdown, felt hopeless and despairing"). This is congruent with the black underpinning of the tree.

*Person (I).* It is usually assumed that patients who draw the opposite sex first are projecting an identification with that sex. The term "identification" in this context is ambiguous and can be very misleading if we do not know whether the identification trend signifies phallic-assertive drives, a wish for the prerogatives of the male sex, orally determined possessive and exploitative

---

[2] Post-Drawing Interrogation.

motivations, or more complex combinations of these components. There has been no evidence thus far to suggest a wish for masculinity, and the appearance of the figure would certainly fail to confirm such a wish. It would be more logical to assume that opposite-sex figures drawn first indicate basic object-relation problems and that the underlying identification factor has manifold transference ramifications rather than a desire to take over the role and function of the other sex.

The figure (in right profile because she is left-handed) looks like an adolescent in spite of her statement that he is 38, and it is interesting to note that the therapist, upon first meeting her, commented, "I estimated her age at about 16 and was surprised when she admitted to 23." The impression of youthfulness is increased by the infantile hands, shortened arms, bowtie, boyish lines of the face, and underdeveloped nose. The emphasized bowtie in conjunction with the grotesquely raised crotch indicates sexual anxiety which is handled by elimination of disturbing sexual attributes (castration?) leading to desexualization. The stance of the figure appears to be pleading and welcoming in an indecisive manner, while the constricted and partly internalized arms hint at her feeling that accepting and welcoming gestures on the part of others are definitely limited and restricted, with implication of a similar inhibition on her own part.

The drawing is outstanding in its almost studious avoidance of genitality and its emphasis upon a passive-receptive childish conception of a male who cannot be a sexual threat.

*Post-drawing Interrogation and Supplementary Data.* In answering a request for an identification she remarked, "I thought of my psychiatrist for a moment and my medical doctor and what men generally mean to me. Just my impression of men." The implications of this comment need no elaboration. As she continued she altered the impression to "a waiter because I put the bowtie in and from the waist down he looks like a cowboy." The condensation of *service* functions supports an interpretation of an intensely recipient orientation with herself as the egocentric supplicant and demander of narcissistic and oral supplies. The cowboy reference would seem to express a recognition of masculinity rather than servility and devotion, but one might conjecture that this concept is probably associated with a romanticized notion of rough male gallantry in an emergency and diffidence in close quarters. The status-whittling process continues: "He's not too bright, so he's satisfied with what he does. . . . I'm thinking of the waiter now." and finally, "I wouldn't like that person. He doesn't appeal to me because he's not masculine looking." There is apparently a very confused and unstable conception of masculinity in this patient which would make it difficult for a man to play a consistent role in response to her demands.

Her relationships with therapists have been stormy ones, and in their course she clearly demonstrates what appears so quickly in her drawing. Her insatiable demands are exemplified in the following chart entry; "Patient expressed anger at the therapist because he was 5 minutes late starting the session. She expressed feelings of jealousy: "Maybe you think my troubles are less important because your other patients have families and maybe children of their own and it is more important to help them. I get jealous because everyone has families and belongs except for me." The stance of the figure projects this feeling and is further confirmed by a recent outburst in which she complained: "There's something about you that annoys me, I feel you're stubborn, you're too ethical, I don't have the impression you're a good doctor, you're not interested in me as a person, just interested in pure science, you're not attached to me, you're selfish," etc. Her previous therapist mentions the vicissitudes of the transference relationship in the course of which the patient made constant efforts to find out as much about his personal life as possible. He states; "This ambivalence, not only to the therapist but to adults in general was one in which she was only able to form a close relationship after she had 'extracted everything' from them, but even after that it could be noted that she was still extremely hesitant in her relationship because she seriously questioned whether adults could really help her in any way." She told another therapist that her hospitalizations have been her chief source of satisfaction. "I daydreamed of romance with doctors and that kept me alive."

She entered into an impulsive liaison with a young man who was undergoing psychiatric treatment whom she recognized as *boyish and immature* and who had a chronic illness which the therapist suspected might be congenital lung cysts on the basis of her description. There has never been any sexual relationship with him or with any other man and she expressed in one of her sessions "some ambivalence about sexual intercourse before marriage, but generally feels that she would like to avoid sexual activity." The likelihood of any man being able to gratify her is very dim in light of her basic conception of men which is so involved with castrative attitudes, fantasy preoccupations, and a search for father figures. At one time she made the statement that because of her problem she "would never be happy even though she attained some of her most cherished goals such as graduation and marriage" (1953). She recently broke off with this boy.

*Female (II).* This drawing projects a combination of narcissism, sadness, the faltering uncertainty of a child first learning to walk (stance), feelings of marked insecurity concerning her ability to maintain herself and to reach goals (tiny feet), hostility (jagged fingers), helplessness and trends toward inertia (drooping hand), and sexual inhibition (collar barrier). Although she has glamour aspirations there is marked lack of confidence in her ability to live out such intentions (coiffure which seems to reveal areas of baldness). She does not feel herself to be a mature woman (breast omission) but entertains romantic notions which point to fantasy ego formation (ante-bellum Southern Belle skirt). The peculiarly twisted right arm and the segmented left indicates those same inhibitions as were projected in the male figure-drawing and underscores a distinct hiatus between impulses and their expression. Patients who draw arms in this way are frequently subject to blocking in their therapeutic sessions and feel themselves swept by compulsions which increase their feelings of helplessness. While mouth accentuation suggests narcissistic enhancement within the normal range, the dark shading would also point to some anxiety concerning her dependency needs. The figure as a whole would therefore seem to stress an unrealistic self-concept linked with chronic self-rejection and pessimism, brooding fantasies, and the feeling of being a little child whom others must care for and support (little girl feet underneath a big girl skirt).

*Post-drawing Interrogation and Supplementary Data.* Ambivalent identification is inferred from her statement, following denial of any association, that "it could remind me of myself or my mother." Self-hatred as a derivative of the hatred of the intro-

jected mother is supported by her response to a sentence completion item (My mother and I . . . "hated one another"). The figure
is looking into a mirror and feels "that she looks pretty, but doesn't
feel pretty. She can see that she's dressed pretty but her feelings
don't correspond with that and she's aware of that." This comment can be correlated with her statement that the figure is
"young in spirit but old in age, around in her forties," a further
indication of conflict with the mother figure which is blurring
her self-concept. It is a "disturbed" figure, with the "hands hanging in air, people don't stand that way, not happy," which corresponds with feelings of isolation and ego fragility as expressed
in a therapeutic session ("I have no feeling of permanency, like
I'm hanging, my feet aren't touching the ground"). Such feelings
also suggest an uncertain contact with concrete aspects of reality
and hints at suicidal fantasies. The figure, like herself, "doesn't
even know what she needs, she needs help."

The oral need stems from early deprivation which is projected
in her Rorschach responses and takes precedence over more
permanent mature heterosxual relationships (VI, "swinging doors
like cowboys come in and out of in these saloons"; VII, "looks
like animals you see around Easter time, stuffed animals"), although the cowboy-saloon theme hints at concealed promiscuity
fantasies which may be related to her persistent efforts to extract
something from all her therapists. It should be noted however
that these seductive gestures are of pregenital origin in light of
their childish insistence upon being the focus of attention. At
one point the therapist remarks, "She expressed hostility toward
the new therapist in the group situation because of his 'coldness.'
During discussions it was apparent that she meant she did not
feel he was giving her sufficient personal attention." In the TAT
a detailed foster-child fantasy attests to her unabated need to
search for and find a good father.

Her fantasy ego formation began quite early in life. She recently related a favorite daydream of her childhood in which she
saw herself in a white wedding gown being married to a prince,
an obvious Oedipal fantasy which is restated in the flowing skirt
of the figure. But her basic detachment from people and her
difficulty in establishing interpersonal relations (which are
brought out in predominance of (H) and (A) figures in the
Rorschach) intensifies this trend and is brought to a vivid climax
in her TAT story to 8 GF:

"This is a story of a professional model and the great men she sat for. This woman has had some of the greatest artists paint her and there's no way of paying her; if she doesn't want to pose for an artist she won't. She refuses to name the sum until the portrait is finished and there is written guarantee that this sum will not be revealed to any other artist. She has been painted 500 times and each piece is a masterpiece. This woman lived 500 years ago in Rome, Italy and there is now a gallery, the Lu Lu La Rhein gallery, and no prints are allowed to be made, so if one wants to see the painting one must go there. No one knows about her personal life. The only way they communicated with her was through her sittings. Other than that her life is a complete secret."

The splendid narcissistic isolation projected in this story has grandiose elements compatible with her "mansion" drawing.

*Conclusion.* The final step in evaluating this H-T-P would be to integrate the findings into an organized psychological report and without reference to the treatment history, but to do so would be beyond the scope of this study. My main purpose was to demonstrate an interpretative procedure with a technique which provides rich material in so short a time as to make its inclusion in the test battery a must. The detailed clinical verification shows an impressive correspondence between the H-T-P and independent data, which should not be surprising in view of the fact that all the material comes from the same patient. It might be argued that there is danger of ad hoc interpretations, but in routine clinical practice all interpretations are test-confined and the final report is derived solely from projective and expressive techniques. If these tests have something to offer they should stand on their own merits and not as pale reflections of the case worker's or psychiatrist's observations and interpretations. This study was attempted to show that the H-T-P can reveal fundamental aspects of the patient's personality and struggles and that such insights can often be made available to the therapist prior to the first treatment session.

## REFERENCE

1. Meyer, B., Brown, F., and Levine, A.: Observations on the House-Tree-Person drawing test before and after surgery. *Psychosom. Med.*, 17:428-454, 1955.

CHAPTER 13

# THE CASE OF R: BEFORE AND AFTER THERAPY

### John N. Buck

The patient, R,[1] was referred for psychological appraisal by one of his college professors after R had remarked to the professor (in a chance conversation) that he was contemplating suicide.

R was born in a small town twenty-two years ago, five hours prior to his twin sister. R was said to have suffered a mild injury at birth. R's mother became seriously ill after giving birth to the twins, and for a good many months the children were cared for by their father.

When R was three years of age, he inadvertently knocked over a kerosene lamp and set fire to the family home which burned to the ground. His family, apparently without intent to traumatize, dubbed him "firebug" for some time thereafter. About a year later the house caught fire again while the patient was the only one in the home. He doesn't know how the house caught fire, but has always felt that somehow it was his fault. That same year the third and last child, a boy, was born to R's parents. R's mother by then was in good health and was able to breast-feed the younger brother (much to R's discomfiture).

When R went to school, it was to a school whose principal was his mother. He was found to be sinistral; promptly converted to dextrality by the simple expedient of many spankings. He remembers having many quarrels with his younger brother during their early childhood, and almost invariably R was held by his parents to have been in the wrong. R feels very strongly that his mother favored the younger boy. The mother was the dominant figure in the household. R tended to identify with his father who, when things became too unpleasant, left home for a time.

When R and his twin sister entered the second grade, the

---

[1] All names of persons and places have been altered to preserve the patient's anonymity.

mother (for some reason which R never fully understood) sent R and his twin sister to live with her mother. Once again R felt severely rejected.

R had the usual diseases of childhood—none serious; a number of minor accidents.

When R was six, he and a group of small boys engaged in mutual masturbation. When he was eleven years of age, he was introduced into heterosexuality by an experimentally-inclined girl some years his elder. When he was twelve years of age, he had fellatio performed upon him by an older boy with whom he was spending the night.

R describes himself as having been a perfect little gentleman up until he was twelve or thirteen, and having secretly despised himself for it. In grammar school he was always at or near the top of his class—and so was his brother. However, after R entered high school, he began to rebel more and more strongly against his brother's almost uncanny perfection (which infuriated R), and by the time R graduated from high school, he was near the bottom of his class.

One day while R was in high school, his brother teased him about something which enraged R so that he grabbed a kitchen knife and went after the brother who ran upstairs and locked himself in the bathroom, then went out the window, across the porch roof, and down a tree while R was trying to kick the door down. R feels sure that if he had caught his brother within five minutes of the time he picked up the knife, he would have killed him.

After graduating from high school, R entered a military college where he did fairly well for about six months; then he was "shipped" for violating the rule that one must not tell a lie. The lie in this case was told in defense of two classmates. R was permitted to re-enter college the following Fall, but a short time later he was "shipped" again for the same offense. He states that he found himself almost obsessed with the idea that he must accept blame if anyone in a group of which he was a member was found guilty of misconduct. After having been "shipped" for the second time, R joined the Reserve Officers Training Corps and was sent to the same college! In a short time he was in trouble again. Each of these episodes was accompanied by a conviction that he had disgraced his family intensely.

After the third episode, R felt that he could not face his

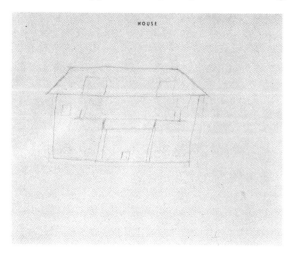

Pre-therapy

family again. He enlisted in the Army, sought and received placement in a Ranger outfit. It was his quixotic idea that if he were killed in action, he would somehow restore the family's good name. Much to his disgust (and additional frustration) the war ended before he got into a combat area, and he was ultimately placed on occupation duty.

R spent much of his time in the Army in stockade because of various infractions of rules.

In the Rangers, R engaged in extensive homosexual and heterosexual activities.

While he was in the Army his childhood sweetheart—a girl whom he had been dating off and on for many years—married and in due course bore a child. R expressed himself thoroughly surprised to find his reaction to be one more of relief than anything else.

Upon his discharge from the Army R re-entered college (not the one in which he had had so much difficulty); found adjustment to prosaic civilian life extremely difficult; resorted to periodic bouts of heavy drinking as an escape mechanism.

At the time of his first interview R had fallen rather deeply in love with a fellow student (female). He complained that he was finding it uncommonly difficult to control his desire for prompt and complete sexual satisfaction when in her company. He felt that marriage was out of the question (for a number of years at least), and he was definitely depressed.

As a matter of differential diagnosis it was essential to determine whether R's hostility and persistent anti-social activity represented psychopathy or character neurosis. It was even more imperative to determine whether R was or was not truly suicidal. The first H-T-P was administered at the second interview.

## POST-DRAWING INTERROGATION

P1.[2]  Is this a man or a woman?
   Started off with a man.

P2.  How old is he?
   Mmn—I'll say about 27.

P3.  Who is he?
   Who? (laughs) I don't have the slightest idea.

P4.  Is he a relation, a friend, or what?
   That's what came from my pencil, my making a mark on paper.

---

[2] *P* questions deal with the drawing of the Person; *T* with that of the Tree; and *H* with the House.

Pre-therapy

Pre-therapy

P5. Whom were you thinking about while you were drawing?
How stupid it was for me to try to draw something like that; how stupid it was 'cause I didn't do a better job.
P6. What is he doing?
(laughs) While I was drawing him you mean?
What is the *person* doing?
Well, he's got on a lounging robe. Evidently he heard some noise, or could be talking to someone. I'd have put a pipe in his mouth, but couldn't draw one.
Where is he?
Getting ready to take a drink of whiskey, mix a nice ginger ale and rye.
Where is he?
Being? Let's put him in his study; after his whiskey, he'll relax and listen to some classical records he put on.
Well, what about the noise you said he might have heard?
The thing came to me then, but he could be looking;

possibly looking to his butler as to what to mix in the line of cocktail.

P7. What is he thinking about?

Thinking how good this drink is going to taste; sit down and be able to sip it. Sit down and listen to Rachmaninoff, Tchaikovsky, or Korsakoff — not too loud. Just relax thoroughly—he's a bachelor, by the way.

P8. How does he feel?

Just likes listening to music. When you listen to music like that, you don't feel it until the music starts. The mood of the music would fix his thoughts.

What type of music?

Pick a record at random, let the music dictate the mood.

---

T1. What kind of a Tree is that?

(laughs) I didn't want to insult God by saying that was like any kind He'd put on earth.

But what kind of a Tree do you think this is?

That would resemble a tree—well, pick a maple. Reminds me of the big one in my Grandmother's yard—real big.

T3. About how old is that tree?

Oh, if this is the one in my Grandmother's yard, it would be—fifty years old?

T4. Is that tree alive?

I see that tree—would you say that the tree was alive in the winter? I'd say it was alive, but it doesn't have all the beauty it could have in the spring or fall.

T5(a). What is there about that tree that gives you the impression that it is alive?

Here it is, as you might put it, static, waiting for spring to give it leaves and life. If he could think, he'd realize fall will make him. He will lose it, but there is possibility the next spring can give me my beauty back again.

Well, what about this static period?

Definite static period during which its job is to stay alive and wait.

T5(b)  Is any part of the tree dead?
       *No!*
T6. Which does that tree look more like to you: a man or a
    woman?
    (Smiles) A woman.
T7. What is there about it that gives you that impression?
    (Blushes) Well, it's—just—more—take a woman, char-
    acteristically built, she has more protruding features
    than a man has.
T8. If that were a person instead of a tree, which way would
    the person be facing?
    At (gestures toward self—pauses)—to me she'd be
    standing facing that way (to the left of page).
T9. Is that tree by itself, or is it in a group of trees?
    By itself.
T10. As you look at that tree, do you get the impression that
     it is above you, below you, or about on a level with you?
     I've got it on a little knoll.
T11. What is the weather like in this picture?
     Typical—well let's say like Thanksgiving Day was
     (clear, rather warm, sunshiny).
T12. Is any wind blowing in this picture?
     None.
     Has it been blowing recently?
     No, it hasn't.

———————

H1. How many stories does that house have?
    Two—with a good attic.
H2. What is that house made of?
    It's a brick, colonial-type job.
H3. Is that your own house?
    It wouldn't be bad if I could be an artist and draw
    what's in the back of my mind.
    Whose house is it?
    No one's.
H4. Whose house were you thinking about while you were
    drawing?
    None in particular; possibly one of the beautiful
    Southern homes you see in the movies.
H5. Would you like to own that house yourself?
    Yes.

Why?

> The idea is—to have a home like that one would be secure—that means a lot to us humans, I understand. Be out in the open with a lot of fresh air—no mountains to hem you in. It could be in the Blue Ridge, but not the Alleghenies. (R went on to say he'd like a den with a music room—baby grand, etc. His fiancée plays. While he was answering this question, he drew the drive in front of his house.)

H6(a) If you did own that house and you could do whatever you liked with it, which room would you like for your own?

> Looking at that house, I'm not single.

Which room would you take for your own?

> I'd like to have upstairs—either right or left, facing the front—either one of the corner rooms.

Why?

> (Long pause) I don't know any particular reasons— just one of those desires (at home he had a back corner room facing, and almost against, a cliff).

H6(b). Whom would you like to have live in that house with you?

> Mary.

Why?

> Because I want her to be my wife.

Why do you like her?

> Partly her personality and the fact that she's almost lived in a vacuum—she's never had the knocks—she's relaxed and direct.

H7. As you look at that house, does it seem to be close by or far away?

> Far away! (Said with a deeply wistful tone.)

H8. As you look at the house, do you get the impression that it is above you, below you, or about on a level with you?

> It's on my level; it's away from me, but it's on my level.

H9. What does that house make you think of, or remind you of?

> Oh, I guess I already answered it to a certain point. It's having security (a place every one wants), a place to get away from the world—live in your own world.

H10. What else?

I guess of a flight into fantasy.

H11. Is that a happy, friendly sort of house?

Very.

H12. What is there about it that gives you that impression?

I don't know—that's the way I'd want it to be: happy for those I know I can trust, and a cold front for those I don't trust.

H13. Are most houses happy and friendly?

Yes, I guess they are, I never bothered to give it much consideration.

H14. What is the weather like in this picture?

Mm—the weather'd be perfect there—trees out in front'd be spring, probably—hedge and lawn'd be green.

---

T15. What does that tree make you think of or remind you of?

Oh, I'd put it in front of the house, now.

But what does the tree make you think of or remind you of?

Nothing.

T16. Not anything at all?

Still nothing, except in line of my Grandmother's tree, as one in front of the house. (He said that his Grandmother lived in the County—rolling country—the tree was on the second drop toward the main highway—he had played under it a good deal. This is his paternal grandmother, but he liked his maternal grandmother best.)

T17. Is it a healthy tree?

Yes.

T18. What is there about it that gives you that impression?

I don't know.

T19. Is it a strong tree?

Yes, it would be strong.

T20. What is there about it that gives you that impression?

I wouldn't want it to be weak.

---

P9. What does that person make you think of, or remind you of?

What? Security. (He commented that for himself, personally, money made no difference, but if he were married it would be different.)

P10. What else?

What?—Nothing particularly—

P11. Is that person well?

I'd say he'd be well.

P12. What is there about him that gives you that impression?

I've never been too sick much in my life. What sickness I've had never affected me to not be able to do everything anyway.

P13. Is that person happy?

Mmn—I wouldn't say he was happy—I wouldn't say he was unhappy.

What mood is he in?

Well, either possibly of trying to relax completely, or in the mood of trying to figure something out.

P15. Are most people that way?

They're human beings and that's it—there's nothing outstanding about them. I don't think they're better than I am or worse, until proven. Like a bunch of cattle.

P16. Do you think you would like that person?

Never having seen him before, I know nothing about him.

What sort of a person do you think he is?

In other words just the image of a human being.

Do you think you'd like him?

I'm more or less indifferent.

What sort of person is he?

I wouldn't say. I never draw opinions of people on first meetings unless I draw on intuition. If drawn on first meeting, it's generally hate. I draw up a sort of caution-barrier against people.

P17. What is the weather like in this picture?

What? (Picking up drawing form) Well, it's, it's in the early evening—must be around 5:30 to 6:00 o'clock —I imagine it has been a pretty day.

P18. Whom does that person remind you of?

That I wouldn't know—honest.

No suggestion of anyone you know?
No suggestion at all!
P19. What does that person need most?
I'd put him in that fortunate position of needing noth-
ing.
Do you really think that would be a fortunate state?
If he lived in nothing, he wouldn't have to think.

---

T12. Whom does the tree remind you of?
No person—the tree itself could remind me of my
Grandmother's yard.
How do you feel about your Grandmother?
One of the few things I can remember as a kid, I
wasn't hemmed in there. (He could do as he liked
there in the afternoons.)
T22. What does the tree need most?
Its leaves.
Why?
Because from that position we left him in awhile ago,
it has everything it needs to make it beautiful.

---

H15. Whom does that house make you think of?
Mary.
Why?
There is no point having a house without her.
H16. What does that house need most?
Doesn't need anything.

---

P20. What kind of clothing does this person have on?
Robe with regular pants, I mean regular trousers under. Bedroom slippers.

---

R described the floor plan of his House as follows: The two
box-like affairs in the roof area were intended to represent dormer
windows. He stated that he had intended to erase the two rectangular openings jutting down from the lower edge of the roof,
but had forgotten to do so. The single, well-placed window in the

second story opens into the room he would take for his bedroom. The two pseudo-rectangles (open at the top) to the right of the second story window, represent porch pillars.

In the ground floor the two windows to the left open into the living room; the door leads into a hallway; the first window to the door's right opens into a den and the one farthest to the right into a music room—back of the music room would be either a *bar* or a *kitchen!*

The omission of bathroom, and bedrooms for anyone else, from the second floor points up his intra-familial conflicts still further.

## ANALYSIS OF PRE-THERAPY H-T-P

### Quantitative[3]

The Raw Good I.Q. is 83, the Net Weighted I.Q., 85. The weighted Good I.Q. is 91, the weighted Flaw I.Q., 74. This relatively low level of function serves to emphasize the magnitude of R's maladjustment (there can be no doubt that he is basically of at least high average intelligence). The 17-point disparity between the Good and Flaw I.Q.'s is definitely pathoformic[4] (inspection of the raw scores, however, shows that his ability to appraise critically is not uniformly that inferior; that his critical failure is most acute in the home situation).

His Good Proportion score is depressed, but not to a greater degree than is frequently found in H-T-P's of college students whose fixation on the more abstract elements of life interferes mildly with their ability to solve more prosaic problems easily and quickly. His Flaw scores for both Proportion and Perspective are pathologically low and imply that his maladjustment is really serious (since it has affected both critical judgment and critical insight adversely).

Of the three wholes, the scores for the House, are most sharply depressed. From this we may deduce that: (1) the subject finds his home and his relationship to those occupying it his greatest source of conflict; (2) he also finds it difficult to maintain smooth and satisfying intimate interpersonal relationships in general.

---

[3] The presentation of the quantitative scoring procedure is too elaborate to have fallen within the scope of this book, but may be found in Buck (1). [Ed.]

[4] Leaning toward pathological.

Hopeful signs in the quantitative analysis are: (1) his flaws are largely of the D1 (minor) type; (2) all his major flaw scores are restricted to the House (implying that his maladjustment is relatively crippling only in a specific situation); (3) his Detail score remains high and he has 29 A-scores (indicating that he is striving to maintain good contact with reality); (4) he has no frankly pathological signs, although there are many pathoformic signs (the means score pattern is contraindicative of a psychotic disturbance).

## Qualitative Analysis

### House

*Details.* One essential detail (chimney) is missing (R feels the absence of warmth in his home; is not well adjusted sexually). Window panes are omitted (he has strong oppositional tendencies). Some overemphasis was placed upon the windows and upon their presentation (this suggests an orificial fixation). The emphasis placed upon the so-called containing lines bespeaks a feeling that he is losing control. The detail sequence was atypical which implies that strong emotional associations were aroused by the drawing process with resultant difficulty in plan formation and execution.

*Proportion.* The farther one gets away from the groundline—reality—the larger the windows become (strongly hostile fantasy is suggested and the inadequate integration of the personality is dramatically portrayed).

*Perspective.* Striking is the very poor organization; it is so poor, in fact, that the presence of a psychosis is suggested. The placement of the House serves merely to point up the fact that in the home situation he tends to behave more impulsively, more emotionally.

*Time.* His time consumption of six minutes, forty-five seconds is excessive; indicates that home for him is an area of great sensitivity. There was an initial latency and there were periodic latencies throughout the drawing, indicative of great indecision.

*Line Quality.* The extremely vacillant line quality is pathological: great emphasis is placed on the containing lines of the roof (the fantasy area); he has presumably fantasied a great deal concerning his home and those within it.

**Criticality.** The diminution of his critical ability is indicated by his extensive erasure without subsequent improvement.

**Attitude.** Throughout his drawing of the Home he was defeatistic; plagued sorely by feelings of inadequacy and inferiority.

**Drive.** Despite his obvious distaste for the task presented and despite his equally obvious feelings of inadequacy, he exhibited a peristence that spoke well for his future.

**Comments.** *Drawing phase:* After drawing his first detail (the House's baseline), he commented, "A House? I haven't the slightest idea of how to draw one; it would be much easier to make a blueprint of one." A little later, after he had completed the outline of the walls and roof, he remarked, "Why didn't you ask me to stand on my head? It'd be a lot simpler! I can think of plenty simpler things, like flying twenty feet off the ground and doing a slow roll; it'd be less exciting and less worrisome." He apparently found the drawing-aroused associations something less than pleasant.

After erasing much of his drawing several times, he remarked, "I'll draw you a Japanese temple." This may be interpreted as indicating his opinion that, so far as he is concerned, his home is in a sense a church, and the rituals that must be observed there are foreign.

In the end, and expressing full recognition of the inadequacy of his production, he said, "*You* won't see what *I* see in this! There's your House. It's one a three-year-old could do a lot better!"

*Post-drawing phase:* to recapitulate his P-D-I very briefly: the House was his ideal home, and must be "out in the open" (he has been frustrated too much already). He saw the House as far away (from a psychological as well as a more material standpoint). His relative social immaturity was sharply pointed up: (1) by his comment that he'd want it to be happy for those he knows he can trust; (2) by his remark that he'd never bothered to give much consideration to the possible happiness of other homes.

*Associations:* His House had the following associations for him: (1) home; (2) security; (3) a place to get away from the world; (4)a flight into fantasy.

To sum up, it was a dream house; something he felt he had little chance of getting.

## Tree

*Details.* He drew his Tree in constricted, cautious fashion; gradually extending the trunk upward, and adding branches on each side as he proceeded showing: (1) a sort of burnt-child reaction; (2) a pathoformic need for symmetry. The phallic-like character of the Tree apparently disturbed him. For he screened his drawing with his left hand much of the time. He accounted intellectually for the absence of foliage by stating that, since it was winter, he'd not draw leaves.

*Proportion.* The Tree is the smallest of the three wholes, expressing symbolically his basic feeling of inferiority. The inadequate, frail branch structure connotes his appraisal of his satisfaction-seeking activity as inadequate, unsatisfying, and poorly co-ordinated. He draws the sun as a tiny, far distant object, which suggests that: (1) he feels that the environment in general provides little warmth; (2) often he and authority are far apart.

*Perspective.* The arc-like character of the groundline implies both an unresolved mother-attachment and a tendency to seek to occupy the center of the "social stage" so to speak. The placement of the Tree below center upon the form page implies that he prefers the elemental and the concrete to the complex and the abstract; the placement of the Tree close to the average vertical midline connotes a specific attempt to maintain intellectual control over his desire for immediate emotional satisfaction and his proclivity for acting impulsively.

*Time.* He took one minute, forty-eight seconds to produce this; not an excessive expenditure of time.

*Line Quality.* In general, the line quality is reasonably consistent; it is definitely superior to that for the House.

*Criticality.* There was almost no erasure; little need for any.

*Attitude.* While he was still openly dubious concerning his ability to draw satisfactorily, he was far more assured than when he was drawing the House which seemed to arouse many very disturbing associations concerning his relationships with his family.

**Comments.** *Drawing phase:* He made no comment while drawing the Tree.

*Post-drawing phase:* To recapitulate his P-D-I very briefly: his Tree reminded him of a woman because of its "protruding" features; it was alive, but static, waiting for spring. Note his change of Person in the statement: *"He* will lose it, but there is the possibility the next spring can give *me* my beauty back again" (his view of the future is by no means entirely dysphoric). His remark that he wouldn't want it to be weak expressed his own fear of appearing weak and his contempt for the weak.

*Associations:* His Tree first suggested nothing; then his grandmother's home which he liked, because there he could do as he wished in the afternoon and there he didn't feel hemmed in (he has always been more or less in open conflict with authority and has felt that he has been unfairly discriminated against).

To sum up, his Tree was a tree of childhood; a tree located in the one place in which he felt he was treated with some consistent justice by an elder.

**Person**

**Details.** Here the sequence of details was a striking thing; first of all R was obviously reluctant to draw his Person below the waistline (sexual preoccupation with maladjustment strongly suggested). He found it impossible to draw visible arms and hands (expressing symbolically his inability to make spontaneous, easy social adjustments, and also his inability to evaluate adequately just what his potentials really are). In effect, the body is nude under the robe; yet he cannot bring himself to draw genitalia (his need for exhibitionism runs into sharp conflict with his strong need to conform).

**Proportion.** The overly large neck implies an acute awareness of body drives with strong effort to control them. The short, stubby legs suggest rather profound feelings of immobility and a lack of autonomy.

*Perspective.* The rigid stance, the averted head, and the suggestion that the Person is at least partially on tiptoe, connote a pathoformic inflexibility of reaction; a tendency to avoid facing issues squarely, to seek satisfaction in irreality. The almost perfect "framing" of the figure on the form page is pathoformic in itself and implies that R is comparably rigid in his relationship with people in general.

*Time.* The time consumption of five minutes, twenty-seven seconds, is mildly excessive in view of the scanty detailing.

*Line Quality.* Emphasis and reinforcement of containing lines imply an acute awareness of a need for self-control. The great and wide variation in line quality suggests that R is rather seriously maladjusted; that, among other things, body cues are disturbing to him.

*Criticality.* As in the drawing of the House, there was a considerable amount of erasure with little of it followed by correction.

*Attitude.* The patient was obviously disturbed and uncertain while he was drawing his Person.

*Comments. Drawing phase:* Immediately prior to drawing the legs, he paused and remarked, "All the way, huh?—what an amazing thing!" And then, emphasizing his sexual preoccupation and the guilt feelings accompanying it, he concealed his Person with his left hand while he drew the legs.

*Post-drawing phase:* A brief review of the P-D-I reveals: (1) marked subjectivity—the drawn person is in a very real sense a self-portrait; (2) his feeling that he can trust a person only after that person has convincingly demonstrated his reliability; (3) his acute awareness of his bachelor status; (4) his somewhat unusual and unexpected willingness to "let the music dictate the mood"; (5) his philosophy that the ideal state is *nothing.*

*Associations:* With his Person he associates security, expressing his own great need therefor.

To sum up, his Person is a thinly veiled self-portrait (idealized somewhat verbally, degraded somewhat non-verbally).

It is obvious that R is badly maladjusted, anxious, insecure, immature, and greatly frustrated; that he is in very real need of therapy. The drawings and the patient's reaction to them do not indicate the presence of a psychosis. The depressed manic-depressive, for example, does not exhibit the drive that R shows; he usually draws very small wholes; he places his wholes either very low on the page (emphasizing the depression of mood), or very high on the page (emphasizing his feeling of overstriving); he does not verbalize freely; his drawings tend to have a minimum of detail; time consumption may be very great; and there is often progressive deterioration of both the quality and the quantity of the drawings from House through Person.

R's House and certain of his comments made while he drew it strongly suggested schizophrenia, but the Tree is of far better quality and is not schizophrenic. And the P-D-I, though it contains several pathoformic responses, is not that of a psychotic.

The patient's anxiety is too patent and too deep to justify a diagnosis of psychopathy. The tentative diagnosis was character neurosis, with obsessive-compulsive components.

At first the therapeutic approach was extremely cautious and essentially non-directive; later the patient was found to be able to accept a rather surprising amount of interpretation and rather carefully veiled direction. After the eighteenth session the H-T-P was administered for a second time, in an attempt to evaluate the effects of the therapy. At that time the clinical picture indicated improvement.

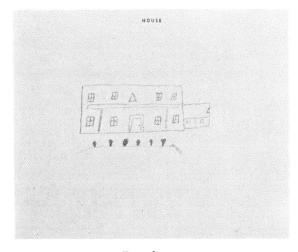

Post-therapy

Post-therapy

## POST-THERAPY P-D-I

P1. Is that a man or a woman?

Man.

P2. How old is he?

Oh, between twenty-six and thirty.

P3. Who is he?

Just anybody—any man.

P4. Is he a relation, a friend, or what?

Mmn—not particularly, no.

P5. Whom were you thinking about while you were drawing?

(Slight delay.) Not any particular person (R chokes),
'cept when I drew the nose in a peak and redrew it,
I thought of the self-consciousness my girl has about
her nose. I thought of that for a split second, I imagine.

P6. What is he doing?

(Long delay) Well, since I drew him with a bathrobe,
we'll have him at home.

Where at home?

In the living room.

What is he doing in the living room?

Well, he could be getting ready to lay down on the sofa and sleep or just rest.

What was he doing before?

Let's see—taking a shower.

P7. What is he thinking about?

Just relaxing.

What has he been doing that he wants to relax for?

I wouldn't know—you could say any type of work in the afternoon or evening, early evening, rather—just relaxing.

P8. How does he feel?

Well, he doesn't have too many big problems to be pondered over—he's able just to relax now—and—

And what?

Just take it easy.

---

Post-therapy

T1.  What kind of tree is that?
       Well, maple came into my mind first.
T2.  Where is that tree actually located?
       I still see it in my Grandmother's yard.
T3.  About how old is that tree?
       Oh! At least fifty years old, I imagine.
T4.  Do you think of this one here as living?
       Yes, sir. (Slightly hesitant.)
T5.  What is there about that tree that gives you the impression that it's alive?
       (Slight delay) I'd want it to be alive.
     Is there anything that makes you feel this tree is alive?
       I was drawing a tree, and consciously I don't think I'd be drawing a dead tree.
     Is any part of the tree dead?
       No—
T6.  Which does that tree look more like to you: a man or a woman?
       (Long delay) Man.
T7.  What is there about it that gives you that impression?
       Strong, sturdy,—I'm—
     I'm what?
       I didn't mean to say *I'm*—just something—
     Do you see any part of the tree that looks like any part of a man?
       No.
T8.  If that were a person instead of a tree, which way would the person be facing?
       Well, his face would be toward me.
T9.  Is that tree by itself, or is it in a group of trees?
       Well, it could be—I see that tree—as by itself, but with, with smaller trees near it. (At this point R indicated there was a large tree to the right.)
T10. As you look at that tree, do you get the impression that it is above you, below you, or about on a level with you?
       On the level.
T11. What is the weather like in this picture?
       Well, it's a nice day.
     What would you call a nice day?
       A little warmer than it is today. Maybe this time of

month, but a little warmer. (Actually it was windy, temperature about 40 that day.)

T12. Is there any wind blowing in this picture?

No, sir.

Has it been blowing recently?

Not any particular reason for me to think that it has.

---

H1. How many stories does that house have?

Two.

H2. What is that house made of?

Frame.

H3. Is that your own house?

No, sir.

Whose house is it?

I don't know. It's situated between Blue Point and Riley going around the Power Plant Road, not direct on Route 21. It is beautiful. I find myself looking forward to passing it going and coming.

H4. Whose house were you thinking about while you were drawing?

That one, and someday I could possibly have one like it.

H5. Would you like to own that house yourself?

Yes.

Why?

Well, it's sitting out, not exactly level, but compared to where I come from it is level. There is a range of the Blue Ridge Mountains in front of it. Not near any big town, but close enough for easy reach.

H6(a). If you did own that house and you could do whatever you liked with it, which room would you take for your own?

If I didn't have any bedroom downstairs, I'd take the upstairs left corner room.

Why?

The way the house is situated there's a nicer view from the left (his left) hand than from the right—the other side is too close to the mountains.

H6(b) Whom would you like to have live in that house with you?

Hmm! (laughs) Do I have to answer that?

You could've changed.

Not that fast! Definitely I'd like to have *her* there. I couldn't have that house until I'd been married a few years because I wouldn't have enough money, and by then I'd probably have a couple of little ones—she wants them that bad.

H7. As you look at that house, does it seem to be close by or far away?

It's not too far away, and it's not too close.

H8. As you look at that house, do you get the impression that it is above you, below you, or about on a level with you?

It's on the level, but it's back—I'm going to have to grub to get it!

H9. What does that house make you think of, or remind you of?

Well, naturally—security.

Why *naturally?*

A man couldn't very well own a house like that and be very insecure. I see that house as permanent, not temporary.

H10. What else does it remind you of?

Not anything special in the past. I can keep it visualized in my mind as more or less a goal to work toward in the future.

H11. Is that a happy, friendly sort of house?

Yes, sir.

H12. What is there about it that gives you that impression?

It just does.

H13. Are most houses that way?

Not particularly, no.

Why?

I don't know. I can't say any definite reasons. Maybe I judge most from the way you do when you first meet a person—some you don't like—some you leave on the fence to go either way. That house has a more aristocratic, but friendly look.

H14. What is the weather like in this picture?

Beautiful sunny day.

What is the temperature?

Oh, the temperature's like we enjoyed last week. The days were very warm. I don't believe any kind of weather or temperature would make that house look bad.

What time of year is it?

This time of year, it could be.

What kind of ground is the house on?

The house is on a level with a gradual, very gradual slope towards me.

---

T15. What does that tree make you think of, or remind you of?

Hmn—nothing in particular.

T16. Not anything?

Still be my Grandmother's tree.

Does it arouse pleasant or unpleasant memories?

Pleasant.

Is that tree healthy?

Yes.

T17. What is there about it that gives you that impression?

Trunk and limbs—I'd hoped to portray that—I mean the trunk and the limbs are—

Are what?

Are very strong.

Is it a strong tree as you've drawn it?

Yes, to me it is.

---

P9. What does that person make you think of, or remind you of?

(Long pause) What? Looks like I'm getting in a rut —I hope I'm not disappointing you—(delay) Just a man with no particular great worries at the moment, anyway.

P10. What else?

(Long delay) Reminds me of a person—well off— by that I mean not necessarily financially well off, but just contented.

P11. Is that person well?

Yes, sir!

P12. What is there about him that gives you that impression?

When I drew him, I didn't have any idea of him being anything other than being well.

P13. Is that person happy?
    Yes, sir, he doesn't have any mental conflicts or phy-
    sical conflicts or anything, he's just—
    Just what?
    Pretty well with the world—thinks it a pretty good
    place to live in.

P15. Do you feel that most people are happy and well?
    I wouldn't want to call that an ambiguous question,
    but it would be hard to answer. Many people look
    happy on the outside, but inside it might be tragic.
    Generally speaking, I think the American leads a
    pretty happy life. I stress *American,* because there's a
    lot of difference on a day-to-day basis between Ameri-
    cans and others. Take the Japanese people, they may
    be happy, but they remind you of a piece of machinery.

P16. Do you think you would like that person?
    Well, he's a person that appreciates and tries to admire
    the beauty in nature, yet he can see the damage that
    nature can bring. He likes classical music—wants to
    understand and appreciate art. He wants to accom-
    plish these things and yet remain a common human
    being. He doesn't feel he's better than any other, re-
    gardless of race, class, or anything else.

P17. What is the weather like in this picture?
    Well, it has been a nice day. It's in the afternoon or
    evening—the temperature is rather warm.
    What time of year is it?
    This time would be all right.

P18. Whom does that person remind you of?
    No one in particular—possibly *I'd* like to be like I've
    described *him.*

P19. What does that person need most?
    That's what makes him so well off—classifying be-
    tween a necessity and a luxury he doesn't need any-
    thing.
    What do you mean by *classifying?*
    Well, you know the sociological definition of *necessity.*

---

T21. Whom does that tree remind you of?
    Could be my father.

Why?

Dad's strong; healthy, I guess you'd call it.

T22. What does that tree need most?

I don't see it needs anything—when Spring comes it will have its leaves.

---

H15. Whom does that house make you think of?

Mary.

H16. What does that house need most?

That house doesn't need a thing—that's equivalent to Mr. Blanding's Dream House.

H17. If these were persons instead of shrubs, who might they be?

(Reading from left to right) My brother-in-law, Mary, Dad, Mom, my twin sister, and my brother. I should've put in another for the baby. (Note: his sister had recently had a child.)

Where are you in this picture?

I'm standing off looking at it.

H18. To what does that walkway lead?

To the left, it leads to the field; to the right, it leads to the road.

---

P20. What kind of clothing does this person have on?

I have him with a pair of pants on under the robe.

What is the material of the robe?

I don't know anything about material, but it's heavy. Not *heavy*, but hard-finished, not rayon or stuff.

Is the bathrobe buttoned?

I was trying to leave the impression that it came together in front.

On questioning R described the floor plan of his house as follows: the window farthest to the left upstairs opens into his bedroom (the room extends through to the back of the house); the second window (reading left to right) opens into a guest bedroom (there is a bathroom back of that bedroom); the middle window he describes as a small French window opening onto the balcony over the porch from the hall (this window he sees as now open); the last two windows open into separate bedrooms (for the children) which extend to the back of the house.

Downstairs (reading from left to right : a living room lies behind the first two windows; and back of that is a music room; the door opens into a hall; behind the third window is a dining-room; behind the fourth, the kitchen.

The wing contains a garage with the attic over the garage fixed up as a place to build model airplanes.

*Supplementary Questions*

1. What about his hands?
    They're in his pockets, conveniently placed there.
2. What is in the right hand?
    Nothing.
3. What is in the left hand?
    Nothing.
4. Why is he on tiptoes?
    That was just my inability to draw him flat footed (anteriorly).
5. What is he looking at?
    Nothing in particular—I just drew him for—
    For what?
    Could be looking at the time before lying down for a nap—speculate on the time he had for a nap before dinner—before getting dressed for dinner.

NOTE:  His concept of his second House is of much higher quality than the first. All in all, this P-D-I suggests that R has in some respects undergone a definite change for the better.

### ANALYSIS OF POST-THERAPY H-T-P

### Quantitative Analysis

There is no striking change in the quantitative scores: the Raw G. I.Q. is 82; the Net Weighted I.Q. 90; the Good I.Q. 94; the Flaw I.Q. 80. While some of this improvement might perhaps be attributed to "practice effect," not all of it can be shrugged off in that fashion. Signs of improved efficiency of function are: (1) the increase in the Net Weighted I.Q. (implying a mild increase in the quality of performance); (2) the six-point rise in the Flaw I.Q. (indicating that R's critical insight has improved); (3) the lessened disparity between the Good and the Flaw I.Q.'s (suggesting that R's ability to accept and to deal with the problems and situations of every-day life is bettering).

The Perspective Flaw score is still depressed, indicating that strong emotional factors within the personality are still interfering with critical insight, but the previously sharply depressed Proportion Flaw score is much improved, arguing for a diminishing of some of the heretofore handicapping rigid attitudes.

The Flaw score for the House is definitely improved, implying a comparably improved intra-familial adjustment, with a lessening of his "chip-on-shoulder" attitude.

The patient may be said to have undergone definite, 'though by no means great, improvement, but it is patent that he is still maladjusted, and that the clinically observed improvement, which is much greater, is to be regarded as tenuous.

## Qualitative Analysis

### House

*Details.* He is still unable to draw a chimney, but whereas before he found it impossible to present door and windows until he had gone over and over the roof and wall, this time he indicated his need and overstriving to make satisfactory contact by drawing the door and the lower windows after drawing the groundline and before producing a wall at all! This suggests that although R's attitude toward his family has altered markedly for the better, he is by no means well-adapted to this new attitude of whole-hearted cooperation, nor is he wholly comfortable in his new role.

He is now able to put panes in all windows save the triangular affair in the upper story (perhaps he still indulges in hostile phantasy about his mother) and the windows in the garage to the right (he still regards the future with skepticism).

He identifies the shrubs in front of his House, from left to right, as brother-in-law, fiancée, father, mother, twin sister, and brother. He can now include members of his family in the picture of his dream house, but their presence induces anxiety, as is indicated by the deep shading. The shrubs were the last details drawn, incidentally.

*Proportion.* His door is larger in this House than in his first, indicating his increased willingness to make sharing relationships, and there is no longer the former great disparity between the windows as to size (satisfaction in the home is no longer restricted to fantasy, and the personality integration is better). The House is smaller, suggesting that R is less acutely sensitive about his status in the family.

*Perspective.* The House is still essentially a façade, 'though he attempts to give depth to the picture with a front porch (he is still too immature in his intrafamilial situation to undertake to substitute tactful evasion for blunt forthrightedness).

In sharp contrast to the vacillation and indecision he exhibited in the first drawing of a House, he produced this House with a fairly coherent plan of action (no longer does he react toward home in a more or less impulsively chaotic fashion; he still has not fully accepted his altered role, but he is able much of the time to exercise the intellectual control that the present placement of the House suggests).

*Time.* His time consumption of six minutes, twenty-nine seconds is pathoformic (his impulsivity in the past has brought him grief—he now exercises over-compensatory caution).

*Line quality.* There is lessened emphasis on the containing lines (he has relaxed somewhat), but the lines throughout still show an unhappy lack of assurance.

*Criticality.* He erased less. When he did erase, erasure was at times followed by mild improvement.

*Attitude.* R was rather tense and anxious. He stated that he knew he had improved, and he insisted that he no longer felt depressed, but it was patent that he was worried about what he might be revealing in his drawings. The confusion of the pre-therapy drawings had been replaced by excessive caution.

*Comments.* *Post-drawing phase:* A summation of his P-D-I reveals that now his dream house has become a specific structure. Mountains no longer symbolize being hemmed in; he can now even express pleasure at viewing them (the female breast symbol no longer arouses unpleasant feelings of having been rejected by the mother). The future has real meaning for him.

*Associations:* He associates: (1) security (a permanent sort of security); (2) a future goal; (3) his fiancée with this House.

### Tree

*Details.* His Tree now has several two-dimensional branches (indicating a feeling that his satisfaction-seeking resources are stronger). In the branch structure there is mild overemphasis on the right side of the Tree—the intellectual-control side. The branches suggest mild hostility, but the hostility appears to be rather well controlled.

The shading of and at the groundline implies the presence of definite, but by no means crippling, anxiety.

He can now indicate the position of the sun with an X (his conflict with authoritative figures has been somewhat lessened). At the time these drawings were obtained, subjects were asked to indicate the position of the sun in relation to the Tree, but not specifically to draw the sun.

*Proportion.* His second Tree is smaller than his first, but the trunk and the branch structure are in much better proportional relationship. The reduced size suggests: (1) lessened sensitivity; (2) feelings of relative inadequacy, but an ability to accept that position without open rebellion.

*Perspective.* The groundline slopes mildly upward from left to right, connoting a feeling of definite, but by no means abnormal, striving. The almost perfect "framing" of the Tree on the page expresses his feeling of rigidity in his new role.

*Time.* Four minutes, three seconds, is definitely slow in view of the scant detailing (he has replaced impulsivity with somewhat excessive caution).

*Line Quality.* The quality of the lines is rather consistent here.

*Criticality.* There was no erasure except for the lowest right branch, which he felt to be overextended (he has a heightened awareness of the advantage of maintaining equilibrium).

*Comments.* He made no spontaneous remarks while he was producing this Tree.

*Post-drawing phase:* His P-D-I comments, "I'd want it to be alive," and "Strong, sturdy, I'm——," illustrate his sharply altered attitude toward the future and his increased feeling of ability to deal with whatever the future may have in store for him, and strongly suggest that he views this Tree as a pseudo self-portrait.

*Associations:* With this Tree, as with the first, he associates his Grandmother's home; the home in which he spent the happiest days of his boyhood. His first Tree was a maple; so is this. But he saw his first maple as a female; this one is a male, whom he identifies specifically as his father (his former hostility toward his father has now largely disappeared, and he is beginning to assume a full-fledged masculine role with heterosexuality replacing the former homosexuality).

### Person

*Details.* His Person has visible arms now—one might more accurately say *miserable* arms, but they are real arms none-the-less. The deeply shaded necklines suggest that he still finds it difficult to control body drives; the heavily shaded hair connotes anxiety created by sexual drives. The lessened jutting of the chin implies that he no longer finds it necessary to proclaim his virility so vehemently.

The bathrobe is given an almost ethereal quality. It was very difficult for a long time for the examiner to determine just what this bathrobe, an unusual article of clothing in the drawing of a Person, might indicate; the patient himself could contribute nothing. Quite by accident the examiner learned that at the military college that R had thrice attended, a student was re-garded as acceptably dressed when he was clad in a bathrobe and nothing else, but felt to be indecently garbed if he appeared in public in trousers and T-shirt! This having been learned, the bathrobe immediately assumed specific significance. Here it appears to symbolize the fixity of R's belief that his behavior while at military college hopelessly disgraced himself and his family. This belief has been as handicapping to the patient in his efforts to make a post-service adjustment, as the bathrobe in the first Person that he drew seemed to enfold and render impotent that Person. The presently transparent bathrobe, then, may be regarded as an evidence of improvement since it is disappearing, rather than as evidence of a pathoformic failure of criticality.

*Proportion.* The spindly, inadequate arms express R's reluctance to tackle the problems presented by social intercourse (but the arms are no longer concealed. This Person is somewhat smaller than the first one—the patient is less hypersensitive than at first, too.

*Perspective.* This Person is standing in a more relaxed position than its predecessor. The stance is broad-based and more secure. However, the figure is rather rigidly "framed" on the form page (implying an equivalent rigidity in social intercourse). The head is still averted (the expression, however, is no longer one of amazement—or of painful inspiration).

*Time.* Five minutes, twenty-nine seconds is somewhat excessive for a drawing of such scant detail.

*Line Quality.* Associations aroused by the drawing of a Person continue to be disturbing to R, and the line quality is highly vacillant.

*Criticality.* Criticism was restricted largely to pauses during the drawing-phase with frequent exclamations indicating disgust at his inability to do better.

*Comments.* *Drawing phase:* He made no comments while he was drawing, but immediately after completing his Person, he remarked, "One of these days, I'm going to come over and really draw you a picture. I *tried* to make that a bathrobe. I don't know whether I did any good or not."

*Post-drawing phase:* To R this Person is relaxing (so is R to some extent); he has just had a shower (symbolic of more than *physical* cleansing); he doesn't have many major problems to ponder over (in recent interviews the subject had exhibited gratifying insight).

*Associations:* His Person makes him think of a man with no particular worries—*at the moment anyway* (this qualifying statement is a healthy one); he reminds R of a person well-off, contented (a state the subject would like to achieve himself).

To sum up then, we find from his second H-T-P that R's attitude toward the future has changed rather strikingly for the better; he is less suspicious and irritable. Although he is still anxious and insecure and doubts his ability to make a success of life, he now sees life as something definitely worth living. Certainly he has improved; certainly he is still maladjusted.

At this point the *clinical* picture showed striking improvement. The subject had become engaged; he had stopped drinking to excess; he had made plans for his future, and his goals were not fictive. He had made what he felt to be an almost unbelievable improvement in his intra-familial relationships. For example, whereas R formerly had been unable to spend more than a few hours in his brother's company without losing his temper, he could now share a room with his brother for a night without becoming openly hostile, and he was even able to bring himself to lend his car to his brother.

Within a few weeks R broke off the therapeutic sessions voluntarily. From later reports it was learned that R was still behaving impulsively and immaturely at times, but he had managed to pass all his courses in college the subsequent semester: the future did not appear to be too dark to him.

It was possible through use of the H-T-P in this case to: (1) solve more easily the difficult problem of diagnosis; (2) to acquire much useful information concerning the dynamics underlying R's behavior; (3) to evaluate more objectively changes occurring after a series of therapeutic interviews, changes the degree of which might well have been dangerously overestimated on the basis of the clinical picture alone.

## REFERENCE

1. Buck, J. N.: The H-T-P Technique. *Clin. Psychol. Monogr.*, 5:1-120, 1948.

# PART III

## CONTENT COMPONENTS

Unit 3
Other Projective Drawing Techniques

## CHAPTER 14

## *SYMBOLISM IN ANIMAL DRAWINGS*

SIDNEY LEVY, PH.D., *and* RICHARD A. LEVY, M.D.

"SYMBOLISM IS A PRIMITIVE but effective way of communicating ideas" wrote Supreme Court Justice Jackson in a recent decision (1). The present writers agree that symbols are an effective means of communication but they are not necessarily primitive. Symbols may range from primitive forms of expression and communication to the most exquisitely subtle and complicated forms found in art, literature, dreams, folk-lore, rites, and religions (2).

The human mind seems to function more comfortably with concrete images than with verbal abstractions and there is a continual tendency to translate complicated ideas and experiences into such symbols or images. These images are always more finite and limited in form than the ideas, emotions and experiences which they symbolize. However, the symbols are often multidimensional and capable of representing or potentiating a variety of responses which contain both generic and specific elements arranged in unique context and configuration.

Thus an advertising poster displaying blue ocean, palm trees, and a South Sea Isle maiden adorned with a lei is a symbol which evokes the generic idea of repose and pleasure, but the specific meaning perceived by the beholders vary so that one may focus on the maid, another on the lei, another on the peace, and another, perhaps, on the ethnology of Polynesians. Such responses can generally be arranged along normal curves of distribution, each representing a different dimension of subjective experience, or a different intensity of such an experience.

The interest of the senior writer in animal symbology was quickened in connection with a case of multiple or dissociated personality (a phenomenon with inherent fascination fully explored in recent literature (3) which came to his attention in 1945 at Westover Station Hospital, Westover Field, an installation of the Army Air Force). There a patient was being examined for military court-martial for "impersonating an officer" and for being "AWOL." The clinical facts, very simply, are as follows:

Private X was arrested in San Francisco wearing the uniform of a Colonel in the Air Force. He had been living at an exclusive hotel where he ran up a substantial bill on the basis of his army status. He had recently become engaged to a wealthy, young, social debutante and was associating with, and living the life of, a wealthy member of a privileged social group. The hotel became concerned with the size of the cumulative bills and initiated an investigation which led to the eventual intervention of the Military Police.

The present writer was called in by Colonel Frederick Le-Drew, Psychiatrist-in-Charge at Westover Station Hospital, for psychological consultation. As a result of clinical interviews, sodium amytal interviews, and projective testing, it became apparent that the soldier led two compartmentalized lives in each of which he was unaware of the other. In his "real" life he was a private in the Air Force, married, had four children, and his family lived in extremely straitened circumstances; his wife, according to the patient had an inferior I.Q. and came from an economically, educationally, and socially underprivileged family. He was depressed by his life, hated it intensely, but because of ethical considerations and feelings of insecurity, felt unable to change the circumstances. There were periodic fugue states from which he would emerge like a butterfly from its chrysalis (in this case a social butterfly) to find himself in the uniform of a colonel, and so on.

Most of the absorbing details of this case are not relevant to the present study, but there are some germane facts pertaining to *horses* that are intriguing and pertinent. The writer at that time was experimenting with a test which he called "Draw An Animal and Tell a Story Test."[1] When this test was administered to the subject, the animal he drew was a *horse*. In his life as a

---

[1] "Draw any animal you wish. Then make up an interesting story telling *all* about this animal."

Colonel he rode saddle-horses along a bridle path every morning and evinced great love for and interest in horses including those associated with pari-mutuel machines. In his real life he had always had a *horse phobia* involving many symptoms, including anxiety and terror at the sight of horses, real or pictured; allergic reactions if he came near a horse or any object which had been in contact with a horse. He also reported recurring, long-standing nightmares involving being pursued by wild horses whom he had to kill for self-preservation.

His *phobic* and *phyllic* reaction to horses, together with the fact that he drew a horse on the projective test, caused the writer to conclude that the horse had some personal, special and symbolic significance. As a partial test of this hypothesis, during the course of a sodium amytal interview it was suggested to the patient that the next time he was asked by the interviewer to draw an animal he was to draw anything *except* a horse. On a subsequent examination when he was asked to draw an animal he drew what he labeled "a horse-like animal, not a horse but looks like it"! This suggested to the examiner the presence of a strong set of intrapsychic forces with a valence for whatever *horse* symbolized.

### LITERATURE

Obsessed with the question "Why a horse?" a search was made of the literature in an effort to learn more about animal symbology in general and the meaning of a horse in particular. This initiated ten years of reading and research which led through fascinating terrain. The psychoanalytic and anthropological literature (4) had reported the significance of animals in phobias, dreams, rituals, totemistic practices, and primitive religions. Freud (5) and others have recognized for a long time the significance of animals as symbols and projected embodiments of unscious drives and feelings.

In *Totem and Taboo,* Freud (6) describes the practice engaged in by primitive tribes of erecting an animal totem which became both sacred and forbidden. His psychodynamic explanation was that the totem animal was a symbol on to which was displaced certain forbidden feelings actually experienced toward a parent or sibling. These feelings, according to Freud, related in general to murder and incest. Nowhere does he deal with the question, "Why does *this particular animal* become the totem?"

## UNIDIMENSIONAL CAUSALITY

Freud, Stekel, Jung (7) and others have discussed the appearance of animals in dreams and phantasies and their symbolic significance. For a full discussion of Freud's analyses of animal dream symbols, see *Interpretation of Dreams* (8). In general psychoanalysts tend to follow Freud's lead in identifying certain formal characteristics of animals which, by the principle of "pars pro toto," symbolize some object or activity having a similar formal characteristic. For example, Freud thought that the snake was the most important symbol of the male organ and when Steckel protested that every symbol, including the snake, was potentially bisexual the former patronizingly dismissed the suggestion by stating that it was rather difficult to imagine that anything with the shape of a snake could represent other than a phallis.

Argument along this dimension, the sexuality of a symbol, has continued even to the present date. Roheim (9) states that the rainbow-serpent symbol in Austria is the male symbol when it stands erect, and the vaginal symbol when it is swallowing. Opler (10) and Weakland (11) have continued investigation of the bisexual potentiality of symbols which Freud[2] considered unquestionably phallic. Most recent studies, including those of Roheim, Guttman (12), Opler and others tend to conclude that animals as symbols may be bisexual in potential.

[2] It has become an all too prevalent practice in recent years to debunk Freud. The writers wish to dissociate themselves from this practice. Although it is true that he did not discover all the psychological truths to the end of time, and in his pioneering explorations he occasionally changed his views and at other times was inconsistent, it is equally true that his work is the foundation stone of modern psychology. Horney, Sullivan, Fromm, Adler, Jung and others have extended, expanded, refined and modified but the conceptual level of recent modifications is derived and subordinate and not as nuclear as Freud's discoveries of unconscious motivation, defense mechanism, dream interpretation, and so on. This is not to deny the need for continual investigation, refinement and modification.

Formal psychological experimental research into the meaning of animals in dreams, fantasy, and projective responses has been extremely limited. In 1945 Goldfarb (13) investigated the meaning of animals in children's Rorschachs. In this research he explored, among other hypotheses, Freud's belief that animal phobias of children were related to the totemistic practices of primitives.

In 1947 Yoder (14) investigated the use of animal characterology by Shakespeare. Yoder states ". . . the Aesopic tradition exemplified one type of animal analogy, attributing to animals the characteristics of men . . . Shakespeare . . . had employed animal analogy as a technique of character portrayal and had employed it more extensively and more intensively than his predecessors."

The chief criticism derives from the fact that workers have tended to approach animals as symbols from a *unidimensional* point of view focusing usually on the masculine-feminine component, and occasionally on other components, such as the active-passive, or the oral-anal, and so on. The present writers believe it is more rewarding to recognize the *multidimensionality* of all symbols including animal symbols. We have collected in excess of 8,000 animal drawings from varying populations including patients diagnosed as psychotic and residing in mental hospitals, prisoners in state and federal institutions for having committed major crimes, randomly selected female adolescents, male adolescents, male adults, female adults, clinic patients, various occupational groups, such as scientists, artists, musicians; various clinical entities including male and female homosexuals, obsessive neurotics, hysterics, and others. We have personal stories associated with more than 2,000 of these drawings. We have intensive psychoanalytic case histories associated with animal drawings from 102 different patients undergoing psychoanalytic treatment. After evaluating all of the above data we wish to present a theory of symbol formation with respect to animal symbology as follows:

1. Every animal symbol is the resultant of a *field* of intrapsychic and external forces.

2. Animal symbols are potentially multiple-dimensional and ambiguous.

3. Perceptual abilities, tendencies, and associations vary in power, complexity, subtlety and precision, just as do intelligence and the I.Q.[3]

4. Relevant dimensions to a particular subject cannot be determined a priori by the psychologist.[4]

5. Any particular animal has both generic and specific dimensions.[5]

The following section presents the Levy Animal-Drawing-Story (LADS) Technique and the resulting normative data, derived tables, and analyses thereof based upon 7,346 drawings secured from: (1) randomly selected adult males; (2) randomly selected adult females; (3) male prisoners; (4) male institutionalized psychotics; (5) female institutionalized psychotics; (6) male adolescents; (7) female adolescents.

The interests of the present writers, like most clinicians, are predominantly centered on the *individual*, his problems, conflicts, resolutions, character structure and psychodynamics. It is recommended to those of like mind that they peruse rather rapidly the normative data, than go directly into the following individual case studies before returning to more intensive and leisurely study of Tables I through VI.

### THE LEVY ANIMAL-DRAWING-STORY (LADS) TECHNIQUE

1. Materials used: 8½ x 11 blank unruled paper.
   Pencil preferred to pen.

2. Directions:     Please draw an animal, any animal that you wish. Go ahead and draw.

3. After drawings are completed give the following directions:

---

[3] Experience with the Rorschach has shown how varied responses may be to a particular area, let us say D (commonplace) area. To some people a given area is just "a dog," to others it is "a speedy dog, like a whippet," to another it may be "an alert, friendly, large grey dog with tight curly hair and two dark patches on the side, with a short, straight tail, an alert look in his eyes, ready to run and catch the ball which his master is about to throw."

[4] Freud made the error of deciding that the form of a snake was the relevant dimension, and that the symbolic meaning was necessarily phallic. Stekel and others moved in the right direction but rather mincingly.

[5] Delineation of this and the related propositions will be made in connection with discussions of specific animals in following sections.

Write in the upper right-hand corner your (a) age, (b) sex, (c) the kind of animal you have drawn, (d) list other animals you *might* have drawn, (e) under the animal drawing give it a pet name.

4. Further directions: (This section is optional).
   Turn the drawing over and write an imaginative story about this animal.

After the data are collected they may be evaluated in three ways, *viz.*, (1) normatively, (2) formally, and (3) symbolically. The following section presents frequency distribution and derived tables.[6] For formal analysis of the graphological, size, placement and other aspects the reader is referred to Hammer's chapter on Expressive Aspects of Projective Drawings. Additional formal interpretative principles applicable specifically to animal drawings are described below. Principles of symbolic interpretation are given in association with the individual case studies which follow the section on normative data.

## ANALYSIS OF SPECIFIC ANIMALS

### Ram

The writer engaged in an experiment similar to the Rorschach-Oberholzer (15) "blind diagnosis." A psychoanalyst who had been working with a patient in analysis for 18 months sent to the writer a drawing of a *ram* (Figure 1) and its associated story administered according to the LADS technique described above. The only data accompanying the drawing and the associated story were the age, fifty-two years, and the sex, male. It is suggested that the reader study the animal drawing and the story before reading the drawing analysis.

The following story was given verbally by the subject of this experiment in his analyst's office where it was tape-recorded and transcribed.

This is an experienced old boy, leader of his tribe who knows the terrain with the intimate knowledge of the geographer and naturalist. He knows how to follow the seasons of the year in

---

[6] Acknowledgment is made to the following persons for substantial assistance in collecting drawings: N. Fruman, A. Kasper, W. J. Levy, B. E. Tomlinson, D. G. Weinick, A. S. Wodin, and C. Z. Horowitz.

Figure 1

order to find areas of plentiful provender. He knows how to make adjustments for the irregular and unexpected. He also knows well the peculiarities of his wards. Their proclivities in general, and their strengths and weaknesses in particular. He is fond of releasing them in their areas of strength and shepherding them in their weaknesses. He makes a special point of knowing all their personal likes and dislikes and surprising and pleasing them with his knowledge and appropriate applications of it. He has a fierce and protective pride in his large family because he has been responsible for their welfare and growth since he was a young man, and they have learned to trust him. He has guided them away from useless entanglements with neighboring and less crafty bands of animals; he has defended them when necessary, never giving ground to destructive marauders if he could not dissuade them by knowledge and craft. He bore proudly the scars of such combat. Every morning before the work of procuring food, settling disputes, finding new territories for new families, supervising the care of those giving birth, the young, the sick and the aged, he experiences tremendous stimulation by running to the topmost peak among the Empyrean skies and taking a long view of the neighboring valley and crags, deriving not only sensual gratification but laying plans for future moves and expansion. He allows himself, however, a limited amount of time for this self-indulgence. There is much work to be done, and without a backward glance he returns to his flock and gets on with the business.

Every evening after all the work is done he returns to the peak and sees the panorama in a new setting—by starlight and moonlight—and he experiences a mixture of awe and exaltation, of mystery and mastery, of humility and pride. As he stands there looking off into the neighboring lands, he often wonders about the problems and the events which are being experienced there. His wondering quickly leads to plans for the future, for the morrow of the next season when he will see and explore.

As he returns to his tribe he makes plans for sport and play for tomorrow because he knows that they are not capable of the same discipline and stamina that he demands of himself. There must be periodic relaxations, play and sport. He wisely arranges that every game be not only a source of amusement, but an educational growth or physically maturing activity.

At last he goes to sleep with a feeling of great warmth and security because he is home with his own family and on his own land.

*Report of the Writer Based Upon the LADS Technique:* This animal is one which is rarely drawn. It occurs in the order of frequency of approximately one in 8,000. We conclude that the patient is an unusual person, an hypothesis supported by other aspects of the drawing, such as the placement of the figure, the firm continuous lines, the controlled aggressiveness of the animal, the nature of the details, the surrounding scenic effects, and the story itself.

Being "unusual" may place one at either end of a continuum. In terms of ego strength this man is at the extreme upper end. Let us first deal with intellectual aspects. This man is a very superior intelligence. The placement of the animal, the proportions, the communication of tri-dimensionality of the animal body, the perspective (mountain peaks and space), the accuracy of essential details, the effective communication of the essential idea, all indicate a very superior intelligence. Together with the story, the nature of the language used, the ideas suggested, the emotional subtleties involved, would indicate the I.Q. to be well above 140.

The quality of the intellect suggests the presence of both theoretical and practical orientation. The animal is placed very close to the center of the page, indicating a person who is neither withdrawn nor too responsive to external pressures. It is slightly to the left and above center, suggesting a thoughtful man with high aspirations and comfortable feelings of being adequate to his position in life. There appears to be no need to take refuge in withdrawal, (placement in a corner or to the extreme left), or in lower levels of performance (lower placement or sketchy details), or to compensate by being uncomfortably high (reaction formation).

The animal's placement amongst mountain peaks and his preoccupations as presented in the LADS story suggest a man who likes ideas, speculation, reflection, and theory. The representational nature of the drawing and its details, the turning away from speculation to practical problems in the associated story, suggest a balance between idealism and practicality. Since this animal is essentially action oriented, the implication is that the subject is not so much a dreamer as a man of action.

Many details are included but there is no obsessive overconcern with non-essential detail. Thus, cloven hoofs, hair and other non-essential details are not present. Whatever details are included have a direct communicatory value in terms of the essential experience which the subject is portraying. Many other details may have been included which are more related to obsessive concern associated with anxiety and neurosis (the principle of the return of the repressed through obsessive detail). This lack of concern with meaningless, ritualistic or petty detail, suggests that although he is critical and precise, he is not pedantic.

The sketchy nature of the mountains as compared with the emphasis on the animal, the graphology and the story suggest that the patient is flexible, curious, and adaptive, rather than provincial, rigid and narrow. The drawing and the story further communicate a suggestion of directness and discipline. There are no digressions. The drawing is clearly not that of a skilled or trained artist (in the narrow sense), therefore the effective communication is not simply the result of learned skill, but has deeper roots in the personality.

Up to this point the writer has been looking for evidences of pathology. There appear to be no signs of unusual anxiety in its direct form (sketchy broken lines, constriction of perception and association, etc.) There are also no signs of boundup or displaced anxiety. There are no obsessive compulsive symptoms, no hysterical or disorganized aspects, no fragmented ego, no withdrawal, or attack on reality or distortion of it, no psychotic misperceptions, and no evidence of character disorder.

By inference from the flexible line, the placement which is neither bound to the self (left side), nor overly influenced by the environment (right side), this patient has a rich, free but not overly labile emotional life. He communicates well and this suggests a practiced empathy with others. The story and the animal suggest a person who is energetic and a leader and who is concerned with nurturing others. This is the first suggestion of conflict in the area of identification. The stroking is bold, firm, predominantly angular; the animal as symbol and as actually portrayed is essentially male and aggressive. There are horns and a beard. There are no signs of impotence, or castration. However, there is a slight emphasis on the pectoral muscles indicating a need to "mother" as well as to "father." Essentially this patient is a strong, integrated, superior, effective, potent male who tends to be somewhat mothering.

Although he has a valence for ideas and generalization, he is not an over-intellectualized person without roots in reality or action. He is predominantly a man of action. Although he is reflective, he is no Hamlet. He seeks upper levels of action and thought (the mountain peaks, and story content). But he deals not only with theories, policies and ideas, but with their effective implementation. He has a strongly developed curiosity ("looking off into the neighboring, etc."). His story suggests a strong proprietary interest and sense of home and roots, as well as a desire to explore other places and spheres of activity.

There are residual evidences of conflict, such as that between being father or mother, between thought and action. The former conflict appears to be resolved by identification with the father (see ram legends below).

At this point the writer began to speculate about the reason for patient seeking analysis and about his profession or vocation. In view of the absence of pathology, the first thought that suggested itself was that the patient was in what was formerly called "a didactic analysis." But the action orientation, lack of obsessiveness and other data quickly contradicted the likelihood of his being an analyst in fact or in training. The writer confesses inability to determine the problems which led the patient to seek analysis. With respect to speculations about his profession, I found myself thinking of president of a large corporation such as General Motors.

Although at first inclined to consider favorably the idea of his being the head of a large corporation, I gradually relinquished this thought. The aggression was so completely directed primarily toward nurturance and protection that I thought he would be a most unusual industrial executive. Other thoughts that suggested themselves were occupations such as administrator of a hospital, the head of an orphan home, a director of some organization similar to the Ford Foundation (I found myself thinking of Hutchins, but Hutchins from newspaper reports of him is more conflicted and less nurturing than this patient seems to be). Because of the combination of scientific (geography, nature study) interests and leadership qualities I thought of a position similar to that held by Oppenheimer in the Atomic Energy Projects. This patient is obviously not as introspective a person as Oppenheimer and is much more comfortable with other people and with action. This is as far as speculation will carry me. He is a leader of an organization, he is very intelligent, has wide interests, and is interested in the care and nurturance of people.

In order to fill in the above picture with generic data, let us explore the meaning of "a ram." In Egyptian history and theology (16) the ram is the sun god. Note the sun in the drawing. The hymn of Hibis (17) goes as follows: "Thy ram dwelleth in Mendes . . . he is the phallis, lord of the gods. . . ." Compare the Christian rites of the sacrifice of the ram with the Mythraic (18) sacrifice of the bull. In most theologies and legends the ram is the symbol of the sun god, of power, potency, fatherhood, fertility, rebirth, regeneration. (In Persian mythology there is a deviation of this wherein the ram replaces the serpent in the story equivalent to the Garden of Eden legend.)

*Response of the Psychoanalyst to the Previous Report:* The patient whose drawing and story I submitted to you is a fifty-two year old male, married twenty-five years, has four children. He is President of a large University; in the past has been an educator, head of a research organization, and during the war was the Director of an overseas economic and relief mission. He is well educated, has a number of degrees, including a Ph.D. in Literature and several honorary degrees. He has been educated in American, French and English universities. He came into analysis largely because of intellectual curiosity. He read Freud's *Interpretation of Dreams,* was impressed with it and became aware of applications to some of his own dreams. He concluded this was a basic and frontier area of human understanding. Decided to learn more about it. Analysis has revealed that he is a mature, strong, well integrated individual without severe conflicts or symptoms. There is perhaps a trifle more brooding and lonely quality to the man than is suggested by your account.

The writers of this chapter would like to make some further comments about the ram drawing. We wish to point out that had a unidimensional interpretation of the ram as a phallic symbol been made much meaningful material would have been lost. There are many animals which may serve as phallic symbols, such as a bull, snake, bird, etc. Our hypothesis is that the particular animal is specifically determined. Thus the question arises—why was a ram selected rather than one of the other phallic animals? For this patient a ram was an animal which occupied empyrean heights, lonely, a father and mother to his tribe, an explorer, aggressive, not for the mere sake of aggression, but in the interests of leadership and nurturance, reflective, with a long view of things. The ram also suggests certain cyclic aspects, such as the return of spring, a regeneration of hope, virility and action. So it is with every animal dreamed or drawn. One must seek all the dimensions, generic and specific, appropriate to the meaning which each has to its creator.

### Raven

This raven (Figure 2) was drawn by a 17-year-old male, college freshman. The raven is drawn approximately once in 5,000 times. Therefore it is an unusual drawing and this subject is not an average young man.

The generic meaning of all flying birds is essentially the expression of a wish to escape from a stressful and unyielding situation. It includes a feeling of tension and containment and the wish to *physically* escape therefrom by action. A *ram* reacts

Figure 2

to such a situation by aggressive attack, an *insect* by anxiety and avoidance, a *bird* by (1) physical flight or (2) by an intrapsychic transmigration as exemplified in the legend of the phoenix which arose reborn from its own ashes.

At one level of meaning, a bird is a symbol for a phallis. Thus the German word for bird "vogeln" and the Italian word "l'uccello" both idiomatically mean penis. For other examples of the symbolic identity between bird and phallis see the *Meaning of Animals* (2).

Note that in Table I birds occur with greater frequency amongst prisoners and adolescents than amongst other groups. The prisoners' wish for physical flight is too obvious to require comment. Adolescents require more careful study. The adolescent is in a period of transition in which there is a great intensification of sexual impulses and superego demands. He can no longer indulge to the same extent in previously childish (id) impulses and irresponsible self-indulgence. Since he has not had long experience with this new intensified conflict, his ego defenses are not sufficiently practiced or mobilized to dominate the conflict. Therefore it becomes essentially a superego-id conflict with resulting feelings of guilt, tension, depression and anxiety. In this situation the ego is poised between the unusually strong demands of the id for sexual gratification in relation to forbidden objects, and of other gratifications tabooed for him. The chief restraint against these forbidden drives is his own conscience (superego) and the external representation of it in the person of his father. Therefore the father is experienced as the source of prohibitions which really emanate from his own psyche. This results in intense feelings of hostility toward the father usually repressed and experienced as depression. In his progressive development toward maturity, the adolescent may unconsciously renounce his claim on mother who has been the source and recipient of his love, and may resolve the unconscious conflict with father by oral incorporation and resulting identification with father.

Let us examine the drawing of the *raven* presented by this adolescent boy. The most unusual aspect of it is the word "Nevermore." This suggested to the writer the poem by Poe (19), an association verified by the young man. The poem in part is as follows:

"Be that word our sign of parting, bird or fiend!" I shrieked upstarting—

*The Clinical Application of Projective Drawings*

TABLE I

FREQUENCY DISTRIBUTION OF 7,346 ANIMALS DRAWN BY
(1) RANDOMLY SELECTED ADULT MALES, (2) RANDOMLY SELECTED ADULT
FEMALES, (3) MALE PRISONERS, (4) MALE INSTITUTIONALIZED
PSYCHOTICS, (5) FEMALE INSTITUTIONALIZED PSYCHOTICS,
(6) MALE ADOLESCENTS, (7) FEMALE ADOLESCENTS.

| Animal | Adults | | | | | Adolescents | |
|---|---|---|---|---|---|---|---|
| | (1) N = 1042 | (2) N = 1026 | (3) N = 1029 | (4) N = 1080 | (5) N = 1020 | (6) N = 1070 | (7) N = 1079 |
| Alligator | — | — | 3 | — | — | 13 | — |
| Anteater | 9 | — | — | — | — | 2 | — |
| Amelgonia | — | — | — | — | — | — | 3 |
| Amoeba | — | — | — | — | — | 5 | — |
| Ant | — | — | — | — | — | — | 3 |
| Antelope | — | — | — | — | — | 2 | — |
| Ape | — | — | — | — | — | 10 | 6 |
| Bear | — | — | 3 | — | 34 | 2 | 6 |
| Beaver | — | — | — | — | — | 2 | — |
| Bee | — | — | — | — | — | — | 3 |
| Beetle | — | — | — | — | — | — | 3 |
| Bird | 17 | 56 | 105 | 160 | 51 | 176 | 173 |
| Buffalo | 9 | — | — | — | 17 | — | — |
| Bull | — | — | 6 | 20 | — | — | — |
| Butterfly | — | — | — | 20 | — | 2 | 8 |
| Camel | 17 | — | 6 | 20 | 17 | 8 | 6 |
| Cat | 178 | 362 | 156 | 120 | 255 | 39 | 165 |
| Chicken | — | — | 12 | — | 17 | 5 | 3 |
| Chinchilla | — | — | — | — | — | 2 | — |
| Cow | 17 | — | 33 | 20 | 17 | 13 | 3 |
| Crab | — | — | 3 | — | — | — | — |
| Deer | 17 | 6 | 9 | — | — | 15 | 3 |
| Dinosaur | 9 | — | 6 | — | — | 10 | 14 |
| Dog | 332 | 294 | 183 | 180 | 153 | 174 | 224 |
| Donkey | 34 | 13 | 33 | 40 | 17 | 13 | 6 |
| Eel | — | — | — | — | — | 2 | — |
| Elephant | 42 | 19 | 24 | 80 | 17 | 34 | 25 |
| Fawn | — | — | — | — | — | — | 3 |
| Fish | 9 | 13 | 3 | — | 51 | 70 | 41 |
| Fox | — | — | 3 | — | — | 8 | — |
| Frog | 9 | — | — | — | — | 2 | 3 |
| Giraffe | 26 | — | 9 | 40 | 17 | 15 | 3 |
| Goat | — | — | 12 | — | 17 | 2 | — |
| Grasshopper | — | — | 6 | — | — | 2 | — |
| Hippopotamus | — | — | — | — | — | 2 | — |
| Horse | 196 | 106 | 156 | 220 | 102 | 244 | 160 |
| Kangaroo | — | — | 6 | — | — | — | — |
| Leopard | — | — | 3 | 20 | — | — | — |
| Lion | 17 | — | — | — | — | 5 | — |
| Llama | — | — | — | — | — | — | 3 |
| Mice | — | 6 | 18 | — | — | 15 | 11 |
| Mink | — | — | — | — | — | — | 3 |
| Mongoose | — | — | — | — | 17 | — | — |
| Monkey | — | — | — | — | 17 | — | — |
| Octopus | — | — | — | — | — | 5 | 6 |
| Ostrich | — | — | 3 | — | — | 5 | 3 |

TABLE I—Continued

| Animal | Adults | | | | | Adolescents | |
|---|---|---|---|---|---|---|---|
| | (1) N = 1042 | (2) N = 1026 | (3) N = 1029 | (4) N = 1080 | (5) N = 1020 | (6) N = 1070 | (7) N = 1079 |
| Ox | — | 6 | — | — | — | — | — |
| Panther | — | — | — | 20 | — | 2 | — |
| Parmicium | 9 | — | — | — | — | 13 | 8 |
| Penguin | — | 6 | 3 | — | — | 5 | 6 |
| Pig | 9 | 13 | 66 | 20 | 17 | 5 | 3 |
| Porcupine | — | — | 3 | — | — | — | — |
| Possum | — | — | — | — | — | 2 | — |
| Rabbit | 42 | 88 | 69 | 20 | 119 | 33 | 110 |
| Raccoon | — | — | — | — | — | — | 3 |
| Shark | — | — | — | — | — | 8 | — |
| Sheep | 9 | — | 12 | 20 | 34 | 2 | 8 |
| Skunk | — | — | — | — | — | — | 6 |
| Snail | — | — | — | — | — | 2 | — |
| Snake | — | 6 | 45 | 20 | — | 60 | 19 |
| Spider | — | — | — | — | — | 2 | — |
| Squid | — | — | — | — | — | 2 | — |
| Squirrel | — | — | 3 | — | 17 | 2 | 3 |
| Teddy-bear | — | 13 | — | — | — | — | 11 |
| Tiger | 17 | — | 3 | 20 | — | — | 3 |
| Turtle | — | 19 | 6 | — | 17 | 8 | 6 |
| Weasel | — | — | 3 | — | — | — | — |
| Whale | 9 | — | 3 | 20 | — | 10 | 3 |
| Wolf | 9 | — | 12 | — | — | 10 | — |

"Get thee back into the tempest and the Night's Plutonian shore!
Leave no black plume as a token of the lie thy soul hath spoken!
Leave my loneliness unbroken!—quit the bust above my door!
Take thy beak from out my heart, and take thy form from off my
    door!"
       Quoth the raven, "Nevermore!"

Just as the poem suggests the poet's despair over a lost love, so this drawing suggests the patient's despair and depression over a renounced love. This renunciation results not only in feelings of despair, but also rage and a wish to achieve the forbidden object without at the same time offending the superego. There is a South African myth (20) as follows:

There are certain rocks or caves that only open at a magic word. If the rock does not want to open, it answers, "The rock will not open to children, it opens to the *swallows* that fly in the air."

Jung (7) points out that no human power can open the rock,

TABLE II

PERCENTAGE OF POPULARS

Combined Percentage of Three Most Popular Animals
(Cats, Dogs and Horses)

| Male | | Female | |
|---|---|---|---|
| Adolescents | 43% | Adolescents | 51% |
| Prisoners | 48% | | |
| Psychotics | 50% | Psychotics | 50% |
| Normals | 68% | Normals | 74% |

Table II indicates that normal adults (randomly selected) have a significantly higher percentage of popular animals than do institutional psychotics, prisoners, or adolescents.

only a magic word or a bird. This expresses a neat resolution of the superego-id conflict. The cave opens (that is, the wishes are gratified), but the child is not responsible and therefore cannot be punished. It is a bird who accomplishes the miracle. Here again, we have an example of the return of the repressed in symbol form. Although the bird in the myth is supposedly responsible for the gratification, it obviously represents the libidinal drives of the child himself.

Let us examine the *raven* drawing in detail. There are evidences of strong, masculine, phallic drives as follows: The pencil pressure, the firm lines, the prominent pointed beak, and the emphasis on the claws, as well as the bird symbol. The placement of the bird crossing the center line and going over into the right side of the page suggests the action orientation, that is, a flight away from the self. Thus, this young man is resolving his internal conflict by a flight into action. We may predict that this man engages in strenuous physical activity, such as athletics, travel and so on, and relatively little introspection. When there is introspection it is of a slightly pessimistic guilt-ridden quality. The emphasis on the beak is expressive not only of aggression, but of orality. The closed beak, the absence of any orifices suggest a reaction formation to his oral drives. Summing up, we have here a young man with very strong phallic and oral drives who strongly represses these drives and diverts them into action and physical flight; who is slightly pessimistic and guilty. The resolution of his basic conflict is in favor of the superego.

By derivation we may expect this young man to be extremely conscientious, to be somewhat rigid in his morality as a reaction formation, to be self-denying particularly in the oral area. We would, therefore, expect him to have a tendency to renounce activities such as smoking, sweets, and other oral gratifications. The repressed hostility resulting from frustration of his impulses will be expressed not orally (insulting remarks and so on), but rather in physical action. He is the kind of young man who slaps friends hard on the back, who tends to be a little too firm in his hand-shake, and so on. The proportions of the bird and the use of space suggest an orderly and disciplined person. The prominence of the rump area (the tail) suggests anal emphasis and since his major defense is repression and denial, (there are no orifices in the drawing) there will be great stress on cleanliness and on holding things in. You might expect this young man to be a rather quiet person. Whatever aggressive and boisterous impulses there are will be very carefully directed into socially acceptable channels. There will be a flight away from all aggressive activity as a reflection of flight from his own aggressive feelings.

### Birds

Although all birds symbolize flight, action orientation, the wish for phallic drives, various specific meanings vary with the individual bird. There is a tremendous difference between an eagle and a canary, or between a hen and a vulture. There are nurturing birds, cannibalistic birds, birds of prey, parasitic birds, singing birds, exhibitionistic birds (peacock), defenseless birds (sitting ducks), peaceful birds (doves), female birds (pigeons), long-necked birds (which will be discussed in the section on the giraffe), and so on. Each bird has the generic meaning of all birds plus the generic meaning of his particular species of bird, plus the specific meanings attributed to it by his particular creator (the dreamer or the drawer).

### The Seahorse and the Cat (Complementary Drawings by Husband and Wife)

The seahorse and the cat (Figure 3) were drawn by a husband and his wife. The story presented by the wife who drew the seahorse is as follows:

Figure 3a

Our little seahorses grow to be no longer than one inch. The male—honestly—is the one who gives birth to these little fellows, probably about a quarter of an inch, hundreds of them. In case you don't believe this, note that the female lays the eggs in the male's pouch. When he swells up he looks pregnant, like any decent female; and when time for the births arrives, he emits the little ones in what looks like actual birth pangs. The minute the children arrive they take off into the deep on their own and if they survive it's practically a miracle.

The story presented by the husband who drew the cat is as follows:

This animal is a cat. Cats are famous in history and are the quintessence of femininity which explains why most women hate them. Men, on the other hand, love them and frequently meet for the purpose of feeding the kitty. Have I hurt anybody's felines?

Figure 3b

TABLE III

ANIMALS WHICH SIGNIFICANTLY DIFFERENTIATE BETWEEN
MALE AND FEMALE

| | Normal Population | | Adolescent Population | | Psychotic Population | |
|---|---|---|---|---|---|---|
| | Male | Female | Male | Female | Male | Female |
| Cats | 17% | 35% | 3% | 15% | 11% | 25% |
| Horses | 19% | 10% | 22% | 14% | 20% | 10% |

This table indicates that cats are drawn from two to five times as often by females than by males; and horses approximately twice as frequently by males than by females. Thus, one might conclude that the cat is predominantly a female symbol; and the horse somewhat more equivocally a male symbol. This is fully discussed in the sections on the *cat* and the *horse*.

Reference to Table III reveals that there is a significant sexual difference in the incidence of *cats*. The cat is essentially a feminine animal reflecting a strong female identification. Not only the normative data presented above, but myths, legends, rituals, literature (2), and clinical data reinforce this conclusion. Of the 102 patients in analysis who have been studied there are only nine *cat* drawings from males. Of these nine, seven had a long history of overt homosexual relationships, one had some history and the ninth was psychotic. The evidence from these three areas points in the same direction.

*Seahorses* have a frequency of one in 5,000 drawings. The associated story presented by the wife indicates in very thin disguise that she has reversed the sexual roles. The male is the one who gives birth and the female the one who implants the eggs in the male. The idea of the male as the sexual receiver is not a novel concept (11). The drawing itself with the hollow phallic-like snout (similar to an elephant's trunk) is also structurally similar to a uterus. The present writers have often found in the phantasies and dreams of psychotic patients, of sexual deviants, and severe neurotics, an unconscious confusion between the sexual organs. Thus some women in this category unconsciously phantasy their genital apparatus as a phallus, which impregnates the urethral opening of the male. In order to express in a reinforced way this wish, note the way in which the subject emphasized the priapic tail. Attention is also called to the line flattening out the curvature of the stomach, another evidence of reversal of sexual role. The size of the drawing indicates considerable narcissism. The autism and immaturity of this subject's phantasy is further suggested by the fact that this drawing' is almost entirely in the upper left quadrant of the page. Since there is very little evidence of overt anxiety in this drawing, the presumption is that the sexual conflict does not take the direction of neurosis, but rather psychopathy such as is found in a character disorder or in psychosis. The comblike areas on the rear of the head and lower back indicate a somatic preoccupation with those areas, probably manifesting hypochondriacal symptoms. This is often found as a tenuously maintained defense against loss of self-identity and regression to a fetal-like attachment to mother. This subject is probably a character disorder with sexual deviation, some hypochondriacal preoccupation with body narcissism and possessing the possibility of an underlying repressed psychosis.

The *cat* drawn by the husband and the associated story indicates the basic feminine identification of this man. His hostility to women is suggested by his story. (The use of wit as a defense has been thoroughly described by Freud.) His drawing is in the extreme upper left-hand corner of the page. The animal itself is very small and requires the support of a fence. This suggests that the person is very autistic, feels extremely up-in-the-air, inadequate to life's problems, and requires artificial support by props and devices. The cat is presented rear view consistent with the suggestion of a passive, homosexual problem. The emptiness of the cat, the lack of identity, the communication of "catness" by the use of external outline suggests that this person feels himself to be empty and little more than a facade. The curving tail suggests impotency, the sharp point a devious underhanded hostility. The basic self-concept is that of a phallic female.

## Cat (21)

Amongst males, cats are the third most popular animal coming after dogs and horses. Amongst randomly selected male adults 17 per cent draw cats, amongst adolescent males only 3 per cent draw cats, amongst male psychotics 11 per cent draw cats. This is true in spite of the fact that in our cultural experience cats are a domestic animal, almost as prevalent in the home as dogs. In each of the aforementioned groups, the female component draws from two to three times as many cats. Therefore the writers conclude that one generic meaning of cats in drawings, dreams, and so on is *femaleness*. This is substantiated by such idioms as "a catty person," "pussy," "kitten," as applied to a woman.

Historically, the Egyptians venerated the cat; it was a crime to spill the blood of this sacred animal. When a cat died in a house all the people of the dwelling shaved off their eyebrows as a sign of mourning (castration symbol?). For the Egyptians the cat symbolized the moon. Both the moon and the cat are almost universal symbols of nocturnal activity and fecundity, coldness, remoteness and femininity. Often the cat goddess became identified as the female of the god Ra. This symbolism strongly suggests that the cat is a mother symbol.

In Egyptian theology, the cat was known as "the eye of Ra" with the special quality of being occult and hidden (2). This suggests that the cat is no ordinary symbol of motherhood but has the special quality of being hidden, remote, mysterious, cold, and distant. In Roman myth the modification of Diana known as Vesta, the goddess who guarded hearth and home, was robed in a mantle made from cat skins. Note also the parable of the virgin and the cat which is related to the old folktale of Cinderella.

It has been suggested that the English word "puss" is derived from the name of the goddess "Pasht," a form of the Egyptian Isis. In every culture the cat goddess is essentially the feminine "principle of the deity" and usually the virgin goddess who, although she bestows fertility, is not emotionally involved in the process. In Heraldic symbology the cat is the emblem of freedom, mystery and independence. The cat is unlike the dog in its relations with people. The cat's attachment to human beings is of a different quality from that of the dog. It is more autonomous, detached, self-centered, independent, self-sufficient, resistant to affection and interdependency.

In myth and literature, cats are often synonyms for amorality. The cat appears only once in the Bible, in the deuterocanonical Book of Baruch—and then it is only to symbolize treason and lying. The association between cats and witches is well known. The cat is often regarded as cruel and cunning (cat and mouse game). It is interesting that in iconography, saints are accompanied by virtually every animal in the bestiary except the cat.

Another generic quality of the cat symbol is detachment and self-centeredness. In the experience of the present writers, the cat drawing always represents at the generic level the symbol of a cold, distant, detached, self-centered mother.

Specific cat drawings vary along many continua. We have a series of cat drawings along the continuum representing self-centeredness with autonomy at one end and extreme narcissism at the other. Amongst the other qualities described in the previous paragraphs none is universally applicable to cat drawings but one or more are frequently associated with cat symbolism.

## Snakes

Since the "Garden of Eden" the *snake* has played an important role in the religions, myths, literature and preoccupations of the human race (2). Therefore, it is an astonishing fact that according to Table I only six snake drawings were among the 2,068 collected from the random male and female adults, and all six were from females. Three times as many snakes were collected from institutionalized psychotics and approximately thirteen times as many from both male prisoners and adolescents.

In the dreams of people undergoing analysis snakes occur with great frequency during its course. Toward the termination of analysis, once again, the animals in dreams stabilize and occur in accordance with the original frequency distribution.

Freud stated rather categorically that when snakes appear in dreams, religious rituals or art they symbolize "the male principle." To him the snake is the prototypical phallic symbol. Stekel and others suggested it was ambipotential with respect to sex. Research into mythology indicates that a snake has had a variety of meanings ascribed to it, amongst which have been the following: symbol of death; guardian of the treasure of life; the world of instinct; danger; sensuality; forbidden knowledge; the fear of consequences of breaking the incest taboo; death; world destruction; impotence in old age; physical disease; an abnormally active unconscious; in youth fear of life; in age fear of death; a harbinger of psychosis; instrument of sacrifice; regeneration; the archtype of life itself; the devouring mother; the source of life; the creator and worker of miracles. Most of the meanings are derivative and can be subsumed as special cases under three basic meanings, *viz.*: (1) the source of life (the procreative principle); (2) the source of death (the punishment principle); (3) the source of forbidden knowledge (the libidinal principle, i.e., the unconscious).

Several examples of snake stories secured by the LADS technique are as follows:

A thirty year old male in psychoanalysis gave the following:

> This snake is a harmless gartersnake with his mouth wide open. Some big he-man skin diver comes along and shoves his spear into the open mouth. The snake can hardly breathe and his heart is beating to beat the band. He is almost exhausted but finally the guy takes the spear out and he swims away and rests on a bed of rushes.

At this stage of this patient's analysis his passive homosexual desires, as well as the associated feelings of guilt and danger, were prominent. However, shortly after this stage had been worked through it became very clear that the "skin diver" was his phallic mother who was in effect "the guardian of the treasure of life." This represented the patient's wish to reestablish his oral dependency on mother. As is so often the case, the orally oriented homosexuality is derived from, and a disguise for, the wish to become an orally dependent infant.

Another patient, an unmarried woman of twenty-six, gave the following dream:

> In my dream I lay transfixed in my bed without any ability to move. I saw the window open and the head of a tremendous boa constrictor slowly entering. I wanted to scream and run, but my muscles had a will of their own, they kept me where I was. The snake slowly approached me, I could see its strong sinewy body, it came closer and closer and I could hardly breathe. It wrapped itself around me, squeezing, and I was panting for breath. I woke up.

For this patient the snake represented a condensation of the father image and her own subjective reactions to it. Subsequent analysis revealed that her avoidance of marriage and strong social attachment (non-sexual) to women were a defense against these forbidden drives. Her associations to the dream were related to her father's coming home from work, picking her up and hugging her so tight that she could hardly breathe. She remembered how big and strong he was. The snake in this dream represented the father, sexuality, tabooed wishes threatening to flood her consciousness, feelings of guilt and excitement. Subsequently patient worked through these feelings, became free of her guilt, married and shortly thereafter reported the following dream:

> I walked into my room and was confused for a moment because there was someone there. I began to laugh with amusement when I saw a blue snake grinning at me and wagging its tail. I followed it into the bedroom and couldn't stop laughing when the snake crawled into bed.

## Horse

The writers' explorations in this field began with the question "Why a horse?" A question which continues to perplex us. Reference to the frequency Tables I and III indicates that from 19 to 22 per cent of males and 10 to 14 per cent of females draw a horse. It is one of the three most frequently drawn animals for both sexes.

In mythology and folklore the great preponderance of stories regard the horse not as a sexual symbol, but rather as a symbol of a friendly, active helper. In our experience most drawings contain this generic element, that is to say, the drawer sees himself as a helpful person, a servant, subordinate, aid, worker, friend, beast of burden. Note that energy at man's disposal is measured in horse power.

In our experience, a secondary psychodynamic explanation represents the harmonious relationship between the ego and the id. This is not universally true but it is more true of the horse symbol than of any other of the animals listed in Table I. Occasionally the horse has been regarded as the goddess of the underworld (that is, of the unconscious). For example Hecate, the

TABLE IV

ANIMALS WHICH DIFFERENTIATE PRISON FROM NORMAL

|  | Prison Male | Normal Male |
|---|---|---|
| Pigs | 6% | 0.7% |
| Bird | 8% | 2 % |
| Snake | 4% | 0.0% |
| Rabbit | 7% | 4 % |
| Dog | 17% | 32 % |

Table IV clearly differentiates the prison population from the normal population as a result of a greater preponderance of self-denigrating animals, timidity (rabbits), and wish to escape (birds). The stereotype of the criminal as an aggressive, destructive, hostile person appears to be contradicted by these data. A stereotype closer to the truth may be one characterized by self-contempt, timidity, tension and a desire to escape.

horseheaded goddess, was the ruler of the underworld. Other aspects of the horse as a representative of the unconscious appear in legends and myths picturing him as a clairvoyant, prophetic, a mysterious pathfinder, and so on.

When horses appear in an energetic or dramatic form of action they almost always symbolize a fructifying principle; for example, Pegasus struck the fountain of Hippocrene from the earth with his hoof. There are many old wives and folk superstitions which suggest that pregnant or unfertile women feed oats to a horse as a good luck charm.

The writers have heard and read statements by several of their colleagues that the horse "is a symbol of castration fear," "a symbol of an oedipus conflict." These statements have the same degree of relevance and redundance as a statement that a man is a human being.

One study (22) states "the interpretive significance of the *horse* has received consistent and unreserved empirical verification. Its essential meaning has been found to be that the individual possesses some greater-than-average component of opposite sex drives, all the way to strong latent or even overt homosexual characteristics."

Although this has been true of a substantial *minority* of our horse drawings, it is not a universal symbol. There must be some reason why, although it so often represents the vitality of the unconscious, it relatively infrequently represents either the essential male principle or female principle. The structure and activities of the horse are apparently sufficiently sexually ambiguous to permit its frequent use by those who are themselves ambiguous.

The chief generic meaning of the horse, however, relates to ego characteristics of action, work, service, help, and so on. In fewer cases it represents the unconscious and danger (wild horses, nightmares). Less frequently it represents the mother principle. The formal analysis of horse drawings is especially important.

Space limitations prevent more complete discussion of the animals listed in Table I. For such a discussion the reader is referred to the work previously cited (2).

## SPECIAL ASPECTS OF DRAWINGS

### Oral Attachment

Analysts and clinical psychologists have become increasingly aware of the nuclear importance of the process whereby an individual gradually loses not only physical but psychological dependence on his mother. It has rarely been sufficiently understood by workers in other fields that physical separation after the separation of the umbilicus was not necessarily followed by psychic separation. Recent literature (*The Silver Cord*) has dealt with

TABLE V

DIFFERENTIATING VALUE OF ANIMAL ORIENTATION

|  | Facing Right | Facing Left | Front View |
|---|---|---|---|
| Prisoners | 23% | 64% | 11% |
| Normals | 16% | 66% | 18% |
| Psychotics | 11% | 81% | 8% |

Animals which face to the right appear to have the same significance as a white space (S) response in the Rorschach, i.e., it suggests an oppositional tendency. Prisoners are more oppositional than normals and psychotics less so. The prisoner's opposition appears to stem from his feelings of being a rejected, unattractive, misfit—that is, it is a reactive opposition. The psychotic person apparently has given up almost completely the effort to oppose the press of unwelcome circumstance. As a sidelight it may be noted that scientists and other creative and pioneering people often manifest more than an average amount of oppositional tendency.

TABLE VI

COMPARISON OF FACTORS WHICH DIFFERENTIATE BETWEEN
ADOLESCENTS AND ADULTS

|  | *Male* Adolescents | Adults | *Female* Adolescents | Adults |
|---|---|---|---|---|
| Popular | 43% | 68% | 51 % | 74 % |
| Snakes | 3% | 0.% | 1.7% | 0.58% |
| Birds | 16% | 1.% | 16 % | 5.4 % |

Table VI reveals the struggle of the adolescent for conformity. His intense feelings of fear and guilt (snake) and a desire to find physical release by escaping (birds) is suggested.

Table VII and the accompanying illustrations show the body distortions which tend to reflect psychotic states. (See Figure 4.)

this problem in its acute form but few realize its existence to considerable degree in everyone. If one could fully measure the degree of "self-separateness and independence" of all individuals we would have a normal curve of distribution representing every degree from fetal-like dependence of the infantile psychotic character structure to the very rare and perhaps only theoretical instances of complete psychic separateness and independence of the mature man. It is the present writers' opinion that this is the basic psychological problem in man, rather than the oedipal conflict or the question of sexual identification.

This dependence having been originally a physical attachment (an umbilicus), subsequently an oral attachment (breast or bottle feeding), it is not surprising to find that symbols representative of such an attachment condense both these in symbol formation. For example drawings of the following animals: (a) sucking insect; (b) whale; (c) elephant; (d) anteater; (e) giraffe; (f) seahorse. Among our collection of drawings we have a series arranged along a continuum from strong oral attachment to relative independence as revealed by the mouth parts.

*Negativism*

Most drawings face to the left. Table V indicates the distribution of orientation left, front and right. Orientation to the right has a meaning similar to the use of white space (S) on the Rorschach, i.e., it represents an oppositional quality. The precise value of this quality is determined by other factors in the drawing since opposition ranges from the negativism of the catatonic to the trail-blazing of the scientist; lack of opposition ranges from mature cooperation to empty, slavish conformity.

### Self-concept

Animal drawings, like human drawings, represent the person's feelings about himself. Feelings of largeness, clumsiness, awkwardness, incoordination, are often related to the previously described insufficient sense of separateness. Drawings which portray this quality include elephants, bedbugs (Metamorphosis by F. Kafka), and whales. Feelings of insubstantiality and flightiness by butterflies; of self-denigration by pigs,. goats and rats; of hate and fear by drawings of monsters and anthropoids; of timidity by rabbits; of being queer (schizoid) by fish (out of water); of repressed hostility and its attendant guilt and embarrassment by long-necked animals (who swallow hard).

### Blacking and Filling

Filling in the entire body or blacking it is an obsessive-compulsive mechanism. This mechanism in drawings follows exactly the same pattern as it does in behavior and fantasy. There is a continuum ranging from effectiveness as a defense mechanism (see ram drawing), through hypochondriacal preoccupation with the body to the transparency of body parts which reflects a loss of self-image in psychosis.

### Psychosexual Fixations

By examining the kind of animal and the particular way it

TABLE VII

SEVERELY DISTORTED BODY OUTLINES *

| | |
|---|---|
| Psychotics | 27% |
| Normals | 5% |
| Prisoners | 10% |

* See Figure 4.

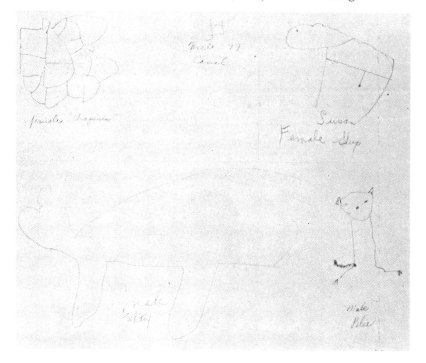

Figure 4

is drawn, one is given evidence about psychosexual areas of difficulty revolving around oral, anal and genital parts.

A continuation of the discussion of animal drawings, although from a somewhat different vantage point, is offered by Hammer in his chapter on Doodles.

### REFERENCES

1. Jackson, Justice: In Commager, H. S.: *Living Ideas in America.* New York, Harper, 1951, p. 539.
2. Levy, S., and Levy, R.: *The Meaning of Animals:* as symbols in dreams and drawings, literature and legend, ritual and religion, art and projective techniques, Vols. I and II. In preparation.
3. Cleckly, H., and Thigpen, C.: *Three Faces of Eve.* New York, McGraw-Hill, 1957.
4. Frazer, J. G.: *Totemism and Exogamy.* London, 1910, 4 vols.
5. Freud, S.: *Basic Writings of Sigmund Freud.* p. 904.
6. Freud, S.: *Totem and Taboo.* New York, Norton, 1952.
7. Jung, C. G.: *Collected Works,* Vol. 5; Symbols of Transformation. (Bollingen Series XX.) Pantheon Books, 1957.
8. Freud, S.: *The Interpretation of Dreams.* Basic Books, 1955.

9. Roheim, G.: *Psychoanalysis and Anthropology.* New York, Internat. Univ. Press, 1950.
10. Opler, M. D.: Japanese folk beliefs concerning the snake. *Southwest. J. Anthropol., 1:*251, 1945.
11. Weakland, J. H.: Orality in Chinese conceptions of male genital sexuality. *Psychiatry, 19:*237-247.
12. Guttman, S.: Bisexuality in symbolism. *J. Am. Psychoanalyt. A.,* p. 280, April, 1955.
13. Goldfarb, W.: The animal symbol in the Rorschach Test and an animal association test. *Rorschach Res. Exch., 9:*No. 1, March, 1945.
14. Yoder, A.: *Animal Analogy in Shakespeare's Character Portrayal.* New York, King's (Columbia Univ. Press), 1947.
15. Rorschach, H.: *Psychodiagnostics.*
16. Breasted, J. H.: *A History of Egypt.* New York, Scribner, 1948.
17. Brugsch, H.: *Religion und Mythologie der alten Aegypter.* Leipzig, 1885, p. 354.
18. Heidel, A.: *The Gilgamesh Epic and Old Testament Parallels.* Chicago, 1946.
19. Poe, E. A.: *The Raven.*
20. Frobenius, L.: In Jung, C. G. (7), p. 246.
21. Howey, W. O.: *The Cat, In the Mysteries of Magic and Religion.* Castle Books, 1956.
22. Schwartz, and Rosenberg: Animal drawings. *J. Orthopsychiat.,* p. 738, 1955.

## CHAPTER 15

# THE DRAWING COMPLETION TEST

### G. MARIAN KINGET, PH.D.

THINKING OF a way to start this modest contribution to a work on projective techniques brings to mind something I said a few years ago which has since become an anecdote among my colleagues. It happened at the time I joined the institution with which I have the privilege still to be associated. As part of the ritual marking the installation of a new member, I was asked to speak to the staff and graduate students about my work with the Wartegg Drawing Completion Test. I had already learned that, in America, such occasions call for an introductory note of humor. However, having grown a bit weary of the all too obviously laughter-triggering little joke, I decided to say something which, though funny in itself, would draw visible reaction only to the extent that the listeners were acquainted with the subject, thereby telling me something about my audience and turning the occasion into a slightly more mutual affair. Thus, with the gravity of the author speaking about his first book, I announced that I had "the privilege of presenting a work for which the field of clinical psychology has, in the last five or ten years, been feeling a growing need" and, pausing a comma-worth, adding: "another projective technique." The general laughter and applause arising from the floor made it plain that the inflation I was referring to was far from being in-group information but that it was known even to those whose kinship with the clinical branch goes little beyond membership in the APA.

The moral of the story is clear. Projective techniques have come to be recognized as not only too numerous but as too alike underneath the variety of their media. The initial enthusiasm over their striking and often ingenious forms has made room for an awareness of the necessity for selection. For while a reliable diagnosis requires application of a variety of techniques the contribution of every single technique cannot be greater than its individual value and this value—despite all efforts at objectification of the instrument—remains greatly dependent upon the worker's mastery in its use. Acquiring mastery takes time and systematic study—which puts a limit to a worker's repertoire.[1] Furthermore, excessive variety may endanger objectivity for it tends towards giving every diagnostician his private set of means. Healthy conditions of personality testing require, therefore, a balance between variety and restriction. Hence the necessity to take stock of the crammed diagnostic toolshop and to pick out those means which offer the greatest promise in terms of validity, reliability, selectivity, simplicity, economy of application, and similar criteria.

With the foregoing idea in mind I will use this opportunity for making a general presentation of this (in the United States) relatively little known test, bringing out its characteristic assets and merits rather than presenting an account of any particular study involving its use.

## ORIGIN AND DEVELOPMENT

The originator of the test is the (East) German psychologist Ehrig Wartegg. From the date of his first publication on the subject (6) it can be inferred that he devised the blank in the late twenties or early thirties. In 1939 he published his work "Gestaltung und Charakter," (7) a highly developed approach to the evaluation of personality based upon drawings obtained by means of his blank. Shortly after its publication I became acquainted with the test and, intrigued by the diagnostically promising appearance of the blank, I set out to familiarize myself thoroughly with its use according to the principles expounded in Wartegg's work. Soon I was forced to the conclusion that the blank was not merely another ingenious device but an excep-

---

[1] This would seem to be true especially in regard to techniques using different media. It applies less to tests whose medium falls within the same category as, for instance, the group of tests presented in this work since thorough familiarity with one drawing test is likely to generalize easily to others, thus making for an economically gained and adequately buttressed diagnosis.

tional creation on a level with the unsurpassed Rorschach ink-blots.

At the time I became acquainted with it (1943), Wartegg's work had not been the object of any known research. Carried by the enthusiasm one is bound to develop when seeing the response material the blank is capable of producing, I ventured into the rather bold enterprise of submitting Wartegg's system to experimental verification—or, at least, to a first approximation thereof. The extensive research which this project involved and which took a number of years to be completed led, beyond its original aim, to the accumulation of a vast amount of new data and insights. As the stage was thus set for further development, I attempted to extend the test's diagnostic value from the typological level on which it was originally conceived to the level of individual diagnosis. To this end I concentrated upon discovering the psychological correlates of the *single* drawing variables, i.e., the characteristics of content and execution which, thus far, had been used primarily *in clusters*. This operation resulted in shedding considerable light on the meaning of individual differences and thus contributed appreciably to a sharpening of the test as a diagnostic instrument. In its present form it makes, of course, no claim to finality, the nature of projective techniques being one of incessant improvement and growth. However, it is probably safe to say that it has now attained a degree of development which cannot fail to make its use and further research a rewarding experience.

## Construction of the Test [2]

*The Population.* One of the characteristics of the test is the fact that, contrary to most projective techniques, it was developed entirely on a normal, that is, a functioning, non-hospitalized population. This lends it not merely a distinctive feature but perhaps also a distinctive merit. Indeed, the investigation of the basic make-up of normal individuals by means of the products of their free activity is an uncommonly challenging enterprise. For the

[2] Because the published data regarding the procedures followed by Wartegg in the first phase of development of the test are scanty and general I will, in the following, report mainly on my own work.

range of differences in the creative products of normal individuals is incomparably greater than that of psychiatric groups—individual differences within the latter notwithstanding. Those who know the difficulty of providing meaningful, individualized interpretations of material produced by normal subjects in response to established tests may perhaps appreciate what is entailed in the construction of a new test on the basis of such plurivalent material. The difficulty did not, however, come as a surprise. It was foreseen and accepted as part of one of the tasks which confronts the profession today, namely, the reversal of a trend established in the pioneer days of clinical psychology which tended to evaluate the normal in terms of the abnormal instead of the other way around.

Whether Wartegg's use of a normal population was planned or accidental we do not know. We do know, however, that it consisted of children and adults of both sexes examined in connection with problems of educational, vocational, and military screening. No exact figures are given but it is apparent that the number of subjects examined in connection with the basic work on the test must have been considerable. The subsequent phase of development, which I undertook (3), used a group of 383 adult subjects, (187 males and 196 females whose educational and occupational background ranged from grade school educated manual workers and homemakers to college students and professional people). This group, in contrast with much psychological work done on normal populations—which, for practical reasons, often show an unrepresentative predominance of college students—was selected in such a way as to form a representative sample of the socio-economic structure of western society, that is, reflecting the marked predominance of the middle classes, and the relative predominance of the lower over the professional class.

*The Validation.* As in most verification and validation work the central difficulty concerned the establishment of an adequate criterion. The difficulty was particularly great in this case because the diagnostic blueprint used by Wartegg had no parallel among existing tests. As was already mentioned, his system was basically typological. Consequently, his scheme of personality investigation was devised primarily for the purpose of identifying the three types distinguished in his system, namely, the vital-emotional, the rational-volitional, and the integrative. Making up the schema were the traditionally recognized "basic functions": emotion, imagination, intellect, and volition (the latter term has been substituted here for the term activity), each of which was further subdivided in two contrasting aspects (see bottom part of Table III) making for a total of eight aspects from which to investigate the personality.

As can easily be seen from this brief description, Wartegg's diagnostic schema was considerably different from that underlying all other personality tests. While this is not a deficiency in itself, it did preclude the use of these tests for the purpose of comparison and posed the immense problem of constructing a criterion *ad hoc.*

An easy way out of this difficulty would have consisted in taking the core of Wartegg's work, namely, the blank and using it in combination with a more common diagnostic blueprint. This idea was, however, abandoned because it was felt that progress in the field of diagnosis was better served by the chain-work approach in which every researcher aims, at least in part, at verifying, clarifying, and possibly improving the work done by his predecessors instead of starting an independent course of action, the result of which is a confusing profusion of creativity and a lack of solidity.

What gives the validation its particular solidity[3] is the multiple character of the criterion used. Indeed, because of the deficiencies inherent in any one particular test—especially new tests—a set of three different approaches was used to neutralize the effects of subjectivity, inconsistency, inexactness, and unreliability which inevitably affect, to some extent, the kind of tests finally decided upon. These were a forced choice test, a questionnaire, and a rating scale. The first two were taken by the subject, the latter was given to one or several persons who knew the subject well.

---

[3] In his preface to the book *The Drawing Completion Test,* Percival Symonds writes: "I discovered that here was not only another study which attempted to give an experimental basis for the interpretation of the projective elements in drawing but one which surpassed all of the previous attempts at such validation and provided for the first time really convincing validation data and an interpretation of the projective elements of drawing on satisfactory evidence" (p. v).

The content of each of these tests was made up strictly in terms of Wartegg's definitions of the components of his personality scheme. The questionnaire and rating scale presented a great number of interlocking questions, the forced choice test consisted of concept-pairs selected in such a manner as to reflect the subject's affinity for either of the two polar aspects of each of the basic functions. The validity of the criterion tests was not taken for granted. Each of them was built according to regular methods of test construction—an operation which was somewhat facilitated because of the possibility for mutual cross checking of their content.

## THE BLANK

Because the particular properties of the blank represent one of this test's major credentials for admission to the round, a relatively substantial part of this article will be devoted to a discussion of its characteristics and of the data which support its claim to exceptional diagnostic potentialities.

For a given material to be suitable as an instrument for personality testing it must satisfy two basic conditions. It must lend itself to free activity by the subject and to systematic evaluation by the examiner. These two requirements are obviously not easy to reconcile. Systematic evaluation presupposes criteria on structure, and structure constitutes an obstacle to freedom. The Wartegg blank combines these conflicting conditions with uncommon effectiveness. To the subject it presents a situation which is as free as a given material, compatible with the requirements of a test, can be. To the examiner, on the other hand, it offers a highly structured situation, providing him with numerous and varied criteria for evaluation. These apparently mutually exclusive characteristics call for some clarification. A brief attempt at such now follows.

### Qualitative Factors

By qualitative factors is meant the whole of attributes related to the particular form (curved or straight, large or small, etc.) of the stimuli appearing within the drawing spaces. A simple glance at the blank suffices to recognize that: (1) each of the stimuli

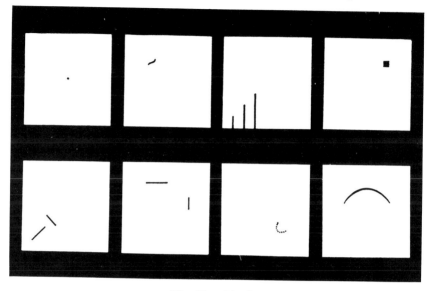

The Test Blank

has a form very much of its own which gives it individuality, and (2) the forms of the individual stimuli are greatly varied.

These form-qualities are of two kinds. Some of them are objective in the sense that they are inherent in the physical structure of the stimuli. For instance, Stimulus One has the objective qualities of being round, relatively small, and centrally located. Other form-qualities have a strictly phenomenological or Gestalt value; that is, they are attributed to the stimulus by the perceiving subject. The latter type of quality may be relatively objective (in the statistical, not in the physical, sense of the word), or it may be relatively subjective (perceived by only a few, or even one single subject). The wavy line of Stimulus Two, for example, is generally perceived as supple, mobile, even animated—occasionally as crawling or even as humorous. These Gestalt qualities give the stimuli a certain affective or "mood" value which causes them to appear as more or less attractive or unattractive to the subject. In objective terms this means that he finds certain stimuli "easy," others "difficult," to deal with, thus revealing his affinity—and respectively his lack of affinity—for the qualities symbolized by these stimuli. Following is a brief indication of the qualities most commonly ascribed to each of the eight stimuli.

| *Stimuli* | *Objective Qualities* | *Gestalt Qualities* [4] |
|---|---|---|
| One | round, relatively small, exactly central | delicate, light, insignificant, alive, drifting |
| Two | curved, round-edged, off-center located | supple, mobile, loose, alive, waving, flowing, crawling |
| Three | elements are straight, equidistant, regularly increasing, peripherally-located | stiff, strict, austere, methodical, constructive, progressive, growing |
| Four | square, intensely black, corner located | heavy, solid, massive, static, material, somber |
| Five | straight, contrary oriented, peripherally located | dynamic, conflicting, aggressive-resistant, goal-oriented |
| Six | straight, at right angle, unequal, off-center | plain, matter-of-fact, uninspiring, awkward, unbalanced |
| Seven | dotted, half-circular, peripherally located | delicate, refined, fussy, lively, complex |
| Eight | broadly curved, upwards located, downwards bent, relatively large tapered-off ends | smooth, easy, restful, fluent, flexible, organic, sheltering |

**Masculine Stimuli and Feminine Stimuli.** While the stimuli are qualitatively highly diversified they can nevertheless be organized into two categories according to the similarity of some of their predominant qualities. Thus we have the group of the curved and dotted and the group of the straight and square stimuli. Wartegg calls these respectively the feminine and the masculine groups. As used here, these labels do not refer to any Freudian symbolism but simply to the supposedly greater affinity of women for the world of animate reality whose organic, round, flexible, and growing quality is symbolized by the curved line, and the corresponding greater affinity of men for the world of

---

[4] Only the Gestalt qualities with the highest degree of objectivity (i.e., most frequently mentioned) are listed. The order of their listing reflects roughly the order of frequency with which they are mentioned by the subjects.

**Belgian subject.** This set of drawings points to a typically "feminine" make-up. The content of the drawings reveals an orientation of the interests towards home, children, flowers and decorative objects. The execution is marked by abundant use of shading, strong lines, extreme carefulness and a concern for harmony and embellishment of a rather conventional style.

This combination of characteristics indicates an emotionally rich, generous, sensitive and friendly personality, well endowed but void of intellectual ambition, conservative, candid and somewhat seclusive. A fairly strong but gently disciplined vitality makes for a happy balance between spontaneity and control, productiveness and relaxation. Though solidly rooted in reality and well adjusted to her small-town environment, this girl shows a somewhat naïve romantic-idealistic outlook.

objective reality with its technical-constructive properties more aptly symbolized by the straight lines.

The individual's affinity for the qualities represented by either of these groups of stimuli appears to constitute a valuable criterion for judging the relatively masculine or feminine character of his personality. Conclusions of this kind are, of course, not based upon *single* cues. Like all other conclusions drawn from this test they are based upon a *twofold pattern* of responses whose detection is made possible by the double-barrelled structure of the blank. To a variable extent every conclusion is based upon the relative consistency of the subject's positive responses to sets of stimuli pointing in a given direction *and* upon the corresponding consistency of his negative responses to sets of stimuli pointing in the opposite direction. More concretely, for a given subject to be diagnosed as having a predominantly feminine make-up, he must not only respond to the feminine group of stimuli by producing predominantly organic content—life, nature—and by tending to give them precedence in the order in which he makes the drawings, but he must also respond to the masculine stimuli by producing no or few man-made objects, technical abstractions, etc., and by otherwise failing to show affinity for the qualities represented by these stimuli. In summary, every conclusion is founded, so to speak, upon proof and counterproof.

In connection with the tendency of non-representational lines, such as those here used, to be associated with certain types of subject matter, it may be useful to refer to the work of Krauss (4) and of Hippius (2). In their experiments each of these researchers asked his subjects to represent concepts by means of mere non-representational lines and other graphic elements. Among

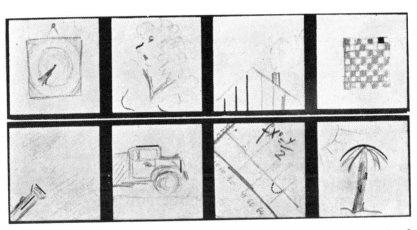

**American subject.** This is the way a young American male has completed the testblank. The content shows mainly commonplace objects, a mathematical graph and the picture of a girl with abundant hair and marked features. The style of drawing is supple, casual, simple and void of any concern for embellishment or superfluity.

Both in content and in execution, this set shows a typically "masculine" make-up. Main characteristics of its author are his realistic-practical orientation, his dynamic approach and healthy aggressiveness. Ambitious, efficient yet relaxed, he seems to be the kind of person who sees his aims clearly and achieves them with relative ease.

A strong zest for life appears directly or indirectly in several drawings. An intelligent, well-rounded and matter-of-fact person, of a type that tends to be centered exclusively in tangible reality.

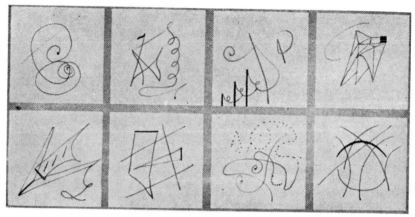

**Canadian subject.** In sharp contrast with the preceding drawings, which all pictured reality, this set made by a Canadian girl contains nothing material, either animate or inanimate. The execution shows a predominance of curved lines, capricious loops and criss-crosses.

These abstractions suggest a predominantly emotional and dynamic make-up, unconventional, independent, rather creative but not very stable or practical. Basically flexible and adaptive, this girl is, however, conflict-prone and liable to react aggressively. (Testblank completed and returned by a *Life* reader.)

these concepts were emotions such as joy, anger, or fear, abstract notions such as harmony or progress, concrete materials as glass or gold, and even colors. The results showed that certain types of lines tend to be associated with certain categories of subject matter—a conclusion which was amply confirmed by the findings of this test. It appears thus that seemingly meaningless stimuli may actually exert considerable influence upon the direction of the subject's associative activity. Hence the importance of *a balanced representation of a broad variety of stimuli* for a testing tool of this type to be free from implicit direction and suited for a broad exploration of the projective activity.

## Organizational and Quantitative Factors

Task variety is but one of the requirements for the diagnostic validity of projective activity. Freedom of action is another. This requirement is sometimes taken too narrowly. It is too easily believed that when we present the subject with certain non-representational material and with the instruction that he may make "anything he wants" out of it that we are giving him complete freedom. Actually he is free only in a negative sense, in that he does not have to meet any particular predetermined standards. In a positive sense, however, the subject's freedom—in terms of the range of subject matter from which he may choose his response—is determined by the ease with which the testing material can be worked into a broad variety of things. This is a consideration which does not always seem to be taken into sufficient account in the construction of testing material of this kind.

The amenability of non-representational stimulus material for completion in a variety of items, that is, its plasticity, is determined mainly by organizational and quantitative factors. By this is meant the size, number, location, and structure of the stimuli. The structure factor is present only in complex stimuli such as three, five, six, and seven in the above blank but plays a very important role. Indeed, the distribution of the elements of such stimuli over the drawing space may tend to fall into certain configurations which pre-figure, more or less, certain kinds of subject matter. Take, for instance, Stimulus Eight. If a horizontal line were drawn underneath it, extending somewhat at each side, the configuration thus produced would almost inevitably suggest a hat or a rising or setting sun. The result is, obviously, a serious reduction of the projective value of the drawing. When the configuration is highly suggestive, the stimulus may be completely devoid of diagnostic potentialities. Another and more insidious way in which the projective activity can be hampered is through irregular scatter of various elements over the drawing space. In this case their integration into meaningful drawing may be so difficult that it becomes a function of the subject's intelligence. Especially when the stimuli contained within the drawing space are of different kinds (e.g., straight and curved or broken), projective activity may practically be precluded.

## THE DIAGNOSTIC MECHANISM

One of the unique assets of this test is the fact that it provides three different sources of data, making for a threefold approach to the interpretation of the results. Most distinctive among these sources is the Stimulus Drawing Relation (SDR) or analysis of the manner in which the subject responds to the form-qualities of the stimuli. The next source of data consists of the *content* or specifically projective aspect of the drawings. This source is available due to the fact that the subject is allowed to draw what he wants—and thus to associate freely—instead of having to perform a given theme. Finally, because of the emphasis placed upon the characteristics of *execution* this test also taps the expressive or performance aspect of the drawings.

## The Stimulus Drawing Relation

As was indicated earlier, the stimuli appearing on the blank serve as a series of varied tools for exploring the individual's make-up and as a series of checks upon the information brought out by each of them. To know which of the qualities carried by the stimuli have been responded to, we have to examine the Stimulus Drawing Relation. This is a double operation consisting of noting on the one hand the stimulus qualities which the drawings emphasize and, on the other, the qualities which they disregard and of translating the product of this analysis into psychological terms.

Let us examine a brief, simplified, and incomplete sample of this operation, taking some types of drawings often encountered in response to Stimulus One and noting their diagnostic implications. It should be emphasized that, at this stage of the analysis, such implications are merely pointers which need to be validated or rejected through cross-checking against the information derived from the SDRs of the other stimuli and from the other two sources of data. Frequently encountered responses to Stimulus One are the following:

*a) A Wheel:* A drawing like this shows that the stimulus is perceived in its two essential qualities, namely, in the centrality of its location and in its roundness. Such a response may be considered tentatively as indicating a matter of fact, objective, realistic, practical, and outspoken masculine make-up. It may further be inferred that while the subject tends to have an eye for the essential and a disregard for trivia (the centrality, not the smallness of the dot is emphasized), he is somewhat lacking in integrative ability (failure to integrate the stimulus into an independent whole such as a carriage). There is also the possibility of low emotional capacity (the roundness of the stimulus is used for representing mechanical, not organic, reality).

*b) The Center of an Old-time Clock:* In this case the conclusions would be basically the same as under a). However, the fact that the subject completes the stimulus in a self-contained whole and shows a concern about style would point in the direction of a better balanced make-up, with greater integrative and emotional capacities, a more refined sensibility, and a less unilaterally masculine make-up.

*c) A Rain Drop:* If the subject draws a scene representing, e.g., a little girl sheltered by a large umbrella, and reduces the stimulus to one of many raindrops filling the upper part of the drawing space, he emphasizes primarily the smallness of the dot and disregards completely the characteristics it derives from its position within the field. In other words, he recognizes the nature of the stimulus (roundness, smallness) but overlooks its function. Indeed, he changes the stability, the importance and individuality it derives from its central position into looseness, insignificance, and commonness. The conclusions tentatively derived from a SDR like this would point to an emotional, imaginative, predominantly feminine make-up (the value of the stimulus is entirely subordinated to the subject's need to create a certain mood, a certain picture of life and nature), to a person with a warm, reality-related, kindhearted outlook, possibly endowed with a gentle sense of humor (amusing contrast between small child and large umbrella).

*d) The Heart of a Flower:* A solution of this type emphasizes the roundness and smallness of the stimulus; it does not entirely disregard the centrality of the stimulus but shifts its value from the abstract-geometric to the concrete-organic plane. Such a SDR would tend to indicate a strong predominance of sensibility over the intellect, to an unaggressive, somewhat romantic (in the case of a male subject, possibly sentimental), markedly feminine type of integration.

*e) The Intersection of Two Diagonal Lines:* This type of response emphasizes the exact central location of the stimulus to the extent of completely denying its roundness. Such a response points to a unilaterally, intellectual, abstract-logical, over-controlled, unimaginative make-up.

The above examples could be multiplied to characterize the predominantly dynamic, the aggressive, the withdrawn, the impulsive, and other types of personality. However, as was indicated before, the diagnostic inferences made on the basis of the responses made to the individual stimuli can be raised to the level of conclusions only when the implications of several responses converge towards the same meaning.

## The Content

The subject matter of projective material is a commonly used source of data in personality testing. It represents a product of the subject's free associations and lends insight into the predominant orientation of the subject's attitudes, needs, and pressures.

The specific contribution of this test to the analysis of content lies in the systematic and differentiated way in which it organizes the practically unlimited realm of content and, especially, in the corresponding psychological indices which it supplies. Since the use of content matter in the interpretation of projective material is well known and since the subject is too complex and extensive to be discussed within the assigned limits, the presentation of this part of the diagnostic procedure will be limited to Table I.

The organization of this table has not only logical but also diagnostic value. The four major divisions in which it is organized (indicated respectively by Roman and Arabic numerals and by capital and small letters) represent steps in the interpretation of the particular drawing. Thus, a drawing representing a horse is considered in so far as it falls within the category of: (1) Representational Subject Matter; (2) of Reality Reproduction; (3) of Natural Objects, and (4) of the Animate variety.

## The Execution

Drawing tests in general have the great advantage that they yield a directly observable, lasting product which can be viewed globally and immediately, that is, without the detour of symbols

TABLE I

| MAJOR DIVISIONS IN WHICH THE TEST DIFFERENTIATES THE CONTENT OF DRAWINGS |
| --- |

I. *Non-Representational Subject Matter*
    1. Scribblings
    2. Abstractions
        a. Symmetrical decorative drawings
        b. Decorative free line structures
        c. Technical drawings

II. *Representational Subject Matter*
    A. Reality reproductions
        1. Natural objects
            a. Animate nature
                People
                Animals
            b. Inanimate nature
        2. Man-made objects
            a. Utility items
            b. Ornamental objects

    B. Fantasy products
            a. Positively toned themes
            b. Negatively toned themes
            c. Symbolic themes

or the lapse of time. Because of this they are excellently suited for the study of performance as well as of content.

The attention given by diagnosticians to these two kinds of resources, execution and content, has, however, been rather unequal. The interpretation of free drawings has been too unilaterally focused upon content, that is, upon the properly projective aspects, while their execution, or expressive aspect, has remained largely unexplored. Content alone is, however, insufficient for a reliable and differentiated interpretation. Subjects of widely different personality·structure draw the same things—human figures or heads, animals, flowers, buildings, decorative drawings, or other familiar items. However, the same content always shows differences in execution. A given object may be represented in relatively small or large size, may be vaguely sketched or sharply outlined, carefully or casually treated, shaded, or detailed; the lines may be strong or weak, straight or curved, fluent, broken, etc. The characteristics of the execution thus lend unmistakable individuality to otherwise common subject matter.

The work done with this test showed, moreover, that execution offers a more reliable diagnostic basis than content. While the latter tends to uncover the subject's interests, his affinities, needs, and concerns, the execution informs about more fundamental aspects of his behavior such as the intensity of his drive, the strength of his control, his basic tenseness or relaxedness, his flexibility, lability, tenacity, and other highly permanent elements of his make-up.

One difficulty in regard to the diagnostic use of the characteristics of execution is the fact that their meaning is not immediately apparent—as opposed to content whose symbolism is easily understandable and remains largely identical from one test to another. It is one of the special merits of this test that it provides an extensive analysis of execution variables along with their psychological indices. These variables pertain mainly to the:

*Coverage:* Full, empty, expanded, or constricted.

*Type and quality of the lines:* Straight or curved, fluent or rigid, continuous or discontinuous.

*Pressure:* Strong or weak.

*Treatment:* Careful or casual.

*Structure:* Organized (spacially or logically) or detailed.

*Shading:* Light or dark.

A number of other variables such as Movement, Repetition—in all, twenty-two scorable variables.

The meaning of the single characteristics is, of course, not to be understood as unequivocal and invariable, like that of dictionary listings. It is to be modified constantly as a function of the ever-changing constellation in which the variables appear.

*Scoring*

Strictly objective scoring presupposes the existence of precise standards or norms. Free drawings, like all products of creative activity, do not permit establishment of rigorous norms. The accuracy achieved in matters as subtle as these is, therefore, only approximate, especially where the single variable is concerned. However, when a great number of variables are involved, the total scoring may attain surprising objectivity. For such to be the outcome, two conditions must be present: first, the things to be scored must be adequately defined; second, a means must be made available for methodical and easy recording of the scores. The test provides both of these.

The scoring occurs by means of a special scoring sheet (Table II) and uses a three-point scale. Scores are indicated by symbols (one X for every point) rather than by ciphers. This procedure is intended to reflect as directly as possible on the scoring sheet the constellation of characteristics contained in the drawings. The distribution of the symbols over the scoring sheet thus creates a pattern of filled and blank areas which provides an immediate communication for the trained examiner. This abstract pattern is not intended as a substitute for the original product. It is only an aid for highlighting its characteristics which, in the drawing, through intimate fusion with one another may be functionally absorbed or enhanced thus tending to distort the interpretation. Another advantage of this procedure lies in the fact that, through the effect of the spaces left open it provides, so to speak, a negative of the product. This clearly shows the characteristics not represented in the drawings. The absence of certain characteristics, though generally not as significant as their presence, is nevertheless a worthwhile aspect of the material, capable of clarifying and emphasizing the trends evidenced in the material.

### The Interpretation

The total scores obtained by the variables appearing in the drawings are then plotted in the interpretation blank (Table III) which is organized according to the relations found between the drawing variables and the psychological variables here explored. The result of this operation is a curve called the personality profile. This curve is often mistaken for the final product of the test. Actually, it represents merely a first organization of the data, a typological picture which must subsequently be individualized through a series of steps. First, the total scores making for the

| CRITERIA | Total Score | Drawings 1 | 2 | 3 | 4 | 5 | 6 | 7 | 8 | | Drawings 1 | 2 | 3 | 4 | 5 | 6 | 7 | 8 | Total Score | CRITERIA | |
|---|---|---|---|---|---|---|---|---|---|---|---|---|---|---|---|---|---|---|---|---|---|
| NATURE Animate | | | | | | | | | | | | | | | | | | | | Fancy | FAN-TASY |
| Physiognomy | | | | | | | | | | | | | | | | | | | | Phantasm | |
| Inanimate | | | | | | | | | | | | | | | | | | | | Symbolism | |
| Atmosphere | | | | | | | | | | | | | | | | | | | | Original | AB-STRACT |
| OB-JECTS Utility | | | | | | | | | | | | | | | | | | | | Symmetric | |
| Ornaments | | | | | | | | | | | | | | | | | | | | Asymetric | |
| Style | | | | | | | | | | | | | | | | | | | | Technical | |
| Movement | | | | | | | | | | | | | | | | | | | | Careful | SHADING |
| COVERAGE Full | | | | | | | | | | | | | | | | | | | | Casual | |
| Empty | | | | | | | | | | | | | | | | | | | | Light | |
| Expanded | | | | | | | | | | | | | | | | | | | | Dark | |
| Constricted | | | | | | | | | | | | | | | | | | | | Orientation | |
| Organization | | | | | | | | | | | | | | | | | | | | Closure | |
| Detail | | | | | | | | | | | | | | | | | | | | Parts | |
| LINES Curved | | | | | | | | | | | | | | | | | | | | Scribbles | |
| Straight | | | | | | | | | | | | | | | | | | | | Duplication | |
| Strong | | | | | | | | | | | | | | | | | | | | Repetition | |
| Soft | | | | | | | | | | | | | | | | | | | | Schematism | |

Table II. Scoring Blank

| Anim. Phys. | Ina. Atm. Sof. | Phys . Orna. | Expa. FAN. | OBJECTS | Organized | Aim. Mov. | Emp.Con.Stroi. |
|---|---|---|---|---|---|---|---|
| Expon. Curv. | Sy. As. SHA. Pa | Styl. Organ. | Orig. Asy. | Detail | Technical | Ful. Strong | Stro.Clo. Rep. |
| Casual | Scri. Sche. | Symmetr. | Dark | | | Dark, Orie. | Duplic. |
| | | | | | | | |
| | | | | | | | |
| | | | | | | | |
| | | | | | | | |
| | | | | | | | |
| | | | | | | | |
| Open | Seclusive | Combinative | Creative | Practical | Speculative | Dynamic | Controlled |
| EMOTION | | IMAGINATION | | INTELLECT | | ACTIVITY | |

Table III. Interpretation Blank

profile must be analyzed. For instance, the total score for the outgoing pole of the Emotion variable may be made up of scores for Animate Nature, Expanded Coverage, Curved Lines, and Casual Treatment. However, each of these variables also has a specific significance. Hence, two subjects having a total score of twenty for Outgoing Emotion may nevertheless be very different, depending on whether the scores are represented mainly by the first two or by the latter two of the above mentioned variables, or by any other combination of same.

The picture thus obtained must then be further differentiated by Combination with the data conveyed by the Stimulus Drawing Relation and the order of execution of the drawings. Finally, the data have to be interpreted as a function of certain basic data such as the subject's age, sex, level of education, or type of occupation. Blind diagnosis is, of course, feasible and may be of interest for theoretical purposes. In practice, however, because of the plurivalent nature of projective material such is not advisable as it detracts from the validity and usefulness of the diagnosis.

## SOME PRACTICAL ADVANTAGES

Probably few diagnostic tools have the potentiality to provide the wealth of material yielded by projective drawings with so little expense of time and effort on the part of all involved. Economy of application is probably this test's most striking practical advantage, too. Indeed, the administration takes none of the examiner's time. As for the interpretation, the average time needed to process the results as described above is about one-half-hour, generally less. Moreover, short-cuts can be taken which may reduce the interpretation time to a few minutes. This is possible especially where the examiner is familiar with the test. In such cases, a simple glance at the set of drawings is capable of conveying important information. This amenability to rapid interpretation is particularly useful for purposes of screening or differential diagnosis where, instead of a full personality picture, only certain specific points need to be examined.

Another asset of the test is that it lends itself without any change in instructions or scoring for application to groups as well as to individuals. Furthermore, the test has certain properties which makes it suitable for administration to a large variety of subjects. First, due to the fact that it was developed upon a normal population, it is applicable in vocational guidance, selection, and other instances where a normal population is tested. This suitability for a large population is also furthered by the nature of the blank, which due to its "neutral" character does not tend to threaten the subject. It does not arouse his anxiety by the strangeness of its appearance, diagnostic "transparence," or by the "childishness" of the tasks to be performed. This may explain to some extent the favorable response which the material generally elicits from adults as well as from children. (The test was applied to a considerable number of children, taken in groups ranging from kindergarten through the sixth grade, and revealed a surprising receptivity on the part of these young subjects. It was also administered to a number of psychiatric patients who produced highly characteristic drawings.)

Finally, because of the precise and differentiated nature of its material, the test is particularly suited for research purposes.

The great variety of perceptions which the stimuli are able to elicit makes it apt to reflect very sensitively the changes which may occur in the subject under the influence of psychotherapy or any other significant learning.

## REFERENCES

1. Berger, E.: Der Sandersche Phantasietest im Rahmen der psychologischen Eignungsuntersuchung. *Arch. ges. Psychol., 103:*499, 1939.
2. Hippius, M. T.: Graphischer Ausdrck von Gefühlen. *Ztschr. ang. Psychol., 51:* 257, 1936.
3. Kinget, G. M.: *The Drawing Completion Test.* New York, Grune & Stratton, 1952.
4. Krauss, R.: Ueber graphischen Ausdruck. *Ztschr. Psychol.,* Suppl. 48, 1930.
5. Sander, F.: Experimentelle Ergebnisse der Gestalpsychologie. *Ber. über d.10. Kongr. exper. Psychol.,* 1928.
6. Wartegg, E.: Gefühl. *Neue psychol. Studien, 12:*99, 1934.
7. Wartegg, E.: Gestaltung und Charakter. *Ztschr. ang. Psychol.,* Suppl. 84, 1939.

CHAPTER 16

## THE MOST UNPLEASANT CONCEPT TEST

## A GRAPHIC PROJECTIVE TECHNIQUE FOR DIAGNOSTIC AND THERAPEUTIC USE

M. R. HARROWER, PH.D.

### INTRODUCTION

SPITZ (6) HAS RECENTLY stated that "the list of projective techniques grows longer daily." While this may be considered psychological, if not poetic, license, there is nonetheless some truth to the remark. One has only to look, for instance, at the long bibliography in Frank's *Projective Methods* (1) to realize the numerous additions in this field since Frank himself coined the term in 1938 to describe the Rorschach test and the Thematic Apperception Test. What justification is there in further adding to this ever-growing list? This must be the question which any experimenter asks himself before devising and advocating yet another projective method.

For introducing to others a test which has proved of value to this writer over a two-year period, the reasons are as follows: the test is extraordinarily quick and simple to administer; it can be handled and administered to large groups as easily as to a single individual; there is no scoring; classification can be instantaneous; yet, like the handling of the Man-Woman Drawing, as described by Machover (5), a wealth of information can be gained in a short time. This test has proved of diagnostic value in many cases, and it has proved useful in other cases for quickly eliciting the core or focus of the psychological disturbance. With all other drawing techniques, it belongs to that class of material which can be transmitted in the original and in its entirety to the therapist, so that he can have the actual data, over and above the psychologist's comments and evaluation. In this connection we have made a point of taking carbon copies of all drawings in our testing interview and relating our evaluative comments to these illustrations. Finally, such material can be used with the patient as an objective point of departure in therapy and can be used for comparative purposes at various stages. A description of this method, called Projective Counseling, appears elsewhere (2, 3).

## MATERIALS

This chapter deals with the accumulated experience gained from the study of 500 cases on whom psychiatric opinion was available and to whom a full battery of already established psychological techniques was also administered. Each of the 500 patients studied received the Wechsler-Bellevue, the Rorschach Test, the Man-Woman Drawings, the Szondi Test, and in many cases independent evaluation of handwriting by an expert graphologist. In this instance our aim is to make the technique and procedure available to others and to make suggestions in view of our present findings.

### Subjects

The 500 individuals whose drawings comprise the subject matter for this study may be described as follows: individuals who are experiencing psychological difficulties and who are seeking psychiatric assistance in their handling of them. In contrast to this, the 450 individuals who comprise our control groups were persons with no overt psychological symptoms. We wish to make it clear, however, that we are refraining from presenting statistics on the differences between "normals" and patients. This is a deliberate omission to focus attention on an unsatisfactory state of affairs in experimental clinical procedure. Who are "normals" and who should constitute "control subjects?" In experimental psychology, the psychology of the laboratory and of the academic world, the experimenter can readily divide rats which are to run mazes or persons who are to learn under different conditions into "equated groups," and sit back comfortably in the knowledge of satisfactory scientific procedure—exposing one group to certain controlled variables to which he does not submit the others. There is a grave danger, however, that, in order to find "controls" for experimental clinical projects, the too academically trained psychologist will consider all those *not* in his particular clinic or hospital or *not* referred to him for examination as "normal persons" or persons without psychological difficulties.

There are many pitfalls and fallacies involved here, however. If one takes as "controls" an unselected group of individuals and contrasts them with the particular patient group under study, one may well find, on more exhaustive scrutiny, that among the "controls" are persons who also have sought or are seeking expert psychiatric aid elsewhere. There are individuals who have successfully completed or are undergoing an analysis. Into which group do these persons fall? Do they then cease to be "normals?" Are they to be classified as "normals" when they take the test under some conditions and "abnormals" when they take it under others? It is not necessary to belabor the point, provided that a warning and explanation are conveyed. And while certain differences between our especially referred group and our random sample group exist, the test is not advocated for screening the normal from the abnormal, the adjusted from the maladjusted, but rather to highlight the type and extent of a given psychological problem and its manner of expressing itself, this latter providing a clue to other, inter-related psychological processes in all persons.

### Instructions for Administration

To the individuals to whom this test was given, the instructions were always as follows: "What is the Most Unpleasant Thing that you can think of?" or, alternatively, "I want you to think of the Most Unpleasant Thing that you can imagine." Then, after a slight pause, the examiner continues, "And now I want you to draw it for me," and at this point he hands the subject a drawing pad and a pencil. He then adds the further instructions, "You can draw it in actuality, schematically, or symbolically, whichever you please." When the subject returns his drawing, he is asked to describe it and give free associations to it.

The paper used in all cases was standard 8½ inch by 11 inch. A carbon underneath provided a second copy and also gave interesting clues as to pressure, erasing, and shading. Originally we also asked for a drawing of the Most Pleasant Concept, but found in this instance much more trivial, banal, and stereotyped expressions which rarely, if ever, provided important information.

## RESULTS

### Reactions of the Subject to the Test Instructions

We may estimate the subject's readiness to respond on a six point scale.

1. The subject immediately takes the pencil, looks at the examiner in a somewhat accusing or penetrating fashion, and promptly draws some idea, concept, or object, as if, by the question, the examiner had triggered a response which was waiting for the word "go." This over-speedy reaction is frequently accompanied by a spoken or gestured question on the part of the patient, "How did you know I had this unpleasant thought?" The graphic products of persons who respond in this way are frequently of a symbolic type, epitomizing a state of mind or psychological experience (see Figures 4, 5, and 6).

2. Type 2 may be considered the "average-speedy" type in the sense that the subject ponders for a few seconds, as though surveying a series of possible alternative answers, then without ado or conflict, he records his decision, sometimes with some slight apologetic comment that, although he cannot draw well, it will be seen what it is that he is attempting. This type of reaction correlates highly with what have been determined as "popular" answers in this test (see Figure 1).

3. The third type of response may be called the "average-slow." This is similar to Type 2 except that the subject is more hesitant in making his decision; he puts up a greater barrage of defense in terms of his inability to draw satisfactorily. Frequently the lines of the drawings are tentative here. The subject requires reassurance in order to continue.

4. Reaction Type 4 may be described as slow and disturbed. Here the subject knows what specific and personally oriented experience he wishes to portray, but finds its portrayal so disturbing

that he cannot bring himself to commit it to paper. Repeated reassurances are necessary, and much encouragement is useful.

5. This type of delay reaches its extreme at a point where there is refusal to commit the highly disturbing idea to paper. Of our series of 500 cases we found several persons who were unable to complete or continue the test despite all help and pressure. In one instance a moment of panic-like anxiety was evoked. Concerning the nature of this, an interesting account was given the following day by the patient to his therapist.

6. Reaction Type 6 is failure, but of a different order. The individual here literally "cannot think of anything unpleasant," and despite encouragement and finally such suggestive questions as, "Are there really no unpleasant things in the world?" cannot bring himself to enter into the test situation.

No statistics are available at this writing on the distribution of our 500 subjects, since these various types of reactions emerged slowly in the experimenter's mind in the course of the work with the test. However, one or two generalizations are in order. The more normal, or let us say the performance of persons who are less seriously disturbed (when correlated with other test findings and psychiatric evaluation), correlate with Reactions 2 and 3. A certain amount of hesitation, a laughing comment on inability to draw with, nonetheless, a courageous attempt to conform to the test instructions, would seem to equate with a minimum of psychological disturbance at the time of the testing. This is also brought out in the study of random groups in which this is unquestionably the prevailing reaction.

On the other hand, instantaneous portrayal of an idea which seems to have been waiting for expression, extreme reluctance to portray an idea because it is too disturbing, the inability to find anything unpleasant in the world—these have correlated with more seriously disturbed individuals when, again, they have been appraised by the total test battery or by psychiatric evaluation.

### Content: The Subject Matter of the Most Unpleasant Concept

What does the subject draw in this test situation? Do we find 500 different ideas of unpleasantness? By no means. Are there

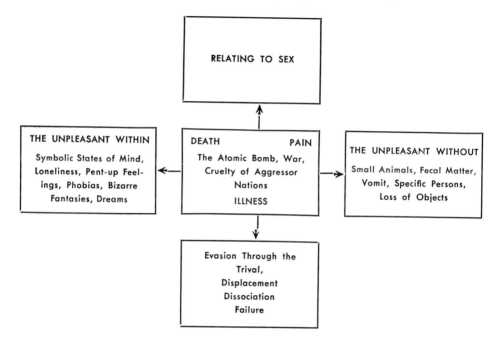

types of answers which can be considered as "popular," psychologically neutral, relating to an unbiased and somewhat objective
appraisal of the unpleasant? It would seem so. We have attempted to bring an initial state of order to our findings by introducing five major divisions or classifications of our material, with
various subdivisions. We will deal first with a discussion of the
major groupings and then consider the subheadings in detail.
As a starting point, the following diagram may be considered as
showing graphically the different "directions" in which the unpleasant may lie.

We may start from a neutral central area which is highly
realistic, impersonal, logical, and universal. I have called this
area: "War, the Atomic Bomb, or Cruelty of Aggressor Nations."
It is impossible to quarrel with the legitimacy of this area as a
Most Unpleasant Concept. Moreover, it will be noticed that in
this instance the word "unpleasant" has been expanded to its
maximum capacity to mean "terrifying," "terrible," and "terrible
to *many*." We have put as an outer ring to this neutral area those

drawings which represent death, pain, or illness. While one cannot quarrel with the legitimacy of the unpleasantness of a violent death, nonetheless this group has a little less of the universality of the first group in that the individual is concerned with his own death rather than the death of many, or he is concerned with the death of someone close to him.[1]

A further look at the diagram shows that, on the arrow to the left, there is a large group of answers which may be considered as *The Unpleasant Within*. Here all objectivity and universality are lost, and the individual is concerned with his own particular psychological "hell." I have grouped here *symbolic* portrayal of states of mind, bizarre fantasies, recurrent dreams, expressions of phobias, etc.

The arrow to the right in the diagram points to the *Unpleasant as Located Outward* but now attached to some specific and definitely non-world-shaking event. Again, there are grades of legitimacy here, the house on fire having greater validity, one might say, than a small bug to harbor or contain human distress and misery. Diagrammatically represented as going in a different direction from the "neutral area" we have listed such examples as "Evasion through the Trivial, Displacement, Dissociation, and Failure." And, in yet another direction, "the Unpleasant Located in Sex."

A comparable diagram drawn for the control subjects would show no drawings which could be classified as "relating to sex," no displacement or dissociation, and no failures. The Unpleasant Within, though represented in terms of loneliness and phobias, is less frequently given than with persons seeking help for their difficulties, and bizarre fantasies are minimal. The majority of responses, therefore, for the "normal" groups are distributed between the central block and the Unpleasant Without. "Popular" responses may be found for specific groups. Thus, as indicated elsewhere (4) a group of patients with multiple sclerosis showed

---

[1] It should be noted that merely to consider these concepts as the "popular" does not mean that in each and every case specific and interesting associations which may be vitally relevant to the psychological problem may not be elicited. We are using this block of associations merely as a starting point to contrast other types of reactions.

# TABLE I

CLASSIFICATION OF REACTIONS ON "THE MOST UNPLEASANT CONCEPT TEST"
OF 500 CASES UNDERGOING PSYCHOTHERAPY

| Classification | Remarks |
|---|---|
| War, the atomic bomb, or cruelty as expressed by aggressor nations | Characteristic responses of "better personality integration" as reflected in the Rorschach Test, lack of distortion of thought processes as reflected in the Similarities test of the Wechsler-Bellevue. In the case of the majority, drawn somewhat crudely but realistically; does not correlate with the psychiatric evaluation of borderline psychosis. |
| Death<br>By plane<br>By drowning<br>By hanging<br>By gashing<br>Death of a specific person<br>Coffin as symbol<br>By automobile accident | Associations here are much less neutral and universal than to the above. Among this group are the drawings of extremely disturbed persons, as well as those with less acute problems. |
| Pain and illness | Given by individuals with actual, distressing physical symptoms and pains (*i.e.*, from Boeck sarcoid) by conversion hysterics, hypochondriacal individuals. Apparently of no diagnostic value. |

## The Unpleasant Within

| | |
|---|---|
| Symbolic portrayal of a state of mind | A highly significant and interesting group, correlating closely with borderline psychosis, distortion of thought processes on the Wechsler-Bellevue, and bizarre concepts on the Rorschach. Not found in the "control" group. |
| Loneliness | Often symbolically expressed and therefore, in a sense, a subgroup of the above. However, there is less of the bizarre quality to the drawings and such responses are found in persons other than borderline cases. |
| Bizarre fantasies and dreams | Again, some similarity with the symbolic portrayal of a state of mind. Often extremely revealing in the uncovering of crucial material. Closely related to the type of free association which may be elicited to original or bizarre answers on the Rorschach Test. |
| Psychological imprisonment | The extraordinary uniformity of this experience can be seen in Figure 13, where five of the six cases are illustrated. |
| Being awakened | This rather interesting subgroup appeared in cases where other test material and clinical findings indicated withdrawal tendencies. |
| Phobias | Common phobias, such as fear of high places, fear of enclosure in a small space, etc., are given. We have included here, also, supersensitivity as expressed in fear of disapproval reflected in facial expression. |
| Very specific personal experiences | Usually highly traumatic experiences; in three of six cases the incident was repressed until time of examination (see Summary and Conclusions, Paragraph 1). |

TABLE I (*Concluded*)

| Classification | Remarks |
|---|---|
| Fear of aggression. Fear of results of agrression (torture, mutilation). Aggression towards children | Of particular interest is the subgroup "Aggression toward children," given by five women and relating to their own children. In one instance a fascinating slip of the pen occurred in the written description. Subject spoke of the fear of killing her child which would "completely accomplish me . . . I mean, ruin me." |

### The Unpleasant Outward

| | |
|---|---|
| The small animal as scapegoat | Almost invariably a neurotic and frequently a specifically sexual problem was found to exist in persons who selected the animal as the Most Unpleasant Concept. Snakes were given most frequently with bugs and spiders in second place. In the one instance where the animal concept was "contaminated," *i.e.*, a spider which had a human expression and was part human, the patient was known to have had several schizophrenic episodes. |
| A house on fire (a house disordered) | A house on fire bears a close relationship clinically to the diagnosis of hysteria. It was given exclusively by women. On the other hand, the two patients whose concept was a house disordered were borderline cases. |
| Specific persons | Usually the problem in this case was very close to the surface—intense antagonism against the mother or mother-in-law was expressed in this way. One depressed individual showed herself as the specific person. A deteriorated organic case drew Hitler. |
| Fecal matter and vomit | |
| Loss of objects, and failure to achieve desired ends or objects | |

### The Unpleasant as Sex

| | |
|---|---|
| Sex Organs—The concept of homosexuality | Castration fears were exemplified frequently by drawings of individuals who had "lost limbs" (see Figure 12). Overt expressions of the idea of homosexuality were given in two cases. There was evidence of severe psychological disturbance in both cases. |

### The Unpleasant Evaded

| | |
|---|---|
| In the extremely trivial. In the weather. Through complete dissociation. Through displacement | Of particular interest are those cases which we have called "dissociation" where the individual is quite unaware of why he drew what he did. For example, a forest, or the moon and a hedge, were not unpleasant to the individuals concerned, yet they drew them without any feeling that they were not complying with the test instructions. By "displacement" we mean the deliberate portrayal of an object which carried some of the characteristics of the idea the individual was afraid to portray. Thus, for example, the dead fish, unpleasant because of its smell, hid the real object, the mother's menstrual pads and their smell. |

### Failure

| | |
|---|---|
| Idea too disturbing to convey. "There is nothing unpleasant" | |

a marked tendency to list the death of their nearest or closest relative as their Most Unpleasant Concept.

Having diagrammed the "direction" in which the unpleasant may lie, a more detailed breakdown of the findings is presented in Table I.

## ILLUSTRATIVE MATERIAL

The illustrations which follow have been selected as expressing as well as possible the material epitomized in the above tables. Needless to say, it has been possible to reproduce only a fraction of those which would have made the reading of this chapter more interesting. Moreover, in making our reproductions as simple line drawings, we have lost a great deal of the interesting variation of shading and quality of line.

## THE MOST UNPLEASANT CONCEPT IN PSYCHOTHERAPY

During the past five years a new form of psychotherapy, described as Projective Counseling (2, 3) has been developed. This method uses the patient's own productions on the projective tests as material comparable to dreams or free association—material, that is, which gives a direct clue to the patient's problems, anxieties and unacceptable attitudes. This material may, at the correct time and in various ways, be used by the therapist to give the patient insight.

The Most Unpleasant Concept has proved of value within this framework. Sometimes a single drawing may be presented to the patient at successive stages and free associations asked for. Sometimes the patient may be asked to redraw his most unpleasant idea, and the changes and the concepts can be utilized advantageously. Sometimes the drawing may, in and of itself, trigger associations which sharpen the patient's awareness of his problems.

One case may be of interest here where the patient, a girl of twenty-five, drew a hearse on thirteen successive occasions. To begin with, the explanations or associations for this drawing were entirely trivial ones, for instance, that she had driven behind one when coming to her analytic session; or that she lived not so far from an undertaker's office. There were associations to the effect that some station wagons looked like hearses, until finally, defenses gave way, and key material was suddenly given and accepted by the patient. As subsequently developed, most of the patient's difficulties lay in her inability to face the fact that she was afraid her mother's death was due to her having left sleeping pills within her mother's reach. Her final association to the hearse was, of course, that this was the hearse that had taken her mother to the funeral.

A more dramatic series of associations, given promptly when the patient was first confronted with her original drawings, came

Figure 1

Showing an imaginative presentation of war and the atomic bomb by a gifted 13-year-old girl.

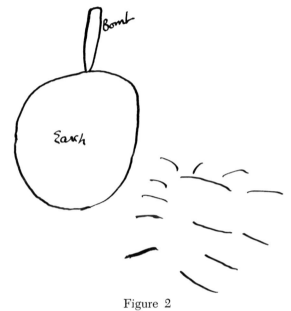

Figure 2
A symbolic representation of war and the atomic bomb drawn by a person
with an acute sexual problem.

from an exceedingly gifted woman who had been literally imprisoned in her apartment for over a year, due to her terror of
stepping on feces were she to venture into the street. Even within
her apartment her entire life was spent preventing possible contamination from dirt, and many hours of each day were spent in
frenzied scrubbing of herself and the furniture.

The patient had drawn what is reproduced in Figure 16 and
had described it as being simultaneously feces, a penis, and the
figure of a woman. In the therapeutic approach it was decided
to confront her directly with this confusion, and she was asked to
discuss her production in the light of the question of what it
could mean when one and the same thing could symbolize or be
these three different things.

The suggestion that she discuss her drawings was prefaced
by an important explanation—that her capacity for this type of
symbolizing indicated her artistic ability—and further, that she
had the type of mental equipment demonstrated by many gifted
artists and imaginative individuals. In this way the depleted ego
of the patient was strongly reinforced by this "authoritative" in-

formation derived from her showing on the test as a whole. Subsequently the patient and therapist referred humorously to her
"creative unconscious," that part of her willing to give clues
around which therapy could proceed.

The patient had three immediate memories on being asked to
react to her own drawing, memories which showed the lack of
adequate boundary lines or demarcations in her experience. She
produced three scenes from her past life which were discussed
and developed: She first thought of herself as a small child who

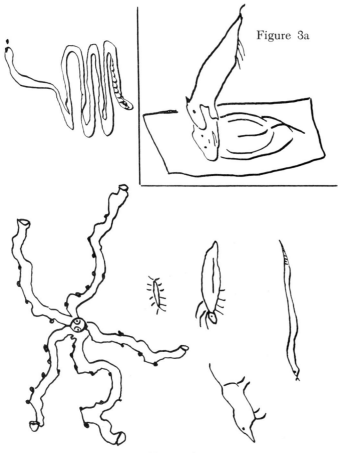

Figure 3a

Figure 3

Drawings of snakes, bugs and octopi, showing neurotic preoccupation with
the Unpleasant Without. Fig. 3a. Introduction of a bizarre feature in a
borderline case "Rat eating a baby's face."

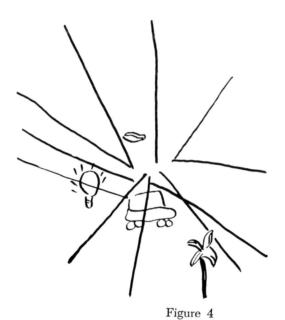

Figure 4

Symbolic portrayal of a mental state representing psychological isolation (the Unpleasant Within).

had been left with a boy baby sitter. During this period she had been subjected to his attempts to get his penis in her mouth. Mostly surprised rather than afraid, as he approached her from above, her remembrance was that she saw feces hanging down and about to drop onto her face. There was, therefore, a penis-feces confusion, a combination of disgust and fear.

Her second memory related to the day on which her present terror of feces in adult life had suddenly started. She had been walking on the street with her husband who had inadvertently stepped on feces. She had taken off his shoe to clean it, when they had returned home, and had from that moment become a prey to the nightmare of terror and contamination in which she now lived. She further remembered that it was on this same day that she had discovered that her husband had been unfaithful, and that as she had seen him about to step on the dirt the idea of squashing or stepping on his penis had entered into her mind. Thus she readily acknowledged and exemplified the lack of boundaries between the feces and penis concept.

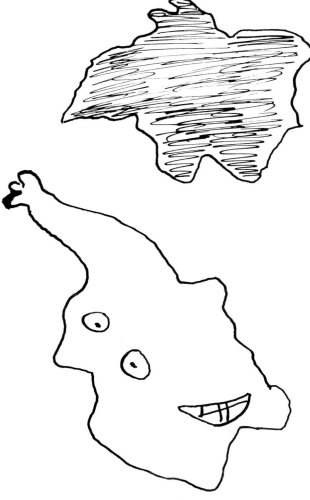

Figure 5

Drawings of "soft, clutching, learing shadow" epitomizing fear to the person.

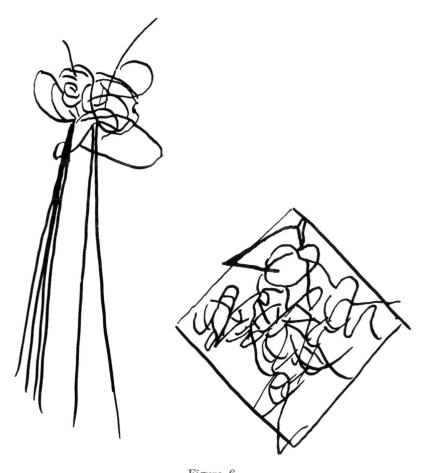

Figure 6

Drawings symbolically portraying tension and confusion.

Discussion of why feces and a penis could nonetheless also be a woman's body evoked considerable anxiety. Before the patient could continue with the associations that came to her mind she needed considerable reassuring, again with reference to the authoritative statement of what the test had shown. As subsequently became quite clear, the patient's extreme anxiety centered on her own unrecognized homosexual trends and her disgust at her own body for her active sexual longings. At this point she needed constant reassurance that "she was not a Lesbian," and that "the tests did not show she was a Lesbian." When reassured she was able to produce the final memory which she felt the drawings had evoked, namely, the confusion between the pleasure which she experienced on certain occasions at the arousal of pleasant feelings from the touch of a woman's body and her own heightened guilt and disturbance at what such feelings might mean. She related a memory of her older sister lying on top of her and moving in such a way as to "produce a warm, comfortable feeling." At the same time she had the child's fear that a grownup would enter

Figure 7

Drawing classified as portraying a symbolic state of mind.

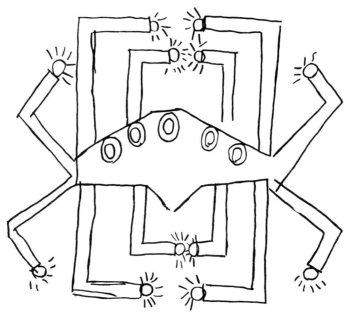

Figure 8

Drawing interpreted by patient as "A mechanized octopus with tentacles of steel and naked light bulbs for claws. The circles in his body seem to be subway straps, and now that I can see it again, the pattern of the tentacles also form a brightly-lit corridor, bare-walled and bleak."

and discover her in this masturbatory play. A second comparable experience in later life related to the guilt associated with the pleasurable feelings following the touch of a woman friend's hand.

These associations were the start of therapeutic sessions in which the patient brought to light much relevant and insightful material. Projective counseling in this case was an adjunct therapy or, one might say, ran a parallel course to the patient's being independently treated by hypnosis by Dr. Lewis Wolberg. At the time of writing this patient has been able to go out of her apartment. There is, in fact, a startling and dramatic improvement.

## SUMMARY AND CONCLUSIONS

A new five-minute projective device called "The Most Unpleasant Concept Test" is described. Based on a qualitative analysis of the results obtained from 500 subjects undergoing psychotherapy, a tentative classification is outlined showing the basic types of concepts portrayed in this collection of drawings. It is concluded that this test would make a valuable addition to a diagnostic personality appraisal battery for the following reasons:

1. This procedure, when imbedded in a series of other projective techniques which are less direct, has the interesting effect of shock or surprise. Frequently, completely forgotten experiences are recovered and recorded, to the subject's own surprise. For example, an early memory of incestuous relations with a parent was an unexpected psychological discovery in the sense that it had been completely repressed for a long period. Drawing two people in bed, the individual suddenly stated, "Oh, that is me and my father!"

2. This test allows a deeper insight to be gained from answers given to some of the other projective techniques. For example, a subject who gave a highly unusual answer to the butterfly on

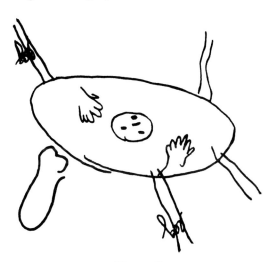

Figure 9

This drawing was described by the subject as follows: "Disintegration of the personality—loss of selfhood. Would mean loss of vision. The head within the circle signifies recession—more than recession—submersion of consciousness, of sensation, of feeling. Limbs, helter skelter and any-which-way signifies destruction of purpose and direction; excentric to the circle to show existence of movement and contact, but indiscriminate and uncoordinated movement, and blind, unfeeling contact."

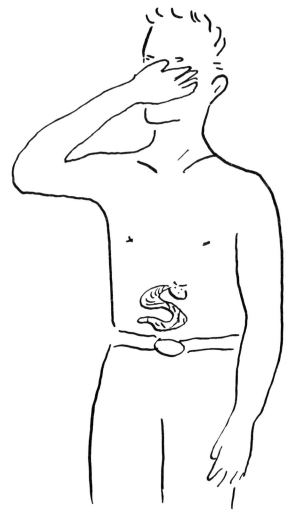

Figure 10
Drawing representing the mono-delusion:  Snake in Stomach.

Card III of the Rorschach, namely, "two doors at the end of a long corridor," made a very similar drawing in the Unpleasant Concept Test, but added two prison cells at the near ends of the corridor in which he and a friend were incarcerated. Associations to this were highly revealing in terms of guilt in connection with homosexual activities.

3. The portrayal of bizarre fantasies seems, in some instances, to provide relief to the individual concerned. It is somehow a sharing of a state of mind which has eluded description. Now both the examiner (in his role of therapist) and the patient can refer objectively to "my state of tension."

4. Progress in therapy is most interestingly revealed in longitudinal sections as the individual passes from one buried un-

Figures 11 and 12

Drawing representing the phantasy "the eyes of God in which are reflected the burning of souls in hellfire."

Drawing representing the paranoid idea of "others laughing at me and rushing my downfall."

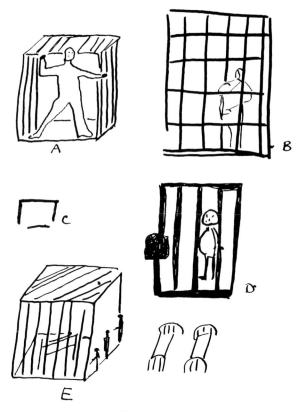

Figure 13

Drawings portraying the state of mind called "psychological imprisonment."
Drawing C, reflecting early schizophrenia, represents "an ice cube in which I
am imprisoned, unable to reach my children." Drawing D was drawn by a
man who had defrauded the government of over one million dollars in taxes.

pleasant experience to another. In connection with this, the test
may frequently foreshadow material which is subsequently
brought to life.

5. One of the advantages of this test is its diagnostic value.
By and large, our point of view in regard to "diagnosis" is that it
is the least important part of the contribution of the projective
techniques. Nonetheless there are certain cases where an underlying schizophrenic process must be confirmed or ruled out before
further treatment can be decided upon. Inclusion of this test in

the battery has, we feel, strongly reinforced our objective evidence in such cases. We refer here to the symbolic portrayal of states of mind as reinforcing the "borderline" diagnosis and, conversely, to the "small animal" drawings as consistent with the neurotic picture.

Figure 14

Drawing representing fears of various forms of aggression. Drawing B by a girl terrified by her own homosexual desires; drawing C by a latent homosexual; drawing D by a patient rated by his therapist as "the most masochistic person I have ever treated," who accepted unbelievable humiliations from his wife and considered the Most Unpleasant Thing to be a Woman attacking a man (note the enormous index finger, possibly a phallic symbol, on the woman).

Figure 15

Drawings portraying unpleasant mutilation concepts related to homosexuality. Drawing A is an overt expression, while B and C reflect the repeated occurrence of castration fears shown by persons lacking an arm or leg.

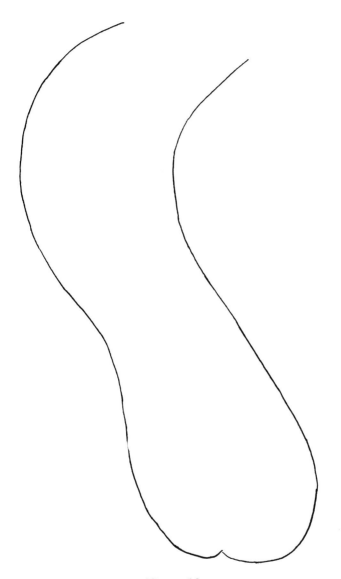

Figure 16

## REFERENCES

1. Frank, Lawrence K.: *Projective Methods.* Springfield, Thomas, 1948.
2. Harrower, M. R.: Projective counseling. *Am. J. Psychotherapy,* January, 1956.
3. Harrower, M. R.: In *Contemporary Psychotherapists Examine Themselves,* Werner Wolff, editor. Springfield, Thomas, 1956.
4. Harrower, M. R., and Kraus, Jane: Psychological studies on patients with multiple sclerosis. *Arch. Neurol. & Psychiat., 66:44-57,* 1951.
5. Machover, Karen: *Personality Projection in the Drawing of the Human Figure.* Molley Harrower, editor. Springfield, Thomas, 1948.
6. Spitz, René: The role of training in psychoanalysis in the development of research in clinical psychology, in *Training in Clinical Psychology.* New York, Macy, 1947.

## CHAPTER 17

## RECENT VARIATIONS OF THE PROJECTIVE DRAWING TECHNIQUES

EMANUEL F. HAMMER, PH.D.

ONE INDEX OF the positive reception of a new clinical tool is the plethora of modifications which spring up around it. The previous chapters have devoted themselves to a presentation of the major projective drawing tools; the present chapter is devoted to a description of recent modifications, the merit of which only time, usage, and further experimentation can prove.

### DRAW-A-FAMILY

The technique of least recent vintage of those treated in this chapter is the Draw-A-Family procedure. This drawing approach consists of giving the subject pencil and paper and merely asking him to draw a family. The technique sprang up so rapidly and gained such quick popularity among clinicians, via word of mouth, that its authorship is undetermined. Various people in different geographic regions have been given credit for innovating the techinque, but priority has not yet been established. Perhaps, like many worthwhile inventions, it sprang up simultaneously in the minds of different people.

This technique is most popular in its use with children, where a determination of the essential relationship to one's parents and siblings is of prime importance. A child who feels that he is the favorite child will draw himself quite differently in a family constellation than will the child who feels neglected, rejected, or hungering for attention.

At times, children will omit their brothers and sisters from the depicted family. Children who do this have invariably been found to suffer acutely from sibling rivalry. They attempt sym-

Figure 1

bolically to eliminate the disturbing competition by not drawing such competitive figures into the family unit.

The size of the various figures is perhaps the most important
variable gained from the draw-a-family procedure. For example,
an exaggerated depiction of a huge mother-figure in these drawings (when the mother is actually not the taller parent) suggests
a dominating, matriarchal figure; if the father is represented as
an insignificant small figure, hardly larger than the children, it
implies that his status is perceived as barely exceeding that of
theirs.

It is not by accident that a six-year-old boy draws himself
and his three-month-old sibling the same size. The subject feels
that the baby is strong competition and endangers his hitherto
exclusive position in the family. When he draws a family, the
child may draw himself very near his mother, or he may put
the rest of the family together in a group and himself apart,

giving clear expression to his feelings of painful rejection and isolation.

Figure 1 was drawn by a twelve-year-old child, a neighbor of the writer's. This illustration of a relatively healthy response to the draw-a-family request, may serve as a base line against which to view the later clinical illustrations. The subject is an only child and represents himself as such in the drawing. The size of his own figure and its apparent age are appropriate, as is the size of both parental figures. A picture of contentment and activity is conveyed, although some detachment—and this parallels the writer's observation of the subject's family—is evident in the representation. Each person is engaged in some isolated activity, rather than interacting with the others.

The mild suggestion of emotional distance between family members might focus itself into sharper perspective if the drawing is compared to Figure 2. Figure 2 conveys a feeling of closer family interaction and solidarity. This is reflected not only in the greater closeness between the positions of the various figures,

Figure 2

Figure 3

but also in the fact that each is not absorbed in his own activity. The only deviant depiction in this essentially positive picture, is the massive immaturity of the subject expressed by his need to label the child in the mother's arms as himself. The subject, at the time of testing, was twenty-six years of age. Thus, regressive needs to be back in his mother's protective arms defines, and limits, his present adjustment. The subject was referred because of his alcoholism. He apparently leaned on alcohol as he had learned to lean upon his mother, in a flight away from assertive maturity. The oral needs implied by his alcoholism are consistent with his strong dependency needs reflected in his Draw-A-Family response.

In sharp contrast to Figures 1 and 2, Figure 3 reflects intense feelings of withdrawal from family interaction. The picture was drawn by a forty-two-year-old male, who had retreated from interpersonal contact into a schizoid shell. This absence of emotional exchange within the family setting is clearly represented in his depiction of the four family members, each in their own corner of the page, not even sharing the same plane. The patient sketched four individual people rather than four people in one integrated setting. The self-absorbed quality reflected in the eyes, which are mere empty sockets without a pupil with which to look outward at others, reinforce the schizoid implications of the patient's retreat as conveyed by his Draw-A-Family response. The acute feelings of insufficiency and inadequacy conveyed by the flimsy arms and legs, and most particularly by the petal-like fingers, may explain part of the subject's need to find some security in the solutions of withdrawal and isolation.

Figure 4

Figure 5

Other elements of interest to the clinician employing the Draw-A-Family procedure are whether or not the subject includes himself in the picture (as an index of his own feelings of belonging), draws one parent with a stern or forbidding facial expression and the other with a kindly one, or puts—as one subject recently did—a tree between his father and himself but has the mother figure standing close by on the subject's side of the tree.

One eleven-year-old boy, with intense feelings of rejection, drew a family of Martians, as if to reflect his firm conviction that only in so distant a place could he expect family closeness and interaction. Along with his expectation that acceptance and family closeness could not be achieved in this world, the subject also, of course, reflected his tendency to seek gratification in fantasy. His escape into fantasy was the only solution left him for his aching hunger for emotional warmth and interpersonal relations.

Thus, the Draw-A-Family procedure has been found to be the projective drawing parallel of the TAT. It is particularly useful where the clinician is interested in the patient's perception of himself in the family and/or his perception of his relationship to parental and sibling figures, and it is generally maximally rewarding for the short time expenditure involved.

## DRAW-A-PERSON-IN-THE-RAIN

The use of the Draw-A-Person-In-The-Rain modification has also been spread by word of mouth, and so far as the writer is aware has not been written up in any publication. This procedure, like the Draw-A-Family request, is a simple one. The subject is merely asked to draw a person in the rain.

Credit for this innovation has been ascribed by some to Arnold Abrams and by others to Abraham Amchin. Again, it may

Figure 6

Figure 7

be a case of a fruitful idea occurring simultaneously to more than one person.

The Draw-A-Person-In-The-Rain device attempts to get a picture of the body image under conditions of unpleasant environmental stress, as represented by the rain; and this drawing frequently provides useful information when compared to the subject's drawing of a person in the Machover technique.

Figures 4 and 5, both drawn by normal subjects (the first by a fourteen-year-old male and the second by an adult male), are presented to afford a base line from which to judge the deviations in the drawing of the clinical population later presented.

By contrast, the Person-in-the-Rain offered in Figure 6 can be seen to depict a subject somewhat more prone than the two previous subjects to employ withdrawal as a characteristic reaction to environmental stress. Under the stimuli of the stressful situation, the subject withdraws relatively more within his umbrella, pulling it down around him as a protective shield. From this, then, we may deduce that this subject is more likely to

Figure 8

Figure 9

withdraw from adverse conditions than are the two subjects who drew Figures 4 and 5. This interpretive deduction was supported by his Rorschach protocol which was replete with content such as "turtles," "caves," and the classical "ostrich" (the traditional symbol of a creature who handles frightening situations by withdrawal rather than fight or active flight).

The drawing of a person in the rain shown in Figure 7 illustrates a reaction suggesting feelings of being under the heaviest of environmental stress conditions. The subject literally presents a downpour as a reflection of his own felt situation in an unhappy and pressurizing environment. The drawn person is relatively less well defended against the environmental pressures than were the preceding persons drawn. He has neither rainhat nor umbrella to ward off the unpleasant aspects of the environment; and he stands with hair pasted down around his face and with the rain beating upon his bare head.

This drawing was obtained from a subject who entered therapy shortly after a series of traumas had occurred. Within a period of two years, this thirty-two year-old male's mother died, his business failed and his wife left him. The environment is painted by this subject, as dousing him heavily in unwelcomed, unpleasant atmospheric conditions. His only recourse, as he sees it, is to stand there in unprotected fashion and take it.

Figure 8 was drawn by a latent schizophrenic girl of twenty-three. Under conditions symbolizing environmental stress, she reacts with a loss of identity and a blurring of the boundary between herself and the outer world. A hint of her feelings of depersonalization is caught and reflected by the Draw-A-Person-In-The-Rain technique, and emphasized by her spontaneous comment that the figure is neither male nor female, but "sexless."

Figure 10

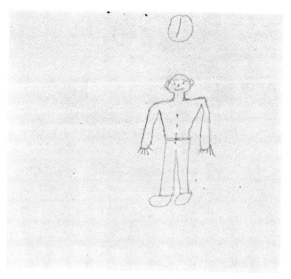

Figure 11

As examples of a reaction at the other end of the stress continuum, it is of interest to note Figures 9 and 10, drawn by subjects in the terminal stages of therapy. Figure 9 was drawn by an adolescent boy who had been in psychotherapeutic collaboration with the writer for approximately a year and a half, and Figure 10 by a twenty-five-year-old male who was in the terminal stage of a two-year therapy span. Both reflect buoyant and cheerful feelings along with the view that the gloomy and unhappy period of their adjustment is coming to a close. In Figure 9 the drawn person already folds the umbrella, for just a few drops of rain are felt to remain in his life situation. Figure 10 depicts a rainbow in the background as if the amount of environmental stress that remains is analogous only to, in the patient's words, "a summer shower." And this, he feels, can be enjoyed rather than felt as something to flee from or against which to protect oneself.

Another subject drew both Figures 11 and 12, the former in response to the request, "Please draw a person," and the latter in response to the request, "Please draw a person in the rain." A comparison of the two figures shows that a paranoid-toned disposition is brought to view only in the latter drawing, in response to a stimuli suggesting conditions of environmental stress. The implications of the over-alert hypervigilant ears which stand up in Figure 12 would not have been deduced from the Draw-A-Person procedure alone. Thus, we get a representative picture of the subject's response to "non-stress" and to "stress" conditions. It is the integration of the two reactive tendencies that describe the *latency* of the patient's paranoid elements, in that the pathology does not become evident in the "non-stress" condition but only in the "stress" condition.

Figures 13 and 14 were drawn by a man incarcerated for armed robbery. Under the stimuli representing stress, the inadequacy feelings hidden by the blustering front in the drawing of a Person (Figure 13) give way and come directly to the fore (Figure 14). In the latter, the legs become weak and puny, the arms inadequate, the facial countenance laughable—all in all, the opposite of the former compensatory large and overly capable figure (note particularly the long arms) in Figure 13. Thus, we may predict, that the subject, in everyday situations, will be

Figure 12

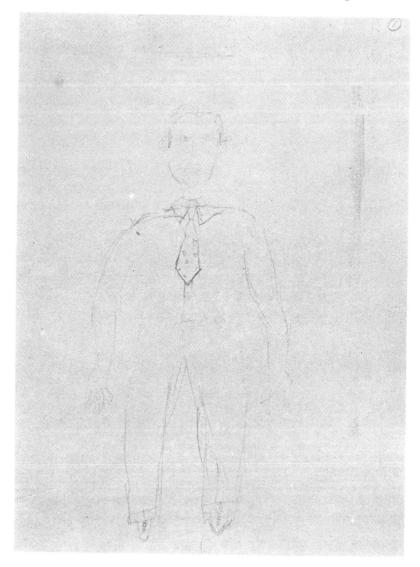

Figure 13

likely to employ compensatory maneuvers to present himself as more adequate than he feels. Under conditions of stress, however, his compensatory front may be expected to crumble revealing the full-blown inadequacy feelings beneath.

Figures 15 and 16 represent the Draw-A-Person-In-The-Rain reactions of other subjects whose defenses also crumble under pressure. In Figure 15, the umbrella withers or disintegrates away, leaving the drawn figure unprotected. In Figure 16, the subject is so overcome by the stimuli representing stressful con-

Figure 14

Figure 15

ditions, that he totally "forgets" the umbrella and quite directly indicates his feelings of being vulnerable and without adequate defenses against adverse environmental conditions. Both subjects are borderline schizophrenics.

Figure 17 was drawn by an obese male who entered therapy

with this obesity as his presenting symptom. His Draw-a-Person male figure was presented with the rest of the page blank. When, however, he drew his Person-in-the-Rain, he added the background of a candy store as a reflection of his oral needs which came rapidly to the fore under conditions of environmental stress.

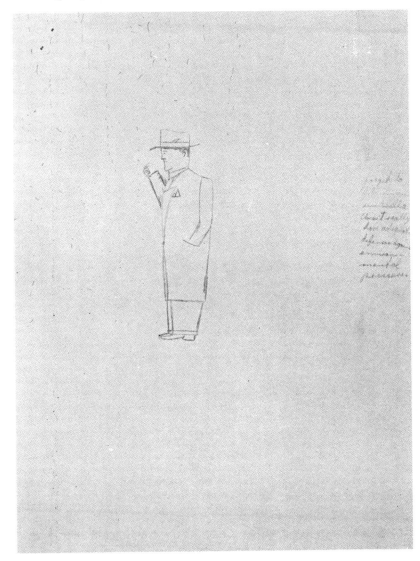

Figure 16

Figure 17

Other reactions to the Draw-a-Person-in-the-Rain request include: the grandiose response of the person in Figure 18, oblivious of the rain; the indications of low frustration-tolerance of Figure 19 drawn as cursing in response to adverse conditions; the contamination of fusing the umbrella with the cloud on the part of the hospitalized schizophrenic who drew Figure 20; the feelings of being inadequately defended against environmental stress in the subject who sketched Figure 21 with the umbrella being knocked out of a protective position over the head of the drawn person; the reflection of the subject's characteristic reaction of denial to stress conditions evident in Figure 22, where

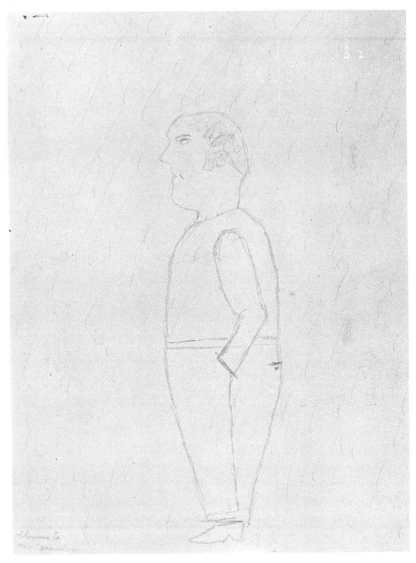

Figure 18

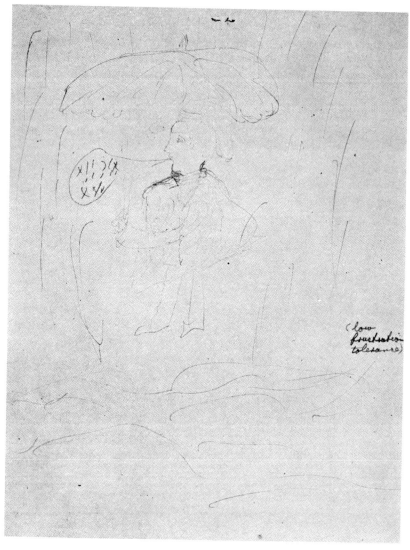

Figure 19

the adult male subject drew a nine-year-old boy walking in the rain with one foot off the curb in the puddles (on the Rorschach the patient also gave evidence of his flight into immaturity and denial, the former in his high preponderance of *FM* over *M* responses and the latter in his tendency toward color projection on achromatic cards); and phallic exhibitionism suggested by Figure 23 in which the hand holding the umbrella is distinctly located directly at the genital region (the subject who offered this drawing was an exhibitionist incarcerated at Sing Sing, who in his drawing reflects his characteristic response to stress conditions

Figure 20

Figure 21

by attempting to prove himself more phallicly adequate than he feels).

The Draw-a-Person-in-the-Rain technique, then is a drawing modification which attempts to get a picture of the body image under conditions symbolizing environmental stress, and frequently provides useful information when compared to the subject's drawing of a person under standard conditions.

## THE ROSENBERG DRAW-A-PERSON TECHNIQUE (10)

In this experimental modification of the "Draw-a-Person" Test, according to Levy (8), the subject is given complete freedom to change his completed drawings in any way that he wishes. By using a carbon copy, one may retain the unchanged or original drawings for comparison with the changed copy.

The subject is given a stapled set of two sheets (with carbon paper between them) on which to do his drawing. Standard directions for the "Draw-a-Person Test" are given, and a modified inquiry is conducted following both male and female drawings in accordance with the Machover technique.

The examiner then tears off the top sheet of each set of drawings and retains the carbon copy for comparison with the changed

Figure 22

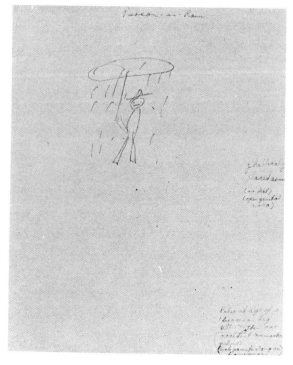

Figure 23

copy. He gives the top sheet back to the subject, stating: "Now you may have complete freedom to change, mar, or mess up, erase, cross out, or do anything you wish with the drawing you have made. Feel as free as you like to change the drawing in any way you wish. Now go to work on your drawing and make it as different as you would like." Changes are requested for the drawings of both the male and the female in the same way. Finally a post-drawing-inquiry is conducted asking about the changes made.

"*Value of This Modification.* In view of the fact that only preliminary work has been done with this technique, I can suggest possible clinical values only.

"1. *Index of hostility:* The aggressive, hostile individual may project his feelings against the human figures he has drawn. The degree and type of change may represent hostility against the self or parent figures. This may be similar to the play-therapy techniques in which children may mutilate dolls representing mother or father figures.

"2. *Rigidity-plasticity factors:* The loose, labile individual will

Figure 24

Figure 25

be willing to change his original drawing, while the rigid person will be unable or unwilling to make any changes.

"3. *Dynamic elements* (complexes, etc.): Sexual disturbances, serious concern over different parts of the body, reflections of core conflicts may come through.

"4. *Diagnosis of serious maladjustment:* The nature and degree of the changes made may provide a basis of differential diagnosis between moderate and severe emotional disturbances.

"*Illustrations of the Method.* D, aged 29, was hospitalized because of complaints of depersonalization and loss of affect. His

Figure 26

Figure 27

woman drawing was that of a voluptuous nude figure, which he promptly changed into a 'devil' when asked to make any changes he wished to. He added a devil's horns, cleft feet, tail, hair on the body, and sharply pointed teeth, and when asked in the inquiry about her, called her a 'nymph.' Further inquiry revealed that he meant 'devil.' His male figure, a dressed, well-integrated drawing, was converted into a cowboy, with high heels, and boxing gloves on his hands. Possible interpretations: great hostility against women; association of sex with moral sin; concern over masturbation" (8).

Figure 28

Figure 29
### THE EIGHT-CARD REDRAWING TEST [1]

The Eight-Figure Redrawing technique of Caligor (2) requires the subject to make a series of eight drawings of the human

---

[1] For a presentation of Caligor's quantitative approach to structural aspects,
the reader may be interested in Caligor's recent book: *A New Approach to Figure
Drawing* (Springfield, Thomas, 1957).

figure, basing each drawing upon the previous one which can be seen through a sheet of onionskin paper. Thus, the subject sees his first drawing through the paper on which he draws his second figure. The second figure then shows through the next sheet laid over it for the third drawing, and so on. Instructions are to "change it in any way you like."

Figure 30

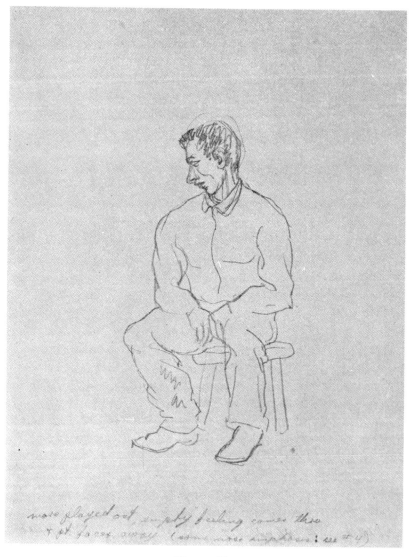

Figure 31

The results of Caligor's study raises pertinent questions concerning the assumption that the sex of a single figure stresses the subject's sexual identification. Caligor seems to show that the true level of sexual identification lies deeply buried under the beginning drawings and has various emphasis on different personality levels. The subject's eight redrawings thus constitute an attempt to plumb deeper personality layers.

There is nothing sacrosanct about the use of eight redrawings, however, and at times the present writer has employed this technique utilizing a lesser number.

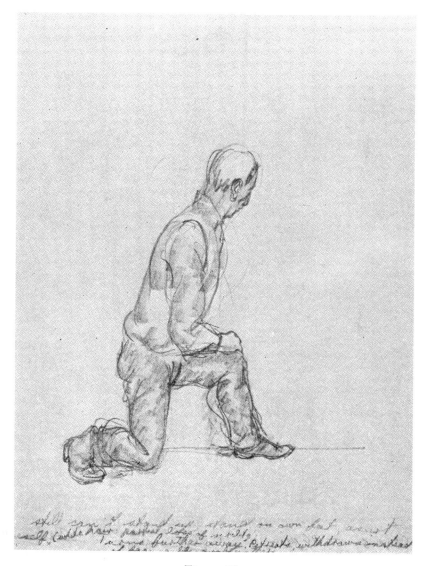

Figure 32

Figure 33

The case presented, at this point, had been asked to enter the redrawing procedure to the point of rendering only six, rather than eight, modifications. Nevertheless, the drawings support Caligor's hypothesis most dramatically.

The subject, a thirty-year-old male, was examined in connection with his commission of a robbery offense.

Because of the large number of drawings entailed in the carrying out of this redrawing technique, only brief mention of the central shift in theme will be made. For his first figure drawing, the subject offers a stereotyped concept of the All-American boy, clean-cut, athletic, and wearing a badge of virility, the Life Guard uniform (Figure 24). For his next drawing, he then extends the

Figure 34

Figure 35

theme (Figure 25) in a still more virile direction: a cowboy with guns ready for quick use. Here, then, he retreats to a more immature level of compensation, and we note that glasses appear on the drawing as an initial clue to the feelings of inadequacy, and less athletically-perfect capability, apparent somewhat beneath the surface of personality tapped by the first drawing. By the next drawing (Figure 26), the subject is still proving his masculinity by offering a concept of a G-Man but the glasses still remain as an index of feelings of being a less-than-perfect physical specimen. The drawn male is in need of a shave as a reflection of the subject's continuing lowering of his reflected self-

Figure 36

Figure 37

esteem. In the next picture (Figure 27), the former hint of lowered self-esteem becomes actuality, for now the male is a hobo in tattered clothing, extending his hand for a hand-out. He badly needs a shave, and he is becoming bald (an index of feelings of still greater lack of virility). The subject then follows this drawing with one (Figure 28) in which the male is still more bald, has a

rather ridiculous nose and chin, and wears "crossed" eyes implying further that this is someone to be laughed at and ridiculed,
rather than respected. By this last drawing (Figure 29), he descends to the deepest layer of his self-concept, thus far, and
presents a picture of still further self-degradation and disdain.
The drawn male is even more bald than before, has a still more
ridiculous countenance, and is said to be sixty years of age—all
this in sharp contrast to the beginning picture of the youthful,
energetic, clean-cut Life Guard.

As we follow the subject from the surface layer down through
the depths to his core of self-disdain, we get a reinforced picture
of his negative self-concept which lies beneath his compensatory
efforts to prove himself possessed of more worth than he actually
inwardly feels.

The drawings of the next subject illustrate the previously expressed view that subjects with artistic capabilities frequently can
reveal more about themselves in their projective drawings than
subjects without such capabilities.

This subject, a thirty-six-year-old male, entered therapy because of alcholic addiction and an inability to succeed profession-
ally. He had had some art training, was judged capable and
promising by his teachers, but suffered too much inhibition to
allow for accomplishment in this field. He felt resentful toward
himself for working below his intellectual and artistic level as a
construction worker doing predominantly physical and unskilled
labor.

Because of his artistic ability, eight redrawing sheets, rather
than six, were prepared for his use. He began by drawing a
person seated (Figure 30), immediately reflecting his inhibited
energy and lack of drive. The unkempt attitude and the attire
(which appears to be an underwear shirt) mirror his low self-
esteem and feelings of lack of acceptable status. The drawing
caught the strained, tense, worn expression which the subject
himself customarily wore. The excessive shading served as the
graphic correlate of the subject's diffuse anxiety.

To move onto more speculative levels, this shading may be
indicative of specific bodily anxiety, as suggested by the fact
that the hands appear attracted to the genital region. Most people when sitting and resting on their forearms would place the
forearms closer to the knee. The drawn person's hands, however,

appear pulled back to the genital region suggesting the *possibility* of either ambivalent feelings about compulsive masturbation or a position of genital defense, or both. The question is raised as to whether the subject anticipates damage being done to his vital bodily parts and whether this might exert some of the inhibiting effect upon his efforts to prove himself a man occupationally.

The sensual mouth emphasis expresses the oral yearnings of alcoholically-addicted patients.

By the next picture (Figure 31), we find the person more played-out and empty. The shading which was too profuse in the previous drawing, is now totally absent, and what is perhaps more conclusive, the subject begins to turn away from a full face view toward the viewer (and interpretively, we might speculate, toward the world). The figure still sits, and also still has the hands attracted to, or protecting, the genital area.

By the next drawing (Figure 32), the projection of the subject's feelings suggest that he has been able to find a core of energy and drive within him, and the drawn figure attempts, or at least gets into a preparatory position, to stand. It is of interest that the subject can not make the transition from a sitting to a standing position in one drawing, but must have an intermediate phase, apparently to muster what small energy he does have at his disposal. The efforts at asserting himself and finding independence (represented by the symbolization of "standing on one's own feet"), are at the expense of having to turn still further away from the viewer, connoting his ready tendency to retreat or withdraw instead of face reality problems. It is only concomitant with withdrawal that he can attempt assertive efforts. This interpretation was supported by the psychotherapeutic collaborative work with the patient in which it was found that he spent considerable time fantasizing about assertive and status-gaining efforts, but could not yet attempt this in reality.

As we continue to sit in on the drama of the patient's efforts to free himself from inhibiting forces and to achieve some degree of independent and assertive status, we find that in the next drawing (Figure 33) the person is able to stand on his own feet, but only at the expense of a total turning of his back upon the world. The subject describes the drawn person as "peeing against the wall," suggesting—against the backdrop of his problems in assertion—that he can achieve independent status only on an infantile level of defiance (in accord with Freud's theory of the urethral-erotic character structure) and at the price of the total withdrawal symbolized by the full back presentation.

Following his feeble attempts at primitive assertion and defiance, the drawn person (Figure 34) now collapses into a beaten, defeated position. We may then deduce that whatever small efforts the patient can mobilize in assertive directions, can be short lived only. Along with the patient's defeat of his efforts toward independent status, we find that he retreats into alcoholism and its induced state of anesthesia, for the drawn figure is now described as "drunk, dirty and disorderly." The self-disdain that accompanies his defeat is eloquently apparent in the projected labels of "dirty" and "disorderly." White hair again appears in the drawing as a further indication of feelings of absence of virility and masculine capabilities.

In passing, it may be of interest to note that the little finger of the left hand is drawn in a bent position, consistent with the way the subject himself always holds this finger. This is an interesting detail which tends to support the general thesis of self-portraiture in projective drawings.

Following the defeat reflected in the drawn person, energy is again mobilized. The subject is certainly one who will not indefinitely accept a vanquished status but will continue, in sporadic bursts, to engage in the fray. In Figure 35, he has managed to convey some self-esteem in his self-concept. He presents a more acceptably dressed male who apparently holds down a job and is not relegated to the status of the previous "bum in the street." The hair-line is still receded, reflecting the subject's feelings of reduced masculinity. The subject manages to find some ego strength within him for the drawn person now stands, after the previous collapse, although he does need something to lean upon, to support him. One hand is still back at the anal area, just as it was in Figure 33. In both these drawings, particularly by a subject who has had some art training, the hand would more naturally fall away from the body in a direct vertical line, rather than be drawn back to the anal area. We wonder then if the patient doesn't fear anal attack and doesn't have some unresolved homoerotic conflicts which further handicap his efforts to achieve status as a male and also feed his need to retreat into alcoholism. By the next picture (Figure 36), the patient apparently has stayed away from his negative self-concept as long as he could. The respectable job, as suggested by the previous picture, is given up for a position of leaning, this time not only on a physical object but also on alcohol. (The glass in the drawn person's hand is labeled "beer.") Thus, the drawings tend to parallel the subject's own capacities in real life and we see that he cannot maintain efforts toward occupational achievement for long. He then seeks not only escape into alcohol but also into withdrawal, for the drawn figure again faces away, and begins to turn his back on the world once more.

In the last picture (Figure 37), the subject again attempts to fight off his symptomatology and to attain some occupational rung. He is able to achieve, however, only a compromise on his ambitions, for his inhibiting forces demand a voice in the end product. Thus, while the drawn person is now a waiter, some one who does earn his own living rather than loll around in the streets, "drunk, dirty and disorderly," the figure is foreshortened, as a reflection of a male of less than full stature.

The subject ends his communication of his body image to us on a submissive, spirit-broken, dejected, round-shouldered, weak, ineffectual, bald note. The hang-dog attitude and the servile aspects of the patient's self-concept are sketched clearly into the drawing as well as described by the subject's comment that the drawn figure is "waiting for someone to give him an order." Thus, the subject seeks a compromise for his conflicts in a submissive, appeasing, minimally-active role in life. As speculations, we still have the question of whether he employs this appeasing way of proving himself and his impulses non-threatening and conciliatory as a defense against his expectations of bodily mutilation, hinted at by the hands frozen in a pelvic defense position on Figures 30 and 31, and in defense of the anal area in Figures 33 and 35. The skirt effect in this last drawing (Figure 37) is a bit too long, as if displaying the feminine aspects of his conciliatory role. The shoulders are now more like a female's than a male's.

The subject's final solution, then, is a compromise. He tells us in the Eight-Card-Redrawing Test, administered at the beginning of therapy, that he hopes for some capacity for standing on his own feet and achieving some occupational success, but that it will have to be at the price of maintaining a feminine-toned, non-assertive role. He shows us that efforts at assertion can only be short lived and expressed on a primitive and defiant level. Dependency needs are prominently expressed by his having his drawn person lean on physical objects as well as on alcohol. A ready tendency to employ withdrawal is shown and will have to be reckoned with in the ensuing psychotherapeutic work.

As the final example of the utility of the Eight-Card-Redrawing Test, just the first and last drawings of a patient psychologically diagnosed as a pre-psychotic will be presented.

Figure 38

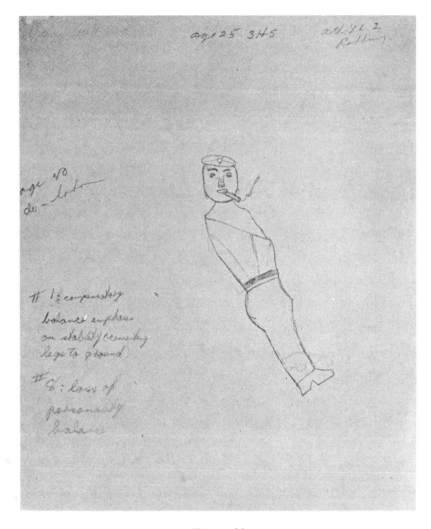

Figure 39

Figure 38 was his first drawing. Compensatory efforts to cement, or somehow anchor, his footing are revealed. There is already a strong hint that the body is top heavy and may be susceptible to a loss of emotional equilibrium, but the figure still stands erect. The twisted jacket, whose bottom line loops up on one side and down on the other, suggests that the patient feels that he is out of kilter, prone to feelings of imbalance. In the last drawing (Figure 39), however, the drawn person fully topples and, in doing so, eloquently describes the subject's inner feelings of impending loss of personality balance.

Thus, the first drawing frequently hints at that which the later drawings bring out in full relief.

The Eight-Card-Redrawing Test, then, is a technique which capitalizes on the value of drawing repetition for probing into the personality structure. The efficacy of the chromatic H-T-P, following the administration of the achromatic H-T-P, rests in part upon the same assumption. However, it should be noted that repetition does not always necessarily mean probing deeper. Often it will produce only a sideways penetration, tapping patterns that are no deeper than the previous ones but only expanding in a more or less horizontal direction. One such subject recently began his Eight-Card-Redrawing Test by drawing a picture of George Washington, his next drawing was that of Theodore Roosevelt, his next that of a pirate, then followed a bullfighter, an Indian, Sir Walter Raleigh, Abraham Lincoln, and finally Caesar. The subject was a person who, when drunk, claimed that he came from a titled family, was the son of a baron, and had "blue-blood." His eight-card themes tapped his persistent need for grandiose identification, but can not be said to have tapped different layers of depth of his personality levels.

All in all, however, if the Eight-Card-Redrawing Test is reserved for subjects who appear to enjoy drawing, a rich yield of data may be expected to be the rule rather than the thin exception. In my own experience, I have not found it to be too often worth the time and effort with subjects who do not like to draw. A task which asks them to draw eight figures, in addition to whatever other projective drawing techniques have been administered, serves only to irritate the subject and place an undue strain upon rapport. When used with subjects who take to drawing, however, it may at times prove to be one of the most rewarding diagnostic techniques of the entire projective drawing battery.

## THE HAMMER DRAW-A-MEMBER-OF-A-MINORITY-GROUP TECHNIQUE

Based on the theory that prejudice has its roots in the phenomenon of projection of the negative traits in one's self onto minority group members, Hammer has devised a projective drawing instrument. If people tend to take those traits or attributes which they cannot accept in themselves, and, as a defense, project them onto members of a minority group, then asking a subject to "draw a member of a minority group" may be expected to encourage the projection of the more negative and unconscious side of himself.

Preliminary exploration with this technique suggests that the baser side of one's self-concept is more readily brought to the fore in the drawing of a minority group member and offers a worthwhile comparison with the drawing of a person under standard conditions. The two sides of the self-concept coin are thus more easily seen side-by-side. The technique is of too recent origin to present more fully at this time; the writer is awaiting greater accumulation of data than he possesses at present.[2] Thus far, the approach appears quite promising.

## THE H-T-P IN VERBAL PHANTASY

Diamond (3) has devised what might be labeled a cross between the H-T-P and the TAT in his thematic H-T-P procedure. This appears to be a promising technique for eventually contributing validating data on the graphic H-T-P.

In this procedure of Diamond's, the subject is instructed to write a story in which there are three characters, a tree, a house, and a person. All of these characters, the subject is told, should have real personalities, the power of speech, and be able to communicate their thoughts to one another. The subject is further asked to let his story really tell what kind of a tree, house, and person the characters are, and how they feel about each other.

As an example of normative data yielded with this approach, adolescents tend to give themes expressing worry on the part

---

[2] The cumulative experience of many clinicians, working in varied institutions, is necessary to determine the preliminary worth of a projective approach. It can not be determined in a tight little study as can pencil and paper tests of the more objective variety. Brief mention is made of the Hammer Draw-a-Member-of-a-Minority-Group device as a stimulus to clinicians to use and assemble data with, and on, this technique. It is hoped that they will feel free to communicate with the author when they have accumulated a body of data.

of the tree about its loss of leaves, or its uncertainty about bearing blossoms or fruit, which is met by reassurance from the house. Here the adolescents seem to express their concern about physical maturation, and their need for reassurance on this score.

At all age levels, it was found that the tree tended to be used as a masculine symbol and the house as a feminine symbol. "If we are prepared to accept the fact that the tree will often be used as a phallic symbol, then we must expect that the vicissitudes of the tree will often express castration anxiety. It is a fact that the tree is far more often exposed to danger than either the house or the person." (3)

There was a small group of stories, by boys, in which danger to the Tree was averted through violent retaliation against the threatening Man. Diamond (3) argues: "These may be regarded as expressions of unresolved Oedipal hostilities directed against the father." This theme of violent retaliation did not occur in the stories by other groups, either females or older males, except for one story by a girl in which a young apple tree had been told that it would be turned into firewood if it did not produce fruit within the week. The timely and miraculous appearance of this tree's golden fruit was immediately followed by a bolt of lightning which destroyed the evil female Person and the House.

It was also found that reference to a forest was more frequent in stories by girls than in stories by other groups. This tends to suggest that girls are more likely to view the environment as essentially masculine than they are to identify with an individual male.

Diamond concludes from his study that the Tree and the House have multiple potentiality as symbols. They can be father and mother; masculine and feminine aspects of the self; and, in some stories, Id and Superego (the Tree offers itself readily as a symbol for a "Natural Force," and the House as a symbol for socially established rules of conduct). A striking instance of this latter idea occurred in a female subject's story of a man who imagined he had a house and a tree living inside him. The tree objected that the house impeded its growth; and the house insisted that it was needed to hold the man straight. There are a number of other stories in which the Tree and the House represent conflicting ethical standards, with the Tree standing for free development of the individual, and the House for conformity to social expectations.

Thus, examination of recurring plots gives support to the view that the House and the Tree have certain typical, though not invariable, symbolic roles. This brief device of Diamond's appears to have a high potential for use as a validating approach to the H-T-P, and it is hoped that its quick and easy administration will encourage clinicians to employ it in such research.

## REFERENCES

1. Abt, L. E., and Levy, S.: A psychological study of World War II amputees. New York University, 1947.
2. Caligor, L.: The determination of the individual's unconscious concept of his masculinity-femininity identification. *J. Proj. Tech.*, 15:494-509, 1951.
3. Diamond, S.: The house and tree in verbal phantasy. *J. Proj. Tech.*, 18: 316-325, 1954.
4. Freud, S.: Totem and taboo, in *The Basic Writings of Sigmund Freud.* New York, Random House, 1938.
5. Goldfarb, W.: The animal symbol in the Rorschach Test and an Animal Association Test. *Rorschach Research Exchange*, 9:1, 1945.
6. Gondor, E.: *Art and Play Therapy.* New York, Doubleday, 1954.
7. Guttman, S. A.: Bisexuality in symbolism. *J. Am. Psychoanalyt. A.*, p. 280, April, 1955.
8. Levy, S.: Figure drawing as a projective test, in Abt, L. E. and Bellak, L.: *Projective Psychology.* New York, Knopf, 1950.
9. Opler, M. D.: Japanese folk beliefs concerning the snake. *Southwestern J. Anthropol.*, 1:251, 1945.
10. Rosenberg, L.: Modifications of Draw-A-Person Test. Unpublished Thesis, New York University, 1948.
11. Roheim, G.: *Psychoanalysis and Anthropology.* New York, Internat. Univ. Press, 1950.

# PART IV

# PROJECTIVE DRAWINGS INTEGRATED IN ONE CASE STUDY

## CHAPTER 18

# THE PROJECTIVE DRAWING BATTERY: A CASE ILLUSTRATION

EMANUEL F. HAMMER, PH.D.

BY THIS POINT in the book, a number of projective drawing techniques have been described at considerable length. The reader may well wonder where the busy clinician is to get the time needed for the administration of *all* these drawing techniques. My own solution to the problem of the tight schedule has been to employ a combination of Buck's and Machover's devices—what might be called the H-T-P-P in that it includes a drawn Person of each sex in addition to the House and the Tree—as a two-phase (achromatic and chromatic) core of the projective drawing approach. Then routinely I add supplementary projective drawing techniques much as a clinician uses certain TAT cards [1] habitually with almost all subjects, and rounds out his TAT administration by then adding additional cards—TAT stimuli which most directly pertain to those areas the clinician has a hunch are most worth investigating in this particular patient as suggested by his presenting symptoms, the behavioral picture, the case history, deduced psychodynamic probabilities, the questions to which the psychologist has been requested to address himself (suicide, superego severity, homoerotic orientation, paranoid trends, ego strength, positive resources, etc.), and the psychologist's bias.

The achromatic and chromatic H-T-P-P takes, I have found, an average of forty-five minutes to administer and when the pressure of clinical time is tight, I give the subject the drawings to do following his Rorschach. This sacrifices (a) the relatively less threatening bridge to the projective battery which drawings as the initially-administered technique provide, and (b) the data afforded by an observation of the subject's sequence in drawing

---

[1] Usually 1, 2, 3BM, and 13MF, from what I have observed.

the various items within House, Tree or Person. The advantage, however, is that the drawings may be administered without an additional time expenditure, on the part of the clinician, while he scores the Rorschach responses, tabulates their determinants, computes their percentages, and works out their various ratios. If the subject draws rapidly or if he has provided an extensive Rorschach record, data from the entire range of the projective drawing instruments may, at times, be obtained before any additional time investment is called for from the clinician.

The following drawings, obtained in part in such an instance, are presented to tie together the utilization of the entire projective drawing family in a case illustration.

### IDENTIFYING DATA

The patient is a 51-year-old, Jewish, white male. He was born in Poland, and came to this country when he was about twenty years of age. He is married and is the father of six children. He has had the equivalent of a high school education, and works regularly as a skilled electrician.

### PRESENTING SYMPTOM

The patient had been arrested and sent to Sing-Sing, with an indeterminate sentence because of a sexual approach to an eight-year-old girl. His pedophiliac act (consisting of manipulation of the child's genitals, and exposing his own) occurred one year before he was examined by our research team set up to investigate "the cause and treatability of sex offenders."

At the time I first saw the patient, he was suffering from a depressive reaction and was overwhelmed with guilt. He carried a Bible around with him constantly in the prison. After he got to know the writer, he confided with a flood of feeling, "I would cut off my hands first before I would stoop so low again."

His offense had been precipitated when his wife refused him intercourse for four weeks because of a rash on her thighs.

His only other sex offense, or for that matter any infraction of the law, had occurred fully twenty years previously (before his marriage) and had consisted of an act of exhibitionism. The patient did not recall any of the details of that offense, other than that he had been drunk at the time.

## H-T-P-P

### Achromatic

The patient entered the drawing situation with alacrity, showing the attention-hunger of a sensitive man who has been starved by an emotionally-barren prison environment. He was generally eager to please, grasped instructions easily, and executed the drawings relatively rapidly.

He appeared to have little trouble with the drawing of the House until he got to the chimney. He approached this detail by commenting spontaneously, "I'll put in a real, large chimney." He then drew, erased and redrew the chimney with visibly mounting concern and display of affect. The chimney appeared to represent an emotionally "hot" area for the subject to handle. The essential adequacy, however, of his finished rendition of the chimney bespeaks at least superficial feelings of capability which overlie deeper fears of finding himself insufficient with those protrusions which extend from his own body. That he has grave doubt concerning his phallic prowess seems certain. Yet he is ultimately able to produce a satisfactory chimney, which indicates that his doubts are not overwhelming.

The enlarged quality of the chimney suggests that the patient handles his underlying feeling of phallic inadequacy by the mechanism of compensation (note his later drawings of a soldier and then an officer in the Eight-Card-Redrawing Test)—and for

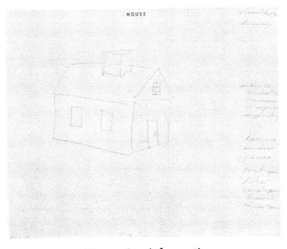

Figure 1: Achromatic

Figure 2:   Achromatic

the most part, this mechanism may be expected to operate relatively successfully. This interpretation receives support from the
extensive period of twenty years duration between the appearance
of his two symptoms, the exhibitionism and the pedophilism.

The House as a whole is adequate and substantial, a reflection
of the intrinsic ego-strength of the subject. His Tree, too, is essentially sturdy and well-rooted, a further indication of the basically
intact integration of the patient's personality.

The conspicuously barred window in the fantasy area of the
House, the roof, suggests that the patient is fearful lest his fantasy
break away from control. This is understandable against the background of the history of his two frank socially-unacceptable sexual
acts. Efforts to constrict and overly-control his fantasy life were
also suggested by his Rorschach patterning.

The windows on the main floor of the House are said to "have
no window panes" and to be "just open holes." Feelings of increased vulnerability to the emotional atmosphere in the environment around him exist hand-in-hand with feelings of being

inadequately defended or protected against this outside atmosphere. The scarring he places on the face of his drawn male (the subject himself has no scars) further shows how acutely he suffers from the social ostracism incurred by his offense.

The reaching of the Tree off the top of the page for what appears to be a considerable distance reflects the patient's tendency to over-extend himself into fantasy in his gratification-seeking. It is this overemphasis upon the fantasy life which then assumes the dangerous proportions suggested by the need for the barred windows in the fantasy area, the roof.

As we examine the growth of the Tree from the bottom to the top, we note that about midway up that part of the Tree shown on the page, there is a sharp constriction in growth and the Tree's trunk suddenly narrows to half its previous width. Whereas a gradual tapering of growth is the expected presentation, the patient's depiction conveys a feeling of an abrupt rationing, along the course of his development, of a previously more bountiful and satisfying emotional fare. This sudden felt frustration of the patient's

Figure 3: Achromatic

Figure 4:  Achromatic

emotional needs (tenderness, affection, etc.), psychodynamic
theory and clinical experience tell us, may be expected to result
in a *fixation* along the path of personality growth. This expectation is confirmed when the patient projects the age range of *"five
to eight"* onto his drawn Tree. If the patient is seen as then clinging to this developmental age range because it was following this
period in his life that he began to starve for the emotional nourishment from his environment that he needed, we can then understand that in periods of stress he would regress to this stage. When
regressed, he then feels emotionally more comfortable with those
of his own developmental level. When sexual needs clamor for
release during such periods of regression, he then discharges them
with a sex object on his own developmental level (his pedophile
object was eight years of age, within the range of his own projected age: "five to eight") and in the immature vein of manual
manipulation, viewing and showing, which were the ingredients
of the sexual offense with which he was charged.

Not only the excessive and sudden tapering in Tree width, but also the sparse growth of foliage testifies to the patient's feelings of inadequate emotional nourishment after the initial childhood period. Further evidence is offered by his post-drawing comment, "The branches are dead." It is only the core—the childish component (represented by the trunk below the place of sudden constriction)—which is alive and well-nourished. His contemporary thirst for warmth from his environment also comes through in the Post-drawing Inquiry period, when he indicates that the Tree "needs sunshine."

Thus, as we view the Tree developmentally from bottom to top, one would suspect (and rightly so, according to subsequent clinical interviewing) that the patient had been emotionally blocked from utilizing the helpful experiences of interpersonal exchange with others once he had passed his childhood period. Hence, he has had to derive much of his satisfaction from fantasy only (the over-extension of the Tree, in fantasy, beyond the page top). Unhappily one cannot short-circuit the developmental path of growth without leaving deep, unsatisfied longings for that skipped period. Hence, in fantasy the patient clung to this circumvented period of his childhood. And when his fantasy erupted into overt behavior, it took the form of immaturity—in an act of pedophilia.

The patient's drawn male Person conveys an atmosphere of dejection, depression, listlessness, feelings of inferiority and loneliness. The limp hang of the shoulders, the somewhat bowed head and the facial scarring all convey the patient's attitude of a beaten, frustrated man. The scar on the face suggests that the patient's recent pedophile act, its detection, his trial and resultant incarceration, and ostracism by family and friends tore a deep gash in his self-esteem.

The scar further reflects both his feeling of being different from those about him, and his feeling that others must be aware of that difference.

The drawn Person's shoulders are loaded down with the weight of guilt.

The drawing conveys feelings of insufficiency, the content of which is a consciousness of absence of support. Affect is of a somewhat cautious type, depressively toned. If we regard the drawn male as a projection, in self-portrait fashion, it is evident that the patient does not possess much feeling of vitality and

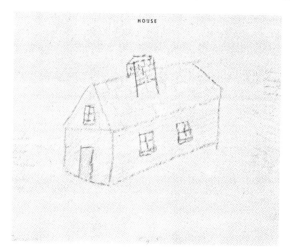

Figure 5:  Chromatic

bouyancy and we may guess that he becomes easily fatigued.

In the Post-drawing Inquiry, he says that the worst part of the drawing is the hands, again suggesting guilt—guilt over that which the hands have done.

The transparency of the feet, whereby one foot shows through the other, reflects the same sort of difficulty in dealing with protrusions that the patient previously experienced in the drawing of the chimney. The feeling of lack of substance which is conveyed by a transparent protrusion may be understood as a displacement of the patient's feelings of phallic inadequacy, and, we might suspect, as a feeling that this is equally apparent to others.

In the drawing of the female Person, the patient indicates that he views females in unappealing terms. He renders an unattractive version of a woman, from her straight, severe hair-do, down to her desexualized breasts and curveless figure. One hand of the drawn female is placed in the "pelvic-defense" position as if to ward off any sexual approach. Thus, the patient perceives adult females as unappealing, in the first place, and as rejecting, in the second place.

In a basically neurotic orientation, the patient implicitly assumes that women are cold, alien, and unloving. He perceives himself as rejected, unloved, and inadequate as a sexual partner.

On top of the subject's underlying view of women as rejecting, the four-week denial of sexual contact on the part of his wife (which precipitated his pedophilic act) only served to confirm and reactivate his feelings of rejection by adult females. Hence, employing substitution, along with regression, he turned toward a child. Here, presumably, he entertained the hope of his sexual advances being more favorably received. Unappreciated by an adult female, he felt that perhaps an immature one would be more impressed with him sexually.

Feelings of rejection by mature females thus join hands with the factors of insecurity concerning his phallic adequacy (the difficulty with the chimney), immaturity and childish fixation (the young sapling drawn with projected age of "five to eight"), and together they forge the motivational mainspring for pedophilia which the four-week enforced sexual abstinence, during his climacteric period, triggered off.

### Chromatic

The chromatic House is rendered in appropriate colors, brownish-orange for the walls, brown for the door, and green for the roof. The choice of bright red for the chimney, against a

Figure 6: Chromatic

Figure 7: Chromatic

background of the more subdued colors employed for the rest of the House, calls attention to the protrusion from the body of the House and recalls the patient's exhibitionism to mind.

Beneath the conspicuousness of the display, however, the chimney appears to dissolve and crumble under the emotional impact of color. Feelings of phallic insufficiency come through more dramatically on the chromatic level, and are supported by the chromatic Tree. Here the patient takes pains to draw in a lower limb stump, at the trunk's middle, which he then describes as "having been sawed off a long time ago." Feelings of castration then explain the compensatory efforts which cloak it on closer to consciousness levels (in the Person drawing): The bushy mustache is added as a badge of virility to hide the patient's feelings of inadequacy as a male.

The feelings of castration so directly revealed in the chromatic House and Tree drawings serve to shed a beam of understanding on the patient's previous act of exhibitionism. Fearing that he was castrated, the patient probably exposed himself to attempt to alleviate the painful castration anxiety. It was as if he courted the screams that his exposure elicited from his female audience. The act of exhibitionism now becomes understandable as having been in the service of obtaining data to deny his felt castration. The patient in effect said, by his act, "Reassure me that I have a penis, by reacting to it."

Twenty years later when his symptomatology again erupted in the form of a sex offense, his castration fears had presumably become more entrenched. This time he had to show his penis to a little girl instead of to adult women. He displayed it to a child because due to his increasing feeling of phallic inadequacy, he thought that only a *young* girl would be impressed.

To return to the chromatic drawing of the House, the fact that the chimney is ultimately adequate on the achromatic level, and appears to crumble only in the chromatic phase, suggests that in situations that do not provide extreme emotional stress the patient is able, largely, to suppress his feelings of phallic inadequacy. Under emotional stress, however, as represented by the impact of

Figure 8: Chromatic

the chromatic drawing phase, his control dissolves. This interpretive deduction receives support from the period of a full twenty years between the patient's original symptom and its later recrudescence.

Although the deeper chromatic level elicits greater pathology in the phallic area, represented by the chimney, the windows, however, look better on the chromatic drawings. This suggests that the feeling of vulnerability to the emotional atmosphere around him, suggested by the achromatic windows minus panes or cross-hatching, is on a relatively recent, reactive basis and is not deeply rooted in the patient's personality. This adds a positive element to this facet of the prognostic picture.

Turning to the chromatic Tree, both the sudden tapering of trunk width and the over-extension of the Tree into fantasy beyond the top of the page reappear. The age projected onto the drawn Tree is "five or six," just about what it was with the achromatic Tree. The use of only two colors, green for the bark and yellow for the leaves, is somewhat few and suggests a mild condition of emotional constriction or timidity.

In the drawing of the chromatic male, we get the distinct impression that black paint, ink or some other such substance has been poured over the Person's head and is running down his face. The patient apparently feels conspicuously and shamefully tainted by his offense. This suggestion of guilt and hypersensitivity to how he appears socially is the chromatic correlate of the previous achromatic scarring on the face. The patient experiences himself as profoundly marked—an outcast.

In the psychosexual area, in addition to the compensatory virility strivings previously noted in the addition of the conspicuous mustache, we observe that one hand is rigidily but noticeably attracted toward the genital region—the area of concern—under the chromatic impact.

Except for this one bit of secondary movement, the Person appears to be holding himself rigidly at attention, legs pressed closely together, arms (particularly the right one) straight and held close to the body. The kinesthetic emphasis in this projection is on the erect posture and on the rigid tension with which the posture is held, keeping the self closed off against the world around. At the same time, the inner impulses are kept under rigid control.

This stance is elicited by the chromatic layer; presumably

emotional situations bring about the defensive reaction of rigidity and hypercontrol—particularly after a recent lapse from this control resulted in the patient's incarceration at Sing Sing.

Patients who project this rigid body posture in their drawings often express an unfree, excessively controlled and basically defensive attitude. Such drawings are offered by people to whom spontaneous relations with others and the world around them are threatening.

In short, the main quality is that of rigid, tense, defensive control in order to keep up a certain appearance of stability.

The chromatic woman is rendered in much the same style as the achromatic one. Both are unappealing, out-of-date, and asexual. Breast and hip contours are absent. To make the woman still less appealing, the patient employs the stereotype of glasses.

Below the waist, the chromatic female appears to fade away, as though this area of a woman is defensively viewed as not real for the patient. This area arouses so much anxiety, that he can not deal with it on the page. (The camera picks up the light yellow lines of the skirt giving it substance that it lacks in the original.)

## UNPLEASANT CONCEPT TEST

As the "most unpleasant thing" he could think of, the patient chose the concept of prison—what might be termed a "popular" response for the population at Sing Sing.

His drawing of this entity (see Figure 9) is, however, bleak

Figure 9

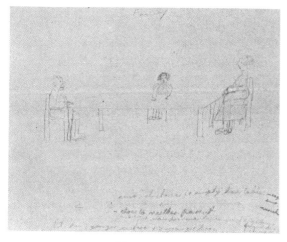

Figure 10

and empty even for a representation of a prison. Most subjects depicting a prison add more signs of life showing through the bars: cot, wash-stand, and a person as the cell occupant. Apparently the patient views prison life as even more dismal and bleak (particularly in view of the adequate detailing on his other drawings) than do his fellow inmates. He is emotionally harder hit by the incarceration. This is consistent with the acute sensitivity he shows by the scarring on the achromatic male's face and the black paint or ink effect pouring down over the chromatic male's head.

## DRÅW-A-FAMILY

In the Draw-A-Family procedure, with adult subjects, the stimulus reactivates one's childhood perceptions of one's family and one's own relationship in it. Our patient draws a family group seated with considerable distance between members rather than a close family unit. The implication of emotional distance between family members is also supported by the empty, bare table reflecting the meager emotional nourishment previously suggested by the abrupt narrowing of the trunk widths of both drawn Trees at one point in their development.

Although the patient felt close to neither parent, he viewed the mother as the more dominant, stern parental-figure. Having, then, a choice between a dominant female or a relatively less significant male to identify with, in his developmental years, he was initially handicapped. He could not pattern himself along wholely male lines, for his male model was seen as a secondary, subordinate figure. Identifying with the father left the patient a legacy of the feelings of inadequacy with which he saw his father assume the male role.

The other alternative would be to identify with the parent who "wore the pants" in the family, but in doing so he would be modelling himself after a female—again an unsatisfactory solution as far as his psychosexual development was concerned.

His shaky psychosexual identification, then, provided the castration anxiety (so dramatically emphasized in the H-T-P) fertile soil in which to grow. The step from confused sexual identification to feelings of insufficiency as a male was but a short one.

### DRAW-A-PERSON-IN-THE-RAIN

Under environmental stress, represented by the rain, the patient tends to employ withdrawal, pulling the umbrella well down about his head so that most of his face is hidden. That part of his

Figure 11

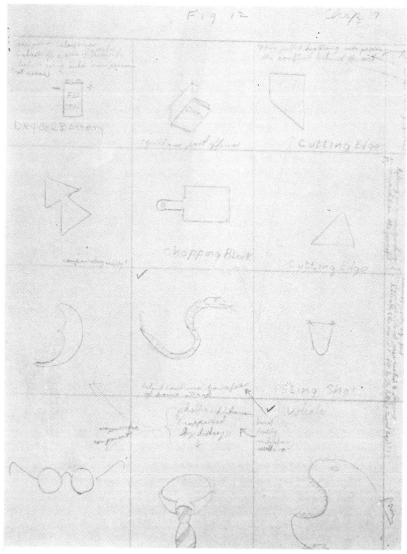

Figure 12:  Drawing Completion Test

face which does show is scarred—repeated evidence of the patient's feelings of being branded a social outcast. The feet, protrusions from the body upon which the patient may displace his feelings regarding his phallus, are again transparent and lacking in substance.

## DRAWING COMPLETION TEST

The patient begins his Drawing Completion Test [2] perform-ance with a drawing of a dry cell battery, falling back on his occupation (electrician) as an area of security to handle the anxiety generated by starting off on a new, unfamiliar procedure.[3]

He next ventures further into a more personal area by drawing a diary. A diary is a record of the past as well as a place where secret thoughts are tucked away. This suggests twin possibilities. The aspect of a diary as a record of the past conveys guilt over his past activities (and thoughts?) which he can not escape. The second aspect of the concept of a diary, concern with private thoughts, brings to mind the efforts to keep his fantasies secret, as well as under control, as evidenced by the barred window in the roof of his House drawing. The barred windows reveal attempts not only to keep the content of his fantasy from spilling out into the outer environment, but—as the diary now suggests—to keep others from finding out about his fantasies. Bars serve to keep others out, as well as things in.

Following the diary drawing and its facet reflecting concern over his past deeds, he is pulled headlong into portraying a hint to the conflicts behind his past offenses. He draws a "cutting edge," and later a "chopping block" and then still again another "cutting edge." This theme weaves its way to the very last drawing response. He closes his drawing completion performance on the same note: a huge fish with savage teeth and dangerously opened mouth. The common denominator behind concepts like cutting edges, chopping blocks, and sharp teeth is the same one that pressed forward in the crumbling chimney on the House and the amputated middle limb of the Tree which "had been sawed-off a long time ago": fear of bodily mutilation or, in analytic terms, castration anxiety.

Imbedded in this context is the ninth drawing completion

---

[2] The series of drawing completion stimuli employed here is neither the Kinget nor the Horn-Hellersberg set but a set devised for our purposes at Sing Sing. The principles employed are essentially the same as not only the Kinget and Horn-Hellersberg techniques, but also Rorschach content analysis since the stimuli are quite ambiguous.

[3] One may speculate as to the meaning of the unnecessary addition of the plus and minus signs as reflecting his present concern with the proportions of "goodness" and "badness" in himself—a preoccupation which has sorely plagued him since his offense.

item, a sling shot. A sling shot is consistent with the immaturity of the patient, previously suggested by his projected age of "five to eight" onto his drawn Tree.

On a deeper layer, one is reminded of the possible strong association of a sling shot in the mind of the subject, at this point a rather religious Jewish individual who had taken to carrying the Bible around with him wherever he went in the prison, even at the price of the ribbing he took from the other inmates. The sling shot, biblically famous as the implement which allowed the boy David to contest and vanquish the huge enemy figure so easily capable of smashing him, suggests the ego strength the patient has displayed [4] in fighting against the threat of castration, rather than giving in to these feelings, by a male authority figure.

To continue into the area of the patient's defenses, the arrow is congruent with the previously noted [5] compensatory mechanisms in phallic areas. The exhibitionistic mechanism, whereby he displays that he is not castrated, is reflected in the drawing of the tie which calls attention to something decorative hanging down from the front of a man. Or if less symbolic levels are preferred, a tie is at least an item of clothing worn only by the male sex and hence, the patient feels the need to display his affiliation or membership in this sex.

The voyeuristic component of the exhibitionism-voyeurism coin is suggested by both the glasses and the moon, the first something to look with, and the other something to look at.

The last item left to discuss in the Drawing-Completion Test is the rattlesnake, poised to strike. If we build upon the empirical structure of experience with the Draw-An-Animal Test, dreams, Rorschach content symbolism, and myths, the depiction of the dangerous qualities of an animal so susceptible to use as a phallic symbol suggests that we look further for evidence that the all male environment of the prison may be stirring up latent fears of homosexual attack. Certainly, the occurrence of latent homosexual fears is consistent with the patient's castration anxiety.

---

[4] Again we recall the compensatory virility strivings suggested by the mustache on the chromatic male, the essential adequacy of the achromatic chimney, the intact personality integration evident in the drawings as a whole, and the behavioral evidence of the long time between the patient's two symptomatic eruptions.

[5] The over-large achromatic chimney, the large, bushy chromatic mustache, and evidence to be presented later in the Eight-Card-Redrawing Test, where he draws a soldier and then a boxer.

Figure 13

## DRAW AN ANIMAL

For his animal concept, the patient chooses a horse [6] whose destructive potential he noticeably underscores. The emphasis on the horse's teeth repeats the previous highlighting of the dangerous teeth in the Drawing Completion Test. The outer world is again and again seen as capable of inflicting instant damage, symbolically mounting—the H-T-P indicates—to castration proportions.

## EIGHT CARD REDRAWING TEST

By this point in the case study, we have observed the subject's performance on a variety of projective drawing techniques, and have gotten to know him to a depth of several layers. To avoid the tediousness, then, of analyzing in detail fully eight more drawings, we will focus on the shift in dominant theme as the

---

[6] The choice of a horse as a representation of the damage-inflicting power of parental figures also occurred in Freud's case of Little Hans (1).

Figure 14

Eight Card Redrawing Test sifts down into progressively deeper areas of the patient's inner image of himself.

By now the patient has submitted himself to projective device after projective device and has begun to come to himself, to muster his defenses. He opens up on a fresh drawing technique with a depiction of a soldier (Figure 14), a man cloaked in the trappings of virile masculinity.

In the next drawing, the patient advances the drawn Person

to an officer (Figure 15). Compensatory defenses deepen and merge with needs for status, prestige and authority. All this at the expense, however, of some mild withdrawal from reality [7] evident in the turning away from a full-face view. After the initial drawing (Figure 14), the drawn Person never again faces full on to the viewer. Instead, he progressively turns away until facing

---

[7] Consistent with the implications of the previously discussed Draw-A-Person-in-the-Rain rendition.

Figure 15

Figure 16

a full 90 degrees from the full-front position. (Once a subject presents the drawn Person facing *beyond* this 90-degree mark, with the beginnings of a back-view appearing, withdrawal of schizoid if not schizophrenic proportions, becomes suspect. The full back-view perspective occurs almost exclusively in schizophrenic conditions ranging from the latent to the overt.)

In his next drawing (Figure 16), the patient recovers momentarily—again, giving evidence of ego strength—before the momentum of his defensive operations causes him to advance to a still more compensatory level in the drawing after (Figure 17). Here, he draws a boxer, a representation, if we follow the cultural stereotype, of the epitome of capable masculinity on display. The movement from soldier, to officer, to boxer not only is evidence of

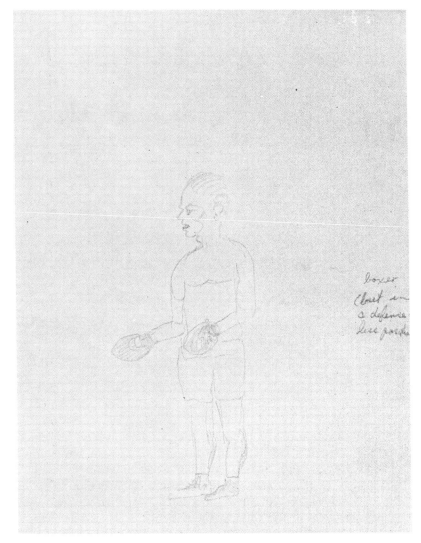

Figure 17

Figure 18

the intensification of the patient's compensatory virility defenses, but also combines at this point with exhibitionism. A boxer performs before an audience and *exhibits* masculinity, much as the patient had to exhibit same by the exposure of his genitals.

At this level of the Eight Card Redrawing performance we get the first hint of the chink in the patient's defenses—or to emphasize the positive aspects in the personality picture, not until this level do we get this evidence. Although the Person *is* a boxer, his hands are dropped to a conspicuously defenseless position. The patient no longer feels adequately defended, and by the next drawing (Figure 18) is no longer on his feet but collapses into a seated position under the rationalization of paddling a canoe.

The choice of a canoe may be multi-determined, in that a canoe is, among the small-boat class vessels, something that is

Figure 19

Figure 20

difficult to control. A canoe is a skittish craft, which twists and turns too readily under the influence of adverse environmental forces. Just the feeling the patient may hold in regard to his own impulses.

In addition, a canoe may have been chosen because it glides along relatively effortlessly, and here it may tend to foreshadow the yearnings "to give up the struggle," and allow the stream of life to carry him wherever it will, which the patient later so graphically highlights in his final drawing (Figure 21) to the Eight Card Redrawing technique.

On the next card (Figure 19), his defenses again momentarily strengthen. He is back on his feet. He is engaged in a sport identified with the male sex. And to go out on a more speculative limb, we wonder whether the theme includes a long, phallic symbol as the patient's last attempt at displaying virility before he gives up the effort entirely in his two terminal drawings.

In the next to last drawing (Figure 20), the patient finally does give up the struggle. He gives up standing on his feet. He collapses into a chair. And he seeks solace and warmth from a large fireplace. At this point, his feet again become transparent, foreshadowing their ultimate fate on the last drawing.

He draws to a close the drama of the increasingly more penetrating views into deeper layers of his self-concept on a climactic note. The drawn Person (Figure 21), now, falls flat on his back. To heighten the effect, the eyes close and the patient spontaneously comments, "He's gone off into a sleep." The patient has given in to an attitude of passive sufferance of whatever life may bring. The cloaks of the role of the soldier, the officer and the boxer, have been stripped from him, and the patient accepts defeat.

Below the knees, he looks amputated. The transparent feet which gave him so much trouble, not only in the present projective test but also in the H-T-P and the Draw-A-Person-in-the-Rain, now disappear. On the deepest personality level tapped they are now not merely without substance, but totally amputated.

The content of the drawing involving the man asleep fulfills the earlier promise of a desire for effortless drifting held forth in the canoe drawing. Also, the withdrawal indications evident in the gradual progression from full face to absolute-profile perspective receives the ultimate in confirmation: the Person retreats into sleep.

Before leaving this drawing, in passing we may dip into a more speculative level. The contour of the body swells into a pregnant-like condition. This hint of feminine psychosexual identification goes hand-in-hand with the "castrated" state of the feet, and calls to mind the suggestion of homosexual fears conveyed by the rattlesnake poised to strike in the Drawing Completion Test.

As we follow the patient down through the hierarchy of his

Figure 21

personality layers, we witness the struggle between the patient's pathology and his defenses. First the one has the upper hand, then the other. It is touch and go, until the very end.

The general trend is, however, an increasing tightening of his defenses until a point where they are evidently stretched too thin. Then they crack. We have to admire the strength of the patient's ego. Compensatory virility strivings increase from cards one to five, and do not really give way until the last two cards, revealing the patient's essential inadequacy, impotency and weakness beneath his compensatory cloak.

To a certain depth in his personality there is a stability of character defenses and a capacity for control. It was upon this positive prognostic element that the writer felt a psychotherapeutic program might be built and therefore engaged the patient in psychotherapeutic collaboration. For, in spite of the classic use of severe neurotic mechanisms, the patient maintains a good deal of personality integration, and has rather good resources to fall back upon. There is considerable strength to his personality, and when he is driven to the point where his defenses crack it is only after a good deal of heroic effort to stave off this ego collapse.

It is noteworthy that at no point does any glimmering of a schizophrenic process reflect itself in the projective techniques

Figure 22: Achromatic

Figure 23:   Achromatic

held up to his personality. Diagnostically the patient's adaptive patterns are securely anchored in neurotic areas. Other positive elements in the prognostic picture include an adequate intellectual level, a need for support, and a load of anxiety which may be expected to serve as a positive force to keep him in the therapeutic relationship. His overwhelming sense of guilt may be an asset when the therapeutic project requires him to gradually face his underlying self, even if it causes pain—in fact *especially* if it causes pain—for in this manner he may feel he can ease his sense of guilt through penance.

His exhibitionistic needs may also be harnessed to the therapeutic task. This neurotic need to openly expose himself to the inspection of others may be exploited to uncover the roots of his other neurotic components. In this manner one neurotic element may be pitted against the others, in the ultimate hope of exploring deeply enough to allow for the eventual resolution of both sets of syndromes.

Finally, his ego can withstand a certain amount of a uncovering type of therapy, if combined with support and acceptance, in the interests of replacing self-tyranny with self-tolerance.

In view of his resources, in spite of his fifty-one years of age and the extensive duration of his conflicts, his mental health still seems to be definitely salvageable, although a great deal of intensive psychotherapy will be needed.

### RETESTING FOLLOWING THERAPEUTIC PROGRESS

After approximately fifty hours of therapeutic collaboration between the patient and the writer, over a period of three and one-half months, a sampling of the projective drawing techniques was readministered. A brief discussion of the picture presented by the data of this retesting is presented to illustrate

Figure 24: Achromatic

Figure 25: Achromatic

the suitability of projective drawings for easy periodic rechecks to appraise progress during the course of therapy, and the sensitivity of these instruments as a reflector of such change.

### Achromatic H-T-P-P

It is reassuring to see several suggestions of improvement: (a) the lessened feelings of vulnerability apparent in the return of window panes and sash to the previous empty square holes for windows; (b) the more solid chimney; (c) the coming into view of more of the Tree with less of it over-extended off the page into fantasy; (d) the projected age of "ten to fourteen" onto the Tree replacing the previous still more immature self-concept of "five to eight"; (e) the loss of the heavy atmosphere of dejection conveyed by the drawn male, the disappearance of gloom and hopelessness, of limpness and the quality of feeling oneself a depressed and beaten man. The shoulders no longer slump; greater relative feelings of vigor return to the body posture. The figure is essentially better dressed, less disheveled, and generally reflective of enhanced feelings of social adequacy and acceptability. A dramatic change in this area of social acceptability is the disappearance of the facial scarring. The drawn male this time looks generally more youthful and confident.

Comparing the drawn female with the earlier one, she looks at least one *j.n.d.* more appealing. Her face is prettier, her hair style is less severe, and she looks more youthful. One hand is no longer in a position of "pelvic-defense," warding off in advance any potential genital approach.

On the negative side, the House is now offered as a facade presentation without the former three-dimensional perspective of depth. Now that the patient has experienced some symptomatic relief—lowered guilt, freedom from depression, and returning self-confidence—he has become hesitant to expose himself further to the scrutiny involved in the process of the psychotherapeutic inventory. In the projective drawing of the House, he presents only a front, keeping the rest hidden behind this facade. Here

Figure 26: Chromatic

Figure 27: Chromatic

the drawings foreshadowed, and prepared the therapist for, the resistance phase brought into the therapy relationship eight or nine sessions later.

### Chromatic H-T-P-P

A comparison of the retest chromatic House with the initial chromatic House closely parallels the comparison of the two achromatic Houses just discussed. The most dramatic improvement is the now adequate and sturdy chimney (Figure 26) in place of the previous crumbling, almost dissolving, chromatic one (Figure 5).

The comparison of the two chromatic Trees reveals that the present one no longer carries a truncated, sawed-off lower limb stump. Now the lower limb is "seen" as growing and in bloom. Life is perceived as returned to it.

The projected age is moved up from the previous childish fixation at "five or six" to an adolescent "fourteen."

The color usage for the Tree moves from the previous constricted use of two to a more expansive five: brown, green, yellow, orange and blue—a harmonious blend of the warmer colors. The emergence of comfortableness with color, and with color subordinated to the form of the drawing, indicates a growth in the patient's capacity for adequate emotional adaptation to the conventional and usual social situations. His increased preference for warm color may be interpreted as a weakening of timidity in affective life and a strengthening of emotional drives, the warm colors being correlates of a more free emotional interest in people. The healthier use of color in the retest H-T-P suggests an improvement in the emotional tone of his thinking and feeling, in general.

The later chromatic male (Figure 28) is drawn larger than the initial chromatic male (Figure 7), reflecting an increase in feelings of adequacy. A noticeable gain in feelings of youth and vigor is also apparent in a comparison of the two drawings. In addition, the patient feels essentially more adequate as a male, no longer

Figure 28: Chromatic

Figure 29:  Chromatic

feeling the need for the conspicuous compensatory mustache.

The feeling of being branded a social outcast, previously suggested by the paint effect spilling down over the drawn Person's head, has now disappeared. This is a parallel finding to the dropping-off of the facial scarring on the retest achromatic Person. In a more speculative vein, the absence of a hat on the retest chromatic male may reflect less felt need to conceal the content of what goes on beneath the hat, his thoughts and fantasies.

Comparing the chromatic females, the present one is strikingly more appealing than the initial one. The patient now finds females considerably more attractive. They are currently "seen" as more youthful, pretty, and with a hair style less out-of-date. They are no longer perceived as old-maid-like figures with glasses.

*Draw-A-Family*

The family unit is now seen in more positive terms. There is less distance between the family members, and the table is no longer bare. In the transference relationship, the patient has re-experienced certain childhood events and appears to have emerged from them with a greater feeling of sustainment and emotional nourishment. The environment is no longer seen as bleak and barren, as on the initial Draw-A-Family production, but as now more pleasurably bountiful.

Comparing the two drawings, we note that the mother-figure is perceived as less stern and domineering than before, and the skull-caps suggest that the patient is turning to religion in his security-seeking efforts.

### Draw-A-Person-in-the-Rain

Changes evident in the drawing of a person in the rain consist of the dropping off of the facial scarring, the addition of substance to the previously transparent feet (in support of the implications of the return of growth to the previously truncated Tree limb), and the tilting back of the umbrella to allow the drawn Person to come out more from his previously greater retreat into withdrawal under this protective covering.

Figure 30

Figure 31

### Draw-An-Animal

For his animal drawing, a horse is again chosen. There is one striking difference, however, in the detailing. The sharply emphasized teeth in the previous drawing are not repeated, suggesting a decrease in the destructive and punitive potential with which others, particularly authority figures, are endowed.

### SUMMARY

A battery of projective drawings was administered to one patient. The data was presented to tie together the entire projective drawing family in a case illustration.

The drawings suggest that the patient suffers acutely from feelings of being branded a social outcast by his offense. The experience tore a deep gash in his self-esteem and loaded him down with the weight of guilt. He labors under the embittered admonition of a severe superego.

Psychogenetically, the drawings suggest that the patient has experienced a feeling of abrupt and sudden rationing, along the course of his development, of a previously more bountiful emotional fare. This produced a *fixation* along the path of personality growth. In periods of stress—such as the precipitating factor of his wife's rejection of him sexually for a period of four weeks—he then regresses to the developmental age range preceding that period in life when he was starved for emotional nourishment from his environment. When regressed, he then feels emotionally more comfortable with those of his own developmental level (felt to be, as the patient projects, "between five to eight years old"). Should sexual needs clamor for release during periods of regression, he seeks to discharge them with a sex object of his own developmental level, as it were, and in the immature mode of manual manipulation, viewing and showing.

The drawings indicate that the patient perceives adult females as unappealing and rejecting. He evaluates himself as sexually inadequate, and suffers from castration anxiety of massive pro-

Figure 32

portions. Hence, he had an additional reason for sexually approaching a little girl—to quiet the inner voice of doubt concerning his sexual adequacy. Rejected by an adult female, he regressively fell back upon the hope that perhaps a little child would be more impressed with him sexually.

Feelings of rejection by mature females thus join hands with castration anxiety, immaturity, and ready regressive channels— taken toegther they forge the motivational mainspring for pedophilia which the four-week enforced sexual abstinence triggered off.

His exhibitionism is also understandable as being in the service of obtaining data to deny his felt castration, via the unconscious mechanism, "Reassure me that I have a penis, by reacting to it."

As to his view of parental figures, the patient presents a picture of having felt close to neither parent. As identification figures, he had a choice between a dominant mother-figure and a less significant father-figure. He could not pattern himself along wholly male lines, for his male model was seen as a secondary figure. Identifying with the father left the patient a legacy of the feelings of inadequacy with which he saw his father assume the male role. The alternative was to identify with the parent who "wore the pants" in the family, but in doing so he accepted a female as a model. Either unsatisfactory solution left him with the shaky psychosexual identification in which his later castration anxiety found fertile soil.

For the most part, compensatory defenses are adequate, with only occasional lapses to inadequate functioning. Other positive factors include essential personality integration and absence of psychotic processes. There is considerable *strength* to his personality, and when he is driven to the point where his defenses crack it is only after a degree of heroic effort to stave this off. These elements forecast a positive prognosis, the validity of which was attested to by the improvement that occurred under psychotherapy and the projective drawing *retest* reflection of this change.

## REFERENCE

1. Freud, S.: Analysis of a phobia in a five-year-old boy. In *Collected Papers*, Vol. III. London, Hogarth, 1949.

# PART V

# RESEARCH AND CLINICAL STUDIES

## CHAPTER 19

# RESEARCH IN DRAWING TECHNIQUES

EVERETT HEIDGERD, M.A.

## INTRODUCTION

RESEARCH PLAYS an even more necessary role in drawing techniques than in any other method of personality evaluation since the use of drawing techniques *superficially* requires very little training. Complex scoring systems can be avoided. Popular magazines have capitalized on the apparent simplicity of drawing interpretation. Sidewalk psychologists freely interpret drawings. For these reasons, hypotheses and different interpretive theories are cheap. To differentiate the good from the bad is often not easy for even the serious and sincere psychologist. The youthful vitality which the clinical field finds within itself, often stirs the inexperienced clinician to accept concepts which have their basis only in recklessness and impulsiveness.

Cynicism and disillusion need not be the major part of the psychologist's attitude toward drawing techniques. Quite to the contrary, the psychologist who keeps his feet on experimentally firm ground and yet willingly utilizes a controlled and professional imagination, will find much usefulness in drawing techniques. The need for active and positive research integrated with the growing clinical use of drawings is therefore obvious.

The area of projective testing finds itself in the middle of the art-science dilemma. Hutt (62) feels that clinical practice is an art and believes that art will always remain an integral part of clinical practice. He believes further that science will become a major portion of the practice in time but as Brown (21) points out, the field finds itself divided between those who call themselves artists and those who call themselves scientists, with each group at the present time having little respect for the other.

Brown suggests that the basic disagreement stems from the nature of projective data which scientific techniques have not been yet able to handle statistically. He sees science as attempting to cope with the problem of quantitative reduction of dynamically organized material by traditional experimental methods. The clinician maintains that projective data has its greatest meaning in its configuration and that experimental analysis tends to destroy this configuration. The clinician therefore, turns to "clinical validation" which the research psychologist labels as fantasy, speculation or assumption.

Much is to be said, and will be said, on both sides of the fence. Many clinicians are "dreamers" who have permitted their dynamic concepts to overwhelm them and have become slaves of these concepts. At the same time, the rejection of the configurational approach by research psychologists will only amplify and extend the limitations of projectives inherent in the exclusive dependence on "clinical validation." Clinician and researcher, have much to offer each other, if projectives are to serve their purpose effectively and efficiently.

Though there is much criticism of the field, there is hardly an author—clinician or researcher—who does not see value in the use of drawing techniques for personality evaluation. Rosenzweig calls drawing techniques "clinically practical." Morris (90) in 1949, in the report of an APA Division meeting says "the method as a whole shows definite promise of developing into a valuable projective technique." Sloan, in speaking of the H-T-P, says that its problems "do not appear to be any more or less than those of other projective techniques now in vogue."

### SPECIFIC PROBLEMS IN VALIDATION STUDIES

Ainsworth (2) has clearly spelled out the problems the unprejudiced researcher faces in attempting to validate projectives. Projective data is the product of a multiplicity of variables. In the traditional scientific investigation, one variable is isolated and explored. This is a virtual impossibilty in the projective test where a response apparently has many possible origins. Not only is perception involved in the response, which in itself is a function of many variables, but also the process of response is involved.

Precker points to this confusion between the "projective" and "expressive" aspects of personality.

It is pointed out further that good clear criteria are practically non-available. Rosenzweig (97) points to the danger of checking one unknown against another as being a particularly useless kind of exercise. Brown (21) questions severely the use of "diagnosed cases" as criterion variables suggesting that all too often a diagnosis is based on completely inadequate data, sometimes a ten minute psychiatric interview. In terms of this criterion problem, MacFarlane points out that correlation between overt behavior and fantasy material is inadequate to show the organizational patterns involved in combinations of explicit and implicit behavior. Ainsworth amplifies this by stating that even when statistically significant differences between *groups* can be shown, that this is of little help in a *specific* diagnosis.

### RESEARCH STUDIES

With these complex problems in mind, attention is turned to specific research studies. For the most part, research dated 1948 and later will be considered. It was in this year that Buck (22) formally introduced the H-T-P, and in 1949 that Machover (85) published her findings. That much had been done with drawings before this date can be verified by the extensive survey and bibliography compiled by Anastasi and Foley (7). References can be found as far back as 1880 when Lombroso and Du Camp (82) studied the occurrence of different forms of artistic expression of the insane. Almost all of these early writings, however, dealt with an unscientific and uncontrolled approach to the use of drawings. It was in 1926 that Goodenough introduced a systematic method of evaluating intelligence through drawings of a man. For a meaningful and a more pertinent survey of the literature up through 1948, Precker (95) has made a worthwhile study. He has reviewed the literature up to that time with particular attention to research. Included are an analysis of the types of research attempted and suggestions for future research. His stated purposes are to synthesize work done and to provide a "vocabulary for future research." Precker makes a brief mention of the H-T-P, which was just being officially born at that time.

## FIGURE DRAWING AND THE H-T-P

By far the most research in drawing techniques has been related to figure drawing and to the H-T-P. As Vernier (109) suggests of all projective techniques in maturation, figure drawing and the H-T-P have stimulated the "usual array of studies of reliability, validity, group norms, differences between groups, and analyses of effects of various factors or events upon performance."

### Reliability

A criterion of reliability with a projective technique is difficult to define. In terms of the holistic approach, is it reasonable to require drawings at different administrations to be exactly the same in some arbitrary ways? It has been suggested that the criterion should be that no conflicting evidence should appear in the drawings but this involves dynamic interpretation and the problem of how an interpretation is made. It has also been suggested that two drawings by the same subject could be quite different in formal or structural characteristics and still reveal the same valid information about the subject.

Gasorek (40) in working with children's free drawings found much conflicting evidence in terms of the consistency and reliability of formal and structural characteristics. His study is helpful in that it does define to some extent what features of drawings in general tend to recur. Albee and Hamlin (3, 5) judged personality adjustment from drawings by a global method and by means of a rating scale and found positive indications of reliability. They state that the use of a rating scale "lends encouraging reliability to judgment." The judges used in this experiment were experienced clinicians with post-doctoral training. This approach to a reliability study therefore, was completely different from Gasorek's approach.

Lehner and Gunderson (77) using the D-A-P [1] technique, investigated both test-retest reliability and inter-rater reliability on

---

[1] Draw-A-Person.

twenty-one graphic traits. Normal subjects were used and results indicated that "relatively high agreement among raters on
graphic traits can be obtained." Test-retest reliability was found
to be generally lower than inter-rater reliability. They suggest, in
some agreement with Gasorek, that many graphic traits show a
strong tendency to remain constant. (These traits are listed in
their report.)

Using a scale designed specifically for rating sexual differentiation, Swenson (105) reports a reliability coefficient of .84 on
drawings judged by trained judges for this particular trait. Without citing the supporting data, Oakley (92) reports his impressions of strong consistency in drawings "over a period of years."

Hammer and Piotrowski (47), employing six clinicians, found
that the reliability in the rating of degree of hostility in the drawings of 400 children, was an impressive .85. The deviation from
perfect reliability was explained by the positive correlation between the amount of hostility interpreted in the drawings and
the degree of hostility of the clinician himself (as judged by the
supervisor). This latter finding will be discussed more fully later in
the chapter.

*Validity*

Validation studies present an initially confusing picture from
which the patient observer may glean many meaningful insights.
Gathering normative data or observing variations in graphic
characteristics with variations in characteristics of subjects along
a continuum is one type of research design which has yielded
helpful but limited findings. Jolles (65-68) in four extensive and
painstaking studies, examined the H-T-P's of over 2,500 children
and found that (in accord with the theory of projection) children
tend to draw their own sex in the drawing of the person. The ratio
of same sex to opposite sex in the drawings, however, varies significantly with age, and also boys differ from girls on this ratio.
In his study of horizontal placement of the drawings on the page,
Jolles confirmed Buck's contention that the psychological center
of the page is to the left of the geometric center, that the mean
horizontal placement varies with age, and that the normal range

for horizontal placement tends to be a function of age. Vertical placement was found to be somewhat above the geometric center with variations similar to those of the horizontal placement.

Using 438 boys and girls of ages seven to twelve, Weider and Noller (111) confirmed the Jolles findings of the sex of the first drawn figure, showing that of the boys, 70 per cent drew their own sex first, while 94 per cent of the girls drew their own sex first. A significantly greater percentage of the girls than boys also drew their own sex larger [2] with slight differences in age levels. A significantly large percentage (61 per cent) of younger children located their drawings in the upper left while a smaller percentage (48 per cent) of the older children locate in that area. This is consistent with Buck's findings that the drawings of regressed adults move back into the upper left corner of the page.

Lehner and Silver (79) found that ages assigned to figure drawings by adults increased with chronological age up to the age of twenty-five after which progressively lower ages were assigned. This is consistent with the principle of projection of the ideal-image. Ages assigned to drawings representing the opposite sex were more variable than those assigned to the same sex. Both sexes tended to assign older ages to male drawings than to female drawings. The authors discuss the possible significance of these findings in terms of the greater status accorded males in our society.

The Draw-A-Person (D-A-P) Test was employed by Lehner and Gunderson (78) to investigate the influence of the subject's sex and age on height of figures drawn. Results suggested that these two factors produce significant variations in height, resulting in a decrease in height of the figure drawn beyond age thirty for men and beyond age forty for women. This seems remarkably consistent with the decline in feelings of bodily adequacy, starting at about these respective ages.

An item analysis of House drawings of children in grades Kindergarten through fourth by Markham (88) provides a collection of normative data. Markham concludes that the House draw-

---

[2] This, as with the previous finding, was related to the fact that girls spend more time with an identification figure of the same sex (mother), than do boys, during the formative years.

ing is an inadequate technique for estimating intelligence but that it can differentiate beween the dull and superior child. She found also that five-year-olds draw vastly different houses from eight-year-olds and suggests that emotional factors may explain some distortions and omissions.

In this general category, we find an interesting study by Lyons (83) who asked his adult subjects to put a scar on their H-T-P Tree and to report the worst and best events of their lives. The correlation between relative height of the scar on the Tree and the relative age of the worst event was .54, significant at the .01 level. Correlation between scar location and the best event was .10, not significant. The distribution of the scars was shown to differ significantly from results of two neutral tasks.

Validation studies which have proved the most popular are those which attempt to correlate clusters of graphic traits with the productions of specifically defined groups. These groups have been defined in many different ways. In some, the subjects have particular physical traits, in others the subjects have been diagnosed in terms of functional disorders. Still other groups have been defined in terms of social or cultural idiosyncrasies. Needless to say, there is much overlapping.

Kotkov and Goodman (73) were able to find graphic signs on the D-A-P test which differentiated obese from non-obese women. Out of an original checklist of forty three items, seven (representing obese characteristics) were found which successfully differentiated the two groups. Their conclusion was that any four of the seven signs in a given drawing would identify the subject as obese and the thesis of projection of the body image in drawings is supported.

Additional support comes from Berman and Laffel (16) who found a significant correlation between body type of the subject and the figure drawn.

Michal-Smith (89) compared the drawings of adolescent subjects having normal electroencephalograms with those having abnormal electrical function. He judged them on the basis of Buck's six scoring categories: Detail, Proportion, Perspective, Time, Criticality and Line Quality. With Line Quality, a significant level of differentiation was found. Beck (14) compared the

H-T-P's of organic defectives and those of non-organic defectives and found that the organics drew more unrecognizable houses and omitted more essential details than the non-organics.

Both Blum (18) and Royal (98) ran into considerable difficulty in attempting to differentiate the drawings of normal and neurotic groups. While Blum's experimental design was adequate, he ran into many contributing sources of error in the administration of his experiment. His conclusion that the D-A-P is not a valid indicator of personality dynamics when compared to ratings of psychiatrists and psychological testing would seem premature. Royal's study involved the use of fifty-four graphic traits, which were hypothesized to differentiate anxiety neurotics from normal subjects. While none of the fifty-four traits did this, a scale of eight of the most discriminating items succeeded in reducing the overlap between the groups to a significant extent.

Giedt and Lehner (42) compared the assigned ages on the D-A-P by neurotic subjects with those of normals. The authors found that both neurotics and normals changed from assigning an age older than the subject's age to an age younger than the subject's age as the chronological age increased. It was found however that the neurotics' point of change occurred at a greater age than it did with the normals. It was found also that there was greater variance in age assignment in the normals than in the neurotics.

Experimental studies attempting to differentiate schizophrenics and normals via the D-A-P and H-T-P techniques are few and conflicting. Using the D-A-P technique, Fisher and Fisher (37) evaluated the drawings of thirty-two paranoid schizophrenics by both a detailed atomistic analysis and total impression. Several raters were used. Results indicated that the majority of the drawings did not fall into the paranoid schizophrenic category. The drawings were evaluated with regard to facial expression and stance. Very little agreement was found among the various raters. It was found also that the trained psychologists showed no greater agreement among themselves than did untrained raters. The authors suggest that Machover's assumptions are dangerous without further research.

On the other hand, Holzberg and Wexler (60) found positive

results using a somewhat different method of evaluation. Using thirty-eight schizophrenic women as an experimental group and seventy-eight nurses in training as a control group, the authors devised a 174-item checklist for evaluating the drawings. They found significant statistical differences between normals and schizophrenics and between normals and each of three schizophrenic subgroups (paranoid, hebephrenic and catatonic). (Reliable differences *among* the three schizophrenic subgroups were not demonstrated.) A later study by Wexler and Holzberg (112), confirmed these findings.

Smith (103) compared the D-A-P creations of forty schizophrenic patients with those of forty general hospital patients. The schizophrenics gave more unusual responses than the normal group. Married schizophrenics mentioned the genitalia more frequently than did the unmarried schizophrenics. The "normals" mentioned differences in genitalia, body shape, hair length, complexion and cosmetics more frequently than the schizophrenics did.

Several studies have been devoted to the area of sexual adjustment as indicated by the H-T-P and figure drawing. In a before and after experiment, Hammer (48) administered the H-T-P at several stages in the process of eugenic sterilization of selected subjects in a state where sterilization is official policy. It was assumed that subjects who undergo eugenic sterilization would be prone to respond with feelings of castration. A checklist of graphic indices of castration anxiety based on clinic experience and psychoanalytic theory was devised. Significant differences were found between "before" and "after" on twenty-six of the fifty-four items compared. Hammer summarizes the statistically significant differences in the following conclusions:

"1. Elongated objects on the H-T-P, such as chimneys, branches, tree-trunks, arms, nose, legs, feet, etc., are susceptible to being utilized as phallic symbols. Circles, triangles, and objects with a vertical split down the center (such as a window depicted with emphasis upon the vertical sash-line and the horizontal sash-line omitted) may be employed as vaginal symbols and serve as reflections of felt castration in the creative drawings of males.

"2. It is in the drawing of these genital symbols that an individual may reveal his feelings of genital inadequacy and castration anxiety. Such feelings may be depicted by his presentation of the symbols as damaged, cut through, broken or otherwise impaired.

"3. The male genital trinity may be symbolized by groupings of three, e.g., buttons, branches, shrubs, doorknobs, etc., produced in clusters of three." (48)

Barker and Mathis (11) investigated the D-A-P characteristics of male homosexuals versus normals. They found that features differentiating the groups were limited but that the pictured hostility towards women was greater in the homosexuals and that this group employed a longer reaction time in identifying the self-sex figure.

Investigating the sex of the first drawn figure in the H-T-P's of eighty-four sex offenders at Sing Sing Prison, Hammer (52) found no significant difference between rapists and pedophiles regardless of the sex toward which the advance had been made. Hammer concludes that "considerable doubt is cast on the projective drawing postulate that the sex of the first figure drawn may serve as an index of the subject's sexual identification or as evidence of psychosexual conflict or sexual inversion." Further difficulty in interpreting the meaning of the sex of the first drawn figure was demonstrated by Mainord (87). In comparing the D-A-P's of college students and unselected mental hospital patients, she found that both groups tended to draw the self-sex figure first but males did so to a more pronounced degree than did females. Mainord suggests that this is consistent with the fact that our society is "predominantly androcentric."

In two further studies, Hammer (51, 54) investigated the characteristics of the Tree drawing in the H-T-P. His subjects in both studies were male sex offenders divided into three groups. They were rapists, homosexual pedophiles and heterosexual pedophiles. It was found that the homosexual pedophiles had a significantly greater incidence of dead Tree depictions than did the rapists. Hammer demonstrated a progression from rapists to heterosexual pedophiles to homosexual pedophiles (the latter deviating from the norm in *both* age and sex of the partner chosen) in regard to the number who drew their Trees as "dead." This progression parallels the increasing distance from an appropriate sex object. Hammer points out that the parallel data tend to support Buck's view that the psychologically sickest people draw their Trees as "dead."

Hammer (51) found also that "the group of individuals engaging in sex acts with female children drew significantly younger Trees (mean of projected age about eleven) than the group of inmates committing rape on adult females." Hammer argues that if we accept the psychoanalytic assumption that pedophiles are people who feel psychosexually immature and thus reach out to another child as it were, then Buck's hypothesis concerning the age of the Tree receives support. "The age with which the drawn Tree is endowed may serve as a rough index of the subject's felt level of psychosexual maturity," Hammer concludes.

De Martino (33) judged the male drawings of homosexual and non-homosexual mentally retarded males and found significant differences in the drawings in the eyelashes and the heels.

Fisher and Fisher (38) investigated the relationship between the femininity expressed in female figure drawings of women and the style of sexual adjustment. They found that drawings of low femininity tended to correlate with the subject's limited heterosexual experiences, more somatic sexual dysfunction and constricted sexual life. Highly feminine drawings occurred in those with more promiscuity but unsatisfying sexual experience. Figure drawings of average femininity correlated with more genuine satisfaction in the existing sexual role.

Culturally defined groups in a broad sense have provided another approach to research in drawing techniques. These groups are particularly difficult to define and in some of the studies it would be incorrect to look upon the given investigation as a validation study of the drawing technique involved. It is rather that the drawing technique is used as a tool in observing the dynamic processes of the groups being considered.

Hammer (49) compared the H-T-P's of Negro and white children in a southern community for the degree of hostility and aggression shown. He found, rating the drawings "blindly," that the mean hostility and aggression rating of the drawings done by the Negro children was significantly higher than that of the white children's drawings. The frustration-aggression theory is supported by this study. On the other hand, if the frustration-aggression theory is assumed, the ability of the H-T-P to differentiate groups differing in their degree of aggression is supported.

Kates and Harrington (69), using only human figure drawings, found no significant relationship between total ratings of aggression and indices of aggression manifested in the figure drawings of juvenile delinquents. Machover's criteria of aggression were used. The authors warn against any premature conclusion however, suggesting that the criteria were not meant to be used in isolation and that this demonstrates the dangers involved in fractionation.

Toler and Toler (108) investigated the degree of popularity as expressed in children's drawings. Working with fourth and fifth grade children, the authors established a criterion of popularity by means of a sociometric device. Figure drawings of the subjects were given to experienced clinical psychologists who were requested to select the productions of the most and least popular. They did so with some success. The authors concluded that there are certain dimensions of personality which seem to be associated with group acceptance and rejection. They conclude also that psychologists are generally able to discriminate between the more and less popular through an analysis of figure drawings.

Anastasi and Foley (9) attempted to use the D-A-P to differentiate the "pass-fail" groups of aviation cadets in the USAF during World War II. An objective scoring checklist failed to differentiate the two groups.

Woods and Cook (114) analyzed the manner of the representation of the hands in the drawing of the person in the H-T-P's of eighth grade students. They compared this graphic trait in groups of different artistic proficiency and found that the way the hands were drawn was a function of the level of proficiency in drawing. This finding suggested limitations in the interpretation of personality factors through the manner of hand representation.

In a somewhat similar study, Whitmyre (113) investigated the significance of artistic excellence in the judgment of adjustment inferred from human figure drawings. Drawings were obtained from psychotics and "normal veterans." Clinical psychologists ranked the drawings according to the level of personal adjustment and to the degree of artistic excellence. Drawings were also ranked by commercial artists for artistic merit. Results showed that the evaluations were highly reliable and that the psychologists used artistic merit to a significant degree in their evaluations of adjustment. Neither artistic excellence nor adjustment ratings by artists or psychologists showed any consistently significant relationship with the experimental and control groups.

In two studies, Jensen (63, 64) investigated the left-right orientation in profile drawing in relation to established reading habits. Profile drawings were obtained from two American populations, a Norwegian and an Egyptian population. Regardless of the direction of the established reading habit or of the amount of practice in reading, the tendency to draw profiles facing left was present in all four cultural groups. Americans from an urban, upper socio-economic class showed a stronger tendency to orient drawings to the left than did Americans from a rural lower socio-economic class. Left handed subjects did not demonstrate the same left orientation in their profiles as did the right handed subjects. The author's primary conclusion is that culturally imposed reading habits do not determine the left-right orientation in profile drawing.

Machover's definition of the head as a seat of social dominance and her consideration of differential treatment of the drawn male and female figures is the basis of an experiment by Cook (31). A questionnaire was administered to male university students to establish a criterion of social dominance. Analysis of the male and female figures drawn by the subjects yielded a group of drawings in which the head of the same-sex drawing was larger than the head of the opposite-sex drawing and a group in which this was not so. The questionnaire differentiated the two groups in a statistically significant way. Considerable overlap existed suggesting that Machover's hypothesis may hold in general but will not hold in each individual case,

An interesting study using a somewhat modified technique was completed by Baumgarten (13). The author obtained drawings from over 200 Serbian children living in Swiss refugee camps in 1942. These children had been subjected to extreme war experiences. Their drawings were compared to those of Swiss and American children. The drawings included were the human figure, something from the imagination, and something from the homeland. Evidences of aggressiveness, hostility or other disturbances were not observed in the drawings.

An experiment by Ochs (93) involving the Goodenough technique demonstrated the misleading nature of an atomistic approach. In a before and after design, Ochs checked the Goodenough drawings of Primary Behavior Disorder cases upon admission to an institution and later when social adjustment was in evidence. Experimental results showed little consistency in changes in the specific scoring items though total scores did not vary significantly. The author points to the fallacy of the notion that the whole is the sum of the parts.

Researchers and clinicians are equally interested in the effect of client-examiner relationship on the projective productions. Sinnett and Eglash (101) analyzed the variation in the size of drawn figures with manipulation of the examiner-subject relationship. They concluded that the size of the figure may very well be of importance in the analysis of the client's relationship with the examiner. In a similar experiment, but using four experienced clinical judges, Holtzman (59) concluded that "no variations in the drawings . . . could be attributed to the examiners' personality, sex, or physical appearance." Highly significant differences were attributed to the sex of the subjects. In a more penetrating and more controlled experiment, Hammer and Piotrowski (47) examined the effect of the examiner's personal hostility and aggressiveness on his interpretation of H-T-P's. Six clinicians served as subjects in judging 400 H-T-P's for evidence of hostility and aggression. Each clinician was administered the Szondi Test from which Deri derived a rating of aggression. Rank order comparisons of the data yielded a positive correlation. The more hostile clinicians "saw" more aggression in the H-T-P's they interpreted.

## DRAWING COMPLETION

The drawing completion tests are less widely known than the H-T-P and the Machover technique, but have nevertheless stimulated thoughtful consideration in clinical circles. Though the technique is primarily of European origin, a very adequate presentation of the background and method is offered by Kinget (71). In the same publication, Kinget presents a very impressive validation procedure. Adults were tested via the described technique and three types of validating data were secured. The validation data or criteria were reduced to workable categories and compared with each of the elements analyzed from the drawing tests. Results were encouraging. In discussing the problems involved in a continuing validation program, the author stresses need for integrated "chain work" rather than "a profusion of creativity."

Takala (107) has developed a quantifiable scoring system for the Drawing Completion Test based on the hypotheses suggested by Wartegg and Kinget. The test was administered to over 1,000 subjects representing seventeen occupational groups. The results indicated that the test differentiated occupational groups and seemed capable of serving as a predictor of vocational success. Correlations with intelligence were low but with drawing ability high. Norms for specific test variables and results of factor analysis are reported.

To investigate the graphic traits in the Drawing Completion Test (D-C-T), Bauer (12) obtained test protocols from male and female subjects in several different experimentally defined groups. Groups included were enuretics, epileptics, "suspected" schizophrenics, psychopaths, mental defectives, and neurologically disordered. Distinctive drawing characteristics are reported for all the groups mentioned except in the neurological disorders.

Analyzing a specific factor, the lack of attention to the starting sign in the drawing completion items, Duhm (34) attempted to work toward a clearer understanding of the processes involved. Over 1,600 subjects divided into groups of younger children, older mentally retarded children, adolescents and adults were asked to take the Drawing Completion Test. The ways in which lack of attention to the starting sign is expressed show variations from group to group.

The Horn-Hellersberg Test, an important drawing completion technique, has been investigated by Ames and Hellersberg (6) in a normative study of the responses of children. Drawings were analyzed in an effort to determine maturational stages of the normal child in terms of test performances. Seventeen developmental stages are reported and results suggest that the test assumes diagnostic value after the subject's age of nine.

Another study by Hellersberg (57) utilizes the Horn-Hellersberg technique to investigate the subject's relation to reality. The method of analysis and the compilation of results provides opportunity for insights and understanding of the technique.

## EIGHT CARD REDRAWING TECHNIQUE

Research studies on the Eight Card Redrawing Test (8CRT) are limited primarily to the investigations done by the founder of the technique, Leopold Caligor. In an early study, Caligor (26) attempted to use the technique in the determination of the individual's unconscious conception of his own masculinity-femininity identification. Results on this study were compared with those on the Blank Card TAT and MMPI. Criteria used for the M-F identification were age and sex of the person with whom the subjects identified. The basis for these criteria is not clearly established.

In a later study, Caligor (27) investigated the ability of the 8CRT to detect paranoid trends. The eight card sequence was compared with single figure drawings at each end of the sequence. The author reported more identifications made on the No. 1 drawings for the coarctated than for the over-ideational subjects. Supporting Caligor's assumption of increasingly greater depth tapped by continued redrawing, the presence of hostility and paranoid dynamics usually increased on the later drawings. The detection of strong paranoid trends was consistently greater on the 8CRT as a whole, of course, than on drawing No. 8 alone.

Using a multi-item checklist, Caligor (28) in another study, found thirty-three graphic indices which successfully differentiated between normals and hospitalized psychotics. In addition, ten selected items were found to differentiate between psychotic sub-groups. The purpose of this study was to develop a more objective and quantitative method of evaluating the 8 CRT.

## OTHER DRAWING TECHNIQUES

Numerous drawing techniques continue to appear and disappear in clinical practice. Often these techniques do not become sufficiently popularized to stimulate serious research. Clinicians may find them useful while researchers do not become interested or find them awkward to handle experimentally. As a consequence, these techniques are presented with a rationale and some preliminary statistical data. Unfortunately the potentialities of these techniques often go undeveloped because further experimental exploration is not done. Others, fortunately, die a quick death after a short and useless life.

Some preliminary normative data for the Most Unpleasant Concept Test has been supplied by Harrower (56). This technique consists of requesting the subject to draw the most unpleasant thing he can bring to mind. The author presents results of a qualitative analysis of over 500 subjects seeking help for psychological difficulties. Reactions to the task and the content of the drawings are discussed. A control group of 400 normals provide a reference. Harrower indicates a deliberate omission of statistics "to focus attention on the unsatisfactory state of affairs in experimental clinical procedure."

No research on Koch's Tree Test could be located. Koch (72) however, has made an adequate presentation of the technique in European journals. The subject is requested to draw a fruit tree and the level of development of the subject and neurotic regressions are said to be shown in the character of the results. The relationship of this technique to the H-T-P is obvious.

The Draw-an-Animal Test is another technique about which little has been written and practically no research attempted. De Graaf (32) describes an animal identification test which is related to this technique. In the technique described by De Graaf, a book with animal pictures is given to the subject. The subject is asked to tell or write a story about the animal he would like to be for a day. The author has found that identification with aggressive animals such as lions, tigers and elephants is often seen in overtly timid children. The choice of a deer is said to be often made by girls with strong wishes for tenderness and maternal care. The horse is reportedly chosen by subjects with a strong cathexis to their work and rather good personality integration. Experimental verification of these hypotheses at present is lacking.

"Doodling" too has many suggested potentialities for revealing personality dynamics. Research with "doodling" has proved particularly difficult to design. Some information was presented by Auerbach (10) who collected the doodlings of patients during analytical sessions. Associations given spontaneously to them were collected at the end of the hour. Auerbach discusses who doodles, when he will start or stop, and changes in drawings during analysis. Experimental design is not present.

The Family Drawing Technique, rather widely used in clinical practice, is another drawing modification presently with inadequate experimental verification. Hulse (61) presents the findings of eight case studies and eleven drawings. Some clinicians have found this type of study very useful while research oriented psychologists are rather critical.

### FREE DRAWING

The use of free drawings as a method of personality evaluation is a field within itself. In it, of course, is much material related to specific drawing techniques. Free drawing techniques would involve a volume by itself and therefore are beyond the scope of this book. The bibliography listed by Levy (81) in *Projective Psychology* will provide many leads for the interested reader as will the survey provided by Anastasi and Foley (7).

### SUMMARY AND CONCLUSIONS

Experimental techniques have provided much hopeful but not yet conclusive data in regard to the use of drawing techniques as a method of personality evaluation. Conflicting results, as with the Rorschach and TAT, have frequently been found. Much of the existing conflict results from poorly and unrealistically developed experimental design as well as unclear definition of terms and concepts. Particular difficulty has been introduced through faulty criterion groups. The need for a clarification of concepts and rationale can not be overemphasized.

There is strong evidence that no single technique will in itself provide a complete and meaningful picture of the subject's personality. Consequently, experiments designed to test a single technique's ability to do this are unrealistic. Those experiments which have somehow incorporated the use of a test battery or the validation thereof, have yielded hopeful results. Central to the core thesis of drawings as a projective device are the studies by Lehner and Silver (79) indicating that one's own age tends to be projected in drawings; by Hammer (54), employing rapists and pedophiles, suggesting that one's felt or subjective psycho-maturational age tends to be projected; by Lehner and Gunderson (77) finding that the height of the drawing is related to the degree of feelings of bodily adequacy; by Lyons (83) uncovering the correlation between age at which psychic trauma was experienced and height up the Tree trunk a scar is placed; by Kotkov and Goodman (74) demonstrating more "obese" drawings by the more obese subjects; by Berman and Laffel (16) who reported significant correlations between body type of the subject and figure drawn; by Hammer (48) finding significantly more indices of castration anxiety in the drawings made by subjects after sterilization than before they knew of the impending operations; by Barker and Mathis (11) who reported greater hostility toward women in drawings by homosexuals than in drawings by "normals"; by De Martino (33) who found more feminine features in homosexual's drawings of a male person; by Fisher and Fisher (38) who uncovered a relationship between the femininity expressed in female figure drawings of women and their psycho-sexual adjustment; by Hammer (49) who showed H-T-P's to differentiate aggressive from control groups; by Toler and Toler (108) who showed that popular and unpopular children project traits associated with this into their drawings; by Cook (31) who substantiated Machover's definition of the drawing of the head area as reflecting the degree of social dominance of the subject; and by a number of investigators (65, 110, 87, 53, 33) who demonstrated that subjects, when asked to draw a person, tend to draw a person of their own sex.

The usefulness and value of drawing techniques cannot be denied. The need for further research and for a clear understanding of the limitations of the technique can also not be denied. There are obvious dangers in the clinical use of these techniques. If researchers and clinicians put their heads together, not only can these dangers be minimized but the techniques will be enriched and developed so that they may yield their optimum contribution to the understanding of human behavior.

## REFERENCES

1. Abel, T. M.: Figure drawings and facial disfigurement. *Am. J. Orthopsychiat., 23:*253-264, 1953.
2. Ainsworth, M. D.. Some problems of validation of projective techniques. *Brit. J. M. Psychol., 24:*151-161, 1951.
3. Albee, G. W., and Hamlin, R. M.: An investigation of the reliability and and validity of judgments of adjustment inferred from drawings. *J. Clin. Psychol., 5:*389-392, 1949.
4. Albee, G. W., and Hamlin, R. M.: The place of judgment in clinical research. *J. Clin. Psychopath., 11:*174-177, 1950.
5. Albee, G. W., and Hamlin, R. M.: Judgment of adjustment from drawings: The applicability of rating scale method. *J. Clin. Psychol., 6:*363-365, 1950.
6. Ames, L. B., and Hellersberg, E.: The Horn-Hellersberg Test: responses of three to eleven year old children. *Rorschach Res. Exch., 13:*415-432, 1949.
7. Anastasi, A., and Foley, J. P.: A survey of the literature on artistic behavior in the abnormal: I. Historical and theoretical background. *J. Gen. Psychol., 25:*111-142, 1941.
8. Anastasi, A., and Foley, J. P.: An experimental study of the drawing behavior of adult psychotics in comparison with that of a normal control group. *J. Exper. Psychol., 34:*169-194, 1944.
9. Anastasi, A., and Foley, J. P.: Psychiatric selection of flying personnel. V. The human figure drawing test as an objective psychiatric screening aid for student pilots. *USAF Sch. Aviat. Med.,* Project Report, No. 21-37-002 Rep. No. 5 iii 30 p., 1950.
10. Auerbach, J. G.: Psychological observations on "doodling" in neurotics. *J. Nerv. & Ment. Dis., 111:*304-332, 1950.
11. Barker, A. J., Mathis, J. K., and Powers, C. A.: Drawings characteristic of male homosexuals. *J. Clin. Psychol., 9:*185-188, 1953.
12. Bauer, L.: Erfahrungen mit dem Wartegg test auf unserer Kinderstation. *Nervenarzt, 23:*52-55, 1952.
13. Baumgarten, J., and Tramer, M.: *Kinderzeichnungen in vergleichend psychologischer Beleuchtung.* Bern: A Francke, 1952.
14. Beck, H. S.: A study of the applicability of the H-T-P to children with respect to the drawn house. *J. Clin. Psychol., 11:*60-63, 1955.

15. Berman, A. B., Klein, A., and Lippman, A.: Human figure drawings as a projective technique. *J. Gen. Psychol.*, 45:57-70, 1951.

16. Berman, S., and Laffel, J.: Body type and figure drawing. *J. Clin. Psychol.*, 9:368-370, 1953.

17. Bialick, I., and Hamlin, R.: The clinician as judge: details of procedure in judging projective material. *J. Consult. Psychol.*, 18:239-242, 1954.

18. Blum, R.: The validity of the Machover DAP technique. *J. Clin. Psychol.*, 10:121-125, 1954.

19. Boussion, Leroy A.: Dessins en transparence et niveau de developpement. *Enfance*, 3:276-287, 1950.

20. Britton, J. H.: Influence of social class upon performance on the Draw-A-Man Test. *J. Ed. Psychol.*, 45:44-51, 1954.

21. Brown, F.: House-Tree-Person and human figure drawings. In Brower, D., and Abt, L. E., *Progress in Clinical Psychology.* New York, Grune & Stratton, 1952.

22. Buck, J. N.: The H-T-P Test. *J. Clin. Psychol.*, 4:151-159, 1948.

23. Buck, J. N.: The H-T-P technique: a qualitative and quantitive scoring manual. *J. Clin. Psychol.*, Mono. Supplement, 5:1948.

24. Buck, J. N.: The use of the H-T-P test in a case of marital discord. *J. Proj. Tech.*, 14:405-434, 1950.

25. Buck, J. N.: Quality of the quantity of the H-T-P. *J. Clin. Psychol.*, 7: 352-356, 1951.

26. Caligor, L.: Determination of an individual's unconscious conception of his own masculinity-femininity identification. *J. Proj. Tech.*, 15:495-509, 1951.

27. Caligor, L.: The detection of paranoid trends by the Eight Card Redrawing Test. *J. Clin. Psychol.*, 8:397-401, 1952.

28. Caligor, L.: Quantification of the Eight Card Redrawing Test. *J. Clin. Psychol.*, 9:356-361, 1953.

29. Chatlerji, N. N.: Schizophrenic drawings. *Samiksa*, 5:32-41, 1951.

30. Cohn, R.: Role of "body image concept" in pattern of ipsilateral clinical extinction. *Amer. Arch. Neurol. Psychiat.*, 70:503-509, 1953.

31. Cook, M.: A preliminary study of the relationship of differential treatment of male and female headsize in figure drawing to the degree of attribution of the social function of the female. *Psychol. Newsletter*, 34:1-5, 1951.

32. De Graaf, A.: De dieren-identificatie test. *Psychol. Achtergr.*, 14:174-180, 1951.

33. De Martino, M. F.: Human figure drawings by mentally retarded males. *J. Clin. Psychol.*, 10:241-244, 1954.

34. Duhm, E.: Die Bedeutung der Angangszeichen in Wartegg-Zeichen-Test. *Psychol. Rdsch.*, 3:242-252, 1952.

35. Feather, D. B.: An exploratory study in the use of figure drawings in a group situation. *J. Soc. Psychol.*, 37:163-170, 1953.

36. Fisher, L. J.: An investigation of the effectiveness of human figure drawings as a clinical instrument for evaluating personality. Unpublished Ph.D. Dissertation, New York University, 1952.

37. Fisher, S., and Fisher, R.: Test of certain assumptions regarding figure drawing analysis. *J. Abn. soc. Psychol.*, 45:727-732, 1950.

38. Fisher, S., and Fisher, R. L.: Style of sexual adjustment in disturbed women and its expression in figure drawings. J. Psychol., 34:169-179, 1952.

39. Gallese, A. J., Jr., and Spoerl, D. T.: A comparison of Machover and TAT interpretation. J. soc. Psych., 40:73-77, 1954.

40. Gasorek, K.: A study of the consistency and reliability of certain of the formal and structural characteristics of children's drawings. Unpublished Ph.D. Dissertation, Teachers College, Columbia University, 1951.

41. Gehl, R. H., and Kutash, S. B.: Psychiatric aspects of a graphomotor projection technique. Psychiat. Quart., 23:539-547, 1949.

42. Giedt, F. H., and Lehner, G. F.: Assignment of ages on the DAP by male NP patients. J. Personality, 19:440-448, 1951.

43. Granick, S., and Smith, L. J.: Sex sequence in the Draw-A-Person Test and its relation to the MMPI Masculinity-Femininity Scale. J. Consult. Psychol., 17:71-73, 1953.

44. Greenberg, P.: The use of the graphomotor projection test in describing the personality of a group of normal girls. Rev. Psychol., 1:469-494, 1952.

45. Gunzburg, H. C.: Maladjustment as expressed in drawings by subnormal children. Amer. J. Ment. Def., 57:9-23, 1952.

46. Hamlin, R. M.: The clinician as judge: implications of a series of studies. J. Consult. Psychol., 18:233-238, 1954.

47. Hammer, E. F., and Piotrowski, Z.: Hostility as a factor in the clinicians personality as it affects his interpretation of projective drawings. J. Proj. Tech., 17:210-216, 1953.

48. Hammer, E. F.: An investigation of sexual symbolism—a study of H-T-P's of eugenically sterilized subjects. J. Proj. Tech., 17:401-413, 1953.

49. Hammer, E. F.: Frustration-aggression hypothesis extended to socio-racial areas: comparison of Negro and white children's H-T-P's. Psychiat. Quart., 27:597-607, 1953.

50. Hammer, E. F.: The role of the H-T-P in the prognostic battery. J. Clin. Psychol., 9:371-374, 1953.

51. Hammer, E. F.: A comparison of H-T-P's of rapists and pedophiles. J. Proj. Tech., 18:346-354, 1954.

52. Hammer, E. F.: Relationship between diagnosis of psychosexual pathology and the sex of the first drawn person. J. Clin. Psychol., 10:168-170, 1954.

53. Hammer, E. F.: Guide for Qualitative Research with the H-T-P. J. Gen. Psychol., 51:41-60, 1954.

54. Hammer, E. F.: A comparison of H-T-P's of rapists and pedophiles; III the "dead" tree as an index of psychopathology. J. Clin. Psychol., 11:67-69, 1955.

55. Hanvik, L. J.: The Goodenough Test as a measure of intelligence in child psychiatric patients. J. Clin. Psychol., 9:71-72, 1953.

56. Harrower, M. R.: The Most Unpleasant Concept Test; a graphic projective technique. J. Clin. Psychol., 6:213-233, 1950.

57. Hellersberg, E. F.: The individuals relation to reality in our culture; an experimental approach by means of the Horn-Hellersberg Test. Springfield, Thomas, 1950.

58. Holsopple, J. A., and Phelan, J. G.: The skills of clinicians in analysis of projective tests. J. Clin. Psychol., 10:307-320, 1954.

59. Holtzman, W. H.: The examiner as a variable in the Draw-A-Person Test. J. Consult. Psychol., 16:145-148, 1952.

60. Holzberg, J. O., and Wexler, M.: The validity of human form drawings of personality deviation. *J. Proj. Tech., 14:*343-361, 1950.
61. Hulse, W. C.: Childhood conflict expressed through family drawings. *J. Proj. Tech., 16:*66-79, 1952.
62. Hutt, M. L.: Assessment of individual personality by projectives: Current problems. *J. Proj. Tech., 15:*388-393, 1951.
63. Jensen, B. T.: Left-right orientation in profile drawing. *Amer. J. Psychol., 65:*80-83, 1952.
64. Jensen, B. T.: Reading habits and left-right orientation in profile drawings by Japanese children. *Amer. J. Psychol., 65:*306-307, 1952.
65. Jolles, I.: A study of the validity of some hypotheses for the qualitative interpretation of the H-T-P for children of elementary school age. I Sexual identification. *J. Clin. Psychol., 8:*113-118, 1952.
66. Jolles, I.: A study of the validity of some hypotheses for the qualitative interpretation of the H-T-P for children of elementary school age. II. The "phallic" tree as an indicator of psychosexual conflict. *J. Clin. Psychol., 8:* 245-255, 1952.
67. Jolles, I.: A study of the validity of some hypotheses for the qualitative interpretation of H-T-P for children of elementary school age. III. Horizontal placement. *J. Clin. Psychol., 9:*161-164, 1953.
68. Jolles, I.: A study of the validity of some hypotheses for the qualitative interpretation of the H-T-P for children of elementary school age. IV. Vertical placement. *J. Clin. Psych., 9:*164-167, 1953.
69. Kates, S. L., and Harrington, R. W.: Authority figure perspective and aggression in delinquents. *J. Genet. Psychol., 80:*193-210, 1952.
70. Keyes, E. J., and Laffal, J.: The use of a graphomotor projective technique to discriminate between failure and success reactions in a level of aspiration situation. *J. Clin. Psychol., 9:*69-77, 1953.
71. Kinget, G. M.: *The Drawing Completion Test*—a projective technique for the investigation of personality. New York, Grune & Stratton, 1952.
72. Koch, C.: Le test de L'arbre. In Baumgarten, F., *La psychotechnique dans le monde moderne.* Paris, Presses Universitaires de France, 1952.
73. Kotkov, B., and Goodman, M.: The Draw-A-Person Tests of obese women. *J. Clin. Psychol., 9:*362-364, 1953.
74. Kotkov, B., and Goodman, M.: Prediction of trait ranks from Draw-A-Person measurements of obese and nonobese women. *J. Clin. Psychol., 9:* 365-367, 1953.
75. Kutash, S. B.: A new personality test: the graphomotor projection technique. *Trans. N.Y. Acad. Sci., 15:*44-46, 1952.
76. Landisberg, S.: A study of the H-T-P test. *Training School Bull., 44:*140-152, 1947.
77. Lehner, G. F., and Gunderson, E. K.: Reliability of graphic indices in a projective test (DAP). *J. Clin. Psychol., 8:*125-128, 1952.
78. Lehner, G. F., and Gunderson, E. K.: Height relationships in the DAP test. *J. of Personality, 21:*392-399, 1953.
79. Lehner, G. F., and Silver, H.: Age relationships on the Draw-A-Person Test. *J. of Person., 17:*199-209, 1948.
80. Levine, M., and Galenter, E.: A note on the "tree and trauma" interpretation in the H-T-P. *J. Consult. Psychol., 17:*74-75, 1953.

81. Levy, S.: Figure drawing as a projective test. In Abt, L. E., and Bellak, L., *Projective Psychology*. New York, Knopf, 257-297, 1950.
82. Lombroso, C. and Du Camp, M.: L'art nei pazzi. *Arch di Psichiatria Scienze Penali, ed Antrop. Crim.*, 1:333-342, 1880.
83. Lyons, J.: The scar on the H-T-P tree. *J. Clin. Psychol.*, 11:267-270, 1950.
84. MacFarlane, J. W.: Problems of validation inherent in projective methods. *Am. J. Orthopsychiat.*, 12:405-410, 1942.
85. Machover, K.: *Personality Projection in the Drawings of the Human Figure.* Springfield, Thomas, 1949.
86. Machover, K.: Human figure drawings of children. *J. Proj. Tech.*, 17: 85-91, 1953.
87. Mainord, F. B.: A note on the use of figure drawings in the diagnosis of sexual inversion. *J. Clin. Psychol.*, 9:188-189, 1953.
88. Markham, S.: An item analysis of children's drawings of a house. *J. Clin. Psycho.*, 10:185-187, 1954.
89. Michal-Smith, H.: The identification of pathological cerebral function through the H-T-P technique. *J. Clin. Psychol.*, 9:293-295, 1953.
90. Morris, W. W.: Methodological and normative considerations in the use of drawings of the human figure as a projective method. *Am. Psychologist*, 4:267, 1949.
91. Muller-Suur, H.: Psychiatrische Erfahrungen mit dem Wartegg-Zeichentest. *Nervenarzt*, 23:446-450, 1952.
92. Oakley, C. A.: Drawings of a man by adolescents. *Brit. J. Psychol.*, 31: 37-60, 1940.
93. Ochs, E.: Change in Goodenough drawing associations with changes in social adjustment. *J. Clin. Psychol.*, 6:282-284, 1950.
94. Oppenheim, S. and Goldwasser, M. L.: Psychological report on Cyprus psychiatric mission. *J. Proj. Tech.*, 14:245-261, 1950.
95. Precker, J. A.: Painting and drawing in personality assessment. *J. Proj. Tech.*, 14:262-286, 1950.
96. Reichenberg-Hackett, W.: Changes in Goodenough drawings after a gratifying experience. *Am. J. Orthopsychiat.*, 23:501-517, 1953.
97. Rosenzweig, S.: A method of validation by successive clinical predictions. *J. Abnorm. & Soc. Psychol.*, 45:507-509, 1950.
98. Royal, R. E.: Drawing characteristics of neurotic patients using a drawing of a man and a woman technique. *J. Clin. Psychol.*, 5:392-393, 1949.
99. Schmidl-Waehner, T.: Formal criteria for the analysis of children's drawings. *Am. J. Orthopsychiat.*, 2:95-103, 1942.
100. Sells, S. B.: Problems of criteria and validity in diagnosis and therapy. *J. Clin. Psychol.*, 8:23-28, 1952.
101. Sinnett, E. R. and Eglash, A.: The examiner-subject relationship as a variable in the Draw-A-Person Test. Paper read at Midwestern Psychol. Assn., Detroit, May 1950.
102. Sloan, W.: A critical review of H-T-P validation studies. *J. Clin. Psychol.*, 10:143-148, 1954.
103. Smith, E.: A study of sex differentiation in drawings and verbalizations of schizophrenics. *J. Clin. Psychol.*, 5:396-398, 1949.
104. Stonesifer, F. A.: A Goodenough scale evaluation of human figures drawn by schizophrenic and non-psychotic adults. *J. Clin. Psychol.*, 5:396-398, 1949.

105. Swenson, C. H.: Sexual differentiation in the Draw-A-Person test. *J. Clin. Psychol., 11:*37-41, 1955.
106. Swenson, C. H., and Newton, K. R.: The development of sexual differentiation on the Draw-A-Person Test. *J. Clin. Psychol., 11:*417-419, 1955.
107. Takala, M., and Hahkarainen, M.: Über Factorenstruktur und Validität des Wartegg-Zeichentest. *Ann. Acad. Science Finl., 81:*(1) Ser. B, 95, 1953.
108. Toler, A., and Toler, B.: Judgment of children's Popularity from human figure drawings. *J. Proj. Tech., 19:*170-176, 1955.
109. Vernier, C. M.: Current avenue of psychological research in projective techniques. *Quart. Rev. Psychiat. & Neurol., 7:*1-4, 1952.
110. Weider, A. and Noller, P. A.: Objective studies of children's drawings of human figures. I. Sex awareness and socio-economic level. *J. Clin. Psychol., 6:*319-325, 1950.
111. Weider, A., and Noller, P. A.: Objective studies of children's drawings of human figures. II. Sex, age, intellingence. *J. Clin. Psychol., 9:*20-23, 1953.
112. Wexler, M. and Holzberg, J. D.: A further study of the validity of human figure drawings in personality evaluation. *J. Proj. Tech., 16:*249-251, 1952.
113. Whitmyre, J. W.: The significance of artistic excellence in the judgment of adjustment inferred from human figure drawings. *J. Consult. Psychol., 17:*421-424, 1953.
114. Woods, W. A., and Cook, W. E.: Proficiency in drawing and placement of hands in drawings of the human figure. *J. Consult. Psychol., 18:*119-121, 1954.

# PART VI

# PROJECTIVE DRAWING IN A
# PSYCHOTHERAPY SETTING

## CHAPTER 20

## *ART THERAPY: ITS SCOPE AND FUNCTION*

MARGARET NAUMBURG

ANALYTICALLY ORIENTED art therapy deals with the release of the unconscious by means of projected spontaneous images into graphic and plastic expression. Art therapy can be employed either as a primary or an auxiliary form of psychotherapy. It is effective with behavior disorders as well as with neurotic and psychotic patients; it is usable with adults, adolescents or children. Art therapy which was originally applied to the treatment of individual patients, is now, also, beginning to be used as a supplementary technique in analytic group therapy.

Art therapy accepts as fundamental to its treatment methods, the psychoanalytic approach to the psychology of anxiety and guilt feelings, as well as to the psychodynamics of repression, projection, identification, sublimation and condensation. Such mechanisms are as evident in the visual expressions of patients during art therapy as in the verbal expressions of psychoanalytic treatment. Spontaneous graphic or plastic expression is released within the transference relation and is dealt with by means of free association.

The process of art therapy is based on the recognition that man's most fundamental thoughts and feelings, derived from the unconscious, reach expression in images rather than in words. By means of pictorial projection, art therapy encourages a method of symbolic communication between patient and therapist. Its images may, as in psychoanalytic procedures, also deal with the data of dreams, fantasies, daydreams, fears, conflicts and childhood memories. The techniques of art therapy are based on the knowledge that every individual, whether trained or untrained in art, has a latent capacity to project his inner conflicts into visual form. As patients picture such inner experiences, it frequently

[ 511 ]

happens that they become more verbally articulate. Through the use of graphic or plastic expression, those who originally blocked in speech, often begin to verbalize in order to explain their art productions.

In art therapy the patient's unconscious imaged experience is transposed directly into another pictured image. In psychoanalytic treatment such inner visual experiences must be *re*translated from an imaged into a verbal communication. Freud made some penetrating observations on this point and its effect on his patients in his *New Introductory Lectures* (1).

"One experiences them [dreams] predominantly in visual images, feelings may also be interspersed in the dream as well as thoughts; the other senses may also have experiences, but after all, the dream experiences are predominantly pictures. A part of the difficulty of dream telling comes from the fact that we have to transpose these pictures into words. 'I could draw it,' the dreamer says frequently, 'but I don't know how to say it.'"

Although Freud made the modern world aware that the unconscious speaks in images, he did not follow the suggestion of his patients, that they be permitted to draw, rather than to tell their dreams. But art therapy encourages just such an expression of inner experience. Objectified picturization acts then as an immediate symbolic communication which overcomes the difficulties inherent in verbal speech. Another advantage inherent in the making of such pictured projections is that such unconscious forms can more easily escape repression by the censor than verbal expressions, which are more familiar to the patient.

By projecting interior images into exteriorized designs, art therapy crystallizes and fixes in lasting form the recollections of dream or fantasy which would otherwise remain evanescent and might be quickly forgotten. With the help of such a pictured record of inner unconscious experiences, the patient is able to observe and grasp, objectively, changes that have occurred during art therapy.

Among the spontaneous designs released during art therapy, a number are found to have diagnostic as well as therapeutic value. Diagnostically they are useful in two ways: either as imaged patterns of responses typical of the reactions of schizophrenic, paranoid, obsessive-compulsive, severely depressed, alcoholic or other patients; or as transformations in art productions which may serve as an objective index of changes in patients during therapy. (Examples of such diagnostic elements are illustrated in the case study of a schizophrenic girl in the chapter which follows.)

The fundamental difference between projective drawings obtained in psychological tests and those produced in art therapy is that test designs are necessarily prompted and those in art therapy are entirely spontaneous. While certain diagnostic elements in art therapy are comparable to some aspects of projective drawing techniques, the therapeutic techniques of art therapy are related dynamically to the techniques of psychoanalysis.

Analysts, psychiatrists and psychologists have become increasingly aware of the way in which art therapy, whether employed as a primary or auxiliary technique, tends to release deep unconscious material more quickly and, in consequence, helps to speed up the therapeutic process. The reason for this lies in the immediate translation of inner experiences into pictures rather than words.

It is frequently assumed that art therapy is only applicable to those who have already evinced artistic ability. Yet the majority of patients treated successfully by this method have neither drawn or painted before. With artistically inexperienced patients, the approach of art therapy is quite different from that used in treating the professional artist. Patients inexperienced in creative expression must be helped to gain confidence in their capacity to express unconscious thoughts or feelings in spontaneous images. They need to be made aware that the unconscious speaks symbolically in terms of rhythm, color and form. (The various techniques by which such patients can be helped to release fantasies, conflicts and dreams into pictures, are discussed and illustrated in the case study in the next chapter.)

A professional artist is most likely to seek treatment by means of art therapy if his neurosis interferes with his creative work. When attempts are made to obtain spontaneous projections of his unconscious conflicts in pictures, the artist uses his specialized skill to distort or repress unconscious material. It is especially difficult to free an artist from the tyranny of his technical knowledge. When archaic forms begin to break through from his unconscious, during treatment, the artist becomes eager to capitalize, immediately, on this new content for his professional work. He must then be persuaded to postpone the application of such unconscious imagery to conscious work until therapy is completed. In beginning therapy, the artist sometimes fears that the authoritative figure of the therapist may try to control his originality of expression. But with the development of the positive transference, the artist comes to understand that whatever he may be able to express spontaneously, during art therapy, is uniquely his own and may later be employed in any way that he wishes in his professional work.

The art therapist does not usually interpret the spontaneous art of a patient, but rather encourages the patient to discover for himself the meaning of his own productions. Even if a patient does not, at first, understand what a series of his symbolic designs means to him, it is possible, by the use of free association and recovery of the moods or circumstances under which the designs were made, to help him eventually to uncover their inner meaning.

The patient's capacity to verify the meaning of his symbolic expression takes place in art therapy most frequently within the transference relation. When the therapist convinces the patient that he can accept whatever is expressed, the patient *begins to project in images what he dare not put into words.* Such pictorial images can escape the denial of the censor in a way that words cannot. If this happens, the patient is faced with evidence of a concretized image of his conflict projected into consciousness in the shape of his drawing, painting or sculpture. When a forbidden impulse has found such form outside of the patient's psyche, he gains a detachment from his conflict which often enables him to examine his problems with growing objectivity. A patient is thus gradually assisted to recognize that his artistic productions can be treated as a mirror in which he can begin to find his own motives revealed.

The autonomy of the patient is encouraged by his growing ability to contribute to the interpretation of his own creations.

He gradually substitutes a narcissistic cathexis to his own art, for his previous dependence on the therapist.

A number of psychiatrists have observed that the techniques of art therapy help to reduce the length of treatment as well as the complications of the negative transference. Two factors contribute to this: first, the encouragement of the patient to make the interpretation of his own symbolic projections; and second, the patient's narcissistic identification with his own art. As his creations improve and he becomes more convinced of his ability to help actively in the therapeutic process, his ego is thereby strengthened and his dependence on the therapist is proportionately reduced.

Some Freudian analysts and Jungian analytical psychologists impose a particular type of interpretation, consistent with their own special approach, upon the art productions of their patients. In art therapy, however, the patient's spontaneous art is not interpreted by the therapist; the patient is encouraged by various techniques to discover, for himself, what his own unconscious projections may mean. For such art is regarded as symbolic speech (2).

As patients become able to associate to the meaning of their art productions, their own interpretations sometimes confirm a Freudian and at other times a Jungian interpretation of their symbols (3-5).

Freudian analysts generally have not been as interested as Jung and his followers in relating the symbolic art productions of patients to analytic treatment. Those who have, usually interpreted individual pictures in the same way as dreams. Recently some Freudians have become increasingly interested in the art productions of their patients. Evidence of this is to be found in publications by Bychowski (6), Stern (7), Kris (8), and Spitz (9).

In discussing the value of spontaneous art in the treatment of schizophrenics, Ernst Kris writes:

"Creative therapy supplies to the relationship (between patient and therapist) a form of anchorage from which it may swing to more archaic patterns and to which it can safely return. . . . The creative activity of the patient offers marked advantages:

the regressive behavior can be meaningfully channelized, the onslaught of the id loses some of its boundless potential since control tends to be recaptured by the ego, a recapture which takes place in the shaping of the material." (8)

René Spitz also offers an affirmation of the value of the creation of spontaneous art in psychoanalytic treatment, when he says:

"Spontaneous art production, discussed with the analyst, facilitates insight into deeply repressed contents for the patient. We are familiar with the rapidity with which distortion of an interpretation made by the analyst, or of a statement or dream reported by the patient, occurs when repression of present material is at work. Such distortion can be counteracted by art production, for there the patient is faced with the unchanging record made by himself. Another advantage of spontaneous art production is that it works with nonverbal means of communication and thus lends itself to the communication of contents referable to the nonverbal stage and to nonverbal functioning." (9)

Art therapy is still confused with occupational therapy by many in the psychiatric professions, as well as by the lay public. In contrast to art therapy, which is analytically oriented, with emphasis on releasing each patient's unconscious conflicts, occupational therapy is concerned with directing the conscious level of the performance of patients in a group; it depends on a process of technical training in the arts and crafts; it encourages the copying and making of standardized products. The class teaching methods of occupational therapy are unrelated to the psychodynamics of psychoanalytic therapy. Art therapy, on the other hand, bases its methods on releasing spontaneous art expression; it has roots in the transference relation between patient and therapist, and on the encouragement of free association. It is therefore closely allied to psychoanalytic therapy procedures.[1]

---

[1] A number of psychiatrists, psychologists, and analysts have expressed the opinion that a specialized type of graduate work is now needed for training art therapists. Plans for offering an M.A. degree in art therapy are now being developed at a major university. The chief psychiatrist at the medical school of this university has initiated a plan for this new graduate degree. Training in clinical psychiatry in combination with advanced courses in psychology, counseling and

## REFERENCES

1. Freud, Sigmund: *New Introductory Lectures on Psychoanalysis.* (Translated by W. J. H. Sprott.) New York, Norton, 1933.
2. Naumburg, Margaret: Art as symbolic speech. *J. Aesth. & Art. Crit., 13:* No. 4, 1955; also as a chapter in *In The Beginning was the Word: An Enquiry into the Meaning and Function of Language,* Ruth Nanda Anshen, editor. New York, Harper, 1956.
3. Naumburg, Margaret: *Schizophrenic Art; Its Meaning in Psychotherapy.* New York, Grune & Stratton, 1950.
4. Naumburg, Margaret: *Psychoneurotic Art; Its Function in Psychotherapy.* New York, Grune & Stratton, 1953.
5. Naumburg, Margaret: *Studies of the "Free" Art Expression of Behavior Problem Children and Adolescents as a Means of Diagnosis and Therapy.* New York, Grune & Stratton (distributors), 1947.
6. Bychowski, Gustav: The rebirth of a woman. *Psychoanalyt. Rev., 34:*32-57, 1947.
7. Stern, Max M.: Free painting as an auxiliary technique in psychoanalysis, in *Specialized Techniques in Psychotherapy.* G. Bychowski, and J. L. Despert, editors. New York, Basic Books, 1952, pp. 65-83.
8. Kris, Ernst: Schizophrenic art: Its meaning in psychotherapy (book review). *Psychoanalyt. Quart., 22:* No. 1, 1952.
9. Spitz, René: Psychoneurotic art: Its function in psychotherapy (book review). *Psychoanalyt. Quart., 23:* No. 2, 1953.

genuinely creative studio work in the visual and plastic arts are to be included. In order to create such a new degree, this university has to overcome the customary departmental specialization usually found in graduate schools; and it is prepared to combine the resources of several disciplines in preparation for a degree in art therapy. This will enable the future art ɹerapist to be better equipped as a member of a team with psychiatrists and psychologists in psychiatric practice.

## CHAPTER 21

## CASE ILLUSTRATION: ART THERAPY WITH A SEVENTEEN YEAR OLD SCHIZOPHRENIC GIRL

MARGARET NAUMBURG

This PATIENT, Helen, a seventeen-year-old Jewish girl, was treated at the New York Psychiatric Institute. She had been hospitalized for four and one-half months before art therapy was undertaken. The case had been diagnosed as schizophrenia, simple type. As the patient had shown little improvement, ambulatory insulin treatment was begun. The girl then showed some signs of improvement; she became more outgoing and cheerful, but she still held aloof from others.

The mother was the informant about both the patient's and the family history. Only the essential facts of the case will be briefly summarized.

The patient had always been seclusive, day-dreaming and shy. During the last months before admission she became increasingly absorbed in herself; she was found talking to herself and showed paucity of emotion; she became slower in response and more forgetful, and was more careless about her appearance and body care.

The immediate reason for her hospitalization was stealing money from her mother. This had occurred over a period of several months. The girl had used part of the money to give her mother a present, and the rest for books for herself. This incident had been reported by the mother to the New York Hospital, endocrine clinic, where the patient had been under treatment since the age of seven. This clinic had tried in vain, for a long time, to persuade the mother that the patient was in need of

---

[1] This paper was presented at a meeting of the Association for the Advancement of Psychotherapy, New York City, December 9, 1955, and at the International Congress of Psychiatry, Zurich, September, 1957.

psychiatric treatment. Only the theft of the money had persuaded the mother to bring the girl to the Psychiatric Institute. The patient had been under treatment for ten years at the endocrine clinic; such treatment was related to the girl's history of multi-glandular disturbance with a precocious menstruation which began at six years; there was also a premature growth and maturity of bones, and the development of numerous nevi.

## FAMILY AND PERSONAL HISTORY

The patient's father, a lawyer, was described by his wife as quiet, serious-minded, withdrawn and indifferent; neither very sociable nor friendly. The mother had worked as a secretary before marriage. The marriage, she stated, was a happy one, and she herself was of an active and easy-going disposition.

The psychiatrist's impression of the mother was the following: "The mother seems to be the decisive influence on the patient's life; she is an attractive, middle-aged woman who (contrary to her own description of herself) makes a rather high-strung and nervous impression. There is a deep conflict between the mother and daughter. It seems impossible for the mother to accept a daughter whose personality make-up is so entirely different from her own and who does not fulfill any of her social ambitions and wishes. There is evidence of sibling rivalry, with the patient showing strong feelings of being pushed out of her mother's life by her twin brothers, who are eleven years younger."

Throughout the patient's childhood and adolescence, the mother overemphasized the girl's physical condition and handicaps and dragged her through all kinds of corrective and curative treatments. In addition, she tried to change the daughter's whole personality by nagging, pushing and never-ending supervision. This led to resentment on the patient's part. There was a continuing struggle against the mother which made it impossible for the daughter to develop her independence and grow up. There are two siblings, a pair of four-year-old non-identical twins; the mother described them as of normal development in spite of the fact that one stuttered and the other one talked baby talk.

There was no history of nervous or mental disease in the family, except for one uncle, who was an epileptic.

Helen was born a year after the marriage. The mother had a normal pregnancy and a spontaneous and normal delivery. The child was breast-fed for five months; she was never a feeding problem and gained weight properly. She started to walk when she was fifteen months, did not do much talking until she was past two years of age. There was early toilet training, no enuresis and no early neurotic manifestations. Her eating and sleeping habits were normal. She was very neat and particular and easy to manage during this period. She was not a very active child and liked to stay by herself. She went to kindergarten, but had few playmates at either kindergarten or school. The mother stated that Helen was always somewhat tense and easily upset.

The patient had the usual childhood diseases. She went through many operations as a child. These included tonsillectomy, the removal of a tumor of the right arm before she was six, amputation of the tip of one toe due to infection, a mastoid and several corrective orthodontic operations. The child, according to the mother, was always very patient and uncomplaining and stood all these operations well. (Some of these traumatic experiences break through in the girl's pictures.) She also developed numerous pigmented nevi which were removed at various times. Her whole childhood was disturbed through a precocious menstruation beginning at the age of six.

The patient was a good pupil, well-liked by the teachers; but she was very shy and did not mingle well with other children. She seemed wrapped up in herself, never listened to anybody, and talked to herself. When asked questions, the patient would answer something irrelevant. She showed no particular affection for either of her parents, but seemed fond of her brothers. The father treated her with complete indifference. The patient did things well under supervision. Her chief hobby was arts and crafts. But for this she showed no originality and copied patterns from books.

## PSYCHOLOGICAL MAKE-UP AND ETIOLOGICAL FACTORS

The patient's psychological make-up from early childhood appears to have been schizoid. She was always shy, withdrawn, preoccupied and absorbed in day-dreams. She did not mingle well and was not very active. She had the physical appearance of a wizened old woman.

*Psychiatrist's Differential Diagnosis and Prognosis (after four months)*

Patient shows typical features of schizophrenia: withdrawn; asocial behavior; interference of thinking with some evidence of intellectual deterioration; mannerisms; symbolic language, and excessive day-dreaming. Except for signs of tenseness and irritability, with a silghtly depressive tinge, her emotional reactions are flat. Though her history has some features of inappropriate behavior this was not confirmed during this period of hospitalization and though she might develop into the hebephrenic type, at present she should be classified as a case of simple schizophrenia.

The prognosis depends on the cooperation of the patient's mother, and the possibility of changing the mother's attitude and bringing her to a real understanding of the situation. (The mother, however, continued to be hostile and intolerant of the patient's responses, always blaming her for her failure to be the kind of social and attractive daughter that she, the mother, demanded.)

*Psychometric Tests*

The patient appeared to be, basically, at least, of high average intelligence, although at the time of the test, at the age of sixteen years and ten months, she was considered to be functioning below her capacity. The patient showed an attention defect as well as an impairment in judgment.

The girl's Goodenough drawings were rather immature, especially her drawing of a man. (The rather "silly" face described is reminiscent of later drawings made in the art therapy sessions.) The figure of the woman showed a better concept with its narrow waistline and flowing skirt. . . . The figure seemed like that of an older person not a young girl. Both figures were small and rather rigid and the treatment of the fingers raises the suspicion of masturbatory activities.

*Rorschach Interpretation*

The Rorschach interpretation of the patient, administered when she was at the age of sixteen years, ten months, was analyzed "blind" by Dr. Zygmunt A. Piotrowski.

Dr. Piotrowski offered two points in his Diagnostic Impression: (1) that the patient seems to be schizophrenic; (2) that the Rorschach record reveals that the patient is sometimes intellectually confused and is little disturbed over it. He added the following summary of personality traits as revealed by the patient's Rorschach Test: (3) There is a strong drive for achievement but its effectiveness is small because of intellectual difficulties and carelessness. (4) The patient produces her ideas quickly, caring little for accuracy. If she discovers an error in her thinking, she tries to change the idea (producing another odd effect) rather than bringing it into closer agreement with reality. (5) There is much preoccupation with her own inner life. The patient would like to be conspicuously successful in life. (6) There is capacity for direct emotional response to environment changes but this response is usually superficial and about the same, no matter what the situation. (7) There is a definite tendency to intermittent depressive moods. (8) The patient tends to become irritated when she is thwarted in her free self-expression and urged to take cognizance of reality. Few of her responses are under the control of rational thinking. (9) The patient seems to be preoccupied with anal and sexual symbols, suggesting a compulsive-obsessive personality make-up. There may be a good deal of confusion concerning sex and the differences between male and female sex functions. (10) There is a rather mild neurotic element which appears secondary to the apparent schizophrenic personality changes.

## THE ART THERAPY SESSIONS

This study was a part of the research project on the application of art therapy to schizophrenia conducted by the writer at the New York State Psychiatric Institute.[2]

The art therapy sessions began with this patient after three and a half months of hospitalization. The girl produced forty-three pictures in the course of the twenty-eight sessions. Some of these designs were made in the presence of the therapist, while many were made on the ward. Stereotyped patterns of folk art were usually copied from books during occupational therapy, but these are not illustrated. The pictures shown are described in the order in which they were made by the patient.

It was extremely difficult to overcome the girl's attitude that

---

[2] Two of these studies have been previously published in the writer's book, *Schizophrenic Art: Its Meaning in Psychotherapy* (New York, Grune & Stratton, 1950).

paints and chalks were to be used only for copying and tracing. What increased the difficulty in freeing the patient's spontaneous expression was her fear of the mother's disapproval of all pictures except saccharine landscapes or pretty place cards for her mother's parties. In the art therapy sessions the girl began, for the first time, to express her repressed emotions. As her spontaneous designs developed, she became increasingly articulate.

Dr. Piotrowski, who discussed this paper when it was presented recently, emphasized that the extent of this patient's ability to express her emotional conflicts, in both pictures and words, during the art therapy sessions, was in marked contrast to her otherwise limited responses in relation to the hospital personnel and other patients.

1. **Washroom Scene on the Ward** *(Drawn two weeks prior to art therapy sessions)*

This vivid and somewhat obscene drawing of a washroom in the hospital is a surprisingly accurate reproduction of the actual setting. The drawing shows a lively and humorous scene, with two girls at the wash basins and two on the toilets. Helen had shown this sketch to her psychiatrist and expressed amusement and satisfaction at having made this picture.

Figure 1

Figure 2

## 2. *"Saturday Morning Blues" (First art therapy session)*

The patient was timid and insecure when she entered the room. But was quite pleased with the copies of illustrations that she showed the therapist. She was encouraged to try out the colored chalks on a sheet of paper.

She began talking about how before the Occupational Therapy sessions on Saturday, she always had the Saturday morning blues. She was asked whether she would like to try to make a picture of this mood. This was a surprising and new idea to the patient and she hesitated to try, saying that she was afraid that she could not do it.

To encourage her, she was urged to forget about the picture and just pick out the colors to fit such a mood. She chose purple, violet, blue and grey. Then she drew a table and a figure standing before it. The eyebrows are purple, the face bright, the sky blue. When asked about the forms floating in the space, a tree, etc., she said these were things that come to her mind as she tries to think of what to do. When asked about the only figure in the picture, she admitted that it was herself.

## 3. *"Happy and An Unhappy State"*

When again she had no ideas of her own, she was asked if she could express other moods in pictures, like a happy or unhappy state. She then drew this picture with a large sun in its center. Asked to explain it, she said that the upper side of the sun in a blue sky represented a happy state and that in the lower right corner, the dark brown color represented an unhappy state. The sun was in the middle.

## 4. *"Anguish"*

This drawing of "Anguish" was produced after the girl had been asked whether she would care to try to express in a picture some feeling that she had experienced. To illustrate, it was suggested that emotions such as fear or anguish or anxiety and many other feelings could be made into pictures. The idea was new to the patient, but she said she would try to make a picture of "Anguish." For this design, she picked out brown, rose, grey and yellow-green chalks. The successive rhythmic forms which she drew began in the lower part of the paper, rose upwards and then bent over on themselves. The colors used by the

Figure 3

Figure 4

girl were muted and delicate. The patient's growing interest in her ability to express emotions for the first time in pictures, led to the therapist's offer of paper for making more such drawings on the ward. She was assured that many professional painters liked to do moods. She did not want to risk doing this, because "Everyone would laugh at me, if I made such pictures on the ward." Asked what kind she usually made there, she said "Illustrated stories." The therapist expressed interest in seeing her art work and assured her that any designs about moods and feelings could, if she preferred, be limited to the art therapy sessions.

## 5. *"Fear"*

This design was one of several brought by the patient to the second session. She was unable to put into words what the picture of "Fear" meant to her. But the small child watched by the great threatening eye is undoubtedly herself. (She later drew several other pictures of a little girl, which she was able to identify as herself.) In all these drawings, the child had golden hair; her own is actually a dull mouse color. Some months later, in relation to another portrait of herself as a little girl, she explained why the hair was golden: Her mother, she said, still had one of her childhood locks, which was that lovely color.

A curious distortion in this picture is a second smaller eye, drawn as one of the child's feet. No reference was made to its special significance by the patient. Two other drawings, one called "Dout" (No. 18) (misspelled for "Doubt"), and the other "Desire" (No. 19), bring in eyes to express fear and threat. These and a number of other designs which will be discussed later illustrate a number of typical aspects of schizophrenic art.

### 6. "Duty"

This too was a design drawn on the ward. No explanations were given by the patient, but we know enough of her patience in enduring much she was expected to accept, especially in terms of many operations. It is noteworthy that this is the first drawing which suggests emphasis on the mouth and huge teeth. Two other pictures drawn much later express the traumatic effect of several orthodontic operations.

### 7. "Death"

At the second session, the patient showed no hesitation but

Figure 5

Figure 6

went eagerly to work on a picture, which she named "Death." Asked about the meaning of this design, she said, "The head in the center is a skull; the house to the right is Life, with its sensations expressed by the eye, mouth and ear. The color, bright blue (at the upper left) is the question of what happens after death. I hope it is something positive." Asked what the brown oblong on the front of the skull stood for, she said, "It's a coffin; the slanting black and red lines over the coffin represent a wound."

Questioning revealed that the sudden death of a distant cousin had stimulated this design. But the girl showed no emotional reaction to that event. When asked whether anyone more closely related to her had died, she said, "My grandfather." She was asked if his death had upset her. "No," she said. "I felt more upset about the death of my kitten, which my brother sat on by mistake and killed. Then we got another kitten which was wild and fierce. Oh," she added, spontaneously. "I'll make a picture of the way I feel about that new kitten."

It is interesting that the mother had reported this incident to the social worker, in order to complain about her daughter's lack of feeling for the grandfather, but that she wept about the

Figure 7

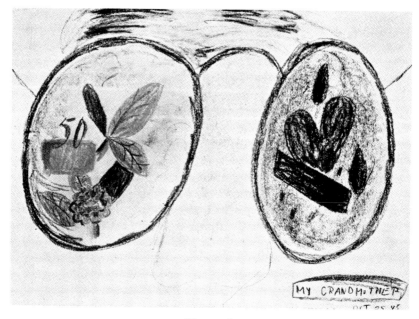

Figure 8

dead kitten. She missed the point that the girl had lost the only creature in the world that she loved.

## 8. "My Grandmother" (Drawn on the ward)

This design, brought in to the third session, was made on the ward, drawn four days after the picture of "Death" (No. 7). It too deals in one part of the drawing with the theme of death; but the death, here symbolized, is that of the grandfather. The entire picture was labelled "Grandmother" by the patient. It is a drawing of the grandmother's nose, wearing a pair of glasses. The girl explained the meaning of the symbols in each lens. About the left lens she said, "The number 50 and the golden leaves represent the golden anniversary of my grandparents last year." (This golden leaf pattern had been adapted from a similar design she had copied from a book.) Pointing to the other lens, the girl said, "That is my grandmother today. The brown coffin stands for my grandfather, who died after the golden wedding. Near it is my grandmother's gray heart; there are tears and red blood drops falling from the broken heart."

This is an interesting example of two schizophrenic mechanisms; the way in which an idea can be expressed in the condensation of a group of connected symbols, and the way the use of a part (the grandmother's glasses) are made to stand for the grandmother. Here, we see how the patient has dramatized her own impressions of the grandparents' golden wedding and the grandfather's death.

### 9. *"Pusy" (Misspelled for "Pussy")*

As the patient dashed in the lines to express the fierceness of the new kitten, she kept up a running commentary: "Claws red, eyes green, tail up in the air. Ready to snap and bite at the slightest thing." Standing before the completed cat, the girl said seriously, "It's not the way a pussy should be, the other one was cute. This one looks the same as the other kitten. I wonder. . . ."

**The Patient Releases Aggression Against the Wild Kitten and Her Own Family.** When shown how to spray fixatif in a flit gun, in order to set the chalk on the cat picture, she laughed aloud as she did it. "It looks as if I might be shooting the cat," she said. "Do you ever feel like having a shot at someone else?"

Figure 9

Figure 10

she was asked. "Oh, brother," she replied, "at lots of others." 'Would you like to use the flit-gun on your brothers?" To this she replied, "Sometimes on my Mother and Father, too." She was encouraged to make pictures about such feelings. "You'd have quite a gallery," she laughed. Now she is able to openly express her hostility, for the first time, against her parents and to enjoy the release.

This swiftly drawn impression of a wild cat has a single red claw, and a boldly upturned tail, attached directly to the neck of the animal. There is no body, yet there is a successful expression of "catness" as well as the wildness of this particular creature.

The use of dissociated parts to express the whole cat and its special nature shows another typical example of schizophrenic response elements.

### 10. "How I Feel About My Mother"

This picture was drawn following a previous session when the patient expressed her resentment about her mother; it was then suggested to her that she try to bring out this emotion, if possible, in a picture. This is how she interpreted the picture. "The mask to the left, that's Mother's face. The dark-reddish-brown, stick-like projection (to the right of the mother), that's the way she tries to run everybody. The broom (yellow and red, behind the pushing rod), that's how she keeps everything clean. The green plate (behind the broom), that's how she tries to make my brothers eat. Black outline figure (upper left), that's how my mother rushes about. Envelope (lower right), a letter, Mother is always being social."

On looking at the picture in the next session, the patient remarked, "My, I hope my mother doesn't see this." Of this she was assured by the therapist.

## 11. *"One of My Twin Brothers, My Mother and Myself"*

This is the way the patient described her picture: "I represented Freddy (one of the four-year-old twin brothers) as a pile of falling plates because of his refusal to eat. The eye is me looking at him. He is held on to my mother by a string. The stick is my mother, and from the stick drop tears. (The brown stick is the same symbol of the mother as in the previous pic-

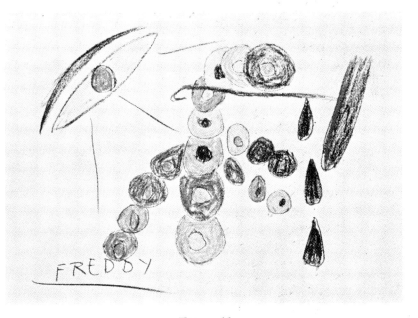

Figure 11

Figure 12

ture.) I've never gone home weekends and not heard one of the twins crying." (Teardrops express this.)

"The bright colors on the plates, that's the brightness and happiness of youth; he's only four years old. That's supposed to be happiness of youth, but I'm beginning to wonder. . . ."

Here the girl repeats the stick as the symbol of the mother's nagging ways, while she symbolizes herself by an eye which watches the family scene. The patient's comment as she finished the picture was, "When I was small, Mother and I were close to each other; but all that changed after the birth of my twin brothers. They were born when I was twelve."

The form of the brother in this design uses the symbol of the green plate, already shown in the previous drawing of the mother. Here the brother's form is made up of a series of circular plates, to represent head, body and limbs, in the way that the jointed wooden dolls are made for babies.

She added that she was more like her father, who was quiet. He was a lawyer. Her parents had been fond of walking and went on long hikes Sundays. And sometimes, when she was smaller, they took her with them on some of the shorter walks. But since the boys were born, her mother didn't go walking. And her father still went hiking, but with a club.

Again, in the picture of the mother and of the twin brother, we have the patient's typically schizophrenic designs; parts are used symbolically to represent a person or an idea; there is also excessive fragmentation shown, in the parts for characterizing the mother; and symbolic abstraction is shown in the way the patient symbolizes herself by the large eye which looks on at the behavior of the mother and twin brother.

## 12. "War, Peace and Sickness"

This and the following designs were made on the ward and brought to the third session.

Questioned as to the meaning of the various parts of this picture, she said, the balls (upper left) are "sickness. The orange lines to the left are men, soldiers. The black and purple are the fire of war." The large yellow and green head, center left, is

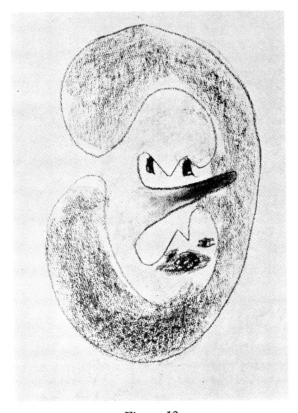

Figure 13

Figure 14

"one who starts war. I was thinking of Hitler," she added, "but it certainly doesn't look like him." The center of the picture, she said, represented "Peace, with sun, trees and water; it's spring." "At the right is the fire and pain and the bravery of the men; the red lines are wounds, more pain; blue tears are heartbreak. The deep red is blood for the wound; the orange lines, more men."

### 13. "Man with Hay Fever": Funny Face (Scribble)

This was one of five drawings made during the previous week on the ward. "I had a cold the day I did this. The man in this picture has a sore nose." This is one of the girl's many grotesque faces, of which the mother disapproved and which she tried to suppress. In such caricatures, the girl was able to release resentment against the mother's unreasonable demands, whether for social graces from her gauche and unattractive daughter, or for the creation of pretty place cards or imitative landscapes.

### First Attempt to Use the "Scribble" Technique

At the sixth session the patient could think of nothing to

draw. She was therefore shown how to experiment with the "scribble" technique. This consists of making a free-flowing continuous zig-zag line which criss-crosses a large piece of paper in unpremeditated ways. As in the use of the Rorschach blots, the patient was asked to discover the suggestion of some object, creature or scene which could then be elaborated.

The girl seemed unwilling at first to try this new approach. "You can't," she argued, "draw if you didn't know what you wanted to do." But soon she became interested in trying it. Her first attempts were extremely simple. The first, "A Bird," is not shown, nor is the next one of "A Flower." Here she began with an original scribble outline and then formed it into a flower, later adding the stamens.

### 14. A Snake

In this picture, supposed to be begun as an unconscious "scribble," there is evidence of a certain controlled idea being directed by the patient. For there are no signs of any accidental or haphazard lines. She was still afraid to allow the unconscious to break through freely.

Figure 15a

Figure 15b

*15a.  Rabbit (Scribble)*
*15b.  "Rabbit" (Second, conscious attempt)*

The patient felt that her first attempt to get a rabbit out of a scribble did not look like one. It made her willing, after this scribble release, to improve upon it by drawing this free design, in which she succeeded in making this rabbit-like picture. She then added red eyes, pink ears and a brown and white body. Here was another of an increasing number of spontaneous efforts by the girl to draw without depending, as formerly, on copying from books.

While at work, she remarked, "Wouldn't it be funny if this turned out to look like a rabbit?" "Did you ever want a rabbit?" she was asked. "Yes, when I was little, I went to a hospital and saw a big white rabbit. I never had one." Here again, as in her pictures of fairy tales and toys, the patient preferred to live in her fantasy world of childhood rather than to accept the immediate experiences of adolescence.

"I saw some little baby rabbits with pink noses, all fluffy like balls, last year," she explained as she drew. "Oh, that reminds me, a pink nose," and she went back to her picture to add pink chalk for the rabbit's nose. She seemed skeptical of the approval given to her about this quite spontaneous picture. But when her drawing was finished, she said with genuine surprise, "Why, it really looks like a rabbit!"

In order to encourage her growing freedom of expression, she was reminded of how helpful the "scribble" technique had been in freeing her. She was, therefore, urged to use it more often. Again she remarked, "But Mother would think these pictures were awful. I would never do any like these at home." She was urged, therefore, only to make such drawings at art therapy sessions or on the hospital ward.

### Conference With the Patient's Psychiatrist About the Mother

The psychiatrist, like the art therapist, had come to feel rather hopeless about modifying the mother's attitude to the

Figure 16

Figure 17

daughter. The girl had reported that the mother hid from her friends the fact that her daughter was at a mental hospital. On weekends, when the girl was at home, she was expected to pretend to the guests, so she preferred to hide in her room, until it was time for her to be spirited back to the hospital.

### 16. "A Wave and Seashore" (Scribble done on the ward)

The original "scribble," drawn in the ninth session, led the patient to develop the large wave. She then decided to add the ship passing through the wave and the scene on the shore. This is a good example of how, by beginning with an image suggested by the "scribble" itself, other imaginative elements can be developed in a picture.

### 17. "Embryo" (Scribble made on ward)

This embryo "scribble" design is the first direct reference to sex offered by the patient. When asked why she had titled it "Embryo," she laughed, self-consciously, and answered, "Why it's just an embryo." This gave the therapist an opening to ask the girl what she knew about birth and sex. She spoke of the way the "sperm" entered the uterus of a woman and told that the baby grew inside of her and then came out. As she spoke,

the patient seemed tremulous and disturbed. Questioning uncovered the fact that the girl's use of the word "sperm" was
derived from a recent talk with the psychiatrist on the subject
of sex and birth.

When asked, in connection with this embryo drawing, what
she knew about sex, the girl shrank back and exclaimed, "I
just can't take it," referring to the nature of the sexual act. An
attempt was then made to deal with the source of the patient's
anxiety.

The patient then spoke of a traumatic experience which had
occurred some years before, when she was going to a Girl Scout
meeting. A man had exposed himself in the subway and she
had been frightened and had run away. It was then suggested
to the girl that her "not being able 'to take it' " about sex information had perhaps been connected with this early fright. "I don't
remember that," she said.

From the unconscious projection of the "Embryo" design it
became possible to obtain, for the first time, some of the patient's free associations about sex.

**Patient's Precocious Menstruation Introduced by the Therapist**

For the first time, the therapist introduced the subject of the
patient's early menses as probably adding to her difficulty in
accepting information about sex and birth. She replied that at
the time of her first menstrual period, her mother told her what
to do and she had thought that other girls had it, also, at that
same age. Only much later did she find out that her periods
came sooner than those of other girls. This was probably (because of precocious menses) a severe trauma for this girl, at the
early age of six.

### Patient's Wish For a Boy Friend

The girl had recently asked the psychiatrist, rather pathetically, whether some day she might have a boy friend. She had
referred to the fact that she never got any new clothes, but only
"hand-me-downs" from relatives. In her fantasies she is frequently a beautiful princess robed in magnificent garments.
The mother's disappointment in having an unattractive and,
from her point of view, inadequate daughter, unable to satisfy
her social ambitions, led the mother to ignore the girl's needs on
all levels.

Figure 18

The patient was now working more, spontaneously, by her-self. To this tenth session, she brought four quite free and original designs. Two of these are illustrated; she called them "Ghost," "Dout," and "Desire." The first two were made from "scribbles." She had nothing to tell about the ghost picture, which is not shown.

### 18. "Dout" (Misspelled for "Doubt")

This picture (with its misspelled title) was said by the pa-tient to concern "fear" and "suspicion." Pointing to the bent figure in the lower left corner, the girl said it shows "Man is a question mark." This figure is poised over a large eye. She ex-plains the tree at the right by stating, "There's doubt, it's not sure that it's going up to the sky." The girl then pointed to the black outline figure (upper center) beside the large green eye with a red center. "It's fear," she interpreted, "running away from the eye." She then explained that the two black outline figures, facing each other in the center stood for "suspicion."

As the patient did not relate how this picture of "Dout" ap-plied to herself, she was reminded that such a drawing might have a personal as well as general significance. She was then asked what her own doubts might be. "I'm afraid," she answered, "that I won't be able to do things myself." She was reminded that part of her insecurity was due to the way her mother had criticized her at home, and that, as she had now begun to discover, she was finding herself able to do many things quite well, on her own initiative.

The patient then referred again to her early childhood. She recalled how much happier she had been at home before the two boys were born; before that she emphasized that she had been the center of attention with her parents. Things changed, however, she explained, after the birth of the twins, for they now received all the attention and she was ignored. The family had then to move to a larger apartment, so that she could not stay to graduate with her own friends at school. She used this recollection as an example of how her needs were ignored for those of her twin brothers.

### 19. "Desire"

The patient offered no explanation of the meaning of her drawing of "Desire" when she brought it to the tenth session. Only when the therapist pointed to each element in the design, did she explain its significance. "The two hands," she said, "are

Figure 19

Figure 20

reaching up to the forbidden fruit, the apple." Asked what the two different hands meant, she continued, "The red, black and green hand (to the right) is going after the fruit. The pink hand (to the left) is a baby's hand. The large blue eye (lower left behind the baby hand) is the eye of the person looking at the apple." Of her own accord the patient added that "The eyes (in the upper left hand corner) are looking down and some say 'Do' and some say 'Don't.' The yellow-green eye expresses jealousy." (It is interesting to note that there are six eyes in this grouping of eyes, and some are paired according to color and others are not.) Asked about the arrows, the girl said, "The black arrows point two ways, toward the fruit and away from it." It is obvious, therefore, that these arrows tell us that the patient is in conflict as to whether or not she should seize the fruit.

As this symbolic design seemed charged with significance to the patient in ways that she had not yet been able to express, she was again shown this drawing at the next session. Pointing to the two hands, the girl was asked for an elaboration of their meaning to her. The dark hand to the right, she described as "a claw." She was reminded that she had, at the previous session, called the pink hand to the left "a baby hand." She was not ready to say more. She was therefore asked whether the "baby hand" might not represent that part of herself which did not wish to grow up. She smiled with embarrassment at the question, but readily admitted "I guess you're right."

This recognition by the patient of her recurrent wish to cling to an infantile state was now reviewed in relation to what she had already admitted about being displaced in her mother's affection by the birth of her twin brothers. It was emphasized that in this picture with its "baby hand" as well as in her fondness for childish toys, daydreams and fairy tales, she was expressing her wish to

Figure 21

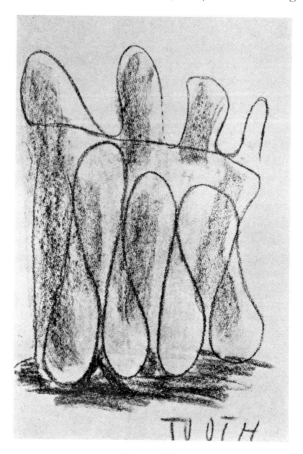

Figure 22a

be a little girl again. She replied to this rather wistfully, "Do I have to give up fairy tales?" The therapist responded to her pathetic plea, explaining that the issue was not whether or not to give up fairy tales, but to come to understand *why* she liked such tales and toys at her present age. She was also reminded that another side of her more mature self was beginning to express a wish to grow up and have boy friends. She could not have those other things in life without making some effort toward getting them for herself. She was also reminded about the need of taking greater personal care of her appearance if she wanted people to notice her; and of not hiding away in a corner at a party, but trying to talk to the people she met, especially the boys.

The patient brought four drawings made from "scribbles" to the eleventh session. Three of these will be considered:

### 20. *"Monkey Shines"*

The basic form on which the patient developed what she described as a monkey, again suggests the basic pattern of her previous "Embryo" (No. 17) design. The shape of the creature recalls a fetal rather than a monkey form. The girl's first remark as she showed this drawing was to say, "It seems like a clown. But it reminds me of a monkey." Then, jokingly, she gave it the title of "Monkey Shines." Her self-conscious behavior suggested that she saw but wished to avoid any possible sexual associations to an embryonic form. Quickly, the patient said, as she pointed to the yellow form in the monkey's paw, 'Yes, I drew that banana after I had added the monkey's arm." Because of the girl's defensive behavior, no attempt was made at this time to relate this design to her previous drawing of a fetal form.

### 21. *"Prehistoric Animal"*

This creature, also derived from a scribble, was related to the patient's recent trip to the Natural History Museum, where she

Figure 22b

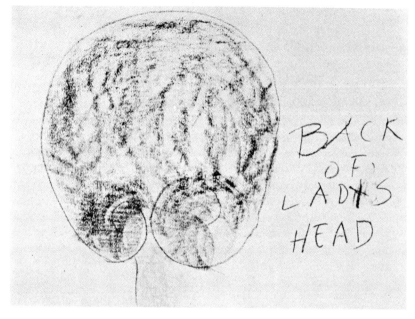

BACK
OF
LADY'S
HEAD

Figure 23

had seen such animals. It is developed with a growing freshness in the use of the colored chalks and the development of design.

### 22a. "Tooth": Expression of Early Traumatic Experiences

There is an expression of grim intensity and violence in this drawing of a huge tooth which rests against a bloody red gum. Without knowledge of this patient's many orthodontic operations as a child, this picture would, in its distortion of form and color, have suggested to any trained observer the effect of some severe traumatic experience.

The girl, when she showed this drawing, offered no spontaneous interpretation of its significance to her. When asked what relation this "Tooth" picture might have to herself, she spoke of the difficulty that she had had with her teeth as a child; she recalled how she was forced to wear a plate for years, and that this had to be adjusted frequently. Now, she added, "I have to wear a bridge." But she was unable to recollect, when questioned, any painful experiences relating to those many orthodontic operations of her childhood. She did, however, recall that both her mother and the dentist had frightened her, when she was small, by saying that if she did not brush her teeth she might lose them. Such fears, she added, were related to those dreams she used to have in which her teeth fell out.

**22b. "Smile" (Drawn on the ward from a scribble)**

This design, although drawn three weeks after the previous picture of "Tooth," is so closely related to the same traumatic experiences of childhood that it is placed here for comparison. For, in this drawing, the memories of those painful and forgotten orthodontic operations of childhood are again released. The "Smile," derived from a scribble, was begun with a central wavy tooth pattern, suggestive of the previous "Tooth" design. In the present picture redness emphasizes the lip formation of the mouth; in the "Tooth" it is, however, the gums that are so red. In this design, the patient invites no pleasurable response from the observer; but projects, instead, an impact that is both grim and painful from her "Smile."

**23. "The Back of Lady's Head"**

This picture was the only one made during the session, after the other pictures, drawn on the ward, had been shown and dis-

Figure 24

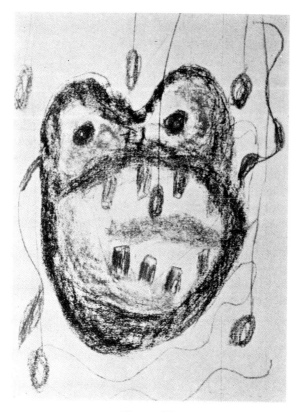

Figure 25a

cussed. The patient began it with a curving form completed in two loops, similar to the "Embryo" and "Monkey Shines" scribbles. It was not possible to judge whether this original shape suggested the picture that evolved from it or whether the girl made this coiled form in order to create the resultant picture, which she later named "The Back of Lady's Head."

As the patient was developing her picture, she said to the therapist, "It's a scream! Wait till you see it." After printing the title, "Back of a Lady's Head," she remarked pointedly, as she smiled, "Did you ever look in the mirror?" The therapist laughed in response to this oblique reference to the way she arranged her hair in double coils. Drawing the *back* of the therapist's head was as far as the patient dared go, as yet, in expressing her growing, positive transference to the therapist.

## 24. "Sea Anemone" (Scribble)

This design, derived from a scribble, was made on the ward and brought to the twelfth session. It has a warmth and freshness of expression in the way the blue violet and purplish tones of the chalks are used. One can see how the twisting central form was the original scribble and how the patient added the stemlike lower part to the anemone shape, and then developed the water movement in wavy cross-lines. The picture shows an increasing release of imaginative expression and a much freer use of color.

## 25a. "Mask of Laughter"

In the twelfth session the patient drew three masks, only the first of these was derived from a "scribble." Following the pattern

Figure 25b

Figure 25c

that the patient discovered within the chance lines of the original scribble, she developed the mask idea in a sideways position. When asked what this design represented, she said, "Laughter, but it doesn't look very much like it. I can't make it go right."

When the therapist asked what the round suspended forms represented, the girl replied, "They're like small hanging balloons. They're the things that tickled him and made him laugh."

### 25b. Second Mask of Laughter

As the patient seemed dissatisfied with her picture, the therapist asked whether she wished to make it again. She responded eagerly to this suggestion and drew a second mask of "Laughter" in a free hand design. She laughed aloud as she was drawing the vast open mouth in this mask, and commented, "It looks like the mouth of a mother calling her child." After saying this, she illustrated her meaning by opening wide her own mouth and shouting "John" to an imaginary child. She gave no further explanation of this mask, until she was asked what the two pinkish forms at the base of the mask represented. The first one, she said, "Is a feather that someone used to tickle his funny-bone to make him laugh. The other (triangular shape) is his funny-bone."

### 25c. "Mask of Unhappiness"

The third mask, the patient said was "Unhappiness." As in the two previous masks of "Happiness" the large mouth is the outstanding feature. In the first and third mask, there is the patient's emphasis on huge and jagged teeth. These three masks seem to emphasize, as did her previous "Tooth" (No. 22a) and "Smile" (No. 22b) drawings, her deeply repressed suffering in the many orthodontic operations she experienced as a child. Such traumatic experiences, the mother had insisted, the daughter had accepted without protest.

The sadly drooping mouth of this mask identifies it clearly as an unhappy state. When the girl was asked the meaning of the pink shape in the upper right hand corner over the eye, she said, "It's a fist that punched the man and made him unhappy."

Such an explanation of the meaning of this external symbolic fist as the cause of the man's unhappiness, as well as the patient's explanation of the role of the symbolic feather tickling a funny-bone to cause laughter, in the first mask, are further examples of schizophrenic thought processes projected into pictorial images.

After completing the three masks, the girl remarked that they were something like Greek masks that she had seen. But she had used this idea only as a stimulus to project the peculiar distortions of her own thoughts and feelings.

### 26. "Decision"

In the sixteenth session, the patient drew this symbolic design which she called "Decision." It was made a couple of days after she had drawn the "Smile" which, it may be recalled, was shown in conjunction with the similar "Tooth" design.

The girl, when asked the meaning of this drawing, explained that she was in conflict about which subjects to take in the hospital classes to prepare her for the Regents' Examinations next fall. Her problem was to decide whether to take History or French.

Figure 26

Her teacher advised that she choose History because it would be easier to cram for the examination. When asked how she felt about the teacher's advice, she protested, "But I like French better." On the strength of the patient's response, she was encouraged to choose French; for she was reminded that she had seldom in her life done what she really wanted to do.

The anxiety of the patient over her studies, due to the mother's incessant effort to push the girl beyond her capacities, caused her to be able to carry only three of the five required studies for the Regents' Examinations. The psychiatrist had agreed to speak to the mother about reducing her pressure on the daughter, but there was little hope of an understanding response from that quarter.

The patient had named this picture of a little girl standing at the crossroads, "Decision." But its real meaning to her proved to be "Indecision." She said that the girl at the crossroads was herself. The golden hair of the child, she explained as the color of her own hair when she was small, even though her hair is now a mousy brown. When asked why she had drawn herself as such a little girl she answered, "I know I like to be boyish." Again, this suggests her longing to return to those first eleven years of childhood, before the twin brothers were born. But to give her support in facing her immediate problems, she was reminded that the other side of herself had expressed the wish to be more grown up and have boy friends.

### 27. *First Impression of Insulin Shock*

The circumstances which led to the creation of this dramatic, and quite schizophrenic picture of the patient's response to insulin shock, are significant.

The girl was very much excited when she came to the eighteenth session. She began immediately to explain how, by a slip-up in hospital routine, she had not been prepared for the first insulin shock treatment. She had, just the day before, begun with a new psychiatrist. A nurse had, by mistake, taken the girl that morning for shock treatment, before the psychiatrist had prepared her for it.

The patient began, immediately, to make a drawing of the insulin shock experience. First, she drew a huge hypodermic syringe, to the left. The needle pointed to the rounded outline of her buttocks, which she drew next. She then made herself (lower

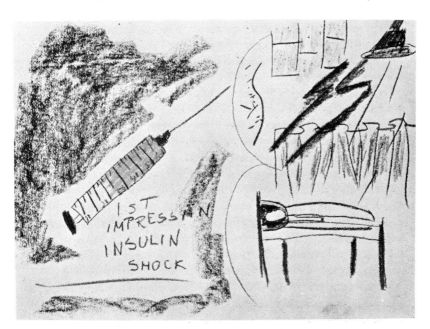

Figure 27

Figure 28

right hand corner) stretched out on a bed. She described how she was covered and bound down to the bed; and how then some arrangement was placed over her head, after the injection and shower. Above the bed she then drew what she described as a shower curtain and the water coming out of the shower. The oblong shapes above the shower curtain, near the top of the page, the girl said showed a view of the ceiling as she lay on the bed. "The shock," she continued, "is shown in the two jagged red lines shooting down near the shower. The shock was the way it all happened before I was prepared. The black (in the upper left hand corner) is the darkness in the early morning when I was taken down to a special room for the injection by a nurse. I only saw my new doctor much later. He explained to me then about shock treatment. He told me that I would have injections every morning and that after a while this would cause a coma."

She thought the picture was finished, but she then exclaimed, "Oh, I forgot something." She then drew inside the outline of her buttocks an undulating upright line. This, she said, stood for her spine, and the red dots she added showed the way her spine felt at the time of the injections.

This is another striking example of schizophrenic thinking

projected into a series of fragmented images as a means of expressing, simultaneously, the inner experience of insulin shock to
the patient and the outer setting of its performance.

## 28. "Anger"

The patient identified the multicolored head as herself in this
picture, which she had called "Anger." In this design, as in the
previous one which she called "Desire" (No. 19), her two distorted hands are reaching out. In this picture the two hands,
which she rightly described as claws, are green and red; in the
"Desire" picture one of the hands was graspingly clawlike, and
the other was what she called "a baby hand." When asked what
the two long yellow forms at the top and the bottom of the paper
were meant to be, the girl called them "rollers." At the lower
left was what she called "a gun." When the patient was asked
to explain the meaning of this picture, she pointed at the objects
she had drawn and said, "Crush, strangle, shoot. The rollers are
meant to crush, the two claw-like hands to strangle and the gun
to shoot."

Now, near the end of the art therapy sessions, the schizophrenic fragmentation of this design leaves no doubt of the girl's long
suppressed hostile and destructive impulses, which she now dared
to release.

### The Final Sessions

After the insulin shock treatment had begun, the patient became increasingly dull and sluggish. While she was still able to
produce some fantasies, she seemed unable to continue in the
expression of original and spontaneous pictures. She now relapsed
into producing a few grotesque faces. And she began, again, to
bring in meticulous copies of designs from books.

### The Patient Becomes Aware of Compulsive Repetition
### in Her Pictures

In the eighth session, the patient began to complain for the
first time that when she made certain pictures, she could not stop
herself from repeating them. As an example of this, she referred
to some autumn scenes she was making at home. In previous
sessions, the girl had denied that she ever copied pictures. But as
a consequence of her increasing sense of security with the therapist and greater freedom in her spontaneous expression, she was
now becoming aware of the difference between her old way of

copying designs and her recent original drawings in which she had begun to express herself. Frequently, after releasing either grotesque faces or animal forms, or expressions of mood, the patient would remark, "Oh, my Mother wouldn't like that!" or "I'd never do such a picture at home." The girl's fear of not winning approval at home was based on the repressive and critical attitude of the mother to her daughter's real interests and original expression; any of the girl's attempts to become herself did not satisfy the mother's superficial social interests and worldly demands. All the mother wanted from the daughter's creativity was pretty place-cards for her parties, or chrome-like landscapes to put on the wall. No wonder then that this rejected and insecure girl had tried to produce such stereotyped pictures to please her critical mother. Gradually, as the patient became convinced of the therapist's interest in her genuine creative expression, she dared to allow a number of traumatic and fantasy experiences to break through in her drawings.

The patient told the therapist that she, now, no longer cared when her mother criticized her pictures adversely, so long as they expressed the way she really felt.

### The Patient's Daydreams, Fantasies and Dreams

When the patient remained uncommunicative, efforts were made to encourage expression of her daydreams, fantasies and dreams in either pictures or words. She would resist at first, saying that her family always laughed at her if she referred to her fantasies. "I often see myself as the possessor of magnificent mansions. I have lots of people with me in my daydreams and we travel all over the world in old fashioned ships. Millions of ships bring me jewels and fabrics and other things from far places." (This girl was never given a new dress and lived in what she called "hand-me-downs" from relatives.)

On one occasion, when asked where she travelled in her daydreams, she said, "If I tried to describe it, it would not seem human." Further questioning brought the reply that "The journeys are not of this earth, but to far away planets."

One of the figures which reappeared in many of her daydreams, she called "the Protector." He offered the patient wealth and power but she refused it. "He was always kind and helped me. Once he offered me a large home." She drew him in several dream pictures in the black costume of a vampire.

In other designs, the patient appeared as a boy in brown knickers and yellow hair. Until her attention was drawn to this male identification, she had not been aware of it. Yet in other fantasies, she was then reminded that she had, also, pictured herself as a young man, boldly leading a robber band. "It's funny," she responded, "how I like to imagine myself in a romantic, swashbuckling role, but I don't like war."

In another daydream, the patient said "I was a little girl in some kind of an institution or home for punishment. The children and everyone else divided into three courts; the Outer, Inner and Middle Court. In the Inner Court were the elite, made up of children of highest rank. I was head of children of the Outer Court. They were exiles. They were popped into the Outer Court when parents of high standing came. Our parents were criminals. We of the Outer Court were looked down on by the other children and had to fight for recognition."

## Conclusion

The decision was made to send the patient back to her family before the summer. The refusal of the mother to cooperate and her inability to grasp the severity of her daughter's illness made it impossible for the hospital staff to do anything to modify the home conditions when the patient returned to her family.

### Patient's Final Contact With the Therapist

In the last session, the patient expressed deep regret at not being able to continue with the therapist. She was urged to continue making pictures about her dreams and day dreams. But she countered, "Why should I? There won't be anyone to show them to." A member of the hospital staff later told the therapist that the patient had remarked, before leaving, "Miss N. was the only person who understood me."

Evidence of the deep need of the schizophrenic to share his fantasy world with some one who can accept and respond to it is shown in this final comment of the patient.

## SUMMARY

This schizophrenic girl who was shy and withdrawn had since the age of six experienced premature menstruation. The mother's increasing rejection and hostility to this wizened and unattractive daughter, following the birth of twin brothers, led to the patient's complete withdrawal into a fantasy world. The mother pushed the girl into endless operations to which she submitted without protest. Only the crisis caused by the stealing of some money by the patient, primarily to buy the mother a gift, made the mother finally willing to consider psychiatric treatment. In spite of the efforts of the department of social work and the psychiatrist, it was not possible to obtain any genuine cooperation from this mother.

While this schizophrenic girl had been, first, at school and then in occupational therapy, interested in tracing and copying designs, she had never been encouraged to express herself in original pictures. The mother, also, disapproved of any of the girl's spontaneous efforts to make grotesque faces at home. She demanded that the girl make "pretty" place cards for her parties or copy landscapes to frame for the walls.

It has been shown how with various techniques, the patient's long-repressed emotional responses were expressed in pictures. These designs began with an expression of a series of moods, never before admitted or expressed to anyone. Among these early designs were "Blue Saturday," "Fear," "Doubt," "Anguish," etc. She was then able to deal, first in pictures and then in verbalization, with her responses to her family; this series included the mother, brother, grandmother and grandfather. In relation to her grandfather, the problem of death was pictured. A design which related to the death of her beloved kitten followed.

Traumatic experiences, first revealed in drawings, concerned the problem of death, recollections of orthodontic operations, the recall of an early sexual threat, and the experience of insulin shock.

Fantasy experiences were projected into pictures as well as stories. In them, the patient saw herself either as a small girl, a boy adventurer or a beautiful princess. Other images of the Self were eventually released in hostile and aggressive designs in which her own claw-like hands became destructive. She also expressed her own regression in baby figures and baby hands which she stated were representations of herself.

There were two expressions of transference released by the patient. One was pictorial and the other verbal. The girl dared express her partial transference by drawing the *back* of the therapist's head. When the art therapy sessions were over, she told one of the hospital staff that the therapist was the only person who understood her.

What could be achieved in terms of art therapy, as well as in any other form of psychotherapy, with this schizophrenic girl, was limited by the mother's refusal to cooperate. It is evident, however, that this inarticulate and insecure patient did gain the ability to express her conflicts with her family and her feelings about herself in original images. She began to show increasing acceptance of her adolescent role. This showed in her original art expression without fear of the mother's disapproval.

The designs are frequently striking examples of schizophrenic thought and feeling. They show the use of a part for the whole in terms of people and objects; an excessive fragmentation of images as well as an elaborate naming of pictures; such means of expression are quite typical of schizophrenic art productions.

In conclusion, I should like to repeat that this type of spontaneous art expression is based on analytically oriented art therapy; such treatment depends on the careful development of the transference relation, and on a continuous effort to obtain from the patient her own interpretation of her symbolic designs. For, in art therapy, the images produced are a form of communication between patient and therapist. The pictures constitute symbolic speech.

## CHAPTER 22

## DOODLES: AN INFORMAL PROJECTIVE TECHNIQUE

EMANUEL F. HAMMER, PH.D.

"THE TRUTH of the unconscious, in contrast to the conscious, position is often revealed in doodlings produced during serious conferences, and this frequently must astonish the doodler" (11). Doodles tend to reflect even deeper layers of personality than do other types of drawings because they are usually produced in a diminished state of consciousness when the focus of attention is on other matters. One's control is lowered and defensiveness, which may at other times be operative, is put aside.

In addition to the doodling produced on the note pad in the conference room, or on the pad in the therapy room, the psychologist may be interested in observing the spontaneous out-of-doors productions of children. During pleasant weather, sidewalks and park pavements are frequently covered with the chalk drawings of neighborhood children, who in absolute spontaneity draw for the fun of the thing and with apparently no other manifest goal.

In the direct clinical context, doodles done by the patient during the therapy session (or outside it, for that matter) can be used in the same way as dream material, irrespective of whether they have content in the common sense of the word or whether they are to be classified as abstract, expressive products. "The drawing corresponds to the manifest content of a dream, and the abstract forms also are basically the expression of human problems and conflicts . . . primitive and important drives make their appearance. Study of such forms is therefore revealing, not only from the point of view of diagnosis, but also from the point of view of therapy." (3, p. 134)

Doodles or other spontaneous and unsolicited graphic productions are of particular value to the clinician working with children, for many a child is unable to express himself adequately verbally because of either some language inadequacy or emotional blocking. The doodles afford the child an excellent means of expressing and revealing his deeper, inner needs, his emotional conflicts, and his fantasy life.

Adults, however, as well as children frequently sit and doodle while they discuss their feelings with the clinician, or they may use the doodling pad—which the writer at one time left alongside the patient's chair by accident and since then has made standard procedure—to illustrate their fantasies, revealing much more to the therapist than they could by relying merely on verbal means of communication alone. At the same time, the use of graphic means in the communication process may help to crystalize the patient's marginal feelings of awareness of that part of his symptomatology which is as yet still diffuse and ill-defined.

At times, the content of the doodles may contribute directly to the therapy process. For example, a child may feel it is not permissible for him to play at being a gangster and beat up the other children on the ward, nor to withdraw into daydreaming aggressive fantasies. But his doodles or other graphic communication having the same content may serve to gratify the child's drives and offer a form of sublimatory release. The procedure allows the patient to get some satisfaction for his aggressive drives without incurring as much guilt.

Bender (3) describes a child who drew a series of pictures of the hospital in which he was institutionalized. In these pictures, the hospital was variously smashed by giants, burned down by fire, and destroyed by bombs which killed the doctors and nurses. When pictures such as these are admired and accepted by the very same clinicians, teachers, and nurses who are destroyed in effigy, the child who produced them tends to lose the feelings of anxiety, guilt or apprehension connected with his aggressive impulses.

Frequently children will draw doodles, the content of which forecasts material that they will later be able to verbalize, but do not yet feel free to discuss. It is as if they were nibbling at communicating the idea graphically and/or symbolically before entering into the more obvious and open verbal level. The writer

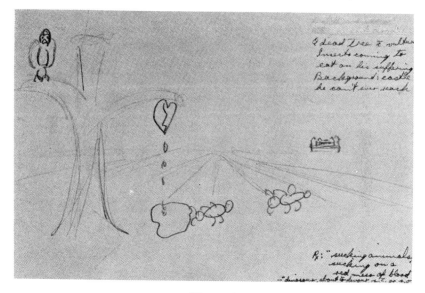

Figure 1

is reminded of an eight-year-old girl who drew a baby Kangaroo in a mother Kangaroo's pouch, as a reflection of her own regressive and dependency yearnings for the care, protection, and prerogatives of earlier stages of development. This craving for closeness to a mother-figure was precipitated by a long vacation the mother took over the summer holiday leaving the child in the care of a governess. The drawing was offered during the first month of the child's therapy, and it was not until three sessions later that she allowed the therapist to discuss with her the feelings reflected in her drawing.

At times the doodles that patients do in an abstracted state while engaged in therapy discussion, serve as an excellent springboard for fruitful associative leads.

One twenty-four-year-old obese male doodled the head of a bear while discussing his relationship to his mother. When asked to associate to the doodle, he began, "A bear leads a happy life . . . nobody ever attacks a bear . . . he's powerful . . . always gets what he wants to eat, never gets hungry . . . gets what he wants . . . does what he wants." In the following therapy session, the patient compared himself to such an animal, discussed his eating binges and total disregard of parental attitudes. The pre-conscious pressing forward of an identification symbol, floated up unwittingly to the level where it appeared on the pad left alongside the patient's chair, and served as an excellent vehicle for eliciting further, related material.

Another patient, a sixteen-year-old male, appeared to have a favorite doodle which appeared again and again on the pad during therapy sessions (Figure 1). When asked to associate to this doodle, he said that the tree on which the vulture sat was a dead tree. The insects were said "to be coming to eat on his suffering," and in the background appeared a castle which he "could never reach." His inner feelings of deadness with the only living core

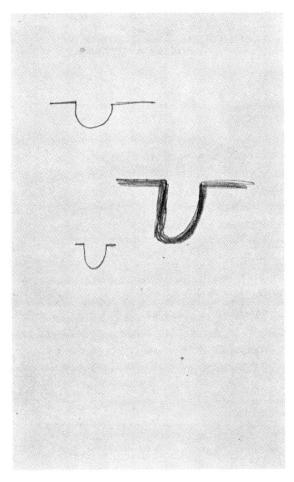

Figure 2

Figure 3

being a dull ache of suffering from which dripped evidence of pain, which in turn only served to attract more suffering, directly described the patient's subjective state as the writer later came to know it. The castle in the background which could never be reached soon found its parallel in dreams in which the essential latent content consisted of a feeling of being unable to attain exalted and renowned status. The patient's intense hunger for achievement placed his level of aspiration so high that feelings of hopelessness of reaching such a level resulted.

Later doodles, in the months that followed, permitted the therapist to keep his finger on the pulse of the patient's shifts in subjective feeling tone.

The more abstract type of doodle shown in Figure 2 was

drawn by a recently widowed woman while she was speaking of her dead husband. The suggestion of the empty vaginal yearnings then led to a crucial discussion of her frustrated psychosexual needs.

Figure 3 was drawn by a fifteen-year-old girl as she was talking of the tensions instilled by her mother's constant nagging and quarreling with her.

Figure 4 was offered by a fourteen-year-old girl, as a reflection of the oppressed feelings which accompanied the content she was simultaneously expressing on a verbal level.

Figure 5 was doodled by a male adolescent, fourteen years of

Figure 4

Figure 5

age. The self-adornment involved in doodling his name, the status needs evident in the United States Navy symbol and in the doodling of something which he had recently acquired as intellectual information (the ameba), and the stream of aggression evident in the content of knife and gun, as well as the expectation of aggression being turned on him by the outer environment (the scarred-up damaged face) all are revealed on the doodle pad.

Thus, graphic correlates of feelings accompanying the material focused on in the verbal communication, diagnostic material (such as are implied in the ghoulish aspects of Figure 6), and a reflection of traits and needs all make the advantage of leaving a pad and pencil alongside the patient's chair a fruitful procedure in psychotherapeutic collaboration which does not utilize the couch. At times the responses on the doodle pad (Figure 7, for example) reflect the emotional panic and lack of readiness, on the part of the patient, for entering an area touched upon in the verbal exploration. The doodling of a person's face hidden away in a corner of the page amidst the confusion and turbulence which churns around the rest of the page, and the lips which emit the word "Help!" warn of the inopportuness of the content area, touched in passing, for focus at present.

At times, more of the expressive aspects than of content material come through in the more aimless doodles of certain types of patients. Subjects who emphasize circles or circular strokes, according to Alschuler and Hattwick (1), tended to be more dependent and less assertive, and showed more effeminate behavior than did subjects who emphasized vertical, square, or rectangular patterns.

Figure 6

Figure 7

Waehner (15) found that few curves and many edges were emphasized by subjects described as overtly aggressive and poorly adjusted. Curved forms with few sharp edges were shown by the well-adjusted, slightly passive, and introtensive subjects. No edges at all were found in the doodles of the more introverted and more passive types.

The data mentioned in Chapter 3 of this book, on the expressive aspects of projective drawings, are transposable to doodles. Placement, size, pressure, stroke, detailing, organizational aspects, motion, synthesis, and the like are variables to be examined by the clinician who attempts to understand doodles, just as he attempts to receive the communication packaged in the expressive aspects of more formalized projective drawings.

In the content area, of course, the rich variety of emotional topics at the subject's disposal allows for highly idiosyncratic, personalized choices. The range of content of a person's doodles may extend from constricted and perseverative to fluid, varied, original and fresh. The former range is found in the doodles of inhibited, inflexible, constricted subjects and the latter in buoyant, vigorous subjects with considerable spontaneity.

Children have been found to show an interest in landscapes when they wish to escape difficult personal situations. Likewise, other children who experience difficult relationships within their family tend to avoid interpersonal areas by immersing themselves in animal content in their doodles. The mentally deficient children seem to prefer simple objects like houses and the like, the forms of which they can more easily master (3). Aggressive content, for example spears, daggers, guns and revolvers, are preferred by delinquent children. The range in content possibility is actually so broad, that a subject has full latitude for expressing his fundamental problems, preoccupations, interests or needs in the recurring themes of his doodles.

Elkisch (6) found that boys of both childhood and adolescent years show a marked preference for doodling machines of various natures; in fact, the representation of the machine outnumbered by far any other content in their drawings. She concluded from her study that boys draw themselves in the guise of a machine. "We have to understand a boy's machines in terms of his interest in his own body, and its relationship to other bodies, as well as an attempt on his part to solve his relationship to reality." The experience of Gondor (8) yielded similar conclusions: "A child who wants to be strong may, in fantasy play, pretend he is a locomotive or fire engine and imitate them. He will draw them with great preference and repeat the drawings." (p. 11) Thus, it is readily observable that a child's inner wishes and desires will be mirrored in his play, in his doodles, and in his other imaginative activites.

Brick (4), studied the spontaneous drawings of 200 school children between the ages of three and fifteen. He observed that pictures of fire and volcanoes are produced by children with acute emotional conflicts. Inanimate movement in the spontaneous drawings of children was found by Waehner (15) to be the graphic correlate of lack of control or of aggressive outbursts. Hellersberg (10) found the same implications for content such as blowing wind, gushing water, explosions and fire. Within the "normal" range, these types of content occur in the upheaved period around puberty. Neurotic trends were found in those who produced morbid images including pictures of destruction, decay and horror. Pre-psychotics also show a predilection for this type of content in their drawings as well as for excessively shaded skies (an expression of their feeling of imminent threat).

Some children draw exclusively doodles whose themes revolve around the core of war, killing, and the like. The implications for aggressive feelings are self-evident. When these children also draw houses, either in their free doodles or in their H-T-P, with doors reinforced and strong locks emphasized, they reflect their feeling that the aggression is perceived as coming more from without than from within. Such children may also draw grates on the windows, window screens, houses with no doors at all or no way to get inside, as a further reflection of their feelings of unreadiness for, and fear of, interpersonal relationships. Anxiety and defensive withdrawal are emphasized. Sometimes in their spontaneous play in the play-therapy room, these children build fortresses or other encirclements around themselves. Such children feel themselves to be too weak or vulnerable to expose themselves to the heavy potential of danger which they perceive in the outer environment. If in addition, they emphasize a rigid pattern of screens, bars or fences in their doodles, this is generally found to point to efforts on the part of the repressive mechanism of these children. When such children also show a preponderance of morbid and horror images in their doodles, it may serve as a warning signal that they feel their relationship to reality is threatened.

When *automatism* enters the picture, the presence of serious psychopathology is all the more likely. On the other hand, it should not be overlooked that in spite of the fact that automatism rules in the drawings of abnormal and psychotic individuals, it can also appear in those of normal subjects when the latter are in a state of diminished consciousness. If one is bored with a lecture, or telephoning, one may begin quite automatically to draw various simple lines and figures, which tend to be repeated rhythmically without any representational intent.

The consistent forming of closures, in drawing, "symbolizes the wish to keep to one's self." (10) The forming of closures occurs, within the normal range, however, in the abstracted doodling which consists of taking already formed lines such as $U$'s, in newspaper print, and merely continuing the $U$ into an $O$. Here this represents merely the exercise of a normal gestalt principle.

To return to the area of content, the writer has observed that a clustering of human heads are common in the doodlings of individuals who feel the thirst of unfulfilled needs for intellectual attainment or status. Adults more frequently draw heads than do children, except children of the mental defective range who so acutely feel the pressure of frustrated efforts in intellectual directions, or non-defective children who are under excessive parental pressure to achieve intellectually.

The single most common content in the doodles of children of both sexes is the boat. Bender (3) relates this to the wish to come into closer relation to the body of the mother and to be carried by her. The use of the ship as a female figure is widespread in literature. Groddeck quotes an old Irish legend in which the female genitals take the shape of the ship's hull, and the male genitals take the form of the mast. An old Irish colloquial term for clitoris is "the little man in the boat." (3)

The Biblical story of the flood and of Noah's ark is repeated in many folklores as the symbol of world destruction and rebirth. The ark with its paired animals has been a favorite children's toy for generations. Psychoanalytic interpretations of dreams support the conclusion that there is a close symbolic relationship between the boat and the mother figure.

The boat is put in a stormy setting, or one in which clouds hang low overhead, by children who experience their relationship to their mother as one creating a dismal and oppressive setting.

Animal content appears so popularly in the doodles and other spontaneous drawings of both children and adults, and the range is so extensive, that the complexity of interpretation in this area deserves a rather detailed treatment.

The preference of patients for animal content in their doodles may be related to the feeling that, in the words of one patient, "I can draw animals better than people . . . I generally distort people." Then with the spontaneous insight that some neurotic patients display, she added, "People have hurt me and animals never have."

The recurrence of animal figures in children's myths, in fables, and in folklore indicate that animals also have certain attributes which make them an excellent medium for the displacement of repressed impulses.

"Many children develop not only a great respect and dread of certain animals but also a marked tendency to identify themselves with the very animals of whom they are afraid." (13, p.58) And this identification is reflected in their content preference in doodles.

It is generally felt by clinicians who employ the drawing of an animal as part of the projective battery that the animal drawing tends to focus more directly than the drawings of House, Tree or Person upon the biological side of the biosocial coin that, roughly speaking, represents the body image. The quantity and quality of basic power wished for by the subject, and/or available to him, can be readily projected in the type of animal selected; that is, in the nature of the animal's characteristics as known through fact or as accepted through legend. The writer feels that like the drawing of the Tree in comparison to the drawing of the Person, the drawing of an animal is "less close to home" as a figure representing the self-concept; hence, the subject can more easily project his negative and ego-alien traits and conflicts onto this drawing with less need for ego-defensive maneuvering. I recall the case of a sex offender who was examined and did not directly portray any of his feelings of castration anywhere in the other drawings, nor in the Rorschach, as clearly as he did in his doodling of an animal with a tail obviously injured or hurt. He then spontaneously commented, "This dog's tail was probably run over or something."

The empirical finding that forbidden, unacceptable or painful feelings can be projected more readily onto the animal than onto the Person is similar to the rationale behind the Blacky Picture Test, The Children's Apperception Test and The Despert Fables. Clinicians, I have found, are beginning to feel that the animal figures on these thematic techniques are more susceptible for receiving the projection of deeper and more negative feelings—with less threat to the subject—than are the human figures of the TAT.

Schactel's (14) observations on the Rorschach Test offers confirming support: "The projection of an attitude or striving onto an animal, especially one that is not human-like, rather than onto a human being may be . . . one of several ways in which repression of this attitude in the subject finds expression in his Rorschach responses." We find the same to be true in the drawing of animal, in comparison to human, figures.

Another sex offender, studied as part of the New York State Sex Offender Research Project, produced the drawing of someone lifting bar-bells for his Person drawing, but at a later time doodled a rabbit.

The subject was a twenty-six-year-old, white, married male who was indicted and convicted of "carnal abuse of a female child." His offense consisted of manipulation of the genitals of an eight-year-old girl. Previous offenses involved four charges, all in less than one month, of assaults on women which the subject described as follows: "I was jumping out of bushes and scaring women and then running off. I had an urge to feel them and then run away."

The drawing of a rabbit with the implied traits of timidity and proneness to flight is certainly closer to the attributes the subject showed in his behavior of jumping out of bushes at the women, and then running away, than is his drawing of a person lifting bar-bells. The latter appears to reflect the subject's compensatory efforts to hide the deeper, more unacceptable levels which were projected in the animal doodle.

In his graphic communication, the subject tapped the same symbolic stream which runs through language and the arts. For example, such idioms as "timid as a rabbit," "free as a bird," "gentle as a lamb," "strong as a horse," "angry as a bear," and so on, may be found in the literature, myths, or language of nearly all peoples.

Certainly, children's fairy tales have anthropomorphized animals and endowed them with the human characteristics that have their roots in the animal's sterotyped nature. Such animals as donkeys, pigs, eagles, etc. possess symbolic meaning even without the support of a descriptive adjective. In the phrase "brave as a lion" the use of the adjective is superfluous. To say that a person is "stupid as an ass" is redundant; calling him an ass is fully descriptive. When we refer to a person as a wolf, a lamb, or a fox, the implied adjectives are self-evident. Even the child is already acquainted with these symbols.

To provide a normative base-line, the writer may mention that he has observed that dogs, cats, horses and other domestic animals are chosen by well integrated, normal people, and constitute a choice comparable to the "popular" responses of the Rorschach Test. The person who is not suffering from emotional disruption can feel close affinity with the animals mentioned, which, in a certain measure, can be assumed to belong to a class constituting "man's friends."

I have found small animals and insects, such as spiders, bugs, and mice doodled by phobic patients. Their choice of this theme for their doodling appears to represent compensatory attempts to come to grips with, and overcome their phobias, much as is done in anxiety dreams. Thus, the patient's choice of his phobic material for doodling appears to constitute a positive prognostic indication, in that in such an instance he is attempting to come to terms with, and tackle his phobic problem.

In an interesting study, Bender (3) has divided the spontaneous drawings of animals she has received from child patients into aggressive and non-aggressive animals. The non-aggressive group included domestic animals such as birds, horses, ducks, rabbits, cats and dogs, while the aggressive group contained jungle beasts. The drawings of the aggressive animals were found to be offered by neurotic children in contrast to the children with mild behavior problems who drew the non-aggressive animals.

Brick (4) found large and powerful animals to be the preferred content of children with disturbed social relations and feelings of inferiority.

The present writer has found large animals to be the preferred theme in the doodlings of males who feel the need to employ compensation to prove themselves more masculine than they inwardly experience themselves to be. Such males choose horses, elephants, gorillas, etc., as a reflection of their compensatory needs.

The famous painting of Goya, *A Woman Carried Off by a Galloping Horse* (Figure 8), easily the most comprehensible of his cryptic work, employs the artist's frequent symbolism of the horse as unbridled, virile passion triumphing when reason loses control and is unseated.

The painting (Figure 9) of a hospitalized, schizophrenic woman who shows herself in the process of offering herself sexually to a virile stallion reflects much the same use of symbolism. With this particular patient, her dreams indicated that the horse symbol represented her powerful father for whom she unconsciously longed in distinctly sexual terms. Myths would appear to support the choice of the horse for virile masculinity in that it is this animal which is chosen to be endowed with the phallic symbol of a unicorn. The writer has encountered the unicorn in

Figure 8

Figure 9

patients' dreams, as a representative of the dangerous phallic father.[1]

In a generic way, one might say that the content of animal doodles have been most frequently associated with either, (a) a facet of the self-concept, or (b) the perception of a facet of parental figures. Certainly we know that children, like primitives, identify themselves and their parents with animals. This shows up in their play as well as in their doodles. The writer recalls one timid, fearful ten-year-old boy on the children's ward of a hospital who ran around with arms outstretched, pretending he was an eagle. Thus, he attempted, through the identification process, to employ compensation and borrow the strength and status of the lofty and fearless bird he chose. Lorand (12) states Ferenczi found that children tended to identify themselves with wild or large animals in their dreams. He felt that the cause of such

---

[1] Just as the mermaid is available to be chosen as a symbol of the immaculate, sexually chaste mother.

dreams, in adult subjects, was "a residue of childhood recollections dating from a time when because we ourselves were so small, all other objects seemed gigantic." One also recalls Freud's famous case of The Wolf Man where the patient was frightened of a devouring wolf which represented his perception of a punitive father.

Freud (7) observed that a person's ability to replace the father by an animal whom he then responds to in phobic fashion, is facilitated by the fact that "children do not as yet recognize or, at any rate, lay such exaggerated stress upon the gulf that separates human beings from the animal world. In their eyes, the grown man, the object of their fear and admiration, still belongs to the same category as the big animal who has so many enviable attributes, but against whom they have been warned because he may be dangerous."

Study of animal doodlings likewise reveal this type of thinking which enables the subject to replace the father with a symbol of an animal.

Bender (3) concluded from her study of animal drawings that children tend to draw aggressive animals if they suffer from a severe superego which leads to a fear of the devouring animal. The aggressive animal may at other times stand for a big, protective father in contrast to the real father's aggressive behavior; or a subject may attempt to overcome a painful situation by identifying himself with the aggressive animal and thus turn against the father; or finally, a subject may choose an aggressive animal upon which he may displace his ambivalent feelings toward a parent, as was seen in Freud's case of Little Hans.

At times, the task of understanding the subject's perceptions, as reflected in his animal drawings, is comparatively easy. The attractive appeal of a figure (Figure 10) with a bountiful supply for his oral needs was left on the doodle pad by an alcoholic patient. Harms (9) reports an adolescent girl, with acute and disrupting Oedipal conflicts, who repeatedly doodled a girl being chased by an elephant with a long trunk stretched out reaching toward her.

At other times, the task of unraveling the communication is quite complex, for we find that the same animal may be suitable

Figure 10

for quite different characterizations. A person may be as true as a dog, while another may be as mean as the same animal. A pig may be a symbol for laziness, but for dirtiness or for gluttony too. Arn van Krevelen (2) cites a few examples:

A young, happily-married woman explained her choice of a dog: "Because a dog is a sociable animal."

Another individual who also employed the dog theme was a neurotic patient, an engineer in his thirties, whose vanity had been hurt by his discovery that his intelligence, which he himself had always rated very high, was not adequate to continue his re-search work. He associated to the dog that this is an animal which "never makes use of his intelligence when he goes to work. . . . I must learn to abandon my attempt at discovering every-thing. I must perform my tasks stupidly just like a dog does."

Another patient, a seventeen-year-old male, who suffered. acutely from unsatisfied needs for an emotional attachment, associated to his drawing of a dog: "A domestic animal highly thought of by people."

A twelve-year-old boy, who stole neurotically in order to invite the attention of his parents who otherwise offered him none, associated, "A dog comes and sits by one . . . because as a dog one is among people."

Thus, while there is some general, or communal, symbolic meaning to various types of animals, it is also equally true that the same animal may be used in different idiosyncratic, highly personalized contexts of representational communication.

It is likely that a further refinement of theme categories, as well as of observed behavior, will lead to a more precise clinical tool where the doodling of animals is concerned. A beginning is offered by David (5) in his systems:

1) Wild animals, including birds, monkeys, panthers, deer, etc., except for animals specifically described as domesticated.

2) Domestic animals including dogs, horses, cats, cows, etc. except for animals specifically described as wild.

3) Associated themes of independence—meaning freedom to do as one pleases and escape from routine. "A bird, . . . I could fly and be free to do as I wished."

4) Associated themes of the "good life"—meaning a life of dependency, ease, and satisfaction of needs without any demands or responsibilities. "A dog . . . easy life . . . eat and sleep . . . no worries."

5) Associated themes of beauty—the object selected is liked or admired for its beauty. "A Peacock . . . its beautiful."

6) Animals liked by people—"Everyone loves dogs."

7) Animals useful to people—"The elephant is a beast of burden."

8) Animals associated with safety—"A gazelle . . . so I could run from danger."

David's refinement of theme categories provides a tool clinicians may be interested in applying to research in the area of animal drawings.

A continuation of the discussion of the meaning of animals in projective drawings is offered by Levy in Chapter 14 and is essentially transposable to the interpretation of animal content in doodles.

## SUMMARY

The writer has found it a rewarding procedure to provide a pad of paper and a pencil by the patient's hand for his use during the therapy session. Doodles thereby elicited: A) frequently forecast material the patient will later be able to verbalize but does not yet feel free to discuss (children, particularly, nibble at communicating ideas graphically and symbolically before entering into the more open verbal area); B) serve the purpose of allowing the therapist to keep his finger on the pulse of the patient's shifts in subjective feeling tone across the span of the therapy session; C) warn, at times, of the inopportuneness of some content (touched in passing on a verbal level) for the receiving of more direct focus at that time; D) serve as an excellent springboard for fruitful associative leads; E) allow the use of graphic means in the communication process which tends to help crystallize the patient's marginal feelings of awareness of that part of his symptomatology which is as yet still diffuse and ill-defined.

It is the writer's experience that doodles tend to tap even deeper layers of personality than do other types of drawings because doodles are usually produced in a diminished state of consciousness when the patient's focus of attention is on other matters, his control lowered, and defensiveness, which might at other times be operative, relatively put aside.

## REFERENCES

1. Alschuler, A., and Hattwick, W.: *Painting and Personality.* Chicago, Univ. Chicago Press, 1947.
2. Arn van Krevelen, D.: The use of Pigem's test with children. *J. Proj. Tech.,* 20:235-242, 1956.
3. Bender, Lauretta: *Child Psychiatry Techniques.* Springfield, Thomas, 1952.
4. Brick, Maria: Mental hygiene value of children's art work. *Am. J. Orthopsychiat.,* 14:136-146, 1944.
5. David, H. P.: Brief, instructional items: the projective question. *J. Proj. Tech.,* 19:292-300, 1955.
6. Elkisch, Paula: Significant relationships between the human figure and the machine in the drawings of boys. *Am. J. Orthopsychiat.,* 22:379-385, 1952.
7. Freud, S.: Analysis of a phobia in a five year old boy, in *Collected Papers,* Vol. 3. London. The Hogarth Press, 1925.

## Doodles: An Informal Projective Technique 583

8. Gondor, E.: *Art and Playtherapy.* New York, Doubleday, 1954.
9. Harms, E.: *Essentials of Abnormal Child Psychology.* New York, Julian Press, 1953.
10. Hellersberg, Elizabeth: *The Individuals Relation to Reality in Our Culture.* Springfield, Thomas, 1950.
11. Jacobi, Jolande: Pictures from the unconscious. *J. Proj. Tech., 19:*264-270, 1955.
12. Lorand, S.: Fairytales, Lilliputian dreams and neurosis. *Am. J. Orthopsychiat., 7:*456-464, 1937.
13. Money-Kyrle, R.: *Superstition and Society.* New York, Julian Press, 1939.
14. Schactel, E. G.: Projection and its relation to character attitudes and creativity in the kinesthetic response. *Psychiatry, 13:*69-100, 1950.
15. Waehner, T. S.: Interpretations of spontaneous drawings and paintings. *Genetic Psychol. Monogr., 33:*70, 1946.

## CHAPTER 23

## SIMPLIFICATION OF THE WORLD AND ITS PROBLEMS IN THE ART OF ASOCIAL DELINQUENT BOYS[1]

LAURETTA BENDER, M.D., AND PAUL SCHILDER, M.D.

SCIENCE HAS helped us to gain a deeper insight into the problems of the asocial child. We no longer believe as Lombroso did that criminal and delinquent tendencies are inborn. Studies of August Aichorn, Lauretta Bender and Paul Schilder and Sylvan Keiser, Fritz Wittels, Franz Alexander and William Healy, and Eleanor T. and Sheldon Glueck have shown that the criminal and the delinquent have suffered from many problems in their childhood. Some of these individuals may also have suffered from organic disturbances in the brain which increased the motor and instinctual drives. But the final form of these drives is always dependent upon the attitude of the parents and the way in which they treated the child in infancy.

Children not only need care but they also need personal appreciation and love. It also appears that the love of one parent is not sufficient. When one parent is loving and the other has no real sympathy for the child, the discrepancy may even be bewildering to him.

A child may perform delinquent acts to compensate for what he has missed in social and emotional experiences. Stolen goods may represent gifts from the loved parent which the child can not get otherwise or, according to psychoanalytic concepts, may represent a sexual experience with a rejecting parent, or they may

---

[1] This paper was originally written by the authors in 1940 as a chapter in the book on *Art and the Problem Child* which was never published as such. Other chapters have appeared as Chapters VI, VII, IX, and XIX in Lauretta Bender: *Child Psychiatric Techniques* (1952) and "Art as a Special Ability in Reading Disabilities in Children," *Journal of Clinical and Experimental Psychopathology*, 12:147-156, 1951.

help the social prestige of the child and compensate for short-comings and deprivations which he has suffered in his family life.

Asocial acts may also serve to get revenge on the parents or to gain attention from them or other authoritative figures. The child may even seek punishment—for he who is punished at least receives some attention from the parents, and the punishment may even satisfy some profound sexual needs connected with suffering. Sigmund Freud and Theodor Reik have shown that some criminal acts are preceded by a deep and poorly understood feeling of guilt which is relieved by the criminal act since the individual then has a good reason for feeling guilty. The feeling of guilt may in turn be relieved by the punishment. In other instances the criminal act serves as a signal of strength, and especially of masculinity. All of these problems develop in a child long before the delinquent criminal act is committed and are the result of deeply rooted conflicts with the parents. When the child has not formed a sufficient attachment to his parents in infancy, he will later on wish to compensate for this lack by social contacts of sufficient strength. The asocial and delinquent child is beset with unconscious problems for which he can find no solution by himself.

It is in *art* that the individual may try to obtain appreciation for and contact with the world which he does not dare to express otherwise.

We will discuss the art work of two boys through which we can demonstrate the conflicts of thwarted personalities.

John was a twelve-year-old boy of Irish-American parentage. His father had been a severe alcoholic who abused and neglected his family until his death when John was ten years old. It also was known that the mother drank and neglected her five children and probably had men visit the home. But it was not possible for the agency, which gave her a widow's pension for the children, to get any conclusive evidence against her. The other children in the home had problems of one sort or another. Two of them were physically ill and one of these died during the time we were interested in John. He had first come to the Children's Court at eleven years of age for truancy from school and failure to come home at night. He was sullen and uncooperative, but was placed on parole. At the age of twelve he got into serious difficulties at school, due to his antagonistic attitude toward his teachers, who, at that time, were all men. This problem undoubtedly reflected his unsatisfactory childhood experiences with his own father. Although our subsequent examinations showed that he was of superior intelligence and able to do work well above the grade in which he was placed, he was doing poor school work, was openly defiant to his teachers and, when disciplined, became violent and uncontrollable.

In Children's Court, when the judge intimated that disciplinary methods would be used in order to force him, if necessary, to conform, he became so unmanageable that an ambulance and several policemen were required to transfer him to the disturbed ward of our hospital. It was some days before any effort could be made to adjust him to our children's ward and weeks before he could be won over to give up his sullen, antagonistic, defiant attitude. It was necessary to cater to his infantile demands that he be given special privileges and that he should not be asked to conform to the routine of the other children. At best, he could not give any expression to his real conflicts and the motives for his behavior. His intellectual brilliance and fundamental charm justified exceptional interest in the child. For weeks at a time his improved school work and apparent happiness and better social attitude appeared to indicate a response to both organized and individual efforts to give him the affection, appreciation and special consideration which he seemed to crave. But after a short period there never failed to appear some surprising example of asocial conduct, such as maliciously sadistic actions towards weaker and more helpless children, defiant refusal to follow school routine, deliberate efforts to fail just at times when promotion and new privileges were about to be granted. He stole, destroyed or lost valuable articles belonging to teachers and their friends, whose homes had been opened to him and, finally, began serious organized stealing with other boys in the community. Although often very productive in his art work, he would become angry if it were admired, and at the best was shy and self-conscious about it. During his more disturbed periods he refused to do any art work and finally gave it up entirely.

In this case the art activity decidedly represents a flight from otherwise unsolved problems. This boy was almost hopelessly delinquent, yet his art productions belong to the most sensitive in our whole group. The majority of his pictures are landscapes with trees, houses and water. There are only a few boats, and one drawing of an Indian standing before a tent. There are no aggressive scenes. Corresponding to the general character of his drawings, dark colors and glowing colors play a very subordinate part in the pictures. Most of his colors are delicate and some of his drawings and paintings are almost ethereal. The pastel of a harvest field (Figure 1) shows the sheaves in a delicate yellow, contrasted with the light green of the fields and the friendly green of the trees. The sky shows a subdued blue and the white clouds which float there increase the peacefulnes of the scene in which there are no human beings. Another pastel (Figure 2) showing mountains and houses in the foreground is interesting since the houses are drawn as if seen from above,[2] in contrast to the perspective of the rest of the landscape.

---

[2] This is consistent with the interpretation presented in the chapter on the H-T-P, that the employment of the "bird's eye view" perspective reflects a defensive rationalization to the effect that one is above the traditional value systems and conventions espoused in the community (Figure 2). [Ed.]

Figure 1
A harvest field, by John (pastel).

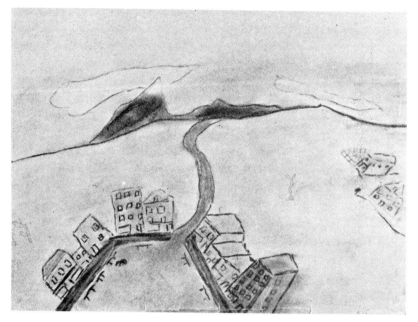

Figure 2

A landscape, by John (pastel).

An aquarelle (Figure 3) used the soft green hills in the background with higher mountains rising in rosy colors. There are white clouds in the soft tints of the sky. The foreground of the picture is formed by a series of trees which are drawn with simple artistry. There are a few lively human figures in the foreground. The whole landscape breathes peace. This picture includes his two favorite motifs which he drew in all kinds of variations. They are trees in a soft landscape, with the peaceful round crown of a subdued green against a blue sky and white clouds and high peaks in soft purple colors capped with snow, against a light blue sky with white clouds. Sometimes houses and trees appear in the foreground, or there may be a stream. The distribution in space is harmonious. There are no strong contrasts. When a human figure appears at all, it is small. The study reminds one of Japanese woodcuts and equals them in simple delicacy.

The boy loved to draw but his flights into peaceful nature did not hinder him from getting into one trouble after another in the real social world. His emotional conflicts were obviously so deep-lying that it was not possible to bring them to the surface. His art problems never revealed the content of his real problems. They were an escape but no real solution. Art has to be more than merely an escape in order to be useful for the artist and, in the long run, also for the community. The approach of this boy to reality in his art is rather naturalistic. However, there are definite form principles which he uses again and again. The trees are drawn according to a simple principle which helped him over his technical inability. It is admirable that he drew only what he could master technically. It is as if he had discovered a few important form principles which were easy to use from a technical point of view, but these form principles served as a successful approach to an important part of reality.

After several months on our service, John was sent home on probation from the Children's Court. The situation at home had not improved and although he sought and received support from both hospital and court personnel from time to time, it was not sufficient to keep him out of trouble, especially rebellion against

Figure 3

A mountain scene, by John (aquarelle).

school authority. Consequently he was soon in trouble again and was committed to a correctional institution for boys. It is inter-testing that he did not resent this and benefited by the two years he spent there. After that he managed to live at home even with the unfavorable situation, to finish school, to work for a while, to enter and serve satisfactorily in the military forces. Afterwards he obtained steady employment and became a husband and a father in a stable family life. Throughout this period he visited the hospital regularly, always at Christmas, when he helped prepare the Christmas tree for the hospital children. He had lost all in-terest in his art work.

Allen was also a twelve-year-old boy with more than average intelligence. He was the only son of a couple who were them-selves very infantile and never made an adult adjustment to their marriage. They were Norwegians and when the mother was preg-nant with Allen she left her husband and returned to her mother in Norway, feeling that she could not endure such an ordeal without her mother. After the child was born, he was cared for by his grandmother during his infancy until the mother felt that she could return to her husband with the child. Then she found that her husband had become used to the idea of taking no interest in his wife and child and would not even support them. The mother then attempted to go to work and placed Allen in a day nursery. His first memories concerned themselves with this nursery and he recalled that he was not liked there and was mistreated. Whether this was an actual memory or merely an interpretation of all his infantile impressions might be questioned. He always felt him-self a burden to his parents and they never really got along with each other. At the time we knew Allen his father was a barge captain and lived on his boat, which was his one real interest in life. His mother was a domestic and, essentially, as devoted to and dependent upon her employer as she might have been upon her mother.

Allen was a serious problem in school. He could not adapt himself to the routine of the other children and frequently was in conflict with them. They did not like him because of his superior and dominating manner toward them and the teachers. Like John, his greatest difficulties were with men teachers. In the argu-ments with them he would become hysterically excited, go home sick and continue ill for many days with severe gastrointestinal symptoms. He continually complained that he was mistreated and misunderstood and situations always developed in such a way as to justify his complaints.

He had been under the care of two child guidance clinics, and two psychiatrists had attempted to treat him and gain some insight into his difficulties which, however, seemed so deep-seated that they defied analysis. Both psychiatrists emphasized his feelings of being rejected by his parents and his antagonism to them and to any other adult who seemed to stand in their place. They also stressed his deeply imbedded distrust of other children whom he may have considered more fortunate than he in receiving love from their parents.

To us he presented a similar picture. His symptoms became more severe with the advent of puberty. He confided in no adults and assumed that they were all his enemies. He was dominating and cruel to other children. Only with a modified routine, which allowed him many privileges and much freedom from restrictions and responsibility and gave him every opportunity for individual success and admiration, did he adjust to a school program that permitted the continuation of his education. Among other things, his unusual artistic ability was discovered and encouraged to the utmost. Since it was evident that no other program would be feasible for him, it was arranged that he attend the hospital school daily from his own home, instead of going to a public school.

Allen was a boy who always felt rejected. He vacillated between giving up and outbursts of activity which led him into very serious difficulties. One can trace his behavior back to a social situation which amounted to being actually abandoned by his parents.

His efforts in drawing and painting were laborious and plodding. He was a very slow worker. The periods in which drawings could be obtained from him were short. There are only a few pictures in our collection. He evidently had the feeling that he had to do justice to details. His ability to draw was excellent, as testified to by drawings in India ink (Figure 4) which were meticulously and carefully done. Like John, he was fascinated by trees, but in contrast he was not interested in merely the general form but in the details. He apparently would have liked to draw

Figure 4

Two drawings, by Allen (India ink).

every leaf. His work was most painstaking. The whole tree is shown in a great number of his pictures, not simply as a total form but also as a sum of innumerable leaves which are drawn in accordance with geometrical form principles. In the same way he would have liked to draw every blade of grass separately and he even showed an interest in the veins of the leaves and ferns. Only occasionally was he capable of suppressing the details of the crown of the trees.

In two of his studies this interest in multiformity is shown. There are a great number of leaves and branches, and leafy vines twine around the tree trunks. The color tones of the trees vary from a light brown to a dark red-brown, but there is nothing sombre about his colors. There is a decided capacity for composition in the paintings. One picture is dominated by a large tree in the middle, but severe symmetry is successfully avoided. The trunks of these trees are emphasized by a light green plant at the base and a soft green vine entwining it. Different colors are pleasantly matched. Some of the foliage is tinted a slightly reddish brown whereas the rest appears in varying shades of green which range from a nearly bluish color to a yellowish one.

The second picture (Figure 5) has two trees standing in the foreground which are also emphasized by stronger colors. Symmetry is again only approximate. In some ways one has the feeling that the boy intended to be more elaborate but that he despaired of ever completing the task and, against his will, gave up his aim of drawing the leaves of the trees in detail. The blues and greens are also pleasantly matched. Behind the great number of smaller trunks appears an empty space. The laborious procedure in his drawings reminds us in some way of the picture of Al-

Figure 5

A forest study, by Allen (water color).

brecht Altdoerfer, a contemporary of Dürer, who wanted to draw every leaf in the German forest. It is evident that Allen had neither the technical nor emotional ability of John. Probably against his will his forest was of a more exotic character, but we cannot be too sure of this, since the India ink drawing shows his interest in exotic landscapes. He soon gave up drawing and painting because the effort was obviously too great. This corresponds with his tendency to go into depressions. In his art he came in contact with an important part of the world but it was a world full of little details difficult to master. His periods of manic excitement unmistakably corresponded to phases in which he gave up any attempt to master that which he would have liked to do in detail. His acts of stealing may have been a further clue to his efforts to simplify his conquest of the world.

Attending the hospital school seemed to succeed for a while, until the increased drive of adolescence threw him into an episode of hypomanic behavior in which all his drives were increased. His cruelty and unkindness to other children knew no limit. He took their few pennies on the promise to use his unusual freedom to make purchases for them, and laughed at them when they asked for the purchases or the pennies. He connived to meet children who were discharged from the hospital and deliberately schooled them in asocial behavior such as sexual activities and carefully planned pilfering of stores, leaving them to take the blame and boasting that he did it on purpose to outwit the psychiatrists who were interested in them and in order to get the children into trouble. On his own part he pilfered an amazing amount from stores. He got home late at night and seemed to need no sleep. He was unaccountably jovial and restless. He discontinued all his work habits and lost complete interest in his art. Necessarily, this behavior led to further hospital care when he was nearly fourteen years of age.

He remained in the children's unit of a state hospital for a year and eight months. During the first year he continued with the same mood swings and psychopathic behavior which we observed. He disregarded authority, and was especially antagonistic to male attendants. He incited the other children to all sorts of trouble, especially running away and stealing. He lied to protect himself. His parents showed little interest in him. However, he slowly improved and made an effort to apply himself to school work and advanced rapidly. He was paroled to his mother when he was fifteen and a half. Although his parents were no better adjusted to each other and the home was unfavorable, he was able to progress in high school and with a minimum amount of social agency support managed to avoid his former asocial behavior pattern.

Paul Schilder has indicated that art work produced in the course of therapy can be used in the same way as dream material whether it contains content or is merely an abstraction. The trend towards abstractions in the productions of these two boys are expressive of their basic problems and conflicts in relation to the unsatisfactory reality of their family life. We can see indications of desires for more fully experienced reality, or for an escape from the reality which they had known, or for an overcompensatory, magical gesture.

## BIBLIOGRAPHY

Aichhorn, August: *Wayward Youth.* New York, Viking Press, 1935.

Alexander, Franz, and Healy, William: *The Roots of Crime.* New York, Knopf, 1935.

Bender, Lauretta: *Aggression, Hostility and Anxiety in Children.* Springfield, Thomas, 1953.

Bender, Lauretta: *Child Psychiatric Techniques.* Springfield, Thomas, 1952.

Bender, Lauretta, Keiser, Sylvan, and Schilder, Paul: Studies in aggressiveness. *Genet. Psychol. Monog.,* 18:361-564, 1936.

Bender, Lauretta, and Schilder, Paul: Art as a special ability in reading disabilities in children. *J. Clin. & Exper. Psychopath.,* 12:147-156, 1951.

Bender, Lauretta: What are the influential factors that predispose the youth of our society to delinquency and crime? Presented at the Law Enforcement Institute on Youth and Crime, New York University, School of Public Administration and Social Service, July 19, 1955. In press.

Freud, Sigmund: *Civilization and Its Discontents.* New York, Jonathan Cape and Harrison Smith, 1930.

Glueck, Eleanor T., and Sheldon: *Unraveling Juvenile Delinquency.* New York, Commonwealth Fund, 1950.

Reik, Theodor: Psychoanalysis of the unconscious sense of guilt. *Internat. J. Psycho-Analysis,* 5: 1924.

Reik, Theodor: *The Unknown Murderer.* London, Hogarth, 1936.

Schilder, Paul: *Psychoanalysis, Man and Society.* New York, Norton, 1951.

Wittels, Fritz: *Die Welt ohne Zuchthaus.* Berlin, Hippocrates Verlag, 1928.

# PART VII

# RELATIONSHIP BETWEEN DRAWINGS AND
# THE REST OF THE PROJECTIVE BATTERY

CHAPTER 24

## AREAS OF SPECIAL ADVANTAGE FOR PROJECTIVE DRAWINGS[1]

EMANUEL F. HAMMER, PH.D.

A CLINICAL TOOL has outgrown its infancy when the key question asked of it is no longer, "Is it good?" Nurtured on a rich clinical diet, with the emergence of experimental studies to add substance to the fare, projective drawings have already taken toddlers steps, for the question presently is, "In what areas, or for what problems are they good?"

In addition, since even the most enthusiastic supporters of a projective tool do not claim that the technique does everything, it seems less tenable to "prove" or "disprove" a test than to find out what it can or what it cannot do, in what areas it has special applicability and in what areas only marginal usefulness.

Piotrowski (28) has ably reviewed the areas of relative advantages for the Rorschach examination, and the present writer will attempt to do the same for projective drawings:

(a) Drawings, basically a non-verbal technique, have the obvious advantages of greater relative applicability to young children. Lauretta Bender (6), in speaking of the functions of play and drawings, states that they serve "as the child's means of making contact with his environment," forming "the bridge between the child's consciousness and his emotional experiences and so fulfill the role that conversation . . . fills for the adult" (p. 13). Flugel (12) also recognized the fact that non-verbal projective techniques are the more productive devices with the lower

---

[1] Expanded from a paper presented at the H-T-P Roundtable, EPA, April, 1955, Philadelphia, and integrated with sections of lectures given at the 1952 and the 1954 Annual Summer Workshop in Projective Drawings, New York Psychiatric Institute.

[ 599 ]

age groups. He states that "our fantasies . . . are among the most jealously guarded of our mental possessions. . . . In the case of the child there exists an additional difficulty—that of his small command of language, which makes it hard for him to communicate his thoughts to us, even when he is willing to do so" (p. 8). Levy (24), employing drawings as an adjunct in the psychoanalysis of children, has also been impressed with the fact that children find it easier to express themselves in pictures than in words.

A *non-verbal* projective test also has relative advantages with (b) the poorly educated, (c) the mentally defective, (d) the non-English speaking as well as the mute, (e) the painfully shy or withdrawn subject, whether child or adult, (f) the relatively barren and underprivileged person of low socio-cultural background who frequently is wracked with inadequacy feelings concerning his capacity for verbal expression, and (g) those of concrete orientation.[2]

(h) Lauretta Bender (6) adds to this list, the case of the remedial reading client: individuals with "reading disabilities often show compensatory adeptness in artistic ability to make articulate their emotional and social problems" (p. 212). The emotional blocks in the verbal areas frequently hamper free Rorschach or TAT performances.

(i) When a subject cooperates consciously and does not resist on a subconscious level, it is generally agreed by clinicians that the Rorschach usually provides a richer personality picture, but when the subject is evasive or guarded, projective drawings have been found to be the more revealing device (19). The bulk of what the Rorschach yields of the subject's personality comes by way of a relatively indirect route. The subject's Rorschach percepts must, first, be translated into and, second, be communicated in, verbal language.

---

[2] A particular individual's Rorschach may not yield nearly so much dynamic or structural material as does his projective drawings, or vice versa. The former condition, the writer has found, is more likely to occur in concrete oriented, more primitive personalities, along with the occurrence of the performance I.Q. on the Wechsler-Bellevue exceeding the verbal I.Q. The latter condition, of the Rorschach (or TAT) protocol providing a richer yield than the projective drawings, occurs more frequently in verbal, "intellectual" subjects, with Wechsler-Bellevue verbal I.Q.'s exceeding performance I.Q.'s.

In drawings, on the other hand, the subject expresses himself on a more primitive, concrete, motor level. In addition to the writer, Landisberg (22) has also found that patients exhibiting guardedness seem more likely to reveal their underlying traits and psychodynamics in the drawings. She states, "They are able to exercise more control over their verbal expression, seem to be more intellectually aware of what they might be exposing on the Rorschach. They tend to lose some of this control in their creative, motor expression (employed in drawings)" (p. 181).

An incident in point was related to the writer by a psychiatrist-colleague who had undergone a psychological examination in being screened for psychoanalytic training. Whereas he was able to withhold Rorschach responses and TAT themes he felt might be damaging to his chances for admission to the psychoanalytic program, he was not able to manipulate his projective drawing productions in a similar manner. While drawing the female Person, for example, he tried to place a smile on her face. But she turned out looking strict and forbidding. Attempting to present his relationships with females in as benign a light as possible, he proceeded to erase and redraw, but each new rendition only gave her face a more formidable and menacing expression than before. In spite of all his efforts, in the end she wore a stern expression. In his own words, "I couldn't control the way she turned out."

A similar case was reported by a psychologist-candidate for graduate school who could not control the size of the female Person's shoulders. The more she erased and redrew, the more over-expanded the shoulders became.

Another case in point (21) was that of an adolescent boy who was brought before a juvenile court on five charges of breaking, entering and larceny and three charges of entering and larceny. Clinically, he appeared as a hostile, aggressive lad who, however, in his drawings attempted to give a benign impression. In the interview following the drawings, he offered the information that he had been "trying to draw a school girl, but the way it came out, it looks like a tough girl that hangs around the river."

These performances underscore the words of Machover (27): "Stereotyped defenses are less easy to apply to graphomotor than to verbal projections" (p. 85).

The present writer's experience with inmates at Sing Sing Prison (19) further supports this view. Incarcerated subjects, for example, because of their basic mistrust and bitter resentment of authority figures in general, remain somewhat suspicious of all personnel employed at the institution, even after years of public relations effort on the part of the psychiatric and psychological staff. Loaded down with pervasive fear of revealing themselves to an authority figure even remotely associated with the prison setting, defensiveness follows, and the inmates dare not "see" anything off the beaten track. The number of their Rorschach responses, for example, tends to drop to a meager ten to twelve with the most frequent record consisting of one noncommittal response given to, and thus dismissing, each card.

Their TAT themes assume a barren quality, remaining for the most part on a relatively superficial and descriptive level. Expressions become stereotyped and the inmate sticks to the "safe" response. Attempts at conformity and undeviating acceptability in his voiced Rorschach and TAT percepts are the rule. Richness of imagination is stifled, and real feeling is hidden behind an obscuring curtain of constant control. The scanty record thus obtained loses the pith and the subtle nuances necessary for full or accurate assessment of the individual type of personality reaction pattern.

In addition, inmates as a group are generally among those subjects who cling, for various reasons, to the concrete. They become anxious and threatened when confronted with the ambiguous stimuli of the Rorschach and attempt to steer clear of real involvement with this type of projective situation, at least insofar as communicating and explaining verbally what it is that they may see.

To illustrate, those offenders who are seen psychotherapeutically after psychological examination often confide to their therapist, once rapport has been cemented in a transference setting, that on the Rorschach they did not reveal everything they saw, e.g., "especially those dirty sex pictures that were there." In responding to the projective drawing task, on the other hand, these patients must reveal something of their sexual adaptation in one of two ways: either in their manner of handling the direct or symbolic sexual areas of the House, Tree, Person figures or else, all the more, by their omitting to draw areas that carry sexual implications, for example, the genital zone or secondary sex characteristics of the drawn Person, the chimney on the House, and the branches on the Tree (18, 19).

Another symptom group found to open up more on drawings than on other projective techniques are the alcoholics. In psychologically evaluating the personality patterns of alcoholics, "drawings, relative to other projective techniques, are receiving increasing attention because they have been found to be . . . difficult to falsify, and in its application there is no barrier of education or language . . . it also requires little time and is simple to give" (14, p. 249).

In general, it may be said that projective drawings appear to the subject to be less threatening (as capable of revealing secrets and forbidden needs) than is the Rorschach which is beginning to be viewed, by the layman today, as a mystical sort of instrument almost on a par with truth serum. Hence, with evasive or resistant subjects, projective drawings frequently appear to be the clinical tool of choice.

Bellak's (5) experience is in the same direction: "The verbal expression of aggression may be successfully controlled when its muscular expression is clearly seen . . . in tests probing the sub-semantic area" (p. 292).

(j) Of late, there have been some interesting observations to the effect that there is a difference in the depth of personality tapped by verbal and non-verbal projective techniques (1, 4, 5, 15, 18, 33-36). With the non-verbal projective drawing it has been found that deeper conflicts frequently press into view more readily on the drawing page. Wyatt (35), in comparing the relative contributions of the different projective techniques to the clinical picture of the, by now, famous "case of Gregor," points out that "in drawings, deeper, more primary, and less differentiated levels of experience are tapped" (p. 468).

In a study comparing drawings with TAT material, Gallese and Spoerl (15) found that "most of the material gathered from the Draw-A-Person Test was inserted on an unconscious level, and represents the more or less unadulterated basic needs," whereas the material on the TAT is, "more likely to be tinged and altered by the familiar techniques of defense" (p. 76).

Wyatt (35) presents much the same view: material from the Rorschach and TAT "seem to emerge from a different level of psychological experience" than do drawing data. "Perception in its adjustive function or dysfunction is involved on a more elementary level (in drawings) than in the tests mentioned before (Rorschach and TAT)" (p. 467). Franz Alexander (1) also elaborates the idea that art has a special affinity to the unconscious mind.

Drawings seem to differ from the Rorschach on the variable of structuredness. Whereas the Rorschach is ambiguously structured, the blank drawing page and just a word ("House," "Tree," "Person," etc.) are relatively even closer to an unstructured state. In Max Hutt's (20) words, "While *all* types of responses may be analyzed for both conscious and unconscious determinants, the more unstructured stimulus is likely to produce unconscious responses of 'purer' quality" (p. 200).

Zucker, in a rather interesting and perceptive little study (36), found that drawings are the first to show incipient psychopathology—and here their prognostic use is underscored—and the last to lose signs of illness after the patient remisses. Zucker concludes that drawings are more highly sensitive to psychopathological trends than are the other projective techniques.[3]

Thus, projective drawings, empirical evidence is beginning to suggest, may constitute a clinical instrument which descends to the deeper layers of experience, thought and feeling.

(k) Within the projective battery, drawings serve a special function by providing a minimally threatening, maximally absorbing introduction to the testing procedure. As the first test in the

---

[3] Hence, negative latent factors foreshadowing a gloomy prognosis are frequently indicated by a set of projective drawings heavy with pathology in conjunction with a relatively clearer Rorschach. The present writer has found that where such a relationship between drawings and Rorschach existed, later follow-up disclosed clinical diagnosis of incipient, latent, prepsychotic, or pseudoneurotic schizophrenic or severe neurotic states (18). Conversely, where drawings yielded a healthier personality picture than did the Rorschach, a reactive maladjustment such as war neurosis, reactive depression, etc., in which latent positive resources were currently over-shadowed by the effects of an emotional upheaval, later frequently proved to be the clinical diagnosis (18). See Chap. 27.

battery, drawings may serve as an easy bridge to the clinical examination; the drawing task allows uncomfortable subjects relatively to exclude the examiner during the initial phase of getting used to the new surroundings and to the stranger on the other side of the desk. To borrow from the observation of a non-professional psychologist, Winston Churchill (8) speaks of draw-ings as "complete as a distraction." He continues, "I know of nothing which . . . more entirely absorbs the mind. . . . All one's mental light such as it is, becomes concentrated on the task" (p. 82).

Duhsler (10) reports that individuals with emotional diffi-culties can be led more easily from drawing to verbal expression. Bender (6) also underscores the special utility of drawings "as a means of establishing rapport" (p. 206). The present writer has found them a good "ice breaker" with the shy or negative.

(1) Drawings are finding special applicability in the area of testing for organicity. Landisberg (22) writes: "Evidence of organicity can be picked up in a more clear-cut fashion from the H-T-P than from the Rorschach, and such evidence may be re-flected earlier on the former test. This, I think, is a result of the fact that the H-T-P, comparatively speaking, forces the individual to use his psychic resources in a much more independent and volitional manner. Blots are blots. The patterns and boundaries may be ill-defined, but they do serve as props. And the organic, concrete as he is, has at least a little to build from. But with just a blank sheet of paper in front of him and just a word to conceptualize from, his basic weakness and shaky response are more prone to come to the fore" (p. 2).

This is consistent with the comment by Schafer (30) that, "There is little doubt as to what you see on the Rorschach card; the ink blot is before you; it is static; its shape, shading and color-ing are clear and fixed" (p. 91). Thus, the relative advantage of drawings in this area springs from the fact that the Rorschach leans somewhat more toward the use of ambiguous stimuli, with drawings more toward the use of unstructured conditions. "The creativity involved in the Rorschach test is exclusively an asso-ciational one. Upon being presented with an unchanging con-figuration, the individual is asked to call upon the content of his ego for a concept which corresponds more or less to the actual shape of the configuration. The individual is not asked to alter reality (as is the case with drawings)" (13, p. 54).

(m) Because of these differences between verbal and non-verbal tools, projective drawings find special applicability with certain other areas of diagnostic groupings. In the latent schizo-phrenic conditions, the individual is not quite sure of himself; he is becoming aware that something about his handling of affec-tively-charged situations is not quite right, and might, even if he could conceive a fairly adequate affectively-charged image, hesi-tate to bring that image forth verbally.

In regard to diagnostic areas, Schafer (30) writes that, "It is not at all rare that the patient, because of a repressive, depres-sive, negativistic, or paranoid orientation, or because of psycho-logical defect, yields minimal responses, that is, responses few in number, brief in extent, and barren in content. This is particularly likely to occur in the Rorschach and TAT" (p. 14). It is with such cases that personality evaluation responsibility is shifted, in a relative way, to the projective drawings in the battery.

(n) In group testing, projective drawings suffer less loss of material than does the Rorschach. In fact, the writer is presently becoming more and more impressed with the fact that projec-tive drawings obtained in a group setting, where there is more emotional, as well as physical, distance between examiner and subject, provide richer and more openly expressed material. Raven (29) obtained parallel results with the Progressive Matri-ces: "The individual test appears to introduce emotional factors which are less operative when a person is allowed to work quietly at his own speed. The group test appears to provide a more reliable sample of a person's output" (p. 9). Studies with other tests (7, 29, 31, 32) have also indicated group testing to be more revealing than individual testing.

Several writers of late have focused on the contaminating influence of the examiner's personality upon the subject's projec-tions. "Depending upon the tester's own personality and emo-tional state, his reaction to the patient, his usual method of ad-ministering tests, his talents and sensitivities and articulateness, and other trends and circumstances, the tester will contribute more or less. . . . He will never be a nonentity in the situation. The patient may exaggerate and over-react to what he sees, but he sees a real person and not . . . a shadowy authority figure. There are, for example, authoritarian testers. There are competitive testers, (and) . . . a variety of 'types' of testers" (30, p. 63). Eysenck (11) elaborates the above view of Schafer's: "Whether the tester is a pretty young girl, a domineering male, or a matured sympathetic woman—all these influences may, and in some cases do, affect a person's scores. They are difficult to control, particularly as the same stimulus—a pretty young girl as tester, for instance—may mean quite different things and arouse quite different emotions in subjects differing in age, sex and marital happiness" (p. 294).

There is some experimental evidence that different testers tend to get different average distributions of Rorschach data from the cases they test (16, 25, 30, 31). Also, studies, in which frustration was imposed in conjunction with the administration of the TAT, indicate that the subject's view of the tester may increase the number of themes of aggression and punishment (3, 9).

In the words of Max Hutt (20), "We must never forget that the (projective test) situation is always a personal relationship no matter how much the observer tries to render himself neutral. In practice, we tend to discount the effects of this relationship upon the end product, and we may perhaps, do so with greater justice when we are analyzing results for certain group situations" (p. 199). Projective drawings which lend themselves more easily to group administration than does the Rorschach can thus be used in this way to reduce the factor of the personality of the clinician being brought into the thick of the projection situation. By the group testing procedure, examiner-subject interaction and the resultant spurious, contaminating influence of the clinician's "type" of personality on the subject's responses—a hotbed of as yet unknown variables—is thus minimized.

(o) Along with the above point, the subject's drawings represent a sample of his behavior which has not been exposed to the possibility of distortion—small as it is—that is always present in behavior-recording procedures that involve patient-examiner interaction. The subject's performance is there, caught on paper.

It does not have to go through the examiner's receptors, his cerebral apparatus with its potential for apperceptive distortion rooted in the examiner's own personality traits and conflicts, and then recorded through the examiner's effector channels. Drawings thus provide a "purer" sample of behavior, especially important for research purposes.

Another research advantage for the projective drawing tool lies in the fact that it is essentially a culture-free technique for anthropological use in the investigation of other societies across the language handicap. The investigator need only be armed with a vocabulary of a few words: "house," "tree," "person," "male," "female" and possibly "animal."

(p) For retest use, projective drawings can more sensitively follow the ebb and flow of therapeutic change with less influence of memory of the previous test performance contaminating the present production. In regard to the Rorschach test, for this purpose, Hermann Rorschach (2) himself stated, "If the test is repeated . . . conscious and unconscious memory effects will contaminate the results" (p. 3). In the task of projective drawings, the subject is less prone to be reminded of his previous projections when confronted with the blank page than when confronted with the same Rorschach or TAT stimuli. Or if he does recall his previous performance, he is less likely to repeat it, merely because he is reminded of it.

This suitability of drawings for retest use is in accord with the observation by Glueck *et al.* (17) that serial testing is useful in checking the impressions of the therapist and in providing indices of the direction of the illness. Tests which are most easily adaptable to retest usage can serve to meet the criticisms of Luchins (26) aimed against the tendency of clinicians to establish a diagnosis at the beginning of psychotherapeutic contact with the patient and thereafter to lack flexibility in altering the diagnostic frame of reference for subsequent viewing of the patient. "It seems to us that the emphasis should not be on the diagnosis, but on the 'diagnostic process' if by this one means a rather continuous assessment of the patient throughout the entire course of treatment" (p. 444).

(q) Projective drawings reflect an impression of the *whole* individual as an organized Gestalt, which is then apparent to the experienced projective drawing interpreter at an extended, per-using glance, without need for simultaneous mental juggling of as many ratios and scores as are necessary, for example, with the Rorschach. The interpreter can step back from the protocol and see it in its entirety. All that has gone into it—every line, every part in its relation to the other parts, making up the composition as a whole—presents a unified effect which he can, more readily than the Rorschach interpreter, see in its total integration. Pro-jective drawings are apprehended by the clinician as a unit; the Rorschach must be taken in part by part.

"The methods of analysis (of Rorschach and TAT) scores, abstracted thema, etc. provide means for ordering the unified, personal productions of the subject in terms of the interpreter's conceptual and experiential framework—in this sense the 'Ges-talt' of the subject's performance is somewhat arbitrarily de-stroyed and distorted in terms of the interpreter's orientation. . . . Behavior must be studied directly in the context in which it is exhibited, not as it suits the convenience of the investigator" (7, p. 129).

(r) In the interest of facilitating interprofessional communica-tion, drawings serve as a useful clinical instrument for psychiatric staff members, untrained in projective techniques, to recognize that there are visible retest body-image changes from one draw-ing to another. The fact that psychiatrists can quickly learn how to empathize with projective drawings stimulates their interest in the psychologist's contribution as a clinical team member. From the psychologist's side, it is easier to explain projective draw-ing findings (on the basis of their evidence) than, for example, those of the Rorschach.

## SUMMARY

In an abbreviated way, one might say that projective draw-ings have the following advantages: (a) they are relatively simple to administer; (b) total response time is comparatively short thus affording rich returns in terms of time and energy expended; (c) they can, therefore, serve as a quick screening device; (d) they afford a minimally-threatening, maximally-absorbing introduction to the test battery; (e) the tests' ease of administration and simplicity of handling make them as easily applicable to testing large groups as to testing individual subjects; (f) a non-verbal projective technique has obvious advantages with young children, the poorly educated, the mentally defective, the non-English-speaking, the painfully shy, and those of concrete orientation; (g) drawings more frequently get under the defenses of evasive and guarded subjects, incarcerated inmates of correctional institutions, etc.; (h) experience suggests that organicity is more readily detected with projective drawings than with the Rorschach; (i) empirical evidence is beginning to suggest that drawings may constitute a clinical instrument which descends to the more primitive and deeper layers of personality; (j) "purer" samples of behavior, for research purposes, are obtained; (k) the quick administration of drawings and their somewhat lessened influence by memory allows for easy periodic retests to check progress in psychotherapy and to focus the therapist's attention on conflicts before they come into view in the psychotherapeutic collaboration; (l) because of the graphic picture of the entire personality as a Gestalt, interpretative relationships between various personality components are more readily apparent to the experienced clinician (that is to say, the psychologist does not have to simultaneously keep in mind a long series of scores, a large number of ratios and various content themes as in Rorschach interpretation, but can see the personality elements and their relationship at an extended, perusing glance); (m) data from drawings are more easily explained to, and more readily understood by, psychiatrists untrained in projectives.

These conclusions are hypothesized from empirical observations only and in no way imply scientifically proven relationships as yet. At the present time, they have proven to possess a pragmatic usefulness. It is hoped that these clinical observations will stimulate research and the gathering of data by psychologists, working in varied installations, in investigation of the presented empirically-derived hypotheses.

## REFERENCES

1. Alexander, F.: In Robert Lindner (ed.): *Explorations in Psychoanalysis.* New York, Julian Press, 1955.

2. Behn-Eschenburg, Gertrud (with Dr. Hermann Rorschach): *J. Proj. Tech.*, 19:3-5, 1955.
3. Bellak, L.: The concept of projection. *Psychiatry*, 17:353-370, 1944.
4. Bellak, L.: *Comments at Society of Projective Techniques Meeting*, New York Psychiatric Institute, January 15, 1953.
5. Bellak, L.: A study of limitations and "failures": Toward an ego psychology of projective techniques. *J. Proj. Tech.*, 18:279-293, 1954.
6. Bender, L.: *Childhood Psychiatric Techniques*. Springfield, Thomas, 1952.
7. Borstelmann, L. J., and Klopfer, W. G.: The Szondi test: A review and critical evaluation. *Psychol. Bull.*, 50:112-132, 1953.
8. Churchill, W.: In Ray, M. B.: You can be an amateur painter. *Coronet*, pp. 82-104, March, 1954.
9. Crandal, V. J.: Induced frustration and punishment-reward expectancy in Thematic Apperception stories. *J. Consult. Psych.*, 15:400-404, 1951.
10. Duhsler, E.: Erfahrungen mit Fingermalerei. *Prax. Kinderpsychol. Kinderpsychiat.*, 1:115-116, 1952.
11. Eysenck, H. J.: *The Scientific Study of Personality*. New York, Macmillan, 1952.
12. Flugel, J. C.: Preface in Griffiths, Ruth. *A Study of Imagination in Early Childhood*. London, Kegan, Paul, French, Trubner & Co., 1935.
13. Fortier, R. H.: The response to color and ego functions. *Psychol. Bull.*, 50: 41-63, 1953.
14. Fox, R.: Psychotherapeutics of alcoholism. In Bychowski, G. and Despert, J. L. (Eds.). *Specialized Techniques in Psychotherapy*. New York Basic Books, 1952.
15. Gallese, Jr., A. J., and Spoerl, D. T.: A comparison of Machover and Thematic Apperception Test Interpretation. *J. Soc. Psychol.*, 40:73-77, 1954.
16. Gibby, R. G.: Examiner influence on the Rorschach inquiry. *J. Consult. Psych.*, 16:449-455, 1952.
17. Glueck, Jr., B. C., Krasner, J. D., and Parres, R.: The use of serial testing in regressive electroshock treatment. In Hoch, P. H., and Zubin, J. (Eds.). *Relation of Psychological Tests to Psychiatry*. New York, Gruen & Stratton, 244-257.
18. Hammer, E. F.: The role of the H-T-P in the prognostic battery. *J. Clin. Psychol.*, 9:371-374, 1953.
19. Hammer, E. F.: A comparison of H-T-P's of rapists and pedophiles. *J. Proj. Tech.*, 18:346-354, 1954.
20. Hutt, M.: Towards an understanding of projective testing. *J. Proj. Tech.*, 18:197-201, 1954.
21. Kott, M.: Personal communication, January 1955.
22. Landisberg, S.: Personal communication, March, 1951.
23. Landisberg, S.: Relationship of Rorschach to the H-T-P. *J. Clin. Psychol.*, 9: 179-183, 1953.
24. Levy, J.: The use of art techniques in treatment of children's behavior problems. *J. Proc. Am. A. Ment. Deficiency*, 39:258-260, 1934.
25. Lord, E.: Experimentally induced variations in Rorschach performance. *Psychol. Monogr.*, 64:(10), No. 316, 1950.
26. Luchins, A. S.: Toward an experimental clinical psychology. *J. Personality*, 20:440-456, 1952.

27. Machover, Karen: Human figure drawings of children. *J. Proj. Tech., 17:* 85-91, 1953.

28. Piotrowski, Z. A.: H-T-P Roundtable Panel, EPA Convention, April, 1955, Philadelphia.

29. Raven, J. C.: *Guide to Using the Progressive Matrices.* London, Lewis & Co., 1938.

30. Schafer, R.: *Psychoanalytic Interpretation in Rorschach Testing.* New York, Grune & Stratton, 1954.

31. Sanders, R., and Cleveland, S. E.: The relationship between examiner personality variables and subjects' Rorschach scores. *J. Proj. Tech., 17:*34-50, 1953.

32. Scherer, I. W., Winne, J. F., Page, H. A., and Lyston, H.: An analysis of patient-examiner interaction with the Szondi pictures. *J. Proj. Tech., 15:* 419-420, 1951.

33. Stern, M.: Free painting as an auxiliary technique in psychoanalysis. In G. Bychowski and J. Despert (Eds.). *Specialized Techniques in Psychotherapy.* New York, Basic Books, 1952.

34. Symonds, P.: *Comments at Society of Projective Techniques Meeting,* New York Psychiatric Institute, January 15, 1953.

35. Wyatt, F.: In J. Bell (Ed.). The case of Gregor: Interpretation of test data. *J. Proj. Tech., 13:*155-205, 1949.

36. Zucker, L.: A case of obesity: Projective techniques before and after treatments. *J. Proj. Tech., 12:*202-215, 1948.

## CHAPTER 25

## RELATIONSHIP OF THE RORSCHACH TO PROJECTIVE DRAWINGS[1]

SELMA LANDISBERG, M.A.

### INTRODUCTION

To INTRODUCE the topic of the relationship of the Rorschach to drawings, I should like to point up the differences in the types of stimuli involved, compare the perceptive and apperceptive processes that come into play, and consider the modes of response in each approach. In the Rorschach the subject is confronted with visual stimuli, which are amorphous and unfamiliar. At first he is asked to tell what the stimuli look like to him, and later, where and how he sees them. On drawings the stimulus is verbal, very familiar, but of a nonspecific character. It consists of: "Draw me the best house, draw me the best tree, and draw me the best person you can." Later, after the drawings are completed the subject is interrogated concerning what he has drawn, in order that he may have the opportunity to describe, associate to, and expand upon his concepts.

In responding to the Rorschach the subject is limited to his interpretation of what he sees within a circumscribed visual field. It is assumed that his visual, memory, and emotional-associational patterns will determine his selection of blot areas, and the construction and content of his responses. What he projects and the way he projects arise out of his psychological experiences, needs, wishes. On drawings, the subject is prompted from a non-specific, familiar verbal cue to create a personal, concrete representation of house, tree, and person. What he draws is a result of the interaction between his visual perception of these objects in the past and his emotional experiencing of them.

---

[1] Delivered at the Round-Table on the Theoretical and Practical Aspects of the H-T-P Technique, APA Convention, Chicago, Ill., Sept., 1951.

The effector mode of response on the Rorschach is verbal. Much of what we learn about the subject's personality comes via a relatively indirect route; through his largely unconscious integration of visual-emotional reactions, which are then translated into and communicated in verbal language. Where and how he sees his percepts are essential in the analysis of the record. But in differentiating between the expressive aspects of this and the drawing situation, emphasis is laid on the fact that he is expected to communicate and explain what he sees verbally. In drawing, on the other hand, the subject expresses himself on a physical, concrete, visual-motor plane. Only after he has completed all three drawings, is he subjected to interrogation.

Both methods promote projection. Despite the differences in the nature of the stimuli, in the perceptive processes, in the media through which the subject relates himself, and the methods of expression employed, both techniques have been found to yield cogent information concerning the individual's personality adaptation; and when used together they provide a rich array of complementary, supplementary, and corroborative data. For various reasons there are some subjects who cling to the concrete and the familiar, who become extremely anxious and threatened when confronted with ambiguous blot stimuli, and who consequently produce meager records. These people are less upset when asked to draw a familiar concept. In this regard a very striking case of an agitated depressive comes to mind.

> Because the level of concentration of the subject was low, and she had difficulty in and disliked verbalizing, and was frightened by what she probably perceived as ominous blacks and disturbing colors on the Rorschach, her responses were few, vague, and stereotyped; she steered clear of real involvement with the test. Since her activity need was strong, however, she expressed herself very forcefully and positively when provided with pencil and paper and requested to draw. Using the pencil almost as an instrument of aggression, she very quickly unleashed in drawing her fury against herself and the world. The quality and movement of her lines and the unmistakable graphic symbolism revealed her high potential for giving way to impetuous, motor impulses, that had as their goal, self-destruction. Although one might have in-

ferred such behavioral possibilities from the Rorschach, one would not have seen her rapid and savage manipulation of paper and pencil. One would have missed the compelling psychodrama that ensued, in her depiction of a crude, womb-like house—showing her obsession with death; in her dart-like tree, with its high-pressured lines directed toward the bottom of the paper, the point closest to her body—baring her ready capacity to aggress overtly against herself; and in her hastily drawn person, into which she projected her self-concept of a washed-out, helpless, broken individual.

Contrasted with this receptiveness to drawing is the fear of motor activity. There are people who are less resistive and more productive when they are in a more passive, spectator role, such as the Rorschach situation permits. In both sets of reactions, nevertheless, whether positive or negative in terms of productivity, the clinician gains valuable information, although a substantial part of his knowledge may derive predominantly from one of the two techniques.

Through use of more than one means of personality appraisal we have the benefit of varied and broader sampling of the individual's interaction with his environment. We are afforded the opportunity of checking the salient findings in one approach against those of another, of locating the problem areas that the individual carries with him from one kind of test setting to another, and finally, of being able to implement certain data so that a more reliable, differentiated, and richer personality picture may be obtained. It would appear that we reach conclusions about personality on the Rorschach through relatively formal and intellectualized constructs, through the clinician's blending of quantitative and qualitative configurational analysis of the selected blot areas, the perceptual determinants, and the content. A more immediate and direct avenue of approach is offered in drawings, in the sense that the clinician has the adavantage of watching the subject adjust to a primary and elemental level of expression, of seeing him in independent action from moment to moment, and step by step, of being able to empathize with or share in this concrete experience in the role of spectator, and perhaps thereby coming somewhat closer to the real life situation.

From the immutable, completed drawings, and our record of the drawing process, we can inspect the qualitative and quantitative aspects of each, weigh one drawing gestalt and its respective verbal associations against the other, and finally synthesize our findings into a complete picture.

## CLINICAL OBSERVATIONS

I should like to present some samples of analogous relationships between two tests, which lack experimental and statistical verification, but which have been found to be clinically fruitful. These must not be regarded as having a 1:1 relationship, but the underlying dynamics appear to be similar.

In the category of ego strength, there appears to be a striking relationship between the drawing of the Tree, and more particularly, the trunk of the tree and the Rorschach measures of ego strength, such as F + %.

In regard to response locations on the blots, a high incidence of whole responses (W) occurs with an over-weighting of the branch structure of the tree. Vague, poorly-articulated W's go along with a dearth of clearly depicted inner detailing in the drawings. The degree of specificity of details on the Rorschach corresponds to the amount of details in the drawings and care involved in their elaboration. An irregular sequence of locations seems to have its counterpart in scattered and autistic placement of details in the drawing whole.

A low number of responses on the Rorschach and poverty of details in the drawings go together. A low number of Rorschach responses with high M seems to correlate with greater responsiveness and concept elaboration on the drawings. People who respond in such fashion on the Rorschach, who are absorbed with their fantasy creations, often succumb to the drawing medium, onto which they more readily project the scope and intensity of their feelings. Early paranoids, for example, with some insight and guardedness, seem more likely to reveal and expand upon delusional material in the drawings. It is postulated that they are able to exercise more control over their verbal expression, seem to be more intellectually aware of what they might be exposing on the Rorschach. They tend to lose some of this control in their creative, motor expression.

With respect to movement responses, it has been found that the quality of animal movement (FM) is linked with the vitality of the tree's branches; that the quality of human movement (M) is related to the posture and motor attitude of the drawn person. Blocked and tense human movement with high m, and high F% usually correspond to rigid, tense boundary lines on all three drawings. A great excess of FM over M has its counterpart in the drawings of the person, where there is usually inadequate attention paid to the head area, and greater focus upon the immaturely formed body and limb areas.

High amount of small c on the Rorschach goes with a high amount of shading in the drawings. High C', indicative of depression, is very often associated with the drawing of a bare, lifeless tree. When there is a combination of considerable C and C, we tend also to find the presence of high-pressured, erratic lines in the drawings, showing the individual's need to do something very actively to relieve anxiety.

How the individual uses color on the Rorschach appears to be related to how open or accessible his drawn house is, how freely and with what control his tree branches move out into the surrounding space, and how the facial expression, body and limb positions on the drawn person relate themselves to the outer environment. No color, or very little use of color, particularly in conjunction with no or very little use of M, is paralleled by a rigidity of lines and an empty, flat quality in the drawings. The presence of high C on the Rorschach seems to be connected with broken-off boundary lines or marked disconnection between integral portions of the drawing. This is carried to the extreme in the "split tree," which indicates a breakdown in defenses, and the danger of inner impulses spilling over into the outer environment. The projection of color onto achromatic blot areas, revealing a denial of felt depression, has its interesting counterpart in the drawings, where, for example, we may find a smiling face appended to a drooping, decrepit body, or unconvincingly life-like leaves joined to a dilapidated tree stump. How the individual handles the last three cards of the Rorschach, the complexities of which are augmented by the introduction of multiple colors, seems to bear some relationship to his reaction to and use of color in the H-T-P chromatic drawing phase, when he is under the impact of this additional emotion-arousing stimulus. How the color is adapted or integrated on the Rorschach, whether in an impulsive or controlled, positive or negative, earthy or ethereal, realistic or artificial manner, has its analogue in the kind and use of color in the chromatic phase of the H-T-P.

Orienting our test material with a view to prognosis, we find, for example, that just as the human movement (M) and color responses (C) are slow in changing on repeated examination, likewise the tree drawing is slow in altering its major configuration. It is the tree, which seems to tap basic, long-standing feelings and self-attitudes, because of its relatively impersonal and neutral conscious connotations, that is more resistive to alteration. Unless the individual has experienced dramatic changes in the life situation or has undergone deep therapy we shall not generally expect any significant changes in the tree.

To illustrate how similar conclusions may be derived from the very different conceptual frameworks inherent in both tests, I should like to cite an example of how inner aggression and the defenses erected against its expression may come to the fore in both approaches. In certain ambulatory psychotics or people with schizophrenic character make-ups the underlying disorganization of emotional and intellectual processes and the intense, negatively-toned feelings are likely to appear more prominently in the house and tree drawings than in the person. It would seem that the last or remaining vestiges of control and self-containment tend to be projected into the latter drawing; that the drawing of a person evokes more conscious control factors than the more impersonal concepts of house and tree. This is related to this kind of person's need to put on an acceptable social front. The Rorschach may reflect this very same phenomenon in terms of the kinds of media onto which this individual tends to project his aggression, the length of time the aggression is sustained, and the amount of distance between the observer (or subject) and the object against which he is aggressing. He may avoid projecting aggression upon living forms and use inanimate or dead constructs or symbols for this purpose instead. His kinesthetic responses may be ridden with passivity or stasis, and may also denote movement at a distance or spurts of movement that die out very quickly.

In presenting these data I have merely made an attempt to suggest some aspects of comparison, which are in no way scientifically proven correlates. At this point they have served as useful frameworks of reference. There are many other dovetailing and high-lighting features that come through in these approaches, but they will vary from case to case, and will require the individual clinician's skill and understanding for their evaluation. It is hoped that these clinical observations will stimulate much needed research to study some of the suggested relationships.

## REFERENCES

1. Buck, John N.: The H-T-P technique; a qualitative and quantitative scoring manual. *J. Clin. Psychol.*, Monograph Supplement No. 5, 1948.
2. Buck, John N.: The Richmond Workshop material on the H-T-P. Beverly Hills, California, Western Psychological Services.
3. Buck, John N.: The H-T-P test. *J. Clin. Psychol.*, 4:151-159, 1948.
4. Buck, John N.: The use of the House-Tree-Person test in a case of marital discord. *J. Proj. Tech.*, 14:405-434, 1950.
5. Buck, John N.: Directions for administration of the achromatic-chromatic H-T-P. *J. Clin. Psychol.*, 7:274-276, 1950.
6. Buck, John N.: The quality of the quantity of the H-T-P. *J. Clin. Psychol.*, 7:352-356, 1951.
7. Klopfer, B., and Kelley, D. M.: *The Rorschach Technique.* Yonkers-on-Hudson, World Book Co., 1942.
8. Landisberg, Selma: A study of the H-T-P test. *Training School Bull.*, 44: 140-152, 1947.

## CHAPTER 26

## SOME RELATIONSHIPS BETWEEN THEMATIC AND DRAWING MATERIALS

Edwin S. Shneidman, Ph.D.

GENERALLY, THERE ARE two ways in which the topic implied by the title of this chapter might be approached in a book of this sort: one way would be to present a résumé of experimental studies from the psychological literature, while the second way would involve the case-book method.

### STUDIES FROM THE LITERATURE

In making a report of studies from the psychological literature which relate thematic tests to drawing productions, one would usually report the nature of the study, the size of the obtained correlations, and a summary of the research findings. Although there are not many studies which relate thematic protocols and drawings directly, some few do exist. Three such studies will be discussed in this present setting.

1. A recent study by Gallese and Spoerl (1) involved twenty-five male students who drew human figures and wrote stories for ten TAT cards. The following is quoted from their study:

> Proceeding on the theory that if two tests are designed for the purpose of determining the needs and conflicts pressing upon the individuals taking these tests there should be the projection of the same needs and conflicts into both tests, an attempt has been made here to check the interpretation of the Machover Figure Projection Test against the Morgan-Murray Thematic Appercep- tion Test. Points of similarity between the two sets of test results will be examined and discussed.
>
> The subjects used in this research were the male students of the 1950 Psychology of Personality class at American Interna-

tional College. As a part of this course the students were required to draw a set of Machover Figures and later to write a story about each of ten pre-selected Thematic Apperception Cards. The Thematic Pictures were projected onto a screen and thus given in a group setting with five minutes allowed for the writing of each story, hence the stories were short. Twenty-five students were used, all of the males in the class.

Each set of Machover figures was interpreted by the senior author, according to the suggestions made by Machover, and the interpretations discussed with the junior author. Then, independently, the same process was used on the Thematic Stories, each being inspected for the one or two principal features of each story as indicative of conflict areas, using the accustomed method of interpretation. Because of the method of giving, the Thematic stories were short, and each showed only a few areas of need or conflict. These two sets of material were then matched and the comparison made in terms of the percentage of instances in which the results of the Machover Test were corroborated in the Thematic Apperception Test protocols.

In terms of percentage of material found in the Machover interpretation and corroborated in the Thematic Apperception Test the range was from 33 to 100 per cent. The mean was 72 per cent agreement between the two. . . .

The remainder of the Gallese and Spoerl article consists of two illustrative cases—one of good agreement between drawing and thematic interpretation and one of average agreement—and a discussion section. The discussion is of interest in the present setting inasmuch as it contains speculations about the different roles of drawing and thematic tests. A section of their discussion follows:

It is especially noted that there is a transformation of the personality factors in switching from one test to the other. Most of the material gathered from the Machovers was inserted on an unconscious level, and represents the more or less unadulterated basic needs. However, in the Thematic Apperception Test the subject can, and does, integrate the needs and conflicts in the total personality expression, and the results are therefore more likely to be tinged and altered by the familiar techniques of defense. For example: a subject would be less likely to express direct hostility and aggressive actions toward his father or mother on a conscious level while writing a story to a TAT card; but a generalized reaction and expression of these feelings can be found in stories dealing with rebellion against society and its institutions, school teachers, and other dominating or superior groups or persons.

2. Katz, in another study (2), using adult male Negro homicide or assault offenders (and non-assaultive controls) as subjects, compared human figure drawings with the TAT (as well as with the Rorschach and Szondi tests). The "Summary" section of his study is as follows:

The present investigation was undertaken to determine whether assaultive aggression is projected into the drawings of human figures, the nature of this projection, and its psychological interpretations. The experimental group consists of fifty-two adult male Negro offenders of sub-normal intelligence, convicted of various charges of assault and homicide and who are incarcerated for their offenses. The control group consists of a similar number of matched subjects who demonstrate no history of assaultive behavior. Supplementary projective techniques also administered to the experimental group consist of the Rorschach, Thematic Apperception Test and the Szondi. A general group case study is also presented of the assaultive aggressive group. It is the opinion of this examiner that this approach contributes more fully to a comprehensive understanding of the individual, his figure drawings, and the dynamics of his assaultive aggressiveness.

In their case histories, it is noted that practically all of the assaultive aggressive subjects were born and reared in the South under the most adverse conditions possible. Most of them were lacking in necessary parental attachments and supervision. Education was negligible and achievement was at a low or illiterate level. Their subsequent work records in New York City were poor and unfavorable associations were formed. There was an almost uniform inability to form satisfactory relationships with the female sex over a period of time. The subjects were easily provoked by emotionally threatening situations, which under the influence of alcohol, led to a relaxing of inhibitions with subsequent physical release of underlying aggressive tensions. . . .

In the Thematic Apperception Test, the results indicate that

ability for establishing sound interpersonal relationships is severely impaired for virtually all of the assaultive subjects. Relationships with the family and parent figures are largely ignored,
or when present, result in hostile reactions. These attachments
with parental and other love objects are highly unsatisfactory
and a source of intense frustration, usually leading to violence.
The stories reflect uniform feelings of frustration and failure due
to hampering outside conditions or to feelings of self defect and
inadequacy. There is an unusually large degree of death resulting
from physical attack and a minimum of verbalized or suppressed
hostility. . . .

Nine drawing features are found to differentiate statistically
the male and female figure drawings of the assaultive aggressive
groups from those of their controls. An additional three drawing
features differentiates only the male drawings of the experimental
groups from those of their matched controls. The interpretations
of the significant drawing characteristics are presented, based
upon the functions inherent within the particular organs or
drawing features themselves, the case history, differences in
the drawings of the control subjects, and the results of the other
projective tests utilized. The drawings show indications for inconsistent motor control, a hostile view of the environment, basic
inadequacy, and strong immature aggressive tensions directly
expressed. It is found that the essential differences in the drawing characteristics are reflected in those bodily features which are
most directly related to and essential for the discharge of assaultive tensions. . . .

A brief study is made of the extent to which present empirically derived drawing characteristics is valid for the groups under
study. The empirical observations of Machover are in agreement
with five of the significant drawing features found to differentiate
the assaultive aggressive from the control groups. Seven of the
drawing characteristics found to be significant for the assaultive
subjects of this study are not recognized or present in the subjects studied by Machover. Twelve other drawing features which
she suggests are indicative of aggression, are not substantiated in
the present study.[1]

---

[1] These data can be further described as follows: (A) the five hypotheses of
Machover which differentiated Katz' assaultive subjects from his control group
were: dark stick lines for fingers and fingers without hands, dark lines, wide
stance, piercing eye, and emphasis on foot; (B) the differentiating drawing

3. One additional study by the present author and others (3) can be reported in which the areas of personality functioning included in one set of drawing interpretations were compared with the areas of personality functioning included in several sets of interpretations of thematic protocols—all on the same twenty-five-year-old, single male Veteran.

Table I shows the percentages of personality items (made about the same Subject's TAT and drawings) subsumed under eighteen areas of personality description. Each separate item of personality description in the one drawing interpretation and in the several TAT interpretations was placed within one of the eighteen categories. These categories grew out of the reports themselves. The "Composite TAT" column represents the mean percentage for the eleven of the fifteen TAT reports where there were twenty or more statements of personality description. The values reported in the Table cannot be assumed to be characteristic of the two *tests* involved but rather must be taken to reflect the characteristics of the (one DAP and eleven TAT) *interpreters.*

Perusal of Table I shows—within the major limitations indicated above—that the *TAT interpretations* emphasized the areas of outlooks, affect, sexual thought, personality defenses, interpersonal relations, and symptoms; the *drawing interpretation* was concerned with the areas of motivations, affect, sexual thought, psychosexual development, self concept, interpersonal relations, and symptoms; while *both* had in common the areas of affect, sexual thought, interpersonal relations, and symptoms.

---

characteristics which Machover had not mentioned were: reinforced hair, large arms and large legs of the male drawings only, large fingers, and arms reinforced and legs reinforced of the drawings of both sexes; (C) the twelve suggestions of aggression by Machover which were not substantiated by Katz' study were: middle placement, mid-line heavy emphasis and pressure, mouth with much pressure or heavy slash line for mouth, dark shading of dress, emphasis on nostrils, speared or talon-like fingers, clenched fist with arm away from body or mitten type hands and fingers, more than five fingers on hand or fingers formed like claw or mechanical tool, toes indicated in figure not intended to be nude, tie drawn as if flying away from body, large figure or heavy line, and vigorous shading of entire figure.

## CASE BOOK PRESENTATION

The second type of approach was referred to as the case-book method. In this type of presentation one would present actual protocols demonstrating the clinical relationships between thematic test data and drawing productions. In this approach one would attempt to point out the significance of "clues" in either drawings or thematic tests for the other set of data. One might say, for example, that when one finds such and such in a Subject's TAT he is apt to find thus and so in his drawing (or vice versa) and that these mean this and that in terms of the Subject's personality. (The danger, not successfully avoided by many present writers, is that the case-book becomes a cook-book). In its best use, this kind of presentation employs the method of precept, in which a relatively experienced clinician performs his task publicly, all the while making didactic asides. Such case-book materials relevant to our present interest can be found in *Thematic Test Analysis* (3) and consists largely of interpreta-

TABLE I

PERCENTAGES OF PERSONALITY ITEMS FROM ELEVEN TAT AND ONE DAP
INTERPRETATIONS OF THE SAME SUBJECT

|  | Composite TAT | Draw-A-Person |
|---|---|---|
| Pressures; forces; press | 1 | 2 |
| Motivations; goals; drives | 4 | 19 |
| Outlooks; attitudes; beliefs | 8 | 0 |
| Frustrations; conflicts; fears | 5 | 5 |
| Affect; feelings; emotions | 13 | 12 |
| Sexual thought and behavior | 9 | 9 |
| Psychosexual level and development | 1 | 9 |
| Super-ego; values; ego ideal | 2 | 0 |
| Self control; ego capacity | 2 | 0 |
| Self concept; insight into self | 2 | 9 |
| Personality defenses and mechanisms | 12 | 2 |
| Reality contact; orientation | 3 | 0 |
| Interpersonal and object relations | 12 | 9 |
| Perception; fantasy; language; thought | 5 | 0 |
| Intellect and abilities | 2 | 2 |
| Symptoms; diagnoses; etiology | 15 | 22 |
| Prognoses and predictions; treatment | 4 | 0 |
| Postdictions | 3 | 0 |

tions by experienced clinicians of thematic and drawing (as well as other) protocols of the same Subject. The Subject in that study was, as stated above, a twenty-five-year-old single, male Veteran. His drawings of a man and a woman are reproduced (3, pp. 223-224) along with a blind interpretation of these drawings[2] (3, pp. 222, 225-226). His verbatim TAT and MAPS test protocols are given (3, pp. 13-16, 20-27) as well as sixteen independent interpretations of these protocols[3] (3, pp. 31-199). Also, clinical and behavioral data such as psychiatric case history, psychotherapy notes, etc., are presented (3, pp. 237-272). It is, of course, not possible in this chapter to reproduce in full (or even in sufficient detail to be meaningful) either the protocols or the interpretations. The reader, therefore, is urged to familiarize himself with the pertinent sections of *Thematic Test Analysis* if he wishes to explore a case-book approach to thematic and drawing relationships.

## POINT OF VIEW

At this point, the question arises whether one should devote continued discussion to experimental résumés or to case book illustrations. The decision, if space permitted, would be to follow neither of these two courses. This is prompted by the point of view which is implicit in the writer's present approach to thematic and drawing materials. This point of view can be described as follows: That the rigorous considerations concerning the validities of the TAT (as well as the Rorschach, MAPS test, etc.) are bedevilled by lack of agreement among experimenters as to meaning of concepts (semantic confusion) as well as by contradictory and incomplete findings (equivocal statistical results); further, that even less systematic research has been done with regard to the validity status of drawings. It follows in the author's reasoning that if the above is accepted, even on a tentative basis, it would not be too meaningful to discuss the interrelationships

---

[2] The drawing interpretation is by Karen Machover.

[3] The sixteen thematic interpretations are by Magda Arnold, Betty Aron, Leopold Bellak, Beverly Cox, Leonard Eron, Reuben Fine, Arthur Hartman, Robert R. Holt, Walther Joel and David Shapiro, Seymour Klebanoff, Sheldon Korchin, Jose I. Lasaga, Julian Rotter and Shirley Jessor, Helen Sargent, Percival Symonds, and Ralph K. White.

between the TAT and drawings on the basis of present knowledge. Therefore, what the reader ought to do is to select several carefully chosen sets of TAT protocols and drawings obtained from various types of subjects which he could use as an exercise in formulating his own notions. This would be done with two goals in mind: to stimulate the reader to think clinically about some of the relationships between thematic and drawing productions and to arrive at his own thoughts about the nature and the complexities of TAT-drawing relationships; and to stimulate the reader to think critically—which is not the antithesis of thinking clinically—about some of the cautions which must be exercised in discussing the relationships between drawings and thematic protocols.

## REFERENCES

1. Gallese, A. J., and Spoerl, Dorothy T.: A comparison of Machover and TAT interpretation. *J. Social. Psychol.*, 43:73-77, 1954.
2. Katz, J.: The projection of assaultive aggression in the human figure drawings of adult male Negro offenders: A study of inmates convicted of homicide or assault by means of human figure drawings, Rorschach, TAT and Szondi. Unpublished Ph.D. Dissertation, New York University, 1951.
3. Shneidman, E. S. (ed.): *Thematic Test Analysis.* New York, Grune & Stratton, 1951.

CHAPTER 27

# THE PROGNOSTIC ROLE OF DRAWINGS IN THE PROJECTIVE BATTERY[1]

EMANUEL F. HAMMER, PH.D.

PROJECTIVE DRAWING TECHNIQUES provide a canvas upon which the subject etches aspects of his inner world, his personality strengths and weaknesses including the degree to which he can mobilize his inner resources to handle his psychodynamic conflicts. In this respect they are similar to other projective techniques. If the projective drawing device is to be given a recognized place in the prognostic battery, it must make a unique contribution to the clinical picture not completely overlapped by other tests.

In attempting to harness projective drawings to prognostic usefulness, it has been found that deeper conflicts frequently press into view more readily on the drawing page than elsewhere. Wyatt (10) explains that "in drawings, deeper, more primary, and less differentiated levels of experiences are tapped." In addition to Wyatt, both Bellak (1) and Symonds (9) have pointed out that drawing techniques tap deeper layers of the personality than the the verbal projective techniques such as the Rorschach and the TAT. I am in agreement with them in their view that drawings per se, on the other hand, do provide a grosser personality picture with less of the nuances filled in. The verbal phases (Post-drawing Interrogation) of the H-T-P, however, frequently provide pertinent data with which to round out the personality picture.

In explaining the deeper though more narrow tapping of the unconscious by projective drawings, Stern (8) writes that "The

[1] Expanded from a paper read at the Prognosis Symposium (Z. A. Piotrowski, Chairman), Eastern Psychological Association Convention, Boston, April, 1953, and printed in *J. Clin. Psych.*, 9:371-374, 1953.

technique used in [drawings] is on a level with primitive pictorial thought. It is of advantage that thus, both as to mode of thinking and of expression, it is on the same plane as the unconscious thought itself. . . . It seems that the affect emanating from a picture reaches into the unconscious more deeply than does that of language, due to the fact that pictorial expression is more adequate to the developmental stage in which the trauma occurred; it has remained more within range of the concrete and physical than has the verbal expression."

To further compare projective drawings with the best known of all projective techniques, the Rorschach, it may be pointed out that drawings tap predominantly effector (outgoing) processes whereas the Rorschach taps predominantly perceptual (incoming) processes. The effector acting out, the carrying through of adjustment potentials, is somewhat more vulnerable to the effects of psychopathology than are the perceptual processes. Zucker (11) found that drawings are the first to show incipient psychopathology, and here its prognostic use is underscored, and the last to lose signs of illness after the patient remisses. Calden (4) in another intensive clinical study has come up with similar results to Zucker. Calden, in comparing a series of Rorschach examinations with a series of projective drawings, writes that the latter "is more sensitive to the subtle developmental changes from month to month, particularly in the area of growing self-awareness and differentiation of behavior" (p. 208). Zucker and Calden both independently conclude that drawings are more highly sensitive to psychopathological trends than are the other projective techniques. Hence, negative latent factors foreshadowing a gloomy prognosis are indicated by drawings heavy with pathology in conjunction with a relatively clearer Rorschach.

The projective drawing performance, then, is generally on notes lower than that of the Rorschach keyboard. Together they orchestrate a rounded theme of the essential diagnostic melody of the subject.

### INTRA-ACHROMATIC COMPARISONS

Another advantage of drawing techniques for prognostic problems lies in the tool's capacity for simultaneous tapping of body-images on different personality levels. It has been felt, for example, that whereas the drawing of a Person taps the patient's degree of adjustment on a psycho-social level, the drawing of the Tree appears to tap basic, more enduring and deeper intrapsychic feelings and self-attitudes. Therefore, the drawing of the Tree has held up as being less susceptible to change on re-testing than the drawing of the Person. Whereas psychotherapy of a non-intensive kind will frequently show improvement in the drawn Person, as a rule only deep psychoanalytic therapy, or highly significant alterations in the life situation, will produce any but minor changes in the Tree.

Also, since it is easier to attribute more conflictful or emotionally disturbing negative traits and attitudes to the drawn Tree than the drawn Person because the former is "less close to home" as a self-portrait as far as the subject is concerned, the deeper or more forbidden feelings can more readily be projected onto the Tree than onto the Person, with less fear of revealing oneself and less need for ego-defensive maneuvers.

A study by Diamond (5) is consistent with this view. Employing a technique in which the subject is asked to make up a story about houses, trees and persons, he found that the tree was the entity most often exposed to danger.

In regard to the H-T-P's capacity for tapping different personality levels, the House appears to lie somewhere between the Person and the Tree on this particular continuum. Focus has been given to the Tree and Person because they represent extremes, prognostically most fruitful for comparison. As may be expected, the prognosis is poorest when House, Tree and Person are all flooded with psychopathology indicators.

Since the drawing of the Tree taps more basic layers than the drawing of the Person, a positive prognosis is suggested by a Tree conveying a healthier picture of the personality than is conveyed by the drawn Person. In such cases latent positive resources are currently overshadowed by the effects of a reactive or situation-induced emotional upheaval. Conversely, a negative prognosis is indicated by the drawn Tree steeped in more psychopathology than the drawn Person. By the Tree conveying an impression of deep psychopathology is meant such depictions as, for example, the Tree consisting of side-lines only, unclosed at the top or the bottom thus giving the impression of a "split Tree," a Tree with broken branches or trunk, a Tree with a scarred trunk, a Tree depicted as toppling over, unconvincing life-like leaves joined to a delapidated tree trunk, and so on.

## ACHROMATIC-CHROMATIC COMPARISONS

A comparison of the chromatic drawings with the achromatic drawings provides another prognostic clue by virtue of their tapping of different personality layers. The pencil drawings tend to convey the characteristics of the patient more routinely employed in dealings with problems of adjustment, whereas the crayon drawings highlight the deeper characteristic organization of the personality when it is subjected to greater stress. The crayon drawing task tends to elicit reactions to, and tolerance for, emotional stimuli, therein supplying an impact similar to the Rorschach chromatic cards in getting beneath the patient's defenses.[2]

The achromatic and chromatic Person drawings often illustrate the relationship between the two phases. The tenuous con-

---

[2] Two essential differences, however, exist between color as a stimulus on the Rorschach and on the H-T-P. In the Rorschach, comparison of the subject's performance on chromatic and achromatic cards carries the assumption that the other elements in the card are held constant. This we know to be not the case for two reasons: (A) The form element of the chromatic and achromatic cards are not parallel. (B) Comparison is not made between performance on cards having a chromatic stimulus with those in which this is the only element absent, but comparison is made rather between chromatic cards and cards in which the shading element is a decided positive stimulus (with considerable impact at times) rather than merely a blot without color. With the H-T-P, on the other hand, essential identity of stimuli is available for comparison of achromatic and chromatic performance. The subject's task is predominantly to draw a series of figures with and without color. The use of pencil for shading, beyond its use for line, is relatively infrequent and secondary. Hence, chromatic and achromatic performance on the H-T-P provides a more pure comparison uncontaminated by differences in form and shading as is the case with the Rorschach.

The second essential difference between the use of color on the Rorschach and the H-T-P lies in the fact that the former provides for a passive reaction to this stimulus whereas the latter demands an active use of the same. It is found, for example, that frequently subjects with only mild Color Shock on the Rorschach exhibit more intense Color Shock on the H-T-P in that they withdraw from a free use of the crayons into a timid or constricted use of one single color, and that color frequently blue, black or brown.

tact with reality in the achromatic drawings may give way to a more frank loss of personality balance, under the impact of color. Incipient or latent conditions are most frequently presented by being hinted at in the achromatic drawings and then more vividly and dramatically overtly portrayed in the chromatic drawings. One subject, for example, presented an achromatic House insecurely anchored on an amorphous cloud-like ground line. This individual's lack of firm contact with reality gave way to an obvious loss of emotional equilibrium when a deeper personality layer was tapped in the chromatic phase of the H-T-P. The house, now, was presented as toppling over. (See Chapter 9.)

One other factor operative in the chromatic phase of projective drawings deserves mention. Due to the associative value of crayons they tend to elicit childhood adjustment levels in adult subjects. It seems almost as if crayons appeal in some degree to the residue of childish layers in the adults' personality, and hence the chromatic drawings stand in relationship to the achromatic drawings somewhat as Piotrowski hypothesizes the FM Rorschach responses are related to the M.

Piotrowski (7) suggests that the FM content indicates the basic attitude which the individual assumed when dealing with others in personally vital matters during his early childhood. This basic attitude is usually presently submerged unless released into overt behavior during states of diminished consciousness such as is induced, for example, by alcoholic intoxication. The M content is defined as indicating the attitude or role in life assumed in the present rather than the past. Hence the FM and the chromatic H-T-P are viewed as tapping deeper personality layers than the M and the achromatic H-T-P, respectively. It is these deeper layers that tend to determine the subject's behavior in moments of relative stress.

Buck (3) feels that the H-T-P's greatest contribution, lies in its capacity to serve, in effect, as a miniature longitudinal study since it demands that the subject at two different time periods (albeit, close together) perform essentially the same graphic and verbal tasks. We are more concerned here with the "psychological time" than with the chronological time between achromatic and chromatic phases. The concept of "psychological time" is used to refer to the great change that so frequently takes place in the subject as a result of his having produced the achromatic set of drawings and having been questioned concerning them. Such a change in certain respects equates the subjective passage of time to a markedly greater amount of objective time. By the time the subject performs on the chromatic phase of the H-T-P he is presumably in a different psychological situation from that which he was in when he began his achromatic drawings. It is this degree of difference, as evidenced by a comparison of his achromatic drawing and achromatic Post-drawing Interrogation answers with his chromatic productions and chromatic Post-drawing Interrogation comments, that may be regarded as a rather fruitful prognostic measure. The examiner can thus compare the two performances both quantitatively and qualitatively thereby providing himself with an opportunity to highlight data indicating the probable degree of permanence of the subject's pathologic features. This measure of probable permanence provides an important dimension for prognostic evaluation.

## SUMMARY

On projective drawings, a positive prognosis is suggested by either:

(A) The drawn Tree conveying a healthier impression than the drawn Person, or

(B) The crayon drawings indicating a better adjustment level than the pencil drawings, or

(C) The drawings yielding a healthier personality picture than the Rorschach.

Where such relationships occurred, a reactive maladjustment such as war neurosis, reactive depression, etc., in which latent positive resources were currently overshadowed by the effects of an emotional upheaval, later proved to be the clinical diagnosis.

On the other hand, a negative prognosis is suggested by either:

(A) The chromatic set of drawings steeped in more psychopathology than the achromatic set, or

(B) The drawn Tree conveying a sicker impression than the drawn Person, or

(C) The drawings carrying negatively-toned feelings more prominently than the Rorschach.

The writer has found that where such a relationship existed, later follow-up disclosed clinical diagnoses of incipient, latent, pre-, or pseudoneurotic schizophrenic or severe neurotic states.

Instances in which the House, Tree, and Person are all rife with psychopathology, or where achromatic and chromatic sets are both flavored with illness, or where drawing and Rorschach personality pictures are mutually flooded with pathology indicators have occurred only in cases carrying the gloomiest prognoses.

## REFERENCES

1. Bellak, L.: Comments at Society of Projective Techniques Meeting, New York Psychiatric Institute, Jan. 15, 1953.
2. Buck, J. N.: The H-T-P technique: A quantitative and qualitative scoring manual. *Clin. Psychol. Monograph*, No. 5, pp. 1-120, 1948.
3. Buck, J. N.: Personal communication, Feb. 1953.
4. Calden, G.: Psychosurgery in a set of schizophrenic identical twins—a psychological study. *J. Proj. Tech.*, 17:200-209, 1953.
5. Diamond, S.: The house and tree in verbal fantasy. *J. Proj. Tech.*, 18:316-325, 1954.
6. Hammer, E. F.: *The H-T-P Clinical Research Manual.* Beverly Hills, Calif., Western Psychological Services, 1955.
7. Piotrowski, Z. A., and Abrahamsen, D.: Sexual crime, alcohol, and the Rorschach test. *Psychiat. Quart. Suppl.*, 26:248-260, 1952.
8. Stern, M.: Free painting as an auxiliary technique in psychoanalyses, in G. Bychowski, and J. Despert (eds.): *Specialized Techniques in Psychotherapy.* New York, Basic Books, 1952, pp. 65-83.
9. Symonds, P.: Comments at Society of Projective Techniques Meeting. New York Psychiatric Institute, Jan. 15, 1953.
10. Wyatt, F.: in J. Bell (ed.): The case of Gregor: Interpretation of test data. *J. Proj. Tech.*, 13:155-205, 1949.
11. Zucker, L.: A case of obesity: Projective techniques before and after treatments. *J. Proj. Tech.*, 12:202-215, 1948.

PART VIII

THE TYING TOGETHER

## CHAPTER 28

## RETROSPECT AND PROSPECT

EMANUEL F. HAMMER, PH.D.

JOHN CHAPMAN, in *Learning and Other Essays,* has observed: "In the caverns of our nature lie hidden various emotions like beasts in a lair. They are shy to the voice of question or of curiosity, and they slink and crouch all the more, if we try to lure them out for inspection. . . . Let no one then wonder at the difficulties that surround all study of the human emotions—blushing giants, vanishing genii that they are."

The preceding chapters in this book have demonstrated that projective drawings enable us to get at least a glimpse of the psychological landscape which is the home of all that is dimly envisioned or dully felt on lower levels of awareness. The "blushing giants" of which Chapman spoke are thus coaxed into view.

It cannot too often be stressed, however, that the interpretive deductions from projective drawings have to be made with caution and treated with objective skepticism mixed with scientific circumspection. The clinical hypotheses—empirically derived—which make up the bulk of this book, still await, for the most part, the experimental verification, which they must have before they can be integrated more fully into the compendium of projective psychology. For the time being, they can be employed only as tentative beacons lighting the path of personality evaluation, and always in company with the other clinical techniques, both projective and otherwise, that guide the clinician in his attempts to understand his diagnostic collaborator, the patient.

In the projective drawing procedure, a standard situation is provided, which offers the clinician an opportunity to observe and compare subjects' behavior. The main intent is to study the effects of the dynamics of the outer situation of the projective technique on the available inner dynamics of the individual. The method chosen is the interrelation of test behavior, drawing performance, and verbal expression.

Thus far, it would appear that projective drawings are now on the path toward slowly but surely acquiring the scientific dignity and clinical prominence that they merit and that their predecessor, the Rorschach, has earlier approached.

It has been found that in drawing, a subject unwittingly tends to project. The concept of *projection* is used here in its broader sense—a broadening which Freud himself later recognized when he wrote in *Totem and Taboo*, "Projection is not especially created for the purpose of defense, it also comes into being where there are no conflicts (p. 857)." Freud further elaborated: "The projection of inner perceptions to the outside is a primitive mechanism which, for instance, also influences our sense-perception so that it normally has the greatest share in shaping our outer world. Under conditions that have not yet been sufficiently determined even inner perceptions of ideational and emotional processes are projected outward, like sense-perceptions, and are used to shape the outer world, whereas they ought to remain in the inner world."

An interesting study by Bellak (2) supports this contention that projection is a phenomena which is broader than the specific defense mechanism which Freud, in his earlier writings, believed projection to be. A number of subjects were given the Thematic Apperception Test under controlled conditions. Then the TAT was readministered under the post-hypnotic suggestion that they would feel extremely elated. It was found that the subjects projected this elation into their stories. This finding could not be subsumed under the content of projection as a *defense* mechanism. Since there obviously was no particular need for the ego, in this case, to guard against the "disruptive" effects of joy or elation, this experiment demonstrates the validity of the broadened concept of the projective phenomena in accord with the view expressed in the quote above from Freud (2).

## PROJECTION AND DISPLACED PERCEPTION

Perhaps the major complication in the unraveling of information kneaded into one's projective drawings occurs in the clinician's attempt to disentangle the phenomena of projection from the phenomena of, what I might term, *displaced perception,* two closely related processes.

It has been observed that man has a tendency to perceive that which he expects, hopes or fears to see (11). In the Rorschach, Klopfer (11) assumes that the subject reflects his fright by the faces and masks he perceives, but that the subject does not project his own feeling—namely fright—on the face or mask seen as one does in what is usually considered projection in the kinesthetic responses. If the subject projected his feeling of fear, one would expect to see a *frightened* rather than a *frightening* face. The psychological mechanism involved here, however, is a kind of displaced perception somewhat different from that involved in projection. In displaced perception, one does not see the environment in one's own image, but sees that in the environment which one expects to see.

Facial expressions drawn in projective drawings, like those recurringly seen in the Rorschach, are at times indicative of the attitude which the subject expects other people to have towards him. This hypothesis is in agreement with Murray's (9) experimental findings that fear makes people attribute maliciousness, rather than fear, to faces in photographs.

Beginning clinicians should be warned that there are no hard and fast rules of procedure that can help them differentiate between the times when the subject is projecting and when he is displacing perceptions. At times the subject will draw what he feels himself to be and at other times, as is the case particularly with a child, he will draw that which he perceives the significant figures in his environment to be.

This knotty problem awaits further study—both clinical and experimental—to adequately set up principles which will allow easier differentiation of instances of displaced perception from instances of projection. Until that time, integrating the entire body of test, behavioral, and case history data and searching for internal consistency will provide the most reliable guideposts.

## THE AMORPHOUSNESS OF PERSONALITY AND SOME CAUTIONS

Another complication exists. The dilemma of the clinician is that in seeking to describe the elusive flame-like spirit of a subject, he must be neat and orderly and logical; and the human spirit, because it is flame-like, dances and flickers beyond order, neatness and logic.

In addition, in projective drawings, as with other projective techniques, it is at times difficult to determine whether a given drawing response reflects overt conscious trends or unconscious latent tendencies. Also there is the constant temptation to consider every line part of the subject's self-portrait. While most elements undoubtedly have symbolic value, not all aspects reflect deep dynamic tendencies.

Glib interpretive analogies and direct transposition of psychoanalytic concepts constitute a particular danger for the beginner. Easy rationalization may lead the inexperienced clinician to express an interpretation in order "to prove" a preconceived impression.

In working with children, it is especially important to learn the symbolic meaning to the child of a given area of the drawing, lest the interpretation be based on adult symbolization (3).

If the study of projection and displaced perception is, indeed, the royal road to the diagnosis and evaluation of personality, this road is still beset with many dangers for the unwary or overenthusiastic investigator: analysis by metaphor, farfetched analogies, circular reasoning, *ad hoc* and *post hoc* arguments.

At the present time, projective drawing techniques are interpreted with the clinician relying predominantly upon intuition. While the *feel* of the artist will probably always remain an integral component of the clinician's armamentarium, it is in efforts to balance the ratio more definitely in favor of the scientific factor over the intuitive element that the greatest hope lies for the most rapid advancement of projective drawings as a clinical tool.

Among other things, we might learn from Freud that the clinician may be as imaginative as he pleases—the more imaginative, the better—in the way in which he brings his data together. But he must not imagine the data.

The clinician who respects his facts enough to evaluate and interpret them, and who presses ever to discover the life behind the data, is the one who usually hangs before us an honest portrait which ends by being a reasonable likeness instead of a figure of *papier-mâché*.

Continued clinical and experimental study, however, is necessary to refine projective drawings as a clinical instrument and to enable increasingly more precise interpretative deductions. Considerable fundamental research is mandatory if we are to avoid the inevitable reaction that will follow the present stage of enthusiasm in which projective tests are accepted uncritically by many and results are generalized beyond the data.

As clinicians are well aware, the clinical use of projective techniques has sped along gradually widening the gap between it and the necessarily slower scientific validation of them. Projective drawings are presently embarking on the thorny path of transformation from an empirical and practical technique to a scientifically and experimentally rooted method of personality analysis. If this transformation is to continue, the chief need at the present time is for further validation. In spite of the recent growth of projective drawings, their analysis still remains more the tool of the artisan[1] than the instrument of the scientist.

Fortunately for psychology there are indications that the iron curtain of insularity between clinicians and experimentalists is being lifted and that a real exchange and integration of ideas is beginning to take place. Clinician and experimentalist have begun to find problems of mutual interest. The studies in the Appendix of the recently published *H-T-P Clinical Research Manual* (4) illustrate this.

When the history of twentieth century psychology is written, it will undoubtedly be characterized as the period when two great streams of psychological thought, one flowing from the laboratory, and the other from the clinic, converged to form a unified science of dynamic psychology.

---

[1] The therapist can prove to himself, and others, how much real grain is concealed in projective drawing data by waiting a few months until he has acquired a great deal of information and feels thoroughly at home in his patient's stream of consciousness. If then, at this later date, he examines the set of drawings, with mind alert to every symbolic possibility, he will almost surely discover that a good deal of what he has learned during the course of the analysis is there, varyingly disguised in the drawings.

Another rewarding exercise is to give projective drawings to those friends whom we know quite well. Thus the intimate knowledge of these people will teach us much about drawings, and present a diverting change from using drawings to tell us about people.

Research, hand-in-hand with clinical study, may provide the criteria for searching interpretation—criteria which may safeguard us against the hazards of wild and gratuitous interpretation but yet allow us to exploit fully the diagnostically and dynamically valuable material that lie in projective drawings. Invigorated research is needed if the nascent science of projective drawing interpretation is not to remain a shriveled version of what it might be.

Projective techniques and dreams remain the chief clinical bridges over which material from the unconscious passes into the hands of the clinician. But these bridges still remain to be anchored more securely in a firm cementing of both reliability and validity.

## DRAWINGS, DREAMS AND THE PROJECTIVE BATTERY

Kris (7) has observed: "In the work of art as in the dream, unconscious contents are alive; here, too, evidences of the primary process are conspicuous, but the ego maintains its control over them, elaborates them in its own right, and sees to it that the distortion does not go too far."

As with the dream, Meyer, Brown and Levine (8) point out, the artistic product is characterized by the stamp of individual signature; like the dream it possesses levels of content, structure, and special language; like the dream it fulfills a function in the psychic life of the individual. The discrepancy between the content of the drawings and the clinical impression obtained on interview is analogous, at times, to the discrepancy between primary and secondary thought processes, or between manifest and latent dream content.

For many subjects, particularly if neurotic or psychotic, submitting to projective techniques, is being severely put to the test. It is, however, particularly the projective drawing and the Rorschach techniques which are so taxing, for they introduce the greatest loss of reality support. By contrast, the TAT introduces relatively familiar situations, and the subjects' stories are subject to conscious and unconscious manipulation on some basis that satisfies the subjects to some degree as to their safety or appropriateness. "For this reason the TAT, which comes closest to real-life situations and fantasies . . . and which is better structured at the same time, . . . is valuable in a test battery. By putting the patient in a situation more like those he encounters in daily life, and in which he has more or less well established modes of response, the TAT helps us get a balanced picture of the patient's adaptive and defensive assets and strengths (12, p. 66)." These assets and strengths may well be minimized or obscured by the Rorschach Test, and even more by projective drawings where the patient has less to lean upon. Blots, although ambiguous, are concrete. The patient at least has something to hang on to! But when he is faced with the blank page and only the concepts of "House," "Tree" and "Person" or "Animal" to conceptualize from, the patient is compelled to fall back all the more upon his own resources and is given less support from outer stimuli. (For other facets of this point, the reader is referred to the chapter on Areas of Special Advantage for Projective Drawings.)

Thus, a continuum is suggested which ranges from dreams, to projective art and drawings, to the Rorschach, on to the TAT.

## THE QUESTION OF PREDICTABILITY

Some academicians feel that if projective tests can not predict overt behavior, they fail the acid test of validity. There are several points to be made in answer to this requirement:

First, it should be emphasized that at this time a high degree of accuracy in our generalizations from projective drawings to life situations cannot be expected. It does appear, however, that we can achieve gross accuracy, particularly if we use a battery of tests, but we must always assume that the projective techniques have not revealed all major personality variables and their patterns of interaction. Also, "We must always make the limiting assumptions that fate often tips the scales of external circumstance one way or the other regardless of the individual's character structure and intentions, and that to a significant extent the prominence of character features and pathological trends depend on external circumstance (12)."

Murray (10) goes even further by pointing out that, "The patterns of the imagination (as revealed in projective tests) and the patterns of public conduct are more apt to be related by contrast than by conformity."

There are several examples available of instances in which the latent and the manifest levels of behavior are inversely related. Oral dependency needs may, for example, be conspicuously evident in the projective drawings. While such a finding may occur in an alcoholic subject who more or less acts out his oral dependency needs, it may also occur in the projective drawings of a striving business executive who is attempting to deny these needs in himself by proving quite the opposite in his behavior.

It is only by integrating the behavioral picture with the projective technique data that the full personality evaluation can be derived. When we view the frustrated oral needs evident in the drawings alongside of the driving, overstriving behavior in the business executive's overt behavior, it is the viewing of these two levels side-by-side which may allow for the speculative prediction of eventual ulcers, but we can not always predict from the presence of dependency needs on the projective drawings the overt form of these needs.

Homoerotic elements reflected in the drawings may be considered as another example. Whether the homosexual orientation, suggested by these drawings, results in inhibited heterosexuality, compensatory Don Juanism, or overt homosexual activities depends, in part, upon the interaction of the basic potential of the subject with the influences in his environment, the latter factors being generally outside the scope of those tapped by projective techniques.

To mention one more example, if the projective drawings suggest extreme aggressiveness, and the patient behaviorally assumes the role of a meek, docile, self-effacing and submissive individual, a comparison of the two levels of data may permit the valuable inference that this subject must suffer from the effects of suppression and/or repression of a significant amount of aggressive impulses. The mild exterior he presents, we may then deduce, is at the expense of creating considerable tensions within him. The viewing of the two bodies of information side-by-side allows us to speculate as to the proneness of the individual for masochistic actions or depressed moods. While, at times, the masochism or the depression is directly evident in the projective drawings, the chief task of projective techniques is not to predict overt behavior, but to tap latent levels of feeling.

Another handicap which interferes with clinicians attempts to predict overt behavior exists in the fact that manifest behavior of any importance is invariably highly overdetermined, the resultant of numerous interacting determinants: identification figures, superego pressures, social and cultural settings, type and strength of defenses, traumatic experiences, and possibly constitutional predisposition would all have a great bearing on the ultimate overt pattern (12). Often, we are able to infer the presence of a powerful trend, kneaded deeply into the personality, but cannot say which of several possible manifest forms it may assume. While it is true that at times the clinician can be impressively successful in predicting overt behavior, he cannot with confidence assume that he can always so interrelate the indicated factors as to predict very specifically the future behavior. The subject's resources and limitations with respect to adaptive, sublimatory activity and achievement are often difficult to take into account. These factors tend to depend so much on situational support and threats, and on other external elements over which the subject frequently has little control (and which themselves cannot be predicted).

The broadest common denominator, then, which interferes with prediction of future behavior and postdiction of genetic events is the operation of multiple determinism, both internal and external. Projective tests merely elicit feelings (and a small sample of behavior) and any conclusions derived from the projective test data are made predominantly by way of inference. Psychodynamic inference "is not something which is built into the tests, but enters the realm of general personality theory." (6) Inferences from projective drawings, then, are not only bound by the extent of the clinician's knowledge of this clinical tool, but also by the limits of our present-day knowledge of psychodynamic principles.

The feelings tapped by projective techniques are, however, fully real. They are as real as that which is seen, in the concrete sciences, through a microscope. Aggression and gore, for example, which flood Rorschach, TAT and drawings, in the battery administered to a subject, are there. If the aggression does not show up in the subject's overt behavior, the conclusion that the aggression does not exist—and that the projective techniques are "wrong" —is never scientifically permissible. The feelings which permeate the projective tests, if consistently and reliably present, cannot be denied. It then merely becomes a question of what the subject does with these feelings.

The validation of projective techniques, it appears to the writer, cannot be asked to stand or fall on the basis of predictive studies of overt behavior—at least not at our present stage of knowledge of adaptive and sublimatory principles.

Whatever particular value the projective drawing techniques— or other projective techniques, for that matter—may have, will be found to reside, not, as some have assumed, in their power to mirror overt behavior or to communicate what the subject knows and is willing to tell, but rather in the techniques' capacity to reveal things that the subject is (a) unwilling to tell, or (b) is unable to tell because he is unconscious of them.

### INTEGRATION OF DRAWING FINDINGS

Perhaps a word of caution is in order. This book is not intended to serve as a check-list of "signs" which can be used in any mechanical or "cookbook" manner. The many case illustrations have been presented to allow the reader to gain a *feel* of personality, in a total way, as it comes through in projective drawings. It is the interrelated pattern of the drawing items which should be focused upon, as they reflect the dynamics of symptom organization in a particular diagnostic integration.

It must be mentioned that drawing elements tend to overlap in the same manner that symptoms in clinically differentiated groups overlap. As with the use of any clinical tool, a grasp of the mere mechanical details of drawing interpretation cannot substitute for knowledge of personality dynamics and clinical syndromes which is the indispensable preliminary capability that the reader must bring to his efforts to master the use of the projective drawing techniques. The integration of the findings, yielded by the projective drawing approach, into some sort of meaningful dynamic picture of the subject depends largely upon the clinician's basic understanding of human personality. For this, no clinical tool alone can substitute.

The dramatic nature of the projective drawing technique, its ease of administration, and the direct method of interpreting from the drawings without the need for intermediate scoring, tend to seduce the novitiate into dogmatic and stereotyped use of fragmentary knowledge. It is to be hoped that the recent growth of workshops and courses in projective drawings, that have been springing up in different geographic areas, will supply the integrating experience necessary to combat this tendency.

## A LIMITATION

The projective, and at the same time identification and empathic, process which is relatively more characteristic of the intratensive subject is also the most important factor in deep rapport, be it with a person, a landscape, a house, a tree, the movement or posture of an animal, and the like.

Therefore, like the Rorschach, projective drawings are generally more revealing with introverted than extraverted subjects. This is perhaps to be expected, since dreams, free association, and other clinical investigative approaches all provide richer yields with subjects capable of reflection and introspection than with those who are predominantly extratensively oriented.

## PRACTICAL USES

Projective drawings, as an instrument for exploring subterranean mental processes, have a specific use at the start, in the middle, and at the end of courses of therapy. Their easy administration allows them to be used as an aid in identifying suppressed or repressed dispositions and conflicts, and in defining the nature of the patient's resistances to these dispositions.

In addition, I have found that projective drawings may be employed as springboards for fruitful associations and the furthering of the therapeutic process. To ask the patient to associate to the stern-looking female drawn, the seated or leaning male, the vulnerable tree bent almost double by the environmental pressures, the tree rooted in a junk yard piled high with debris, or the bleak, desolate, deserted-looking house, for example, provides productive starting points for free association.

Repeated projective drawing administrations during the course of therapy also allow a means of (a) estimating the effects of therapy, or of (b) predicting the subsequent areas to be handled as they emerge closer to the surface.

Lastly, projective drawings have been favorably received as instruments for research and lend themselves quite adaptively to this goal. For a more detailed elaboration of the possibilities of the application of drawings to research and for a breakdown of projective drawing items into a package ready for research applicability, the reader is referred to *The H-T-P Clinical Research Manual* (4).

## BY WAY OF PERORATION

Projective drawings, this book has attempted to demonstrate, constitute a clinical tool which frequently elicits data relating specifically to the way in which a subject sees his "world," approaches it, and handles it. His anxieties and insecurities, his hurts and wishes, his fictions, his needs, his assets and liabilities will determine the elements of his projective drawings. Drawings also tend to mirror the overall configuration of the subject's personality and to supply some insight into the motivations of his behavior. Imbedded in the projective battery, drawings aid materially in differential diagnosis, as a guide to therapy and as an index of its success or failure. Thus, drawings may act as valuable road-markers along two difficult paths: clinical differentiation, and the assessment of the efficacy of therapeutic collaboration.

We have seen, in the uniqueness and drama of the individual projective drawing sets presented, that psychodynamic imperatives tend to force their way onto the drawing page, frequently bursting out from unconscious depths. The interpersonal attitudes of the subject, his emotional history, and the history of his experiences of love and hate will, to some extent, stream through his effector system and break into the outer world, spilling onto the blank page, saturating it with symbolic meaning.

In projective drawings, it is the subject's inner view of himself and his environment, the things he considers important, the things he emphasizes, and the things he neglects to include (and the symbolic meaning of these factors) that interest the clinician. In a figurative way, projective drawings serve as a mirror held up to the subject's inner nature, reflecting his personality strengths and weaknesses, and the balance between the two.

All in all, projective drawings appear to constitute one of the significant workable techniques in answer to psychology's quest for serviceable instrumentalities for personality evaluation.

On the scientist side of the scientist-practitioner coin, the job remains to meet more fully the problem voiced by Allport (1): "The greatest failing of the psychologist at the present time is his inability to prove what he knows to be true" (p. 9).

## REFERENCES

1. Allport, G.: Personality: A problem for science or a problem for art? *Rev. Psychol.*, 11:488-502, 1938.
2. Bellak, L.: The problems of the concept of projection, in Abt, L., and Bellak, L. (eds.): *Projective Psychology.* New York, Knopf, 1950.
3. David, H.: Brief unstructured items: The projective question. *J. Proj. Tech.*, 19:292-300, 1955.
4. Hammer, E. F.: *The H-T-P Clinical Research Manual.* Beverly Hills, California, Western Psychological Services, 1955.
5. Holzberg, J. D., and Wechsler, M.: The validity of human form drawings as a measure of personality deviation. *J. Proj. Tech.*, 14:343-361, 1950.
6. Korner, A.: Limitations of projective techniques: Apparent and real. *J. Proj. Tech.*, 20:42-47, 1956.
7. Kris, E.: *Psychoanalytic Explorations in Art.* New York, Internat. Univ. Press, 1952.
8. Meyer, B., Brown, F., and Levine, A.: Observations on the House-Tree-Person Drawing Test before and after surgery. *Psychosom. Med.*, 17:428-454, 1955.
9. Murray, H.: The effect of fear upon estimates of the maliciousness of other personalities. *J. Social. Psychol.*, 4:310-329, 1933.
10. Murray, H.: Uses of the Thematic Apperception Test. *Am. J. Psychiatry*, 107:577-581, 1951.
11. Schactel, E.: Projection and its relation to character attitudes and creativity in the kinesthetic responses. *Psychiatry*, 13:69-100, 1950.
12. Schafer, R.: *Psychoanalytic Interpretations in Rorschach Testing.* New York, Grune & Stratton, 1954.

# INDEX

## A

Abrams, Arnold, x, 397
abstract drawings, 68, 112
adolescent and adolescents, 36-101-3, 106, 116, 130n., 167, 196, 197, 224-7, 315, 316, 325, 326-7, 333, 335, 340, 402, 436, 489, 565, 567, 568, 571, 579, 580-1, 594, 601
    art therapy with, 518-61
    case studies of, 130-34, 249-60, 323-329, 518-561
adult case studies, 135-161, 261-275, 276-308
    *See also* case studies
age
    assigned to figures, 488
    assigned to tree, 192-3, 268, 446, 452, 458, 472, 474, 493
aggression, 26, 36, 50, 65, 99, 106, 133, 146, 156, 249, 323, 373, 387, 496, 501, 531-2, 563, 568, 570, 571, 572, 576, 579, 586, 587, 591, 594, 601, 603, 607, 614, 615, 618, 622, 624, 644, 646
    of examiner, 496
    *See also* Frustration-Aggression Hypothesis
Aichorn, August, 584
Ainsworth, M. D., 208, 235, 484, 502
Albee, G. W., *quoted* 486, 502
alcoholics and alcoholism, 278, 308, 394, 429, 430, 435, 513, 579, 585, 603, 622, 644
Alexander, Franz, 584, 603, 604, 610
Allport, G. W., 60, 72, *quoted* 649
Alschuler, A., 65, 66, 72, 569, 582
Altdoerfer, Albrecht, 594
ambivalence, 126, 129, 268, 429
Amchin, Abraham, 397
American Crayon Co., 209n.

Ames, L. B., 498, 502
American International College, 620-21
Anastasi, A., 72, 232, 234, 485, 494, 500, 502
"Anger," 556-7
"Anguish," 525-6, 560
animal and animals,
    in doodles, 573-82
    drawings,
        as unpleasant concepts, 373, 387
        symbolism in, 311-42
        *See also* Draw-an-Animal Test
    phobias, 313, 315, 459n., 579
*Animals, Meaning of,* 325, 342
anxiety, 31, 66, 119, 124, 126, 133, 134, 146, 147, 152, 157, 158, 174, 268, 292, 293, 303, 325, 369, 380, 470, 480, 511, 563, 572, 614, 617, 648
Apperception Test, Children's, 173, 575
"apperceptive mass," 141
arms, 99, 108, 109, 126, 128, 131, 133, 146, 159, 186, 273, 301, 403, 491
Arn van Krevelen, D., *quoted* 580, 582
Arnold, Magda, 626n.
Aron, Betty, 626n.
art,
    projection in, 5-17
    symbolism in, 19
    therapy, 511-16, 518-61
    training, 50-53, 86, 166, 513
*Art and the Problem Child,* 584n.
Arthur Performance Test, 238
asocial children, 584-95
    *See also* delinquents
ass, 576
Association for the Advancement of Psychotherapy, 518n.
Auerbach, J. G., 500, 502
automatism in doodles, 572-3
"Avenue of Projection, An," 18